CW00823327

SWEENEY!

THE OFFICIAL COMPANION

SWEENEY!

THE OFFICIAL COMPANION

Robert Fairclough & Mike Kenwood

Reynolds and Hearn Ltd
London

ACKNOWLEDGEMENTS

Many thanks to the following people for their help, encouragement, knowledge and support:

From the Euston Films Flying Squad: Dennis Waterman, Garfield Morgan, Ted Childs, Ian and Troy Kennedy Martin, Trevor Preston, Roger Marshall, Ray Jenkins, P J Hammond, Richard Harris, Chris Burt, Peter Brayham, Tom Clegg, David Wickes, John S Smith, Bill Westley and Johnny Goodman.

From the R&H crew: Richard Reynolds and Marcus Hearn for stitching it up!

The usual suspects: Martin Wiggins, John Herron at Canal Plus Image, Dom Wheeler, Rebecca Morris and Jane Foster at FremantleMedia, the staff of the BFI and Colindale Newspaper Library, Jaz Wiseman, Alison Thomas, Howard Heather, Chris Johnson, Alan Coles, Robert Ross, Henry (not many!) Holland, Stuart Burroughs at Sanctuary Entertainment, Julia Everett, Darren Giddings, Charlie Henderson, Rachel Jones, John O'Sullivan, John Reed, Sanctuary Records, Mike Richardson and the many others who have opened doors, and offered us advice, encouragement and information.

Thanks to Chris Difford and Glenn Tilbrook for 'Cool for Cats.'

The authors are particularly grateful to George Williams for his kind co-operation in the reuse of some material and research from *Fags, Slags, Blags and Jags: The Sweeney*.

Robert Fairclough: My *incredibly* long-suffering wife Rachel: thanks for the typing and transcribing, and for being a ringer for a jack or knave. And to Mum and Dad – sorry about the weekend!

Mike Kenwood: For my family, as always, and for Lisa – unlike Jack 'n' George, we did have some dinner.

Front and back cover pictures © Canal Plus Image

In memory of John Thaw, 1942 - 2002. God bless yer, guvnor.

First published in 2002 by
Reynolds & Hearn Ltd
61a Priory Road
Kew Gardens
Richmond
Surrey TW9 3DH

© Robert Fairclough and Mike Kenwood 2002

The Sweeney is a trademark of Thames Television Limited (a FremantleMedia Company).
Based on the Thames Television programme *The Sweeney*.
Licensed by Fremantle Brand Licensing.

The Sweeney publications (excluding script books) © Ian Kennedy Martin.

A CIP catalogue record for this book is available from the British Library.

ISBN 1 903111 43 9

Designed by Robert Fairclough.

Printed and bound in Great Britain by MPG Books Ltd, Bodmin, Cornwall.

CONTENTS

FOREWORD

HUNDREDS OF YEARS AGO I WORKED WITH IAN KENNEDY MARTIN on a soap called *Weaver's Green*. Sometime after I'd done it, I was standing in a film queue to see *Butch Cassidy and the Sundance Kid* – this is how long ago we're talking about – and Ian was in the queue. He said, 'I'm doing a TV cop series, would you be interested?' and I said, 'Yeah, of course I would.' Tom Clegg, the director who shot Ian's script – 'Regan' – had dossiers on actors; he knew a lot about me, and we'd worked together on *Special Branch*. He decided that he wanted Regan to go and find my character, Carter, sparring in the gym. Tom knew my brother was a fighter, he knew I could fight, and it all came together. Years and years earlier, I'd worked with John Thaw, and he was more than happy for me to play Carter.

John was unbelievably nice to me: we did dopey things like boating on the Serpentine, and went out and had a pint now and again. The Red Cow, Euston Films' local, was an incredibly ugly pub, but we had to go there because it was nearest! It was easier for John during the first series because he wasn't a big star. I think it was among his happiest times, because we could go filming and nobody bothered us. Once *The Sweeney* took off, it got harder and harder to film on the streets because by then people knew who we were. Nevertheless, we always did it. But on that first series, we shot with impunity all over the place. John didn't have any showbiz celebrity on his shoulders, so he was very happy and relaxed about life.

Detective Sergeant George Hamilton Carter was really quite similar to me. A lot of the time, you'd get a *Sweeney* script on the Friday before you started shooting on the Monday, so you didn't have time for great in-depth 'What should my character be?' stuff. You had to learn the lines and go on and do it. We didn't have any rehearsal; you'd do a run-through just before the take. There was no sitting around and talking about characterisation for two weeks.

The Sweeney really was an overnight success. We watched the first episode at John's house – it was the day before his birthday, January 2nd. His Dad came down from Manchester, and we had fish and chips. We'd finished the whole series by then and nobody knew anything about it. It was made at a time when there wasn't the attitude that whatever you did had to be a big hit; now, everybody argues about the ratings. The pressure wasn't that great then, although we knew the scripts were great and we had good directors. We were surprised when it took off as big as it did: always in the TV top ten, and sold to more countries than a UK TV series ever had been before.

The real police always said, 'The problem with *The Sweeney* is that it's too accurate. My wife keeps asking me where I am,' and the heavies would always go, 'Cor, you're just like the geezer who nicked me!' We got adopted by a mob who called themselves the 'Teeny Sweeney'. They were a Regional Crime Squad who were Flying Squad and regular detectives, and they were all plain clothes. If they had a function we'd always turn up and have a drink with them. They'd often drive us there with the lights blazing and sirens going, just to show us how fast they could drive – that was kind of nerve-wracking. And to keep the police sweet, we had to attend a lot of what were laughingly called Policeman's Balls. So, we did a lot of socialising that was forced on us, but some of the real cops became quite good friends of ours.

The team spirit at Euston Films was great. We'd be doing a scene, and if anyone had a better idea, it would get used. The sound guy would say, 'Excuse me, haven't we said all of this in that scene that we did last Tuesday?' You were working at such a speed, that you'd go, 'Hang on, you're right, we can cut this scene down and just get the essentials out of it so it's not just all repetition'. The crew really was amazing; we stuck together 18 hours a day and got on so well.

After the fourth series, John said, 'I wanna have a chat... I think we've gone just about as far as we can go with this. I mean, how many more murders can we invent, how many more ways of breaking into banks can we do?' And he was quite right. On *Minder*, towards the end, every now and then we got a really stupid script in that we wouldn't normally have accepted, but that didn't happen with *The Sweeney*. And also, with all due respect to them, we had seen *Z-Cars* and *Softly Softly* collapse as they were dragged on and on and on. So, John said, 'I don't know about you, but I'm gonna call it a day.' And I said, 'Yeah, I'm with you'. Had it been down to me, I'd have said, 'I'll do another series,' as it was fantastic fun. But John was absolutely right; there's nothing sadder than seeing a great programme go down hill quickly.

I'm very proud of *The Sweeney*, though. It was huge for both John and I and it was a wonderful series to do. In fact, the lady I live with was never a great television watcher, but every now and again I come in at night and she's glued to it. Because it was such high quality, we also had the opportunity to get fantastic casts – really fine actors – who generally wouldn't have said 'yes' to an episode in a TV show; there's a lot of pomposity floating around the acting game. But with our show, they always said, 'I want to be in that because it's good'.

The Sweeney was a joy to do, it really was. When you know you're doing good work, and you're having amazing fun doing it – and you're getting paid – what more could you ask for?

Dennis Waterman
August 2002

SHUT IT!

FOR ITS 15-21 JUNE 2002 ISSUE, *RADIO TIMES* NOMINATED THE TOP Ten TV police they thought could cut it as real coppers. The balance was mostly in favour of recent recruits: DI Pat Chappel from *The Vice* was at number 10, PC Brammel from *The Cops* was at number 3, and Det Supt Michael Walker from *Trial and Retribution* was at number 1. At number 2, nearly 25 years adrift from the officers either side of him, was DI Jack Regan from *The Sweeney*.

Such a high placing in a contemporary poll indicates the unique hold the series – which featured Regan and his DS, George Carter, chasing armed robbers and other villains across a grainy 1970s London – has on British popular culture. A revel in *The Sweeney*'s kitsch seventies iconography of kipper ties, flares and Ford Granadas doesn't completely explain its appeal. Watching any episode today also soon gives the lie to the caricatured view of the series as a simplistic 'blokes and birds' shoot-'em-up, although the fights, car chases and gun-fights are always a high point. Regan and Carter's witty, world-weary cynicism is a window on a Britain full of fuel shortages, IRA bombing campaigns and industrial unrest: in this dour culture, Jack and George were appealing because they were fallible. Minor villains were sent down while major ones got clean away, and the consistently well-written scripts often conveyed real rage at social inequality and injustice.

At the same time, *The Sweeney* was colourful through its inclusion of the vivid and bizarre; villains were comical and eccentric, quoted Hiawatha or cross-dressed, while booze-raddled coppers eyed up anyone in a skirt. The casting was also spot on: Dennis Waterman and John Thaw were completely believable as London coppers, radiating an intensity and nervous tension that was never less than 100 per cent convincing.

The show's attraction may be even simpler than all of the above reasons. 'It's so close to life,' John Thaw said in 1976. 'In a job like a Flying Squad officer, you're close to danger all the time. If you didn't find something to laugh about, or a mate like Carter to clown around with on off-duty hours, you'd go out of your mind.'

The Sweeney also wasn't just a police series: it was an attitude. The rule-bending, work-hard, play-hard approach of the police in the series was also endemic to the series' production company, Euston Films. During the making of the show, these totally committed filmmaking young guns brooked no interference from suited members of the TV establishment and inflexible trade unionists alike.

Sweeney! The Official Companion, which incorporates material that first appeared in the privately published *Fags, Slags, Blags and Jags: The Sweeney*, interviews many of these innovative filmmakers at length. They give the inside story on the making of this British institution for the first time, together with an insight into the history and significance of Euston Films in relation to British broadcasting. Every aspect of *The Sweeney* is covered, from biographies of the leading actors to the series' initial development, through the episodes and films to the spin-offs and merchandise. This book explains why, all these years later, Jack Regan can sit proudly near the top – why not the very top? – of a Top 10 of TV cops.

It seems you (still) can't keep a good copper down.

Robert Fairclough
Mike Kenwood
August 2002

CHAPTER 1

THE USUAL SUSPECTS

JOHN THAW

'He was very funny. One of the luckiest actors in the world – extremely talented.'
Ian Kennedy Martin, Sweeney *creator*

'He did not mind how many takes there were. He was a person who was prepared to do anything to make sure that television was as it should be, and that is how I will remember him – giving 100 per cent.'
Press statement from Colin Dexter, Inspector Morse *creator, on hearing of John Thaw's death*

'John could say a whole paragraph of dialogue in one look.'
Chris Burt, film editor

'It was often what John didn't say in a scene as much as what he did say that carried the conviction in his performance... He was just a very nice bloke, but he didn't suffer fools gladly. If, on a production, there was someone he didn't think was up to the job, he would tell you. He was a very bright man, although he came from very humble origins.'
Ted Childs, Sweeney *producer*

'John and I became huge friends doing the show. It was hard work, and the hours were long. To spend that amount of time together, and to get on for that amount of years, was amazing. And he was just a smashing bloke. And the good feeling on the floor comes from the top: the crew loved him.'
Dennis Waterman, Sweeney *co-star*

* * *

JOHN EDWARD THAW WAS BORN IN WEST GORTON, MANCHESTER on 3 January 1942. When he was seven years old, John's parents split up. His lorry-driver father, Jack, had to work long hours to support the family, and he and his younger brother, Ray, were often left to their own devices. With time on his hands, Thaw took part in several school plays, encouraged by John Lee, a history teacher (and school play director) at Ducie Secondary Technical School in Whitworth Park.

Following brief stints as a porter at Smithfield, Manchester's fruit and veg market, and as a baker's apprentice, Thaw decided to go into acting, enrolling at RADA; as he was only 16, he had to lie about his age to be admitted. 'I think I must have looked older even then,' he later said, reflecting on his characteristic of looking more mature than his years, a trait that undoubtedly helped with his rapid rise to the top of his chosen profession.

With his northern working class background and Teddy Boy apparel, Thaw found it difficult to gain acceptance at the predominantly upper-middle class RADA, but grew more comfortable in his second summer there, making friends with other budding actors such as Tom Courtenay and Sarah Miles. He later qualified with an Honours diploma and made his professional debut at Liverpool Playhouse in 1960, a young man in step with the new wave of British actors like Courtenay, Albert Finney and Alan Bates. His first television appearances followed in Granada Television's *The Younger Generation*, an anthology series that showcased new writing and acting talent. Like his later *Sweeney* colleague Garfield Morgan, Thaw also appeared in several *Z-Cars* episodes, beginning what was to prove a fruitful association with fictional lawmen; he played PC Elliot, a copper whose weakness for the bottle ultimately leads to his disgrace and exit from the force in the episode 'Hide and Go Seek'.

In 1963 Thaw was also on the London stage, at the Saville Theatre in the play *Semi Detached* with Laurence Oliver. At only 20 years of age, he was sufficiently respected as an actor to stand in for Olivier for a week when the latter was taken ill. It was also at the Saville that he met his first wife, Sally Alexander. Thaw subsequently met his second wife, actress Sheila Hancock, through the theatre too, when the pair appeared in the play *So What About Love?* Initially friends, they married in 1973, following the death of Sheila's husband, actor Alec Ross, in 1971. Their union proved to be something almost unique in showbusiness – a long and happy marriage between two actors.

In 1965 Thaw first became known as a major television actor as Sgt John Mann in *Redcap*, a 13-part drama produced by ABC Television in which he was cast as an investigator in the military police equivalent of the CID. In a new twist on the detective series format, Mann traveled the world investigating crimes committed by British troops. Mann was a no-nonsense, angry character, exhibiting stubborn defiance in solving a murder in the first episode 'It's What Comes After', establishing a persona that was a step towards Thaw's defining role as Regan. *Redcap* was Thaw's first success as a TV leading man – a second series followed in 1966 – and the actor himself was praised in the media. Among many positive notices, TV critic Kenneth Easthaugh wrote in the *Daily Mirror*, 'John Thaw is… a rare and welcome example of a very young actor being treated responsibly on TV and given the lead in an important production… [He] is one of TV's best finds.'

The idea of *Redcap* was conceived by *Daily Mirror* journalist Jack Bell, but the editing of the scripts was the responsibility of writer Ian Kennedy Martin, who was to play a major part in Thaw's life for a number of years afterwards. 'I can't believe this to this day,' Ian remembers with a laugh. 'John Bryce was the producer of *Redcap*, the original guy behind *The Avengers*. [He] was a complete nutcase, a wonderful guy. He says, "Right, we've got our lead, John Thaw." I said, "Who's John Thaw?" So we went down to the telecine room, and he starts showing an episode of *The Avengers* ('Esprit de Corps') where John comes in, walks down the stairs and says "Your car is ready, Colonel," and then turns around and walks off. And I said, "You're casting that guy as the lead in this series, for 13 hours of television, on the basis of that?" And he said, "Of course I am!"'

During their association on the series, Thaw and Kennedy Martin became friends and, together with Ian's brother Troy, were drinking partners in so-called Swinging London. 'We were going round with [actor] Nicol Williamson and it was really dreadful – drunk and loose on the streets in Chelsea!' Ian says. 'I had this flat virtually on the King's Road and that was the base from which we'd start. He [Thaw] was just in the process of getting married to Sally Alexander. Sally thought I was likely to be one of his more respectable friends so allowed him out! He had this amazing house. I'd go round there and lolling around the place would be Jacqueline Bisset who was at school with Sally. And there was John in the middle of all this – the nightmare of RADA with his Mancunian ways!'

Thaw also had his first break in the cinema in the early sixties, appearing alongside Tom Courtenay in 1962 in the borstal drama *The Loneliness of the Long Distance Runner*. He consolidated this promising start with a succession of character parts that gradually increased in prominence, in *Dead Man's Chest* (1965), *The Bofors Gun* (1968), which also featured Nicol Williamson, *Praise Marx and Pass the Ammunition* and *The Last Grenade* (both 1970). Thaw's star continued to rise on television too; in 1967 he was joint lead with James Bolam in an ITV serial called *Inheritance*, playing a succession of different men through the generations of a family, starting in the Industrial Revolution and going right through to the 1950s.

With other television appearances in *Bat Out of Hell* (1966) and *Macbeth* (1970) beginning to outweigh Thaw's film appearances, it seemed that even at this stage of his career he was developing a preference for the medium. 'I suppose TV was an area he felt confident in,' *Sweeney* producer Ted Childs speculates, having had a friendly working relationship with Thaw for over 25 years. 'I think he could have been a very successful film actor as well. He just didn't choose to; possibly because there was always a television role being presented to him, he tended to take it, but I don't think John regretted what he did.'

Thaw's most memorable performances in television in the late 1960s and early 1970s were often flawed, angry figures like Mann, although in real life the actor was a shy and courteous man. Ian Kennedy Martin's *The Onedin Line* episode 'Mutiny' featured John as a rebellious seaman, and even his guest appearance as Denzil Davis, a camp professional Welshman, in the Adam Faith series *Budgie* ('Sunset Mansions – or Whatever Happened to Janey Baib?') has understated menace.

One of his most notable television appearances in this vein was in the play 'A Talking Head', which was screened in 1969 as part of LWT's *Saturday Night Theatre* slot. This drama opens with a police station office in which two detectives are arguing about how to handle a case. Thaw suddenly storms into shot and interrupts the pair, snarling 'What a load of crap!', at which point is becomes clear that they are all really in a television studio, making a rather bland police series on which Thaw is a frustrated writer. These railings against the stultifying conformity of the studio-based genre police series are ironic in hindsight, considering the part the actor would play in a mould-breaking new style of TV policing in *The Sweeney*, initiated five years later.

When Ian Kennedy Martin created the part of Regan (an anagram of 'anger') specifically for Thaw in 1973, the actor approached it in his customary committed and focused way. 'He was a 100 per cent professional,' director David Wickes remembers. 'More than anything else in life, he wanted [to get it right], and so he would concentrate every single fibre of himself on it... He was *magic* to work with from that point of view, because he was always *thinking*.'

Right from the start, Thaw had a sound grasp of Regan's compelling but flawed character: 'He's a loner, a very stubborn man,' he said at the time. 'Not a very whole man, not a very rounded man because there's a lot lacking in him... He's marvellous at his job and he can't see himself doing any other work... And because of that attitude of making his work his whole life, he loses out on a lot of things.'

During the filming of the pilot story 'Regan', Thaw contemplated the impact the series would have on his career and home life, while bonding with the crew in the traditional way. 'I remember drinking with John in The Red Cow,' Bill Westley, the second assistant director, says. 'This pub had big red pillars, and John was sitting on his stool up against one of them. We were getting more drunk by the minute and John said to me, "I don't know how I'm going to handle this, my wife seems to think it's *Dixon of Dock Green*." I said, "You what? That's a load of cobblers, whoever's told you that? I'll tell you how these producers see it. In three months' time, they'd love to see you walking down that road and hear people saying, "Oh, there's that bastard, Regan." They want a tough series." With that, he leant forward and said, "Do you honestly see it like that, Bill?" "Yes, I do," I said, and with that he leant back – and he missed the pillar and he fell arse over tit on the floor! He got up as sober as a judge and said, "There was no need to move the pillar, was there?" I'll never forget that. That started a great relationship between John and myself. He was a gentleman and I was what they considered to be a bit of a rough diamond, I suppose.'

The care that Thaw put into the part was exemplified by his research into the real police. 'At that stage, John liked a drink and he used to go off with the cops on his own and ask them questions about their work life,' Ted Childs explains. 'Regan was very much modeled on what he understood a Flying Squad detective, at that time, was like. I remember talking to Troy and John one night about how there used to be quite a close bond between villains and cops. It was almost medieval in the way they related, particularly in that London ambience of villainy. There was a kind of respect for each other, almost like in *The Godfather*. John understood that very well.'

Although the actor said in a 1976 interview 'I hate violence,' he would also work hard to make his fight scenes convincing. Dennis Waterman was more experienced in this area; his brother Peter was a professional boxer known as 'the Clapham Clouter.' 'The real-life John Thaw was very much like the real-life Jack Regan in this respect: he *did* want to throw a punch as well as Dennis Waterman, he genuinely did,' David Wickes says earnestly. 'Dennis would come on and go – pow! – perfectly in the rehearsal. John would wind himself up, go through all the moves [the stunt coordinator] had shown him, and go back to his caravan, pleased as punch that he'd actually done as well as Dennis! And he'd watch and see if he could pick up anything from him. He was a little bit nervous, John, because he did have a bit of a paunch – not a big one, but he had one. It suited the character! But we had to be careful about certain angles on that... he was supposed to be a hard man!'

Of the actor's visible ageing over the course of *The Sweeney*, Tom Clegg recalled, 'It used to annoy John sometimes that the young girls were only interested in Dennis as a lover, and saw him as a father figure. It really pissed him off as he wasn't very old – he just *looked* older.' Like his father, Thaw found his hair started turning grey, and then white, in his thirties and forties. Unintentionally, this added to the human side of the character. 'He was always very good at portraying vulnerability,' Clegg notes, 'which meant he could make the wrong decisions and he would be able to go through all the gamut of emotions. [Regan] wasn't a superhero; he was a guy in there doing a tough, and sometimes shitty, job.'

John Thaw's central performance was three-dimensional and compelling. Shaun Usher observed in the *Daily Mail* that 'Regan is refreshingly muddled and fallible,' and this new style of TV cop made the actor's name familiar to millions of people. Within a month of the first episodes being transmitted, bags full of fan mail began arriving at Thames. Seven weeks into the screening of the series, 150 Bunny Girls at London's Playboy Club voted Thaw top of their Valentine poll; an offer of membership was greeted with a polite refusal, but it was clear, in any case, that romantic interest didn't all go Dennis Waterman's way. And in the *Evening Standard*, Londoners voted Thaw Best Film Actor of the Year for his performance in the feature film spin-off, *Sweeney!*, in 1976.

Like many other actors in the limelight and pursued by the press, Thaw disliked the 'nuisance value', as he put it, of being pointed at by the public, and was reticent about giving interviews. The actor began to value his family's privacy. 'He wouldn't hang around,' Ted Childs says. 'He would always turn up at the parties, he wasn't stand-offish, but he didn't feel, like some actors did, that he had to hang around buying drinks for the crew. He always buggered off home. He valued his own space. Although he was on the A-list, he didn't have to be. He never went to ritzy showbusiness events and getting him to turn up for awards ceremonies was difficult. He was always gracious about it; it just wasn't an important part of his life.'

By the end of the third series, the actor felt there was little more to be done with the character of Regan. He felt strongly that the show should finish while it was at its peak, a view Dennis Waterman concurred with. 'I think the network wanted to hang on to it as it was still doing reasonably well, even though John was a bit iffy about signing up for the fourth series,' Ted Childs remembers. 'He was definitely in two minds about a fifth, and in the end made it clear that the fourth series was the last he would be doing. He was worried about typecasting.' Soon after the news broke that the 1978 series of *The Sweeney* would be the last, Thaw explained to the press: 'I was frightened of going stale. The series started out marvellously and this latest batch is amongst the best we've ever done. But we want to quit while we are winning.' Thaw and Waterman also wanted to spend more time with their families; starting work at 6.00 am every day was beginning to take its toll.

Keen to develop his career in other directions and mindful of being stuck with the image of a TV hard man, a role he had already played twice, Thaw rarely talked about *The Sweeney* publicly after leaving, often discreetly airbrushing it from his own personal history. Years later, interviewed for Radio 4's *Desert Island Discs*, his only comment on the series was that he could never bring himself to play a character like Regan again. A request to sample some of Thaw's *Sweeney* dialogue by the early 1990s indie band Carter the Unstoppable Sex Machine was rebuffed, and the actor was scathing when *The Sweeney* was also repeated on ITV at that time. '[Thames] should be making new shows,' he told the press. 'Not putting out a 17-year-old series which will cost them just a few pounds to show.'

However, in private he was more positive about the programme, as stunt coordinator Peter Brayham remembers. 'I did a film with John's wife called *The Russian Bride* and they threw an end-of-picture party on a boat … I walked on, said hello to Sheila and the cast, and John walked in. "Hello, Peter, how long has it been?" he said. '*Inspector Morse*, I did a few of those,' I said, and from there we talked for an hour, more about *The Sweeney* than *Morse*… And he said, "Wasn't that a great time?" Whether he was reminiscing about the show or the people I don't know, but I know *The Sweeney* was a part of his life that he just loved doing.'

After the fourth and final series, Thaw was keen to make a clean break from *The Sweeney* image by tackling a variety of other work. Only weeks after finishing work on the programme, he took on a BBC *Play for Today*, 'Dinner at the Sporting Club'. Scripted by *Minder* creator Leon Griffiths, he featured as a hardened boxing manager who gets an attack of conscience after one of his young charges proves to be out of his league in the ring. With his wife's encouragement, Thaw returned to the theatre shortly afterwards, appearing with Diana Rigg in Tom Stoppard's *Night and Day*. He subsequently performed at Stratford for a season with the Royal Shakespeare Company, playing Wolsey in *Henry VIII* and Sir Toby Belch in *Twelfth Night*. Another stage appearance was at the Sahftesbury Theatre in *Two into One*.

For much of the early 1980s, Thaw alternated between television and the stage, his television credits including *Drake's Venture* (1980), as Francis Drake, and Hubert De Burgh in the BBC's *The Life and Death of King John* (1984). Two particularly memorable television appearances during the 1980s were in Douglas Livingstone's

Belfast play *We'll Support You Ever More* (1985), where Thaw played a father trying to find out how and why his soldier son died at the hands of the IRA, and John's interpretation of British war leader Bomber Harris in Don Shaw's *How I Won The War* (1989). Thaw was also nominated for a BAFTA for Best Actor in a Supporting Role for his part in Richard Attenborough's film *Cry Freedom* (1987), which concerned the murder of anti-apartheid supporter Stephen Biko.

A curiosity from this period is Thaw's appearance in the drama series *Mitch*, screened in 1983. Created by *Sweeney/Public Eye* writers Roger Marshall and Richard Harris as a new starring vehicle for the actor, Thaw starred as a crime reporter frequently caught, like Frank Marker in *Public Eye*, in the grey area between crime and the law. Sadly, a change of management at London Weekend Television saw *Mitch* shelved for some time. When it was ultimately screened the series wasn't promoted and was buried in a late-night slot. Thaw was hurt by LWT's cavalier attitude, and throughout the rest of his career stuck to his pledge not to work for them again.

Marshall attempted to create a further vehicle for the actor in his series *Travelling Man*, Thaw was interested, but the lead role eventually went to Leigh Lawson. 'We were going to do it, and we had lots of discussions about it, because John lived just round the corner,' editor-turned-producer Chris Burt divulges. '[But] we never quite got it together.'

Instead of playing another detective, albeit a retired one, in *Travelling Man*, Thaw chose to broaden his range by appearing in a situation comedy. (He was no stranger to the form, however, having previously starred with Bob Hoskins in the Dick Clement and Ian la Frenais series *Thick as Thieves* in 1974.) In Eric Chappell's *Home to Roost* he played Henry Willows, a divorced father reluctantly compelled to share a house with his dropout son, played by Reece Dinsdale. (Dinsdale was later cast in the lead role in *Thief Takers*, a 'next generation' *Sweeney* for the 1990s. Significantly, the show's pre-publicity stressed the connection with Thaw from the earlier series.) John received the Pye TV Award for Best Comedy Performance for *Home to Roost*, and Sheila Hancock also appeared in one of the episodes, playing his ex-wife.

Thaw's subsequent return to comedy in the BBC's 1993 series *A Year in Provence* was rather less successful; it was probably the only time his judgment of a TV project proved to be misplaced. 'There were lots of things I didn't put to him because a) I didn't think they were right and b) I knew that he wouldn't want to do them,' Ted Childs says of the actor's instincts in selecting parts. 'Very often people would come to you with an idea from on high saying, "I think this would be a good vehicle for John," and I would say, "He won't do it," and they would say, "But you haven't asked him." Generally speaking, I knew what he would do and what he wouldn't do. He was always very reasonable and sensible, he wasn't petulant about it, he would just make it clear that it wasn't for him and you had to take it.'

1987 saw the television debut of Thaw's most famous characterisation, *Inspector Morse*. Significantly, there was still input from the actor's *Sweeney* days; Ted Childs and Chris Burt oversaw the project, with Burt taking over as producer after his predecessor,

Kenny McBain, died. The new detective had some minor similarities to Regan; difficulty in forming relationships with women, and a dislike of police bureaucracy and doing things by the book. The banter with his sidekick – the more methodical, ever-loyal and put-upon Sergeant Lewis – was also a little reminiscent of the double-act in *The Sweeney*, often revolving round Lewis's marriage.

These superficial similarities were outweighed by the differences. As his friends concede, the actor had mellowed both on screen and off. Rarely reaching Regan's levels of anger and frustration, Morse was a shy, almost reclusive intellectual, enjoying classical music and vintage cars; his drink of choice was a pint of real ale rather than a litre of Scotch. Like *The Sweeney* before it, the series defined a new subgenre of the television detective series; that of the glossy, feature-length mystery set in middle-England – in this case Oxford – adapted from a successful series of novels. *Frost*, *Dalziel and Pascoe* and *Midsomer Murders* have all followed in the *Morse* tradition.

The stories were initially adapted from Colin Dexter's novels, and later either consisted of ideas contributed by Dexter and expanded by other writers, or were original conceptions. Plots full of suspects and red herrings were the norm, often set in local country houses and the cloisters of the various university colleges. Detractors often point out that realism was not the series' strong point, but Thaw's portrayal never failed to depict a believable and sympathetic character. In hindsight, this softened, older and wiser, and less screwed-up 'outsider' figure was the role that really secured public affection for the actor. He was branded the 'thinking woman's crumpet' by the tabloids and won BAFTA awards for Best Actor in 1990 and 1993.

The fondness the British public felt for Thaw was evident when letters were sent to the press expressing worries about Morse's occasional slight limp on screen. It was subsequently explained that this was due to Thaw tripping and breaking his foot while running for a bus at the age of 15. '*Morse* was the nearest thing to John's character,' Chris Burt says, reminiscing about his friend. 'He was very fond of *Morse*. It was just like putting on a comfortable suit for him. He knew that part so well. '

Kavanagh QC, Thaw's next television success, saw him as a senior barrister with a turbulent family life – he had moved from chasing criminals to prosecuting and defending them. (Curiously, Thaw almost refused the role because he didn't like the idea of wearing a legal wig.) The barrister's domestic life also featured heavily in the programme, until in later episodes his wife was killed off. Childs was again involved, and envisaged the character as a crumpled yet charismatic Mancunian (a nod to the actor's own background) with an affinity for life's losers. By this stage, Thaw's characters weren't straying too far from the dogged individualists that had made him a success in the past, a persona which the British viewing public clearly loved him for.

Juggling his commitments, Thaw returned to the National Theatre in 1993-4 in David Hare's *The Absence of War*, playing the part of a Labour Prime Minister loosely modeled on Neil Kinnock. In real life, he and Sheila were both committed Labour supporters, attending party meetings at the branch near their Chiswick home. Thaw was always mindful of the poverty of his childhood but never saw any contradiction between being well-paid and having left wing views, once telling journalists, 'I only get the rate for the job, just like a chippie.'

By the late 1990s, he was one of the highest paid actors on British television, much sought after by both the BBC and ITV. Among his appearances at this time were *The Plastic Man* with Frances Barber and an adaptation of the Gerald Seymour thriller *The Waiting Time*, in which he played a solicitor's clerk embroiled in the intrigues of post-Cold War Germany. Family drama *Goodnight Mister Tom* (1999) won him another accolade, the National Television Awards' Most Popular Drama award, for his portrayal of Tom Oakley, another slightly cantankerous character who rediscovers his conscience. Throughout this time, Thaw continued to work with Ted Childs and Chris Burt. 'He enjoyed working the way he did and he liked being in control, not in any obsessive-compulsive sense, but in the sense that he trusted the people he worked with,' Ted Childs says of Thaw's loyalty to his old colleagues.

In *Monsignor Renard* John played a Catholic priest returning to his native France during the German occupation. This four-part resistance drama was filmed entirely in France and also featured Cheryl Campbell, Juliette Caton and Dominic Monaghan. A second series was planned, but failed to materialise due to cold feet on the part of the series' financial backers. 'What we were hoping to do was, each four episodes would be a year in the occupation of France during the Second World War,' executive producer Childs says ruefully. 'We had a second series lined up, where he is trying to save a Jewish girl from the village, and it was all very good. We all enjoyed doing it and John was very disappointed when it didn't happen. I can see the economic arguments, but they weren't borne out by the evidence.' Given a longer period to develop and find an audience, *Monsignor Renard* could have been Thaw's fifth major television triumph.

The actor continued to work steadily, gently widening his range beyond his established successes. He played double-glazing magnate Jim Proctor in *The Glass* for Granada Television, fighting with his one-time protégé to hold onto both his business and his wife. *Buried Treasure* saw him as a widowed estate agent who finds he has unexpectedly acquired a mixed-race granddaughter. Thaw also proved to be loyal towards two of his established drama series, *Inspector Morse* and *Kavanagh QC*, returning to both in two one-off specials which turned out to be among his final pieces of television work.

In 'The Remorseful Day', Morse was killed off, keeling over and then dying in hospital while on the brink of solving his last case; even the most cynical viewer couldn't fail to have been moved. Sadly, this was to prove an unfortunate case of art imitating life, as only a few months after the last Morse was transmitted, the actor himself became ill with cancer of the oesophagus, and subsequently died at his West Country home on Thursday 21 February 2002.

Right up to the end, Thaw was determined to fight the illness and was talking about returning to work. 'Had he recovered we were planning to do a couple of one-off *Kavanaghs* and we were talking about some new things, but sadly, he didn't survive,' Ted Childs says. Troy Kennedy Martin was also planning to work with his old friend again, as Chris Burt recalls: 'We were about to start... on an H E Bates novella set in 1942. It would have been a nice thing to have done. Then he rang up and said he'd got cancer. But he still hoped that he'd get better. He kept saying, "I'll be ready to do it. I will." Then he just died, very quickly.'

On Friday 22 February 2002, the front pages of every newspaper in Britain were packed with tributes to Thaw. Under the by-line 'Goodbye Guvnor', the *Mirror* editorial summed up the nation's mood. 'Few actors have been as much a part of our lives over the past quarter century as John Thaw... There was always something particularly English about him.' The *Daily Express* simply added, 'He was the ultimate TV actor, loved by millions.'

Johnny Goodman, who took over the running of Euston Films with Verity Lambert and Linda Agran, remembers the optimism the actor continued to show even in his final days. 'I only had a letter from John about ten days before he died. He was optimistic and said he was going to pull out of it and start work again. He ended up by saying he was very much looking forward to seeing me again, even if I hadn't got any more new jokes! That was the last time I heard from him. I got the news when I was in Spain. He was a lovely man, very shy.'

'He was only 59 and there were still a lot of things he could have done,' Ted Childs reflects sadly. 'One thing I always hoped he would do and he often talked about doing was direct. John really understood about film direction. He knew how to work the camera, how to perform credibly, intelligently and convincingly in front of a camera. He knew a lot of the technology, the sound quality and so on, and he had a great passion for serious music, which he always claims he got from Tom Courtenay, and was part of the reason he was attracted to doing *Morse*.'

For some, the most enduring image of John Thaw is of DI Regan in the 1970s, racing through a disused warehouse and slamming villains into iron fencing. For others, it's the morose Morse pondering the intricacies of a murder case in Oxford in the 1980s. For another generation, it's the indomitable Kavanagh, defending his underprivileged clients in the dock in the 1990s. Beginning with *Redcap*, John Thaw remains the only English actor to have had a television success in every decade from the 1960s to 2002, in a career that spanned over 40 years. That all his best-known characters were involved in the prosecution of the law to a lesser or greater degree was not an accident. 'John once said to me that a colleague had told him he was always at his best in a part when he was asking questions,' Roger Marshall remembers. 'I think he took that to heart.'

The posthumous BAFTA awarded by television viewers, and accepted on his behalf by Sheila Hancock in 2002, was a fitting tribute to John Thaw's exemplary contribution to British popular culture.

DENNIS WATERMAN

'Dennis and I went back even further than John Thaw. I knew Dennis very well and what I knew about him was he was a very good actor – because a lot of other people didn't reckon on him.'
Ian Kennedy Martin, Sweeney creator

'I've always loved Dennis, we were great mates for years, but I lost touch with him when he lived with Rula. He was a bit of a rascal and a Jack-the-lad.'
Tom Clegg, Sweeney director

'The thing about [John and Dennis] was that they were both big drinkers. I get a bit lairy after the second double vodka, but they used to steam into that Red Cow pub and watch the strippers!'
Trevor Preston, Sweeney writer

'That they actually liked each other off the set was obvious on the screen. They really did like each other.'
Chris Burt, Sweeney Editor

* * *

DENNIS WATERMAN WAS BORN INTO A LARGE SOUTH LONDON family on 24 February 1947. Like John Thaw, Waterman developed an interest in acting at an early age, but went professional when he was very much younger, enrolling at the Corona stage school. As well as offering drama training, this academy functioned as an agent for its students; Waterman's contemporaries included several other child actors who would go on to become established adult actors, including Susan George, Richard O'Sullivan and Francesca Annis. Waterman made his first cinema appearance in the film *Night Train to Inverness* in 1958, but it was in 1961 that his career as a child star really took off.

In that year he became noticeable in three very different productions. He was cast by Hammer Film Productions in their historical swashbuckler *The Pirates of Blood River* with Christopher Lee and Oliver Reed; he was in the West End, appearing in a production of Meredith Wilson's musical *The Music Man*; and for the BBC he played the lead character in the children's television series *William*, a series of 13 half-hour episode series based on the popular books by Richmal Crompton.

This significant early exposure led to him working in the USA, and Waterman spent 1962 in Hollywood, working on the Desilu Productions series *Fair Exchange* (chaperoned by his mother). This comedy was about two families, one from New York, one from London; the fathers met during World War Two and, on meeting again 20 years later, arrange to swap teenage daughters. Waterman was one of four British actors imported for the series, playing a London lad who suddenly acquires an American 'sister'. The programme failed to win a large enough audience share and was dropped after three months, Waterman returning to England as his green card expired. At least the job had allowed him to see episodes of his favourite Westerns, *Gunsmoke* and *Bonanza*, being filmed; however, he was less comfortable about his presence in the States just as the Cuban missile crisis reached its peak. 'My mother thought the Yanks were just being stupid," he recalled in his autobiography. "She had come through the Blitz unscathed. Even so I did not like the idea of a great big mushroom cloud.'

Following his return to Putney, Waterman's career temporarily stalled as he was by now too old for child parts. Like many others in the acting profession, he spent several years living from hand to mouth, filling in the time between parts with a variety of odd jobs, before securing a regular role in the TV soap opera *Weaver's Green. Sweeney* creator Ian Kennedy Martin was commissioned to perform drastic surgery on the series, starting an association with Waterman several years before beginning his friendship with John Thaw.

'They had used a number of writers who kept introducing new characters and at that moment in time they had about 40 continuously contracted characters and it was getting out of hand,' Ian says. 'The producer said, "What to I do about this?" And I said, "On a thing like this you only ever need six contracted characters. You need young love – which was Dennis and Vanessa Forsyth. You need two standard people the core audience are identifying with – happily married 40-year-olds. And you need two more, people that the audience aspire to be – eg, the Lord of the Manor. And you hire the other people piecemeal."' As for the other 30-odd unwanted characters Ian's solution was simple, and has since become a classic plot device in ailing, overpopulated soap operas. 'We have an enormous fucking fire... And people go into that fire and they don't come out,' Ian laughs, recalling the chaos that filming this scene ultimately caused. 'Norfolk fire brigade sprayed petrol all over this field, threw a match and created a firestorm. There is footage of technicians being sucked into this, like the Dresden bombing!'

Although Waterman's character survived this conflagration, the soap soon folded anyway, and he began taking in diverse adult theatre roles. He was cast opposite Ralph Richardson in Graham Greene's final stage play *Carving a Statue* before taking part in several Royal Court productions. These included *Twelfth Night,* John Osborne's *A Patriot for Me* and Edward Bond's highly controversial *Saved.* This last play, which featured the stoning to death of a baby in a pram, caused a moral panic not dissimilar to that created by Sarah Kane's *Blasted* three decades later. On the strength of his performance as one of the teenagers involved in this killing, Waterman began to receive offers of work in television plays, including *Cry Baby Bunting* and *I Can Walk Where I Like, Can't I?*. The latter featured a ceratain John Thaw in the cast.

Waterman's television work brought him to the attention of director Peter Collinson, who cast him as the male lead in *Up the Junction* (1967). The film was based on the novel by Nell Dunn and had previously been filmed as a BBC television play in

1965, causing controversy with its inclusion of an unwanted pregnancy and a back-street abortion. Suzy Kendall and Maureen Lipman also appeared in the film, which featured a middle-class Chelsea it-girl who cohabits with Waterman's character – Peter – in Battersea. 'It was a massive part,' Waterman acknowledged when interviewed in 1976. 'It had so many facets to it, it gave me a real opportunity to spread myself. That was when people realised, if they ever had realised that I was a child actor, that I wasn't any more.'

Waterman's cinema career continued when he appeared in another Collinson film, *Fright* (1970) – a low-budget British shocker that predated the spate of Hollywood slasher movies by several years. Written by Tudor Gates (who would later write for *The Sweeney*), *Fright* featured Dennis's Corona contemporary Susan George as a teenager left alone to babysit while an all-too-plausible maniac (Ian Bannen) lurks outside. Waterman played the babysitter's amorous boyfriend who gets knocked off in the first reel. Significantly, Waterman's future *Minder* co-star, George Cole, also appeared in the film, but later joked that he couldn't remember working with Dennis on it: 'I guess [Dennis] must have been that body lying face down in the hall that I'd been stepping over for the last three weeks!'

Dennis's other films around this time included another Hammer appearance in *Scars of Dracula*, plus *Man in the Wilderness*, *The Eyes Have It*, *The Belstone Fox* and *The Smashing Bird I Used to Know*. His television work also went on and, in 1973, as a result of a brief appearance in the *Special Branch* episode 'Stand and Deliver', the episode's director Tom Clegg put Waterman's name forward for the role of Detective Sergeant George Carter in 'Regan'. 'I arranged to meet him in a pub in Richmond,' Clegg recalls. 'We talked about boxing, about football, about everything [apart from the programme], but I knew he could do it. He's such a gregarious, generous and talented actor. He'd had a lot more film experience than John had, as he'd been in the business as a child actor. He was the ideal partner for John; he had that lightness of touch.' Having previously worked with Waterman on *Weaver's Green*, Ian Kennedy Martin was also pleased with the choice.

The subsequent success of *The Sweeney* made Waterman a household name. However, as Waterman recalls in his autobiography, things could have turned out rather differently had John Thaw not advocated giving Carter a stronger role in the production. 'The series was written specifically for John, as a vehicle to help propel him up the ladder of success, but it was he who encouraged the writers to make it a double-act. Originally, my character was written very much the second-in-command, always in the background. I'd stand by the door while Regan questioned someone, I'd pass on messages from the office, I'd wait in the car, or look on while he telephoned, until eventually John, of his own volition, started giving me lines of his to say. Finally he went to Ted Childs and pointed out that it was ridiculous to waste a good actor like me. It would be far more realistic, he suggested, if we interacted. The writers noted how we threw lines at one another as if we'd been mates for years, and started writing more dialogue for the two of us. We had that one ingredient that cannot be manufactured – chemistry... That sort of generosity from one actor to another is extremely rare.'

Director David Wickes concurs. 'John was a really generous, giving actor. He would give lines to Dennis… and when we were doing staging, and blocking out scenes, John wouldn't mind if the attention was on Dennis for longer than it should have been. "We'll follow Dennis up to the bar, he brings the two drinks back and puts them down there like that, and we end up on Dennis over your shoulder." He'd go, "OK." Another star would say, 'You do not! You're on *me*, with him out of focus at the bar!"... [But] John would never, ever do that.' Waterman's popularity in what became an almost equal partnership with John Thaw enabled him to tour in a stage production of Bill Naughton's play *Alfie* between series of *The Sweeney*. The part of the archetypal cockney Jack-the-lad could have been tailor-made for the actor.

Having established a good working relationship with Clegg on *The Sweeney*, Waterman worked with him again in the early 1980s on the film *The First World Cup – A Captain's Tale*. This was Dennis's first venture into TV production and was a critically acclaimed one, nominated for an Emmy Award. Through his film company East End Films, Waterman later produced and played the lead in the feature film *Cold Justice* (1989), directed by another graduate of the *Sweeney*, Terry Green. However, this proved less successful: the film failed to find a distributor and Waterman lost a lot of his own money on the project.

Waterman's career was boosted even further by his next major TV series, the popular and long-running *Minder*. Initially Terry McCann, the 'minder', was to have been centre stage; however, Waterman recalls advocating enlarging George Cole's character in a reflection of John Thaw's recommendations on *The Sweeney* a few years earlier. Created by Leon Griffiths, *Minder* took off as Cole's Arthur , the slightly dodgy velvet-collared entrepreneur, resonated with the 1980s' free enterprise culture. Inevitably, the character of Daley would get out of his depth, necessitating Terry turning up and laying out the resident heavy in a spectacular fight scene; not that dissimilar to the climax of many a *Sweeney*. Drawing partly upon his characterisation of Carter, Waterman's Terry was a tough working class Londoner whose interests again included boxing and women.

This second hit series could easily have fallen at the first hurdle, however. The first series didn't do very well, viewing being hampered by an ITV strike. Nevertheless, the decision was made to carry on. 'They went for it and the interesting thing was that the first series did nothing – no impact and no ratings,' the series' executive producer, Johnny Goodman, recalls. 'It came under discussion in the board meeting immediately following the series and [Brian Cowgill, Thames' Programme Controller] said, "Well, we've got nothing else popping up to go, so do another 13." So, the second 13? A little bit better, but no fireworks. At the next board meeting, for some unknown reason it was decided we would do *another* 13. Well, the third series took off like a house on fire and suddenly we were repeating all the old ones, and we became a household name. In America, you make one pilot and if it isn't a raging success, you're dead. To make 26 shows and then a further 13 was extraordinary.'

Minder ran sporadically throughout the eighties. Waterman's final series was screened in 1989, and the programme continued after that with actor Gary Webster taking over as Daly's new protector. As a whole, the series is still fondly remembered as a prime example of entertaining comedy drama.

The theme tune to *Minder,* entitled 'I Could Be So Good for You', was written by Waterman himself with the help of musician Gerard Kenny. Released as a single, it was part of the actor's desire to pursue an alternative career as a musician. Throughout his acting career Waterman has always had a keen interest in music, constantly adding to an ever-expanding record collection and touring Britain in concert with Kenny and Sheena Easton. He made appearances on *The Val Doonican Show, The Harry Secombe Christmas Special* with Cleo Laine, and his own one-hour TV music special, *With a Little Help from my Friends,* also releasing two albums, *Down Wind of Angels* and *Waterman,* produced by ex-Shadows drummer Brian Bennett. In the mid-1980s, Waterman also worked with Roxy Music mainstays Phil Manzanera and Andy Mackay in their band the Explorers; the connection came from Waterman's then-wife Rula Lenska, who had starred in Mackay's TV series *Rock Follies* some ten years before.

By the mid-eighties Waterman was looking for fresh challenges and found one in a four-hour miniseries for BBC 2, *The Life and Loves of a She Devil.* Adapted from Fay Weldon's book by Ted Whitehead, this series also starred Julie T Wallace, Patricia Hodge, Bernard Hepton and Tom Baker. It was an unsettling mixture of black comedy, feminist social commentary and outright fantasy which became an enormous critical and popular success, ultimately spawning a (far inferior) Hollywood movie. Cast in the series as an adulterous husband, Waterman frequently found his off-screen relationships splashed across the tabloids too. He was married three times, to Penny Dixon, Patricia Maynard and Rula Lenska, the latter two making appearances in *The Sweeney* and *Minder* respectivitely.

In 1989 Waterman returned to comedy-drama with the series *Stay Lucky* for Yorkshire Television. Like *The Sweeney* and *Minder,* this series was based around another partnership linked to crime, although in this instance the relationship had a romantic dimension. Waterman played Thomas Gynn, a cockney rough diamond with form, who, after unwittingly acting as getaway driver on a robbery, goes to ground in Yorkshire and looks up his ex, an attractive Northern businesswoman played by Jan Francis. The series ultimately ran for three years but when its original creator, Geoff McQueen, died, the cast opted not to make any further episodes. While this was being made, Waterman also tried his hand at straight situation comedy, with Jim Davidson in the BBC series *On the Up* (1990-2).

1992 found Waterman in Australia, starring in *Jeffrey Bernard is Unwell,* a play written by Keith Waterhouse and directed by Ned Sherrin. This successful tour took in Perth, Brisbane and Sydney. Another change of approach for the actor, the part had previously been played by Peter O'Toole but, as Keith Waterhouse noted, 'Dennis brought to the part a quality of his own, a vulnerability which plumbed the depths of sadness in the role. There is a scene where Jeff is contemplating death, and in his imagination, the friends he has known are with him, awaiting the call of the Grim Reaper. They line up saying graciously, "After you, old boy." "No, after you." Dennis did it with such exquisite melancholy, it brought tears to your eyes.' Building on his association with the writer, Waterman returned to Australia in 1999 in another Waterhouse play, *Bing Bong.*

Shortly before embarking on a UK tour of *Jeffrey Bernard is Unwell*, Waterman completed a hard-hitting two-hour film for Yorkshire Television called *Circle of Deceit*, in which he played John Neil, a retired SAS officer sent to infiltrate the IRA while still traumatised by the murder of his wife and child in a terrorist bombing. The film was directed by Geoffrey Sax and also starred Derek Jacobi, Peter Vaughan and Clare Higgins. A follow-up series of four films, *Circles of Deceit*, followed in 1996, but the actor was less happy with the sequels, feeling that the scripts were inferior. By the middle of the 1990s he was also a regular presenter on the BBC's football retrospective, *Match of the Seventies*; off-screen he is a keen sportsman, playing football, cricket and golf.

While retaining his natural affinity for characters with a street-wise edge, Waterman continues to diversify with parts like the hard-working businessman-turned-killer in the BBC's 2002 drama *Murder in Mind* and the comically debauched dustman Alfred P Doolittle in the recent West End revival of *My Fair Lady*. From child actor with a middle-class accent to gritty cockney to seasoned character actor, Waterman has, like his late *Sweeney* co-star, become a very British icon.

GARFIELD MORGAN

'[Garfield] was good. He portrayed the right amount of self-importance and was always a bit out of touch with what was going on. He was a lovely guy and he accepted all this, like any actor would, and obviously you're not going to leave something that was very successful and gave you work throughout the year.'
Tom Clegg, Sweeney *director*

* * *

ON 19 APRIL 1931, OVER 40 YEARS BEFORE HE WAS TO CREATE THE ROLE of Frank Haskins, Regan and Carter's ulcer-suffering 'guvnor', Garfield Morgan was born in Birmingham. Following brief stints in the services and as a dentist's assistant, he decided on an acting career and enrolled at Birmingham Drama School.

Interviewed in 1976 he remembered: 'I left school when I was 14, hardly able to read or write. I really was very thick and ignorant. It wasn't until a few years later that I learnt reading and writing, and then I regretted not learning more at school. I knew that pretty soon I was going to be conscripted into the army, so I took a job and just waited to be called up. I was a real back-street boy and it never crossed my mind to go into the theatre. But a friend from work, who had bullied me into joining the local youth club, then persuaded me to join the drama group. I didn't want to join at first but when I did I found I really enjoyed acting and being involved with theatre. So I decided that was what I wanted to do as a profession. I had just got a job as an assistant stage manager when I was called into the army. And when I came out, I went to drama school. That's how my career began.'

From Birmingham he went on to act and direct at the Marlowe Theatre Canterbury in 1957-8 and then at the Library Theatre Manchester in 1959 and 1960. Following a two-week stint as Vince Plummer, relief manager of the Rovers' Return pub in fledgling soap *Coronation Street,* he went on to become a regular supporting actor throughout the 1960s and 1970s on television.

One of his early appearances was in 1965, with Judy Parfitt in the 'The New Dimension', the third episode of the ABC-produced science fiction drama *Undermind.* This series, in which a couple investigates mind-control techniques being perpetrated by a secret conspiracy, was *The X-Files* of its day and ran for 11 episodes before slipping into undeserved obscurity.

ITC, the division of ATV that supplied many filmed adventures for the UK and international market, became a semi-regular employer of Morgan over the rest of the decade and into the 1970s. He appeared in an episode of the Steve Forrest series *The Baron* ('Night of the Hunter') and alongside Roger Moore in both *The Saint* ('The Art Collectors') and *The Persuaders!* ('Take Seven'). The original *Randall and Hopkirk (Deceased)* featured Morgan as a worried client in a typically tongue-in-cheek tale in which the ghostly Hopkirk is scared by a fake haunted house ('House on Haunted

Hill'). Morgan's path also crossed that of *Department S,* the home of debonair detective and camp crusader Jason King ('Spencer Bodily is Sixty Years Old'). He played three different characters in ABC TV's *The Avengers,* in the episodes 'Game', 'Take-Over' and 'The Fear Merchants'. 'There were so many [of them],' he reminisces of the almost unbroken run of fantastic, adventurous and sometimes whimsical fantasy and adventure serials. 'Mostly, they were great fun.'

Like Dennis Waterman, his career path crossed John Thaw's prior to *The Sweeney.* He appeared with Thaw in the opening episode of *Redcap* (1966) and later returned in another role, as Sergeant O'Keefe in the episode 'The Killer'. Like Thaw, Morgan also appeared in an early *Z-Cars* episode, the memorable 'Friday Night'. Morgan played a drunk driver, making the transition from bolshiness to remorse and fear of losing his license in the space of a few scenes. *Softly Softly,* the *Z-Cars* spin-off, shifted the action to Bristol, and Morgan played one of his first regular TV roles, appearing with Stratford Johns and Frank Windsor in the early episodes as Inspector Gwyn Lewis.

A more outlandish entry in Morgan's extensive CV was the historical series *Judge Dee* for Granada Television in 1969, in which he also played a regular character, Tao Gan. This series was based on the adventures of a real-life character in China, with Michael Goodliffe in the lead. It was a complete departure from Morgan's previous work, featuring British actors made up as orientals. '*Judge Dee* was, I believe, the first television programme where each episode was recorded over several days following a two-week rehearsal period,' Morgan says of the scheduling of this off-beat series. 'Sadly, it was made in black and white just as colour television was beginning, and possibly suffered as a result.'

Like Thaw and Waterman, Morgan was also comfortable in light entertainment, playing the straight man in a number of situation comedies, such as the Bill Fraser railway farce *The Train Now Standing* (1973) and *Dear Mother... Love Albert* (1969-1972). The latter series, a vehicle for ex-*Likely Lad* Rodney Bewes, featured Morgan as another straight man, factory boss A C Strain.

By now, Morgan's impressive stature and often implacable looks were getting him cast as authority figures or as calculating villains, even in comedy, although being pigeonholed didn't seem to bother the actor: 'I don't think typecasting was a problem,' he says. This impressive run of characters continued with a notable guest performance as KGB agent Lubin in an episode of the Thames series *Callan* in 1969. The producers of American cop show *Madigan* (1972) also made use of Morgan's authoritative persona when he featured as another policeman, a top Scotland Yard cop, in the episode 'The London Beat'. Two years later, and immediately prior to his casting as Detective Chief Inspector Frank Haskins, he was giving orders again, this time as an Israeli general in the film of Frederick Forsyth's *The Odessa File* (1974).

Morgan isn't certain if there was a specific reason the producers cast him in *The Sweeney;* he also guested in *Public Eye,* a detective series overseen by one of the show's executive producers, Lloyd Shirley. 'I really don't know if connections with other work I did for Thames resulted in my being cast. Most (not all) directors and producers like working with people they know and trust.' It was possibly Morgan's appearance in the *Special Branch* episode 'Something about a Soldier', overseen by the *Sweeney* team, that led to his casting as Haskins.

Asked at the time what qualities he had in common with Haskins, he stated, 'Discipline ... In order to be an actor one has to have a large degree of self-discipline. In fact, self-discipline is important if one is going to be a success at any career. I don't approve of an excess of discipline, but a certain amount is absolutely essential. I have no trouble being a boss. After all, it's something I have done in real life: as an actor I am my own boss, and it's a job which has to be done as professionally as if one was running a company.' He went on to qualify this by pointing out, 'I'm far too jokey a fellow to be like Haskins. I know he does have a certain very intelligent type of wit, and when he makes a joke it always comes off, but my humour is much wider... I don't like red tape at all. I've had many brushes with it, and have a healthy dislike of needless rules and regulations.'

Despite his regular billing on the opening titles, Morgan enjoyed rather less screen time than Thaw and Waterman. As director David Wickes observed, the series 'was never a trio, not really. Poor old Garfield Morgan; he didn't have anything like the number of scenes [the other two had]. He was always in a semi-negative position, he was always the restraining influence on Regan, and therefore he became a kind of Johnny One-Note: sometimes he was stitched up, sometimes he was suspended, sometimes he was supportive and at other times he was sceptical. Necessary, but it limited his role; he only had a small, narrow spectrum and he couldn't stray beyond it. Whereas the others roved more, he was rather stuck. I think he was very aware of that.'

Tom Clegg concurs: 'Unfortunately, which has been proved time and time again, characters like [Haskins] end up with very little to do. You've only got two ways to go; either you agree with the guys' coming in with their problems or you oppose it. Normally you oppose it for dramatic reasons. A lot of the scenes they were doing were really repetitive. The guys had to go in for their traditional rollicking from Garfield and then just ignore him and get on and do exactly what they wanted. It's very difficult to write a third character into something like that. You've got two main characters around that story, you've got a team of guys working with them in the Flying Squad, you've got the boss and you've got your guest actors, so you don't have a lot of space left.'

Morgan usually filmed his scenes on Fridays (barring location work), which was generally when the Squad office scenes were shot prior to the Euston team's weekly adjournment to the pub. One development that Morgan was pleased about occurred when writers such as Roger Marshall and Trevor Preston began to give Haskins more to do within the stories. 'They tried, obviously, because it is very frustrating for the actor to keep coming in and playing virtually the same scene,' Tom Clegg noted. 'There was a limit to how much he could do, but unfortunately, if we had to edit an episode that was too long, it would always be those sort of areas that would get cut.'

Despite the limitations of Haskins's character, the actor enjoyed his time on the series. '*The Sweeney* directors were a very diverse and interesting group,' he recalls fondly. 'I particularly enjoyed working with Douglas Camfield (sadly, no longer with us), Tom Clegg and Ted Childs. The crew were an exceptional bunch… The same one for the whole series. The success of the series was always in my view due to Ted Childs and that fantastic, hard-working, talented and very funny team that he put together.'

During the filming of *The Sweeney*, Morgan divided his time between television and the stage. 'During the last series I had returned to the Northcott [Theatre Exeter] as Associate Director and leading actor,' he explained. 'I managed to juggle my theatre commitments in order to do six episodes of the final series during that time.' He starred in *Antony and Cleopatra* (1976) and *A Midsummer Night's Dream* (1977) and directed *Sleuth* and *The Boyfriend* (1977). The same year saw him directing a play by Bristol-based television writers Bob Baker and Dave Martin, *Rat Trap*. This production, starring George Sewell and Dave King, was later remounted for HTV and screened in 1979. 'It was just about OK in the television version, though the director they chose had very little drama experience,' Morgan says now. 'In hindsight, I should have insisted on directing it for television myself.'

Over the late 1970s and into the 1980s Morgan was to return to television in a variety of guest roles, in series such as *Boon*, *Lovejoy*, *Born Kicking* and *Dangerfield*. He also made regular appearances in situation comedies, playing 'The Bishop', one of a trio of con men in *West End Tales* (ATV 1981), Hywel Bennett's landlord in *Shelley* (Thames 1979-1984), the pompous Captain in Johnny Speight's unsuccessful satire of golf club snobbery *The Nineteenth Hole* (Central 1989) and the Party Whip in *No Job for a Lady* (Thames 1990-92).

Rather like George Sewell spoofing his *Special Branch* persona in *The Detectives*, Morgan sent up his Haskins characterisation by appearing in virtually the same role in a series of sketches for the BBC's *Alas Smith and Jones* in 1987, entitled 'Porno and Bribeasy'. His appearance as the grumpy, desk-bound superior in Euston's *Minder on the Orient Express* was also an in-joke; he played an unnamed Superintendent mediating a dispute between warring coppers Rycott and Chisholm as both attempted to 'nick' a certain Arthur Daly. The character later returned in the episode 'Not a Sorry Lorry, Morrie' in 1988, but this time was named Mason, which rather undermined the point of Morgan's casting.

Morgan is still a working actor and director; he returned to the cinema in the Welsh-set *The Englishman who Went Up a Hill But Came Down a Mountain*, which starred Hugh Grant. When not acting, Morgan is a keen horseman and golfer, playing several matches with Dennis Waterman and the Stay Lucky Amateur Golf Society, and taking part in charity events on the golf circuit. He also did public-spirited work with Rick Wakeman as narrator on *The New Gospels*; this was recorded in 1995 at Peel Castle on the Isle of Man as a TV special for Border Television in order to raise money for charity.

Throughout his extensive career, though, his preference has always been for the stage. 'Whilst I enjoy films and television, the theatre will always be my first choice,' he says. Now over 70, he recently appeared in *In Two Minds*, a play by the writer Richard Harris, who once scripted two episodes of *The Sweeney*. Like many other members of the series' production team, the pair's relationship has endured since their participation in that production. 'I played one of the two male characters in what I believe is a very fine play,' Morgan says. 'I have known Richard for some years and have appeared in his other plays and series by him.'

Like many actors, he finds it difficult to choose a favourite role, although he has particular regard for Shakespeare ('Falstaff, Macbeth, Cassius, Brutus, Richard III, Antony in *Antony and Cleopatra* and most recently Gloucester in *King Lear*') as well as works by contemporary writers, in particular Ernest Lehman. 'George in *Who's Afraid of Virginia Woolf?*… may well be the favourite part I've played. Also *This Savage Parade, Misalliance, The Caretaker*.' As a director he enjoyed working on *The Lovers, Henry V, Dr Faustus, The Diary of Anne Frank* and *Sleuth*. '*Sleuth* is in fact much better in the theatre. I quite enjoyed the film but the atmosphere that can be created in the theatre is just something else... The list would go on and on. I've had a great deal of satisfaction and, of course, a great deal of frustration when I thought I could have done it better, but all in all very few real regrets... I do know how lucky I am to have spent my life doing the thing I love.'

While Morgan may not have had as glamorous a role in *The Sweeney* as his co-stars, his quiet authority was central to the series' dynamic. Like Thaw and Waterman, the actor himself has enjoyed a diverse and colourful career above and beyond the series that brought him his biggest audience.

CHAPTER 2

RAW POLICING

'Police on duty were adopting sunglasses and wearing their gloves with the cuffs turned down. They also started driving like bloody maniacs.'
Kenneth Oxford, Chief Constable of Merseyside,
on the influence of 1970s TV cops on his officers

'It's very easy to research because you can't stop policemen talking. Three lots of people can go into any situation demanding answers, and they're lawyers, doctors and policemen. And if you try to research lawyers and doctors it quite difficult unless you have the right legal [or medical] background. When you question policemen, they come out of their shell dramatically. They come up with great, different stories, and they seem to know what you want.'
Ian Kennedy Martin, *Sweeney* creator

'We used to live in Bermondsey when I was a kid. We used to open the front and back door when it was hot, so the wind would go through. The whole family were sitting down to Sunday lunch in the kitchen, my Dad, Mum, sisters, and brothers. Then – bosh, bosh, bosh, bosh, bosh – there were these footsteps – bosh, bosh, bosh, bosh, bosh – down our hallway. One of my Dad's best friends comes in the kitchen says, "Hello Bob, hello Phil," and goes out through the back garden, over the fence and across the square. Next minute, two fucking Old Bill, huffing and puffing, come through and say "Where's he gone?" My father says, "Who, who?" I grew up with that sort of attitude so I suppose it gets reflected in my writing.'
Trevor Preston, Sweeney *writer*

* * *

THE SWEENEY'S FRENETIC TITLES, CUT TO THE BEAT OF AN INSISTENT, driving signature tune, shows rough diamond coppers Detective Inspector Jack Regan and Detective Sergeant George Carter in a car chase with two villains through London's streets, leading to an armed arrest on derelict wasteground. The sequence is at once a slick piece of film editing and an earthy projection of a believable criminal landscape. This chapter looks at how developments in real crime, and the cinematic and TV portrayals of the police, developed to the point where the arrival of *The Sweeney* in 1975 was exactly right for the mid-seventies zeitgeist.

Z-VICTOR 1

The genesis of the fallible, vulnerable, and far-from-perfect Regan and Carter – they swore, they drank, they had personal problems and were dirty fighters – dates back to the BBC series *Z-Cars*, which began transmission in 1962. The earlier series was a reaction against the reassuring, cosy integrity of Sergeant George ('Evening all') Dixon in *Dixon of Dock Green*, which had begun in 1955 and up until the early sixties was TV's premier police series. *Z-Cars'* creator Troy Kennedy Martin saw nothing in it that reflected what he knew about the police: 'I only did *Z-Cars* because I hated *Dixon of Dock Green*. I thought there ought to be an alternative viewpoint and I also wanted to write about young policemen, and that's how it went.'

The new series, set in Merseyside, was indeed a departure from Dixon's tired London beat. It concentrated on the young PCs who drove the mobile police units – the Z-Cars of the title – through a new town called Kirby. They dealt with all the social problems a modern development threw up, from drunken Irishmen to drug addiction, in stories that ran the gamut from comical to harrowing, often at the same time, (a characteristic of Kennedy Martin's writing). *Z-Cars'* accurate snapshots of contemporary urban life reflected the trend for 'kitchen sink' realism initiated by writers like John Osborne (*Look Back in Anger*) and Shelagh Delaney (*A Taste of Honey*).

'What *Z-Cars* did was put an end to 'ello 'ello with slippers on,' says Ray Jenkins, a *Z-Cars* and *Sweeney* scriptwriter. 'They had these guys who sat in police cars, bored out of their crusts, who chatted, partied and talked about women. That realism became a discipline, I'm absolutely convinced. The early writers who were any good on *Z-Cars* learned to do their research and were children of that discipline of neo-realism.' As a result, the regular characters were written in believable shades of grey; they were cynical about their jobs, funny, became emotionally involved in cases and were guilty of racism.

Detective Chief Inspector Charlie Barlow (Stratford Johns) was another innovation. For the first time, a detective was shown to be bad-empered and aggressive, with a problematic home-life. The mould-breaking nature of this character was so successful that Barlow and his Sergeant, Watt (Frank Windsor), were spun-off in their own series *Softly, Softly* (later *Softly, Softly: Task Force*).

Z-Cars eventually lost its edge through being continually reformatted prior to its demise in the seventies. Ironically, by that time its co-creator Troy Kennedy Martin, who along with friend and colleague John McGrath had opted to move on relatively quickly after the programme's inception, saw the show as being just as outdated as *Dixon of Dock Green* had been. However, the radical overhaul of the police's image which *Z-Cars* initiated was an important progression towards the next stage, the development of Jack Regan and his colleagues in 1974. It's no coincidence that one of *Z-Cars'* originators was also instrumental in the evolution of *The Sweeney*.

JACKS AND KNAVES

Apart from believably flawed characters, the biggest legacy *Z-Cars* bequeathed to *The Sweeney* was a feel for authenticity and contemporary relevance in its subject matter. *Z-*

Cars reflected modern policing so accurately, and unflinchingly, that one of its advisers, Bill Roberts, the former head of Lancashire CID, made public how shocked his fellow officers were. 'This was not the way in which the image of the police should be presented,' was the official line, prefiguring the same reaction by the upper echelons of the police to *The Sweeney* 13 years later. Typically, the rank and file in the force loved both series.

The ability of the police series to provoke a reaction, good or otherwise, always came from a firm basis in reality. *The Sweeney* took as its starting point the political changes taking place at Scotland Yard in the early seventies. Ian Kennedy Martin, Troy's brother and Jack Regan's creator, based his troubled DI on a serving officer he knew. 'When my real cop went to Scotland Yard he was in the shit,' the writer says. 'This was the beginning of the focus group and doing everything by the book.' At the time, there was a much closer – perhaps too close – relationship between the police and the London underworld. 'There were members of the Flying Squad sitting in Quo Vadis [a Soho Italian restaurant] and they'd say, "Charge this to Mr Humphries' account,"' Kennedy Martin goes on, referring to the Soho porn baron. 'Their argument was, "We either allow one man to run pornography, or we remove him and leave ten Maltese, 15 Cypriots, a couple of Chinese and a lot of Welshmen killing each other for the big business."'

Such an alliance was obviously open to abuse, and despite the realistic trade-off between the Flying Squad and criminals, corruption was widespread. Ian Kennedy Martin: 'When [Commissioner Robert] Mark came in it all stopped. You were not allowed to drink with villains. My cop said, "Come down to Fulham, I want you to meet some of my officers." Half of them were villains and half of them were Flying Squad officers, and you could not tell one from the other! There were 250 early retirements when Mark came in. My cop, who wasn't bent, was an obsessive policeman, and he was absolutely furious about how Mark put a load of Freemasons into A10 [the police complaints division].'

The conflict between the streetwise old and the bureaucratic new would form the backbone of the series. 'Police from other countries came in at Flying Squad level, guys from the FBI and various other organisations like the South African police. They all knew about the Flying Squad and treated them as an elite bunch of officers who got stuck in and got results,' Kennedy Martin says. 'But at Scotland Yard they were treated like naughty boys. A10 was investigating them and they used to get really pissed off.'

One thing *The Sweeney* did have to back down from for political reasons, like *Z-Cars* before it, was dealing with police corruption: G F Newman's suggestion at a *Z-Cars* script conference that 'Sgt Watt is offered a bribe for £500, which he accepts,' was swiftly vetoed. Arguably, one of the reasons Newman's own *Law and Order* – which dealt specifically with police immorality – got made and transmitted in 1978 was due to a shift in the public perception of the police initiated by the two Kennedy Martin-generated series.

In the interests of maintaining a good relationship, *The Sweeney* production team turned a blind eye to what was really going on in the Flying Squad. 'Most of the information they got was from informers,' producer Ted Childs explains. 'It was usually done on a partly cash deal and partly an insurance recovery reward deal. The guy who put you in the frame gets half of it and the cops involved get the other half. That's how they got all the big houses with swimming pools when they were only on 20 grand a year! There was a lot of that going on, but we had to be very careful that Regan or Carter weren't into that sort of thing. We tried to hint as much as possible but had to be careful not to get on the wrong side of Scotland Yard.' As a result, any explicit references to corruption were restricted to one TV episode and the second *Sweeney* feature film. Authenticity could clearly only be taken so far.

THE CHAPS

While the Kennedy Martins' input gave *The Sweeney* a dose of realism from the police's point of view, one of the show's innovations was to present the opposite outlook. 'Troy and Ian knew the police side,' stunt arranger Peter Brayham says, 'but they didn't know much about 'the chaps', only what the police had told them'. Brayham had grown up in South London and mixed with exactly the kind of characters being portrayed as the opposition in the scripts. A stuntman since the 1950s, his knowledge had been used to give verisimilitude to an armed theft in the 1967 Stanley Baker film *Robbery*. 'I used to run with a crowd of guys who were all boxers and some of the chaps,' Brayham says. 'I used to get involved in fist fights more than anything else.'

The stunt co-ordinator's first-hand experience of the London crime scene added a naturalistic touch to the programme's many fight sequences: 'I always wanted to show what would really happen. You kick a guy in the bollocks, pull his jacket over his head and give him another kicking so he can't see what's coming.' Dennis Waterman praises the sense of real-life Brayham's skills helped enhance in the series: 'Pete was terrific. He knew about street fighting, which was very important. The thing about *The Sweeney* was that we could get beaten up and we could lose cases – we weren't the great big heroes. We could lose in fights and never had to look pretty afterwards, during, or whatever. And Pete had some great guys working round him, so it was always a joy when there was a good action sequence.' Brayham's concern to get the minutiae right also extended to advising how the actors should react to firearms: 'They were drawing their weapons to go out on a raid, and one of the guys was acting Jack the Lad. I said, "He wouldn't be Jack-the-Lad. He'd be shitting himself. I've never been a copper, but I know what the other side is. 90 per cent of the time the butterflies don't stop. That's why they all end up with high blood pressure and pop off quick, because they're under such stress and tension. No one takes it that calm."'

Once the series became established, it had the benefit of the unofficial advisers who drank at *The Sweeney* production team's favourite pub, The Red Cow in Hammersmith. 'The Red Cow was full of villains!' states director David Wickes. 'Half the real Sweeney used to go there, partly because of that. It wasn't strange to see Mad Frankie Fraser in there. The place was like a well you went to with a bucket, because it was *packed* with villains. You'd go in there, and someone'd say, "'Ere, this is George, this is 'Arry, this is Jim... This is what's wrong with your bloody television programme." And they'd lay it on us – they would even harangue the Assistant Editor!'

As well as the hard side of London villainy, the programme's access to what really went on provided an insight into its quirkier side. Bizarre real-life incidents appealed to the scriptwriters (particularly Troy Kennedy Martin, who had always brought a comic and anarchic edge to his writing), helping to make the hard-line tone of the series more palatable and idiosyncratic. Prolific *Sweeney* director Tom Clegg recalls one particular incident: 'A gang came running out of a bank and the get-away driver had got blocked in. So they broke into another one, but it was invalid-modified. The guy didn't know how to drive it properly and they were kangarooing down the road in this three-wheeled disabled driver's car. A lot of the things we put in *The Sweeney* seemed ridiculous, but in reality these funny things did happen.'

Trevor Preston, arguably the series' most influential writer, writing 11 of the series' 54 scripts, also came from a background that enhanced the programme's true-to-life representation of working class villainy. 'You can only write about what you know,' he says. 'I came from that area. Villains were what I knew.' He and Kennedy Martin also gave the series a political dimension: distrustful of the educated upper-middle class that constituted the British establishment, they attacked its representatives in their scripts. 'They were targets,' Kennedy Martin affirms, while Preston adds, '*The Sweeney* was left wing. We couldn't help but feel that way inclined.'

WHISTLES AND JAM JARS

The genuine feel of *The Sweeney*'s mixture of politics, humour and social comment was further enhanced by the use of underworld patter, which again came mainly via Preston and Brayham's first-hand knowledge and experiences. 'We used to take a script and take all the pony [inaccurate] dialogue out of it,' the stunt arranger says. 'When the first dialogue came along, 'rozzers' came up, and I said, "They wouldn't say that. They'd call them the Filth, or Old Bill"; "OK. Let's use Filth or Old Bill." You were changing the dialogue, because there was so many of the 'chaps' there, if you know what I mean – there were a lot of faces amongst the sparks [technicians].'

Cockney rhyming slang had been developed mainly by London criminals in the 1860s to confound eavesdropping bystanders or police, or to warn fellow criminals. Slang had previously cropped up in the Adam Faith series *Budgie,* but this was the first time British TV audiences were fully exposed to a new argot that included jam jars (cars), whistles (whistle and flutes = suits) and poppy (poppy-red = bread = money). This colourful lingo added to the sense of looking into an exotic and exclusive world, a point emphasised by using slang in the series' title. 'We didn't know what to call it,' Ted Childs remembers. 'We were having a drink with a guy from the Flying Squad, we asked him what he called it and he said, "Sweeney Todd." I said, "That's it, we'll have that!" People said, "Oh, totally preposterous title," but it worked.'

The use of authentic slang was a sea change in the fictional presentation of London's working class and underworld. Its effects would be far reaching, later enriching the dialogue of series like *Only Fools and Horses* and Euston's own *Minder,* to films such as *The Long Good Friday* and, more recently, *Lock, Stock and Two Smoking Barrels.*

Although the patter made no concessions to outsiders, Brayham takes issue with the theory that it prevented *The Sweeney* being sold to the USA. 'It's absolute bollocks about the slang. You don't know all the expressions in some of the really great shows on American television. If a guy says 'goddamn/Jesus/motherfucker', you know he's confused and he's upset. You don't have to have the brains of Archimedes or Einstein to work that out.' The lack of a US sale may have actually been due to technical considerations, as *The Sweeney* was shot on 16mm film rather than the US standard of 35mm. That the series was shot on film at all gave it a unique character.

SNALL SCREEN BIG SCREEN

With so many neo-realist elements in its format, *The Sweeney* was clearly a descendant of *Z-Cars.* Its look at the seamier side of life also had an antecedent in Thames Television's *Public Eye,* which began in 1965 and concerned the adventures of down-at-heel private eye Frank Marker. Robin Chapman's Granada Television thriller *Spindoe* in 1968, and the controversial *Big Breadwinner Hog* in 1969, also anticipated *The Sweeney*'s insight into the relationships between criminals. Kieth Waterhouse and Wllis's London Weekend Television series *Budgie* also dealt with London's underworld fraternity, through the misadventures of the young petty crook 'Budgie' Bird between 1971 and 1972.

These series differed from *The Sweeney* as they were all shot on video in studio sets with inserted film sequences; essentially, they were televised theatre. The decision to make the exploits of Regan and Carter on film immediately positioned the series closer to the slickly filmed crime thrillers that came into vogue in the USA in the late sixties and early seventies.

Bullitt, made in 1968, the story of a loner cop in San Francisco, had been memorable for a spectacular car chase shot in recognisable locations without special effects trickery. However, the double-whammy of *Dirty Harry* and *The French Connection* in 1971 were what really redefined the genre. Again, both films featured a lone protagonist, but this time explored the personal and political tensions of operating as a modern-day law officer, with both Harry Callahan (Clint Eastwood) and Popeye Doyle (Gene Hackman) in conflict with their liberal superiors. In both cases, droll dialogue, a realistic mise-en-scène and the cinematic gloss of impressive car chases and action sequences enlivened the moral dilemma. The films' success would inspire TV imitators such as *Kojak, Cannon* and particularly *Starsky and Hutch,* all of which were exported to the UK. Significantly, the basic premise of both films was almost identical to the topical format of *The Sweeney,* devised by Ian Kennedy Martin three years later.

Ted Childs remembers his first exposure to the new US style of fictional policing: 'We'd finished dubbing an episode of *Special Branch* so we went and had lunch in Pizza Express and then decided we'd go to see *The French Connection.* We came out, all excited, and said "Yeah! That's what we should be doing!" Seen in relation to the adventures of anti-hero Popeye Doyle, *Special Branch*, Euston's first filmed series, already looked dated. In hindsight, its blue-tinted title sequence, showing the protagonists DI Craven (George Sewell) and DI Haggerty (Patrick Mower) among the casinos and strip clubs of London, summed up exactly what it was; a fudged attempt at a contemporary police series. As Troy Kennedy Martin put it, it featured 'Patrick Mower, gun in hand, finding missing pearls in the more exotic parts of Kensington.' Reformatting what had been a video/film insert series completely onto 16mm film had, however, given *Special Branch* a fresh look and proved a stepping stone towards *The Sweeney*, the ideal vehicle for Euston's lean and mean approach.

When the production team moved on to *The Sweeney*, the combination of a socially and politically aware, yet idiosyncratic, Brit-crime setting with the US-inspired adrenaline rush of anti-establishment action-orientated cops, created something original – a UK police series infused with a filmic, street-wise style. The objective, cinéma verité style of shooting used on *The Sweeney* was also in keeping with the mood director Mike Hodges created for the British gangster film *Get Carter*, released in 1971. Coincidentally, lighting cameraman Dusty Miller worked on both, bringing to each a style of lighting in keeping with the movie and series' documentary style. The impact of the Michael Caine-starring film wasn't lost on director Tom Clegg, who established *The Sweeney*'s equally downbeat look: '*Get Carter* was an English classic,' he says. 'One of the best.'

The broadcast of the first *Sweeney* series was almost contemporaneous with the premier transmission of the US show *Starsky and Hutch*, which began in April 1975. Both shows featured an attractive male double-act, witty repartee and engaging action sequences, introducing Anglo and Stateside audiences to the underworlds of cockney low-life and pimps, hookers and junkies respectively. The two series' new combination of the gritty and the glossy indicated that the wheel had again turned in TV's fictional presentation of the police. While *Starsky and Hutch* was a logical development from the new generation of cinema cops, *The Sweeney* was even more influential in Britain. Its synthesis of British and American crime cinema production attitudes with the tough realities of modern policing, brought the British police series firmly into the 1970s, establishing a new vocabulary for small-screen crime in the UK.

And, in time, it would be considered as much of an English classic as *Get Carter*.

CHAPTER 3

EUSTON FILMS: FROM THAMES TO TURKISTAN

'It was a brilliant time for me to be working with all that talent. To get away from the confines of studios and get out on the road, because I love location filming. I think it brings its own atmosphere with it. You could build bits in the studio, but on location you know people have sat there and life has gone on there, it has a life of its own.'
Tom Clegg, director

'[The Euston crew] knew their business, they were young, they were ambitious, they wanted to push the envelope, they wanted to try this and do that and do the other… They talked and they ate and they slept and they drank film. It was all they cared about. It wasn't to do with wages, it wasn't to do with career structure, and it wasn't to do with fame. It was to do with, "Why can't we do a four-minute take? Let's see if we can."'
David Wickes, director

'There were two distinct groups of people that made *The Sweeney*, there was the writers and the directors and then there was that crew – and they were a law unto themselves.'
Trevor Preston, writer

'Pranks were a daily occurrence, generally!'
Dennis Waterman, actor

* * *

THE LATE 1960S AND EARLY 1970S WERE DIFFICULT YEARS FOR ITV IN Britain. The 'big bang' of colour television had caused both the BBC and ITV technical expenditure to increase by over 20 per cent; largely this was down to the extra fees run up in lighting and processing colour images. Drama series were hit even harder, in some cases having to cope with a 40 per cent hike in costs. As ITV was not in receipt of any license fee, it had to make expensive new colour programmes for the same amount of money as black and white ones until increases in its advertising rates could be agreed.

Thames Television, a London-based company formed out of a merger between ABC Television and Associated Rediffusion by order of the Independent Broadcasting Authority (IBA), was in no better state than the other independent companies. In 1969 Thames' advertising revenue had fallen, and the companies' financial problems were exacerbated by high levies imposed in the government's annual budget. In the 1970s, after the Independent Broadcasting Authority lobbied for a reduction in these rates, this situation improved slightly, but there was still the double-whammy of rising costs and dwindling capital.

Action needed to be taken to stage a recovery in Thames' programming, particularly in the area of drama. Radical new strategies were needed, and one of the most far-reaching – having consequences in the television industry that are still being felt today – was the creation of a new subsidiary unit of Thames designed specifically to make films for television.

There were several precedents for this decision. One was a proposal by three employees at ABC Television who would later feature in the production of *The Sweeney* – Jim Goddard, Trevor Preston and Terry Green. In the mid-1960s, they had suggested setting up a small experimental production team working with the economic format of 16mm film, called the ABC Nucleus. Another inspiration behind the decision was probably the success of ITC, the Incorporated Television Company Ltd founded by Lew (later Lord) Grade in 1960. His company made programmes for networking by Anglia Television (ATV) and other ITV companies; with an eye on overseas sales, ITC supplied numerous adventure series on the more expensive, US-friendly medium of 35mm film, amongst them *Man in a Suitcase*, *The Persuaders!*, *The Prisoner*, *Danger Man* and *The Saint*.

Additionally, and most significantly, 16mm film had been used before on at least three occasions by documentary director turned drama director Mike Hodges. Hodges had directed a children's serial, written by Trevor Preston, entitled *The Tyrant King* using this medium, before going on to write and direct two television thriller films for adults, also on 16mm. *Suspect* was one of Thames TV's first colour drama productions and was screened on 17 November 1969 as part of the company's first night of colour television.

Following the success of Hodges' two films, it was decided that a small, flexible 16mm film unit could be made economically viable through the employment of freelance writers, directors and crew. 'People will tell you that it was the blinding insight of the management of Thames Television, who saw this great future in making television drama films; the truth was it was a business decision,' Ted Childs, *Sweeney* producer, explains. The companay had plans to rethink how its drama productions were made, as afternoon programming was beginning to start up. 'Thames realised that it was much more cost-effective to use the studios to make little cheap and nasty programmes about origami, and ladies talking about their problems, than to have an elaborate drama production,' Childs laughs. 'Conventional drama is very expensive to make. We used to build these vast sets in the studios, of railway stations with moving trains, and film inserts had to be made because the high priest of engineering had such a big say in those days. It was impossible to make any film for television on less than 35mm gauge.' For a variety of economic reasons, an alternative method of ITV drama production had become necessary.

THE FOUNDING FATHERS

The main players in the creation of the new subsidiary unit were Brian Tesler, Thames' Director of Programmes; Lloyd Shirley, Thames' Controller of Drama; and George Taylor, Head of Film Facilities. All three had had held similar management positions with ABC and had been involved in the making of Hodges' films. Consequently, they knew each other well; Lloyd Shirley and George Taylor were old friends.

'George was the technical bod who would say, "Oh, it's all too dark and you haven't got enough coverage; why don't they ever smile?" Trevor Preston recalls. 'George was the quiet accountant and Lloyd was a more flamboyant character. He used to tell terrible lies about being a professional ice hockey player. I loved Lloyd. He worked like a dog; he was always the first one in the office and the last to leave.'

Sweeney creator Ian Kennedy Martin adds, 'At half ten, quarter to eleven every morning, Lloyd would say, "Is it time for a snifter?" He was [initially] very much an appointee of Sydney Newman, the controller of ABC. Sydney took one look at the BBC and British television, and thought, 'Let's get rid of some of these pipe-smoking sports coats, and let's get some *real* people in.' And he brought all these people in from Canadian broadcasting.'

'He [Lloyd] didn't have that British thing hanging over him,' David Wickes says, 'he just went right for it, and he drove hard. He was a tough bastard, a really hard guy: he didn't suffer fools gladly, and he used to scream and shout. On one occasion, he threw a typewriter out of a window at Thames, and it landed on Brian Tesler's car outside. It made a huge dent in the bonnet, and there were bits of typewriter flying everywhere. Lloyd got what he wanted, he didn't give a damn, and he drove things through.'

With the support of Howard Thomas, Managing Director of Thames, Brian Tesler prepared the relevant financial proposals concerning the new film subsidiary. As Thomas had previously agreed to switch the ABC series *The Avengers* from videotape to film and scored a notable international success with the show, including an American network sale, he was happy to give a green light to the idea of a new film unit. The Thames Board accepted the proposal, and the new company – Euston Films – was born on 9 March 1971, named after the road that housed Thames' headquarters.

While Euston Films had a board of directors, Lloyd Shirley and George Taylor were in ultimate charge of the organisation, even though they continued in their original jobs at Thames. From the outset, Shirley worked with Thames' Director of Programmes, commissioning Euston Films' projects from the company as required for Thames' schedules.

THE FOUR-WALLERS

One contentious aspect of the new company was its relationship with the unions. At the time, the majority of ITV staff were working to the terms and conditions of a contract between unions and management called the Independent Television Companies Association (ITCA) agreement. Under this arrangement, many restrictive practices had built up, including giving at least 96 hours' notice concerning changes to working hours and having to pay large amounts of overtime if productions over-ran unexpectedly.

For ITC's film series, a different arrangement, known as the British Film and Television Producers Association (BFTPA) agreement, had been used. Using feature film production as its model, this contract was more flexible, particularly when rescheduling technicians' working hours at short notice. 'The advantages were that you could do buy-outs up front with Equity, the Writers' Guild and the Musicians' Union,' Ted Childs explains. 'From the point of view of the Association of Cinema and Television Technicians (ACTT) union, you could operate in the same casual way as you did in films.' The BFTPA television films agreement was designed to maximise profits, and Euston were shrewd to use it as the basis for their productions. Ian Kennedy Martin recollects: 'A writer was paid his fee and got an extra 100 per cent, and that was the buyout – they didn't earn anything from it after that. Actors likewise. It meant that [ITC and Euston] could take a product anywhere in the world and sell it for whatever they wanted to with no subsequent rights [issues].'

Uniquely for the time, Thames' new film unit was founded on a television labour force working on short, fixed term contracts. Because of this, the company began to experience industrial relations problems, not least because the ACTT Executive Committee greeted its introduction of totally location-based, 'Four Wall' style of production with hostility. The ACTT were a studio-based union and faced a declining membership following the slump in the British film industry during the 1970s.

'Four-Wallers meant going off with very lightweight equipment – cameras, lights, things like that – to find a suitable building that would suit the particular production,' film editor John S Smith explains. 'The art department and the location manager would set it all up. You could go in there, film, plug into the mains and use their electricity, and afterwards a couple of stage hands would clear the place up and the unit would go off to the next location. This was so much cheaper than going to Pinewood or Shepperton and being locked into their administration and their time scale. So, the unions weren't too pleased with Euston Films when they started up.' Ian Kennedy Martin concurs: 'The union situation was so difficult. They didn't want to make any drama outside of the studios.'

In late October 1973, ACTT executives informed Euston that it was being blacklisted. As a reason had to be given, the Executive cited unhygienic and unsafe conditions in Colet Court (Euston's base of production), stating that Elstree Studios, which EMI at the time were intending to close, should be used instead. The reality for the Euston crew was very different, as Ted Childs recalls: 'The argument that the ACTT used was that we were exploiting their members and making them work in appalling conditions. [But] everyone enjoyed it, we could do what we liked, there was a piss-up every night, and nobody gave a toss.'

The union's sudden announcement was in turn greeted with fury by the Euston crew, who had all begun to enjoy the autonomy the company offered them. The crew led a deputation which fought its way into an Executive Committee meeting and later held a demo outside ACTT HQ in Soho Square. The union was supposed to preserve the employment prospects of its members, rather than destroy them, and several Euston employees, including Chris Burt, Ian Toynton, Eamonn Duffy, John Maskall and Mike Silverlock, all spoke out.

'That triggered the film branch into life and they said, "The television branch isn't going to dictate to our members how they work,"' Childs continues. 'If you got so many signatures the union had to agree to an extraordinary general meeting. They got these signatures and we went to Camden Town Hall. It was a nightmare; there was a lot of screaming and shouting. With the influence of a lot of the leading figures from the film industry present, the film branch decided that if the members of the television branch started dictating to their members how they should work then they would secede from the union. That was the last thing that [ACTT chairman] Alan Sapper wanted, so they reached a compromise.'

Aware that television was a growth industry, and that a fundamental shift in the nature, production and marketing of film material was happening, the membership backed the Euston team's point of view. Film editor Chris Burt, who successfully stood for election, remembers, 'It was Robert Bolt who decided we had to move in because [the union] had been taken over by Trotskyites. We had great big meetings – especially the film branch – and we flung them all out, but somebody had to go and take it over. We were there for about four years, but it was a terrible waste of time, really.' Eventually, ACTT union representatives were persuaded that Euston did not offer any threat to job security in the Thames studios by utilising the BFTPA agreement. It was construed that the company was there simply to handle an overflow situation.

With the dispute settled, the Euston team continued making its first 'banker', the regular product with which it could sell itself. This was the Thames series *Special Branch*, which had already run to two series made on videotape with film inserts. It had proved popular and was a safe bet for the company to commence production with. Shooting of the very first Euston film, the episode 'Red Herring', started in September 1972 with the new regular cast of George Sewell as DCI Craven and Patrick Mower as DCI Haggerty. Geoffrey Gilbert produced the first filmed series and was succeeded on the second by Ted Childs.

'I started off gofering in television,' Childs says, recalling his early career. 'I suppose I was a writer, but got the chance to work in factual television. At the time that Euston Films started, I was making documentary films for *The World at War*, but I had written a couple of scripts that had been commissioned by Lloyd Shirley. I got into Euston when they were making *Special Branch*. Their producer suddenly became unavailable, so I got a call from Lloyd saying, "Listen, how would you like to be a film producer for television?" I made it clear that I knew nothing about it, but thought, "Well, why not?" I took over the second series and managed to bullshit my way through!'

In late 1973 and early 1974 a series of discussions took place regarding the replacement of *Special Branch* with Ian Kennedy Martin's new concept for a series based on London's Flying Squad. Later entitled *The Sweeney*, Kennedy Martin's premise was enthusiastically accepted by Lloyd Shirley and George Taylor, with Shirley deciding that the first script should give the projected new series early exposure as an *Armchair Cinema* production. Euston had begun to diversify with this series of 90-minute feature-length films, which were a development of the *Armchair Theatre* plays Lloyd Shirley had produced for ABC. This first script, 'Regan', was costed at approximately £85,000; a high budget for a TV production at the time, indicative of the confidence the company had in the new project. The other five *Armchair Cinema* films, all one-offs, were 'The Prison', 'Tully', 'Sea Song', 'When Day is Done' and 'In Sickness and in Health'.

Beginning with *Special Branch* and *Armchair Cinema*, the fundamental innovation Euston Films brought about was the decision to shoot as much material as possible on location and on film. This saved money by obviating the need for a studio, and added a new atmosphere of authenticity and realism courtesy of the 16mm medium. The second unique principle was to let directors have the final cut of what they made; getting away from the standard method of making films, imported from America, where the supervising editor and production manager make the final editing decisions.

Lloyd Shirley's input was crucial to developing a totally different style of management to most other television series at the time. 'It seemed to me that you just don't get the best you can for the viewer by engaging a talented director, then putting such strictures round the way they work,' he recalled in the book *Euston Films – Made for Television*. Significantly, Shirley encouraged the crew to take artistic control over the films they made.

Euston had a production base and editing rooms in Redan Place but, starting with the second series of *Special Branch*, it was decided to take a short lease on a larger building. The building chosen was Colet Court, originally part of the St Paul's School for Boys at Hammersmith – it had previously been utilised by Lindsay Anderson for the feature film *O! Lucky Man*. The premises seemed ideal, comprising a front section that held administrative areas and a rear section containing a main assembly hall and several classrooms. 'We gave the prop buyer £50 and told him to come back with some desks and chairs,' Ted Childs says. 'Distance lends enchantment, but it was basically a derelict school with a preservation order on the front, and it's now some trendy offices.' By early 1974, Euston was an established going concern, with the premises and the team that was to make *The Sweeney* both in place.

SWEENEY TODD = FLYING SQUAD

Following the resolution of the behind the scenes discussions concerning the direction of *The Sweeney*, which resulted in Ian Kennedy Martin moving on (see Chapter Four),

Ted Childs was keen to develop further the ethos of making cinema-style films for television. In doing this he had the full backing of his crew. 'Although I trained as a studio television director, I got into film and I wanted to stay in film,' he recalls. 'I was basically full of shit about being a filmmaker, but I knew I believed it and so did the people who worked with me on it. Chris [Burt], Ian [Toynton], Tom [Clegg], the camera crews and the writers; there was a big driving force behind it all.'

Lloyd Shirley and George Taylor had occasional differences of opinion with the team regarding this radical new approach. 'Lloyd had a thing about close-ups whereas Chris [Burt] was more cinematic; we used to have one or two rows about it,' Childs explains. 'Lloyd seemed to think we were a bit too ahead of ourselves, which perhaps in hindsight we were. George [Taylor] was a technician, really. He was always very worried about the exposure and we were always pushing it a bit. We were probably shooting at night when we didn't have enough lights. Again, people like Terry [Green] were keen on this; we used to do what we thought were classy long focus shots. George was always worried that we were using long lenses to their limits and that it would look like washing powder on the screen.'

Despite Shirley and Taylor's initial reservations, the new production philosophy prevailed, even extending to how the sound was recorded. 'I think it was George [Taylor] who insisted that we only needed a [mono] terminal speaker at the dub, because we used to do those elaborate stereophonic dubs that were standard then for movies,' recalls Childs. Although this didn't make any appreciable difference when *Sweeney* episodes were being shown on early 1970s domestic television sets, the point was immaterial: the Euston team were striving for high standards.

Unlike other television series, there was no assigned script editor on *The Sweeney*, another Euston innovation that writers Troy Kennedy Martin and Trevor Preston, in particular, favoured. 'It's a terribly important point not having a script editor, because the one thing we all hated about them was that they are all failed writers,' Preston says. 'In all other forms of television we used to come up against people that couldn't get their own scripts off the ground. So it was wonderful, not having one on *The Sweeney*.' Instead, Childs assembled a team of regular and reliable writers, who would discuss their scripts with each other and with the directors they were paired with. 'We would talk about a difficult bit and Tommy Clegg would come in and he would say, "Look, I can do this, or I can do that,"' Preston elaborates. 'Or I'd say, "Well, I can adjust it so I don't use the car." Tom was the *best* director. You talked to anybody – the cameraman, all sorts of people. It's the way television should be made. It was very democratic.'

Ted Childs sometimes edited the scripts himself, or would reach a mutual agreement on any changes with the writer. 'The good thing was,' Preston continues, 'you could steam into Ted's office at any time and say, "Listen Ted, what about such and such?" He'd either say, "No, it's a load of bollocks," or "Yes, why don't you go away and do that?"' Preston also recalls the producer being very approachable and a fast decision-maker. 'The lovely thing was, if you came up with an idea in three sentences, you knew he would let us do it, because we kept coming up with the goods. You could have an airy-fairy idea in the morning, go and have a drink, a sandwich or a cup of coffee with him and you could be writing it by the afternoon!'

EIGHT-WEEK OBBO

Once each *Sweeney* script was finished, it was made into a completed episode over an eight-week period. This was broken down into two ten-days periods for pre-production and shooting, with a further four weeks of post-production.

The ten days' pre-production involved the location manager liaising with the director to decide where scenes would be shot, preparing the locations and clearing their use with the local authorities and police. The Euston crew tended to choose secluded areas such as disused wasteland and old warehouses, to minimise disruption from the public. Local businesses would have their names disguised with fictional ones; banks usually became the 'National Anglian Bank'. Any extra props not in stock would also be purchased at this time. Two sets of lighting cameramen and assistant directors worked on episodes in rotation, which allowed the production manager, lighting cameraman, assistant director and director to scout locations and sort out problems up front.

The shooting schedule would normally be Monday to Friday over the following ten-day period, with weekends put aside for over-runs or remounted scenes, although this contingency was rarely used. Rushes from the previous day's filming were checked for picture quality, integrated with the sound and assembled into a rough edit. Any muffled dialogue would be re-dubbed – again, a rarity – music and sound effects would be added and a final edit was completed within the remaining four-week post-production period.

As soon as Thames were confident with the progress on the first few episodes, the post-production team were left to edit at their discretion. John S Smith recalls, 'You'd see the rushes from the previous day's filming with the management while the crew were out shooting somewhere. We would synchronise and screen them on Steenbecks [editing machines] and assess them. If the crew weren't around, someone would telephone in and ask if they were all right, and if you said "Yes" you'd start editing. No hold-ups whatsoever.' The film editors also alternated on different episodes. 'You'd assemble the film as quickly as possible,' says Smith. 'The director who was directing the first one would come in after his ten working days, while the other film was being shot, and work with you completing the editing. It was then shown to the Executive Producers in the second week, who would finalise it, and then the film was committed to the dubbing editor and we would also start fitting music.'

On average, five minutes of edited-down, usable material had to be shot every day. Ten days was the standard period also allocated to ITC serials, but these often had a second unit that shared some of the workload. 'You couldn't mess about. You had to move like lightning as you had to film all over London,' director David Wickes remembers. 'I've never seen people work so hard in my life.' Trevor Preston testifies to the strain also put on the writers: 'We all grafted. I nearly lost a marriage because I didn't take a holiday for four years. You just finished one series and you felt like a wet rag and – bang – they wanted the next series to start in three months.' Ted Childs agrees: 'People used to work very long hours, 14 hours a day was average, except on Fridays when we finished about 4:30 and used to go to the wine bar or the pub. But people used to make a lot of money: that was the deal. We didn't want people who wanted to leave early every night. Also, the quicker you made it the less you spent on equipment hire, renting accommodation and hiring cameras.'

The filming each day was prioritised to get the most important shots in the can first. 'With the permission of Ted, Lloyd and George, I would let the directors and the cameramen make the film as in the script up until three o'clock,' assistant director Bill Westley recalls. 'If we were on schedule I would then say, "OK boys, you can now play." So they could do their bit of arty stuff or extra cover – things like that. Providing we got enough stuff for the editor to make things work, I would let them have the rest of the day to themselves. Lloyd and George used to think that was a superb idea. They got their film, and then, with a bit of luck, they got some arty stuff as well that the editor and director could play with.'

Shooting stunt sequences, or fights, was more time-consuming than shooting conventional acting scenes. 'You had to allow probably two stunts in any ten-day episode schedule,' Ted Childs explains. 'If it was a big stunt you'd be lucky to get one edited minute in a day.' This meant that the pressure was on the crew to get the stunt right on the first take. Peter Brayham, the series' stunt arranger, remembers having 'to rehearse and rehearse and rehearse as many times as possible, and you didn't get much time on *The Sweeney*.' However, he was quickly able to tailor John Thaw and Dennis Waterman's fighting styles into what best suited each actor. 'Dennis could throw a punch,' he says. 'His brother was a boxer, and Dennis was pretty natural, so I only had to show him a couple of moves. John was terribly unco-ordinated, but I knew the punches that he *could* throw. John was good for one punch, a grab, and an armlock... I'd use whatever he could do. It didn't matter if he did four or five moves instead of 26. Dennis, on the other hand, you could coach.'

Careful consideration was given in editing the fight scenes to ensure an acceptable level of violence. 'Part of the problem was, because we were filming with a cinematic approach, the action we shot was often quite convincing, while what people were used to on your televised drama was a much more cumbersome and a less convincing portrayal of dramatic violence,' Childs says. 'We were victims of our own success. We were using cinematic techniques and some of the action could look quite compelling, certainly by the standards of what was around at the time.'

Euston's internal control of what was acceptable viewing usually prevailed. 'I think *The Sweeney* went a little bit further than anyone else had gone with the violence,' Peter Brayham maintains, 'but there was a golden rule: we were never allowed to hold a gun to anyone's head. That was a directive.' Editor John S Smith can recall only one occasion when Thames requested a cut to an episode because of violence. 'They complained about one scene, and when we analysed it, it was actually the sound effects that were doing it. As you know, when they punched they always missed, but you would put on something really beefy. So, all we did really was to dub down the sound effects, resubmit it with just one minor picture change, I think, and it was passed, but physically it was the same material.'

The BBC, a public service broadcaster, was more sensitive to public criticism, particularly from Mary Whitehouse's self-appointed watchdog of TV sex and violence, the National Viewers and Listeners Association, an organisation that was particularly vocal throughout the 1970s. Even though the organisation's name was misleading – it was really a minority Christian pressure group with a spokeswoman skilled in PR who provided good copy for the media – it wasn't long before the graphic approach of *The Sweeney* came in for criticism. Mrs Whitehouse, (and therefore her organisation), considered the series 'foul-mouthed, sadistically violent and promiscuous' in its portrayal of the police.

'There used to be an argument that Mrs Whitehouse and her cronies had evidence that it was an emotionally disturbing programme,' Childs remembers. 'In my case, I hoped it was, because if drama isn't emotionally disturbing, people aren't enjoying it. If you made a film version of *Coriolanus*, they wouldn't let you put it on! Much of Shakespeare's drama is very violent, but as it's done in a staged way everyone accepts it, it's not a danger. When you do film and you do it well, it's not the content; it's the way you execute it.'

On a commercial channel and screened after the 9.00 pm watershed, *The Sweeney* successfully weathered Mary Whitehouse's's accusations, although she remained vocal in her criticism of the series throughout its run. A jibe at her expense was included in the episode 'Hearts and Minds', when a pompous nosy neighbour declares, 'I shall write to Mrs Whitehouse!'

THE FORD SQUAD

The motor transport the Flying Squad used in *The Sweeney* was dictated by the constraints of a tight budget. 'We went round all the big motor companies, especially BMC cars who manufactured the Triumphs that the Metropolitan Police used, and we said, "What about a motor?" They wanted paying,' Childs says. 'So we went along to Ford and they said, "Fine, you can have what you like." As time went on, the series became known as the Ford Squad! There was a thing in *Ad Weekly* advertising Fords. They'd used a picture from *The Sweeney* with the headline 'Ford Squad'.'

The manufacturer clearly saw the benefits of this early form of product placement. 'They gave us lorries as well,' Childs elaborates. 'We got a couple of enormous articulated lorries off them we used in some episodes.' According to Peter Brayham, 'The posh cars were the ones Ford gave us because they wanted to sell a few cars, but then every other car was an old one. It's not much different now, unless you do a feature. I used to feel so embarrassed about it, at times. They'd conk out in the middle of the road!'

The non-Ford cars used in the series were bought second-hand to keep costs down, mainly through papers such as *Exchange and Mart*. For authenticity, Jaguars were the preferred choice; many real criminals drove them. They were re-sprayed and rebuilt until they literally fell apart. 'We had no money for cars, no money at all,' Brayham opines. 'And everyone used to think we got cars souped up, like America! I did *Robbery* with Stanley Baker, and I had four Jags, all the cars I wanted. When I got on *The Sweeney* I had one Jaguar 3.4 and one Mark 2 Ford, maybe two! Everything was money.'

One old Jaguar proved so durable that it featured in several episodes in a row; the Squad always seemed to be chasing the same car. 'They were indestructible, which was a factor in why I went for one of those [a Jaguar] in *Inspector Morse*,' Ted Childs comments. 'You could roll them over, all sorts of things, and they survived. Flash villains used them as get-away cars, as they had the acceleration.' After permission had been obtained from the police, car chases were often shot for real in London's streets.

In keeping with the show's overall atmosphere of immediacy and economy, there was no specific rehearsal time for the actors to run through scenes. They would rehearse at every opportunity they could, perhaps while the set was being lit. This was a culture shock to some guest artists, who were used to more preparation time prior to being filmed. 'John and Dennis were very good with people coming in,' Childs remembers. 'ITV drama was normally one or two weeks' rehearsal, but that was because they did very little editing so you needed to have at least a ten-minute run to record. There were very few long-playing scenes in *The Sweeney*. There were interrogation scenes that sometimes went on a bit. We tried not to have a scene of more than a few minutes in length.'

Again with an eye on cost, Euston's Colet Court production office housed the 'Flying Squad office' standing set used in *The Sweeney*. Even though the lease on the building was meant to be a short term one, after acquiring it for *Special Branch*, Euston occupied the premises for several years. The building also provided a contingency in the event of inclement weather during exterior filming. Dennis Waterman recalls that 'We all tended to be somewhat lax in preparing for this [ie, learning the 'contingency' dialogue]. It was only after trying to film in a downpour and hearing the desperate shout from a drenched first assistant, "It's a wrap here, back to the Squad office", that panic set in.'

'We had a director lined up once, Alan Cook, who'd done a lot of *Armchair Theatres*,' Ian Kennedy Martin remembers. 'Lloyd said, "Come up and talk about *The Sweeney*." So he turned up at Colet Court, this junior school, climbed the stairs, went up to the headmaster's study – where you used to be beaten! – walked in, sat down and said, "I can't deal with this!" It was a very hexing place: a Grade 1 listed building, falling down in places, and it had these beautiful doors. Lloyd came in one morning and every fucking one had been stolen! About 40 doors, throughout the building – every single one of them had been nicked! Unbelievable.' Trevor Preston adds: 'Lloyd threatened to fire the whole crew and the next morning the doors were all put back!'

Both cast and crew were prepared to put up with roughing it, such was the singular atmosphere of professionalism and camaraderie. Peter Brayham has fond memories of Thaw and Waterman mucking in with the rest of the team. 'Once, a car stalled in the middle of a chase on a flyover somewhere and it wouldn't start. When it broke down, John and Dennis jumped in and gave me a push. I looked round – there they were, the lead actors! – and I thought, "Yeah, I like this show."' 'It was like a family,' David Wickes confirms. 'We worked till three in the morning, ate rotten junk food, didn't shave, and went down to the one bathroom we had and shared it. It was that kind of world. It wasn't at all the luxury that exists today, that people just take for granted. It was the peer group opinion of you that mattered: were you pulling your weight?'

'The good thing was, we all grew up together as a crew,' Tom Clegg believes, 'and that same crew stayed together for all those years. Apart from everybody working on a project which we were proud of and we knew was of a high quality, we were all great mates. There were a lot of laughs. There aren't as many laughs these days in the business.'

In such a close and hard-working team, pranks and jokes were common. 'They wrote a song about me!' Brayham exclaims. 'It was all about the moves in the fight scenes. I can't remember the exact words, but it was something like *'Tub tub tub/Bop tub twist'* ... One day I walked on the floor and they sang it!'

Bill Westley recalls the laddish treatment accorded Euston's female members of staff: 'We got one to sit on the photocopier one day, she thought it was very funny – mind you, she *had* been to the pub. We photocopied her backside and put it out with all the call sheets, and I think it was Dennis who said, "What the hell's this, the route map?" We used to wind the women up; we used to torment the life out of Mary [Morgan, Associate Producer].'

Tom Clegg remembers another practical joke, this time at Chris Burt's expense. 'The editing room used to be on the top floor, and the office below it was Ted Childs', and Chris [Burt] walked in one morning wearing a brand new raincoat which we all took the piss out of. It was awful. Anyway, Chris went to a meeting in Ted's office, and Ted normally sits with his back to the window, so we put Chris's raincoat on a coat hanger and dangled it down in front of Ted's window for the whole meeting. There was this raincoat going up and down, which Ted couldn't see, while poor Chris was quietly going mental.'

'I cannot remember falling out with anyone,' Westley says, remembering the esprit de corps. 'Yes, we used to have a ruckus and get angry, but it would all be over within ten minutes and we'd all be laughing again.' 'Attitudes were different [then],' Tom Clegg adds. 'At the end of the day we would all have a drink and it didn't matter what time it was. Ideas have legs, and people talked a lot more. Maybe one remembers things from a different perspective, but it was still a lot more fun. I almost wish it were starting again.'

As already noted, the Euston team's preferred venue for relaxation after work was a notorious public house opposite Colet Court, The Red Cow. Aside from the assorted clientele of real London villains and policemen who enjoyed the strippers, The Red Cow was a renowned rock and punk venue in the late 1970s. Retro-mod outfit The Jam played several early gigs there.

David Wickes: 'On a Friday afternoon the whole film crew would be in there, and it was *hilarious*. They used to hate a director who didn't finish by half past four on a Friday. It always used to finish at six o'clock, unless you were going into an extended day, which was very rare, but at 4.30 pm on a Friday, they could get wrapped, return to Colet Court – return was half an hour – and at six o'clock they'd be ready. The whole unit – all of them. If anybody didn't go, it was, "Aye, aye, aye. What's goin' on 'ere? New bird?"'

'The socialising was *so* important,' Peter Brayham says. 'I never drink in the daytime, ever. I would have an orange juice. But Friday night I'd go for a drink with the guys in The Red Cow. It would be nothing to see the producers, Ted, Lloyd and George walk in, and these guys, who'd been working with each other all week, would sit and have a laugh and a drink. I thought it was lovely. It wasn't a piss-up, it was having a drink, y'know? They hadn't had enough of each other's company, and whoever the director was, he would be there.'

The maverick, cockney image of *The Sweeney* was also endemic to the crew. 'The director was always 'guvnor', almost like Dennis was calling Regan 'guv', because he was a higher rank,' John S Smith recalls. 'Anyone of any capacity was called 'guvnor'. The actors were always called the 'la-dis' – as in la-di-da [star].'

From the earliest days of *The Sweeney* being transmitted, the crew were conscious that they had a big hit on their hands. 'I remember when it first went out I was listening to Radio 1,' Chris Burt says. 'I was going to work, actually, and Johnny Walker was on the nine o'clock show, and he had a huge great audience on Radio 1. The first thing he said that morning was, "Have you all watched *The Sweeney*? The best thing I've ever seen on British television. It's bloody great!"'

'It was without question an overnight success,' Dennis Waterman recalled in his autobiography. 'Euston Films had cracked it. *We* had cracked it.' Overseas sales were also surprisingly good for a London-based police show; bizarrely, even some Arab and Islamic states bought the series. The programme rapidly became a UK institution over the next four years. Peter Brayham remembers, 'I used to work with big actors – on films and things – who used to say to me, "Pete, can you get me on *The Sweeney*?" Everyone wanted to be a part of it.'

Considering the programme's appeal, David Wickes speculates: '*The Sweeney* was for the people; *Kavanagh QC* was for some of the people, *Inspector Morse* was for a few more. But you could go into any pub in the East End of London, and you could go into any pub in Birmingham, and you would hear them all talking about it [*The Sweeney*]. It had *enormous* power. It didn't mince its words, and the reason it had this [power] was partly due to Ted, but largely due to Lloyd.'

The fame and the rave reviews did have a few negative aspects, as the cast soon started being pursued by an eager public wherever they went. 'It was one of the first series where the actors became very popular with the public, and led to crowds gathering outside your door,' Tom Clegg recalls. 'There were no such things as caravans for the actors in those days. You'd hire a room in a hotel nearby, or more often they made up in the back of cars. It became impossible for them because the crowds grew so big. They couldn't have any privacy to rehearse their scenes, so it was almost after that point that caravans and winnebagos started creeping in. We were filming with Richard Griffiths [on the final episode, 'Jack or Knave'] just off the Edgware Road in a market, and John and Dennis were outside with a driver and they were *mobbed*.'

GOODBYE GUVNOR

The final block of *Sweeney* episodes to be filmed were made in late 1977 and early 1978, with Lloyd Shirley and George Taylor still acting as executive producers, but now in a freelance capacity. Most of *The Sweeney*'s regular crew were still in place; Chris Burt graduated to directing an episode after working as associate producer on Euston's revival of the Amsterdam-set detective series *Van Der Valk*, made in the hiatus between series three and four of *The Sweeney* in 1977.

During this period, which concluded nearly five years of production with 54 episodes and two feature films, the decision was taken to end the series. 'I was working for Euston as a freelance producer so it wasn't down to me,' Ted Childs explains. In hindsight, he believes it was the right call to make. 'I think it was running out of steam. I did try to bring in new writers and directors to refresh it, [but] I think it was right to end it when we did. The problem with ITV then, more so now, was that they couldn't afford to lose programmes that were working because there weren't enough decent programmes to replace them. There's always that tendency to keep things going beyond their sell-by date.' Chris Burt disagrees, looking at the tendency of American television to protect and invest in its success stories. 'It's the one mistake in British television; in America, they run shows again and again and again, and I felt there was another two or three series to make of *The Sweeney* – I really did. I thought it was a great mistake.'

The decision to call time on the Euston Films Flying Squad was largely that of the lead actor, Tom Clegg recalls. 'It was sad, but there were other things to do. I think Dennis would have gone on but nobody blamed John. I think John just felt it was time to move on and do something else. I mean, four and a half years on one programme? He was a young, ambitious actor. I think it was about the right time.'

With *The Sweeney* coming to an end, changes were taking place in the management of Euston. Lloyd Shirley and George Taylor's remount of the old Thames series *Van Der Valk*, based on the novels by Nicholas Freeling with Barry Foster in the title role, had included the additional challenge of overseas filming in Amsterdam. The ambitious, revamped series indicated the pair were keen to move on to new projects. In 1977, as part of a long-term understanding between them and Thames' management, Shirley and Taylor left to set up a new venture that would make films for other companies, although their old employers would remain a customer.

Johnny Goodman, an experienced producer who had worked on *The Saint* and *The Persuaders!*, was brought in to oversee the production side of Euston. Talking about Shirley and Taylor's departure, Goodman recalls, 'They were getting very successful and decided that they would like to have a bit more of the cake, so they decided to leave Euston Films and set up their own company, while probably still making stuff for Thames. I was brought in to take over from Lloyd and George and, to their everlasting credit, they could not have been more supportive, so the transition was quite smooth. Verity Lambert was now the Chief Executive – she operated out of Teddington – and I was the Executive in Charge of Production at Euston along with Linda Agran, who was the Creative Head.'

Ted Childs cites the departure of his two executive producers as the moment when the maverick film making unit that Euston had been was transformed into a more corporate organisation: 'When Lloyd and George came off the Thames payroll and left, it changed; they got the suede wallpaper in!'

Shirley and Taylor subsequently set up their new company, Seacastle Productions, using some of the established Euston crew, but ran into difficulties. '[It] was a disaster,' Chris Burt says sadly. 'They were about to start making films for London Weekend Television with some Canadian money. They made the first film; it had John Le Mesurier and Beryl Reid in it. Tom Clegg was the director, I was the Associate Producer, Ian Toynton was going to be the editor – [but] the Canadian money didn't arrive. We were all called and told, "You can make this one, but after this it's all over."' Shirley went back to Thames, executive producing other highly regarded series such as *Rumpole of the Bailey* and *Mr Palfrey of Westminster*. Ironically, he would be reunited with George Taylor on another Euston hit that co-starred Dennis Waterman – *Minder*.

THE NEXT GENERATION

Euston built on the company's past success with two series that were a logical extension of the ground broken by *The Sweeney*. 1978's *Out*, a thriller by Trevor Preston, followed the trials and tribulations of a bank robber recently released from prison on his quest to identify the informant who was responsible for his incarceration. *Sweeney* director Jim Goddard, a friend of Preston's, directed, and newcomer Barry Hanson, produced the series. *Fox*, a further Preston series, made up of 13 episodes about a London crime family, followed in 1980, also directed by Goddard. As well as continuity in director and writer, familiar faces such as Ray Winstone, Peter Vaughan, Derrick O'Connor and John Junkin gave the shows a feel consistent with the *Sweeney* gangland developed between 1974 and 1978.

Danger UXB (1979), the next series made, was the first programme to considerably broaden Euston's range, examining the hazards faced by a bomb disposal team at work in London during the Second World War. From period drama, the company explored new territory with the bleak science fiction of *Quatermass*. Shown in 1979, this ambitious four-hour serial was a belated sequel to three BBC series made in the 1950s, *The Quatermass Experiment, Quatermass II* and *Quatermass and the Pit*. Ted Childs produced and several trusted old hands from the *Sweeney* crew worked on it with him, including Laurie Greenwood, Stephen Pushkin, Ian Toynton and Bill Westley. Always keen to diversify, Euston was to attempt science fiction again, in a less serious vein, in the 1980 oddity *Stainless Steel and the Star Spies*; Ed Bishop and Bob Hoskins did the voice-overs for alien robots, but the pilot for this children's show failed to catch on.

The company also resurrected its one-off, feature-length TV film format pioneered in *Armchair Cinema*. Ted Childs produced *Charlie Muffin* in 1979, the adventures of a scruffy, middle-aged spy starring David Hemmings, helmed by cinema director Jack Gold. Another change of style and approach followed soon afterwards with a second feature, *The Knowledge*, about black cab drivers, featuring Nigel Hawthorne and written by *London's Burning* creator Jack Rosenthal.

Also making its debut in 1979 was *Minder,* which became another long-running hit for Euston and remained popular well into the 1980s, featuring Dennis Waterman in another successful partnership, this time with George Cole as small-time villain and con man Arthur Daley. Involving Waterman, Lloyd Shirley and George Taylor, and familiar writers and directors like Tony Hoare and Tom Clegg, *Minder* took on board some of the elements that had made *The Sweeney* popular – the lively depiction of London and its inhabitants, the incidental humour and the (toned-down) violence. It was the closest thing *The Sweeney* had to a natural successor. *The Flame Trees of Thikka,* made in 1981, was a complete contrast, a historical drama with the emphasis on its female characters. John Hawkesworth wrote and produced, and the series broke more new ground for Euston; it was their first literary adaptation and the first production to involve overseas filming outside Europe, in this instance Nairobi.

Ian Toynton had followed in Chris Burt's footsteps by moving from editing into directing, overseeing some episodes of *Minder*. One of his prestigious early assignments was *Widows* in 1983, written by Lynda La Plante, who as Lynda Marchal had previously appeared in an episode of *The Sweeney*. Encouraged to write a script by Linda Agran and Verity Lambert, La Plante's serial concerned four women plotting and then carrying out a wages robbery, using plans left behind by their late husbands (who had been killed attempting a similar raid.) While *Widows* made use of several plot devices and slang terms familiar to *Sweeney* viewers, its main innovation was the concentration on a group of proactive female criminals.

Euston's impressive run continued when *Sweeney* writer Troy Kennedy Martin returned to write *Really – Ace of Spies*. Also shown in 1983, it was based on the exploits of the real-life spy Sidney Reilly, who operated around the time of the First World War; his attempt to engineer the downfall of the Bolshevik government had made him something of a legend in intelligence circles. This lavish historical drama was the most ambitious production Euston had attempted so far. Chris Burt produced, while Jim Goddard and future James Bond director Martin Campbell alternated directorial duties. The relatively unknown Sam Neill was cast as Reilly, complemented by a wealth of character acting talent, including Tom Bell, Kenneth Cranham and the late Leo McKern. 'It was the biggest thing that Thames had ever made at the time – huge,' Chris Burt recalls with obvious pride. 'It started in Turkistan, then went through China and Japan, and then Russia. I'm very proud of it, because it's probably the biggest thing that Thames ever sold around the world.'

Reilly's success was symbolic of how far Euston Films had come in 12 short years. The company was now a world player. Burt and Goddard's handling of a big-budget international production was a long way from filming cops and robbers in Thamesmead.

LAST TRAIN TO EUSTON

With an auspicious and diverse body of work behind them, at the end of the eighties Johnny Goodman, Verity Lambert and Linda Agran all decided to move on. With the original crew, producers and writers all gone, Euston in its final years seemed to lose something of its ability to capture the zeitgeist. Its yuppie drama *Capital City* – one of its last attempts to exploit the contemporary mood – made little impact.

Over the course of the 1980s, television in Britain had undergone a variety of changes, from the introduction of breakfast and all-night television to the launching of Channel Four and satellite networks. Channel Four's programming impacted on ITV's audience, and television in general became more competitive and geared to ratings. In November 1988, MP Tim Renton, then Minister of State at the Home Office, introduced a new broadcasting bill which initiated the deregulation of Independent Television, forcing all ITV companies to reapply for their franchises. As a result of this restructuring, Thames lost its franchise; together with Euston Films, it was taken over and consequently discontinued making and broadcasting programmes in 1992.

'I was never part of the Thames management,' Ted Childs comments on the company's dissolution. 'By that time I was working for Central. I thought it was a bit sad. I would argue that they should have seen it coming ... To be fair to the Independent Television Commission, I think they wanted to give the franchise to Thames because they produced some good programmes. But everything changes; new technology was emerging so it could never have stayed as it was, and I don't think things are any worse than they were then.'

Looking back now that the company has gone, Euston's founder members feel that their team paved the way for many improvements and innovations in the way television has subsequently been made over the last 30 years. 'All TV films have changed now; everyone makes them like that,' Chris Burt states unequivocally. 'We were the first people to change the way of working. The use of locations, the style we used, the quickness, how we contracted actors, how we contracted writers, and how we contracted crew. It all changed and that was the way it was kept.'

'I think *The Sweeney* was the first of the super crews,' Peter Brayham reflects. 'I actually think you could have done a *Sweeney* without a director. The crew were that good.' Of his years on the series, he adds, 'All I can say is they were the happiest working years of my life. The people were 22-carat gold. And nobody minded where the contribution came from; no one took offence. Everybody was looking after and watching out for everybody else.' Chris Burt agrees: 'It was a company that had a great sense of humour; everyone was always laughing when we were making films there. It was several years of great, enjoyable work… It was a really exciting, vital, humorous, *interesting* time, working with great writers and great directors.'

Tom Clegg feels, 'Obviously there were things I would have done slightly differently, but if you could get that same team of people together, I'm certain they would turn out a first-rate result on whatever they were doing. It was just a joy to go into work every day. You had no feeling of, "Oh no, another day, I'll be glad when this is over"... I couldn't imagine working with a better team of people and on a better product.'

'It was the best time for me, it was one of the happiest times I've ever had,' Trevor Preston concurs. 'There was none of that fucking nastiness and backstabbing.' David Wickes pays particular credit to Lloyd Shirley in shaping Euston's unique production style. 'He supported us through thick and thin. And he was *so* successful, the most successful executive Thames ever had. He threw a typewriter through the window and they didn't fire him – they wouldn't *dare*. He was the goose that laid the golden egg. He laid so many golden eggs for Thames; *Special Branch* was one, *Public Eye* was another, *Callan* another, and he went on to do *Rumpole* and God knows how many others. You don't fire Lloyd Shirley, because you know that the BBC would pick him up like *that*... The top brass were *terrified* of him, because he could do anything he wanted, virtually.' Summing up the feelings of many of the people involved with Euston, Wickes says categorically, 'I'm very pleased and very proud to have been part of it. I don't see anything like it now. I don't see any *pathfinding* now.'

The final word on Euston Films goes to Johnny Goodman, who was part of the team that inherited *The Sweeney*'s mould-breaking legacy and went on to steer the company through another decade of success.'The secret of Euston was that if they trusted you and gave you the backing and the authority to do your job, you could sail along and it was all rather lovely. People at the top didn't interfere as long as you were bringing the product in on budget, and the so-called executives – people like myself – were only as good as the people we employed.' He has one overriding feeling about the company's contribution to broadcasting: 'Enormous pride, and enormous respect for the people that gave us the authority and the facilities to do the shows the way we wanted to do them.'

CHAPTER 4

THE OUTCAST: REGAN

'It happened in a strange way, because I'd done four episodes of *Special Branch* and that was right at the end of the series. The news got around that they were setting up this new cops and robbers show. Nobody knew anything about it, who the stars were going to be or anything, so the rumours abounded. Dougie Camfield was going to direct it, Ted Childs was the producer and Ian Kennedy Martin was the deviser.'
Tom Clegg, 'Regan' director

'It's possible to have a really good time as a television writer, but when you see something like this, and when it starts as a major confrontation… then it's going to get very difficult.'
Ian Kennedy Martin, Sweeney *creator*

'I wanted the opening shot to be a vomit-filled puddle in Soho, pulling out to catch John Thaw as Regan tumbling out of a Ford Zephyr!'
Ted Childs, producer

* * *

BY THE EARLY 1970S, IAN KENNEDY MARTIN HAD FOLLOWED IN HIS brother Troy's footsteps and cemented his reputation as a prolific, experienced television writer and script editor. He had worked for both the BBC and Independent Television, and was well known for his track record on *Redcap*, *Z-Cars* and several other series.

By a curious coincidence, Ian had also adapted Bridget Boland's play, *The Prisoner*, for the BBC. Screened in 1962, this play, which starred Patrick McGoohan, Alan Badel and Warren Mitchell, was one of a number of probable sources of inspiration for the famous ITC series of the same name, which was in turn co-created and edited by espionage expert turned writer George Markstein. Markstein, having moved on via the highly regarded spy series *Callan* to become the respected head of script development at Thames Television, was to be a significant figure in the creation of *The Sweeney*.

Having worked on *Armchair Theatre* (contributing a play entitled 'Detective Waiting'), which Markstein and future *Sweeney* executive producer Lloyd Shirley oversaw, Ian talked to Markstein about the future of *Special Branch*, Euston Films' first production. There was a view that it was not a particularly good programme, as Kennedy Martin recalls: 'They had this odd situation where [*Special Branch*] was number one in the ratings and everybody at Euston hated it. They thought it was absolute drivel, these two guys dressed in perfect suits, running around pretending to be Special Branch officers. It was also politically sensitive. The Home Office had been on saying, "Look, we don't want the real stories about the Special Branch."' The real Special Branch were involved in intelligence operations in Northern Ireland, which were too contentious to be written about. At the same time, the programme was not felt to be a realistic portrayal of contemporary policing.

Asked to think about a replacement show by Markstein, Kennedy Martin pitched a script entitled *The Outcasts*, using the Flying Squad as the basis for a new police series. The activities of this Squad, ranging from stopping armed robberies to running networks of criminal informants to obtain information on both forthcoming and unsolved robberies, was felt to provide a strong factual basis for a number of dramatic, varied storylines. These plots would also deal with the internal politics of the reorganisation of Scotland Yard, being instituted at the time under the new commissioner Robert Mark.

Kennedy Martin spent time unofficially researching his idea at Scotland Yard, and the characterisation of Detective Inspector Jack Regan, the main character, was inspired by an 'uncorrupted cop' whom he knew at the time. The first script, now simply titled 'Regan', establishes the DI as resistant to the changes in the way people were being managed within Scotland Yard and continually resorting to sharp practice. Regan is seen breaking into premises without a warrant, pretending he isn't receiving a radio signal from the Yard, and 'borrowing' a gun from the police firing range. At one point, demanding information, he threatens to ensure the villain Tusser gets his sentence extended by alleging the villain hit him. Ian Kennedy Martin reflected in 1993, 'I was around Commander Drury who was about to go to jail and there was this sense that it was very raw, policing in London at that time.'

Written by an author keen to depict a realistic situation, the script eschews simplistic characterisation, as it is made clear that Regan has his faults as well. His motivation in solving the murder of a junior officer under his command, Cowley, partly arises from self-preservation; he needs to obtain a 'result' so that he can extricate himself from any disciplinary action resulting from not supervising Cowley more closely. The other characters are mainly there to create a contrast between Regan's methods and those of his more conventional colleagues. Even his sergeant, George Carter, questions Regan's behaviour and often remains in the background, while the DI's boss, Detective Chief Inspector Haskins, remains indifferent to Cowley's death. He is presented as overly concerned with interdepartmental politics, trying to get Regan suspended as he's convinced he's 'out of control'. ('Haskins was put in as part of the new order,' Ted Childs states. 'Here was an in-house company mandarin who was there struggling vainly to try and control what was going on.') The only copper who seems to respect Regan is the pragmatic Detective Chief Superintendent Maynon, who, in common with the audience, can see arguments for and against the detective's unorthodox ways.

The script concludes in an upbeat manner, with Regan and Carter going for a drink together, while the narrative concerning Regan's position in the Squad is carefully left open for continuation.

Kennedy Martin had also been having thoughts about the casting, and conceived the character especially for his friend John Thaw to play. 'I always had it in my mind that I wanted to make another *Redcap*, and thought John would be the perfect person for it.' He pitched the idea to Markstein, and its content was agreed between the two men, Lloyd Shirley and George Taylor, both executive producers at Euston Films. 'The script was written very quickly and George Markstein story-edited it with input from Lloyd and George Taylor. It took four weeks to write and then as far as I was concerned the script was finished.'

Ted Childs was asked to produce the series following his work on *Special Branch*. He remembers, 'Ian Kennedy Martin came to Lloyd with a premise called *McClean*, about a detective from Scotland Yard who was old school, tough, coming to terms with the new order that the Home Office were trying to establish at Scotland Yard at that time. The view was that this would be a good successor to *Special Branch* and Lloyd and George asked me if I would like to produce it. John Thaw had worked with Ian on *Redcap*. I had a meeting with John Thaw and Ian in a restaurant in Devonshire Street. John obviously thought I was full of shit, which of course I was, but we got on all right.'

Despite differing recollections of the pilot's title, or even the key character's name, the new programme was always intended to be a series. 'What was unusual in those days was that they had agreed to make a series whilst we were doing the pilot,' Tom Clegg, who ultimately directed Kennedy Martin's script, points out. 'The series wasn't contingent on the success of the pilot.' Childs and Kennedy Martin concur with this view. 'It was always going to be a series from the moment I talked about it and delivered it. This was going to be a replacement for *Special Branch*,' Kennedy Martin says.

The development of the series that would eventually be titled *The Sweeney* took an eventful turn, however, when Ian Kennedy Martin and Ted Childs began to have 'artistic differences'. The roots of the dispute appear to date back to when Kennedy Martin and Childs previously worked together on *Special Branch*, on the episode 'Intercept' written by Ian. The writer had not been happy with the limitations imposed on him by Childs, which he felt unnecessary.

'Although it was on film there were severe limitations to it. I wrote one script to see how they shot it and disagreed violently with the way Ted Childs cut everything down,' Kennedy Martin remembers. 'I'd just made a series at Thames Television with James Gadowitz, who was a producer-director... You'd give him a script and if there were 15 locations in a day shoot, he'd just run on with it. He liked the idea, he was a fast-cutting guy. Ted was saying, "We have two bases, each script has to be written with two bases in mind, the morning base and the afternoon base, and all the locations have to be within five or ten minutes of these two." Jamie shot fast and loose and on the run. If you wanted someone arriving outside Buckingham Palace, he wouldn't ask permission to film. He'd get a car to drive towards the gates! And some cops would stop him and say, "You can't do this, what's this camera?" and so on. Ted was more, "I have these rules and they will be followed."'

Childs evidently felt that the logistical restrictions he had specified had to stay in place to allow the production to operate effectively as a viable film series for television. He also stuck to his guns on the issue of using 16mm film, despite misgivings from the IBA concerning its use. 'They were not yet convinced that 16mm could work for drama. New technology was coming in, Kodak was bringing out new stocks, you had the spin-off from the space age, and we had the super-speed lenses and various new lights. We did all sorts of things: we didn't want to have back-projections, so we would build [film and sound] rigs on the cars. We got people like Peter Brayham involved in trying to make the stunts work. But it still had to be cost-effective. At one stage we were making a show for £35,000 an hour. It was made clear to me that if we couldn't make it for that it would be taken back into the studio. We had to take quite a lot of short cuts, but we made it work on quite a tight schedule. We had a formula for doing it, which we tried to stick with.'

'What Ted showed with *Special Branch* was that he could really control the costs,' Kennedy Martin recalls. 'That's how he became important. Lloyd and George were apparently the producers, so when Ted came in, I thought, "Well, this is a line producer."' Perhaps not unreasonably, Kennedy Martin expected to retain significant input into how his creation was brought to the screen. Ted Childs elaborates on the creative disagreements between himself and Ian: 'There are two versions of this story… I was very keen to give it a cinematic view, but Ian was an established writer and script editor and he felt it should be based on television that works – studio-based – although he was very happy for it to be on film. I was more than keen to take it out more and have it on the road. We quarrelled a bit; I'm sure I was quite arrogant in those days!'

It seems the creative tension between the pair was heightened when Douglas Camfield was appointed as director of Kennedy Martin's script. This was a potentially promising combination given Camfield's track record as a director, but, according to Kennedy Martin, the collaboration was stormy and short-lived.

Bill Westley, the experienced second assistant director on 'Regan', believes that 'When Dougie Camfield read the script, he realised that he couldn't do it within the three-week schedule.' However, it appears that the director also wanted to make changes to the existing story. 'Suddenly I was getting called to meetings with them to discuss the script,' Ian states. 'And I thought, "Well, wait a minute, we've *done* the script, George [Markstein], Lloyd, George Taylor and I it sorted it out, so what *is* this?" [Ted Childs, Douglas Camfield and I] were very outspoken in our dealings with each other … I'd go back to Lloyd and George and say "What is this?" and they'd say "Don't worry about it." But I started to *get* worried about it.' Kennedy Martin also discovered that some rewrites unapproved by him had occurred. 'Somebody had written a scene and inserted it in the script. So I went to Ted and said, "What the fuck is this? It's not going in!"'

Matters came to a head when Camfield apparently told Kennedy Martin that he wasn't prepared to shoot the ending as it stood. Ian: 'I said, "Fine – you're fired!" Ted said, "You can't fire him" – and I couldn't, of course. I said, "Well, *I* fucking am!" So he said, "Right, we're going to see Lloyd." And [Camfield] was fired, and that didn't make Ted very happy.' Not wanting to lose Camfield's skills, Childs invited him back later in the series.

Tom Clegg was duly appointed as replacement. 'Dougie had had an argument. I think it was because I happened to be around that I was offered the job,' Clegg says. 'While we were doing it we thought it was okay, but we weren't aware that it was going to be so popular.' The script was then filmed with little alteration, according to Kennedy Martin. 'Tom Clegg came in and he directed it as it was, and he made a very good job of it.'

Clegg's work on the pilot established much of the cinematic house-style of the series that was to follow, employing many naturalistic images of the underbelly of London which at the time were new to television audiences. 'This was the first police series to be done on film, on location, so for once one could open things out,' Clegg notes. 'Dialogue didn't have to happen in a [fake] police station or police car, it was a totally location-based product.' The sweaty, smoky London boozer and the derelict, decaying warehouse, complete with drizzling water and iron chains dangling from the ceiling, have entered into the public consciousness as standard images in many London-set police series and crime dramas on both the small and big screen. As editor John S Smith acknowledges, 'Tom Clegg was the one who kicked it off and he was considered the mentor of it all.'

As the involvement of John Thaw was already established, Clegg and Childs moved on to looking at the other roles. 'Tom Clegg and I had already used Dennis Waterman in *Special Branch* and we thought he would be good as Regan's sidekick; that worked very well.' A car scene not written by Kennedy Martin, showing Regan and Carter driving through Soho, may have been added to enlarge the part of Carter; Bill Westley remembers that '[the pilot] was going to be just Regan.'

While the shooting of 'Regan' was under way, plans for the series continued. Childs produced a series 'Bible' (see Appendix 1) to brief writers on aspects of the series; this was based on his knowledge of the characters used in the pilot script and his production experience on *Special Branch*. Kennedy Martin was meanwhile carrying on with writing the first three scripts for the series. 'The first one was called 'Coming Out', in which a man has been set up by the police to look like a supergrass, to cover for a real grass, so he's running around trying to save his skin.' Arguments were now going on with Childs over the content of these scripts, despite George Taylor's attempts to intercede. 'George Taylor was the head of script development at Euston, and [he] thought, "Well, Ian can handle Ted Childs,"' Kennedy Martin remembers. 'I just thought, "If this is going to be a series, and everything I write is going to be a problem, then I don't want anything do with it – what's the point?"'

By this time it seems the differences in opinion between Kennedy Martin and Childs were so great they could not work with each other. 'Ian had been led to believe that it was going to be his show,' Childs recalls. '[But] it ended up being a question of

him or me, and oddly enough they chose me. So I stayed and he backed out of it.'
Through an oversight, which Kennedy Martin believes was due to confusion between
the Thames offices in Teddington and the Euston Films office at Colet Court, it
became clear, prior to Kennedy Martin's departure, that Euston were actually
contracted to make 'Regan' only as a videotaped production. As Kennedy Martin had
previously signed up to the ITCA agreement, which Euston staff were not signed up
to, it became clear that a deal-breaking mistake had been made, which was only
discovered once shooting on film had already begun. Ian Kennedy Martin: 'A phone call
came from Lloyd, saying, "We've got a problem here." I said, "Yes, you're in production
with a script you don't own!"'

Aware that Kennedy Martin wasn't happy with the way things were developing,
Lloyd Shirley was concerned about this latest difficulty. 'Lloyd said, "I hope you're not
going to take us to the cleaners." I said, "Lloyd, I'm going to take you to the cleaners!"'
The matter was resolved in a congenial manner, with Kennedy Martin opting to allow
the programme to continue in return for a severance deal. Other rights, including
those relating to feature films, remained in his name, and Kennedy Martin parted from
Lloyd Shirley and George Taylor on amicable terms, working with Shirley again on his
1980s police drama film *The Fourth Floor*.

'By that time I had sorted out the contract and I knew that John and Dennis were
going to make it a success. I'd completed what I wanted to do in the sense I knew I
was on to a good thing,' Ian says of his reasons for leaving the show. 'People were
phoning me up about this, that and the other… It was better for me to leave it and go
and write the pilot for other series with the same rights and merchandising.' He was
ultimately not that unhappy with the way *The Sweeney* turned out, being particularly
impressed with the scripts his brother Troy and Trevor Preston wrote for the
programme. Kennedy Martin's main concern, that *The Sweeney* would turn out to be
an inaccurate representation of the police like *Special Branch,* didn't materialise,
although he speculates, 'I think [that] might have happened if Troy and Trevor Preston
hadn't got stuck in.' He moved onto other projects, creating several memorable crime
series such as *Juliet Bravo, The Chinese Detective* and *King and Castle*. He also wrote
scripts for *Colditz* and *The Onedin Line* and his work on *The Knock* gained particular
acclaim in the 1990s.

Despite the professional differences of opinion between Childs and Kennedy
Martin, 'Regan' was viewed as a great success. Interviewed for the book *Euston Films –
Made for Television,* George Taylor stated that 'When *Regan* was transmitted, it was
certainly in the [TV] top ten, if not number one, and we knew immediately it had got
potential. The casting was right – John Thaw and Dennis Waterman as a duo seemed
to work very well.'

Having won the arguments about creative control of the programme, Childs then
began to plan for the first series of *The Sweeney* – as it was now named – which began
transmission six months later. 'Part of the package was that Ian would bring Troy, his
brother, along,' Childs says. 'I knew about Trevor Preston and I got on all right with

Troy. He was quite keen on the idea that we had of making it look cinematic, and so were Trevor and Roger. Tom Clegg and I had been trainee directors together at ABC Television. Terry Green was a graphic designer but was now a commercials director, also at ABC. So that was how we made our team.'

* * *

ARMCHAIR CINEMA: REGAN

Writer : Ian Kennedy Martin
Director : Tom Clegg
First UK Transmission : 4/6/1974 8.30-10.00 pm

CAST: John Thaw (Detective Inspector Jack Regan), Dennis Waterman (Detective Sergeant George Carter), Lee Montague (Arthur Dale), Garfield Morgan (Detective Chief Inspector Frank Haskins), Morris Perry (Detective Chief Superintendent Maynon), Janet Key (Kate Regan), Carl Rigg (Detective Sergeant Kent), David Daker (Tusser), Maureen Lipman (Annie), Stephen Yardley (Detective Inspector Laker), Barry Jackson (Morton), Miquel Brown (Miriam), Peter Blythe (Peter), Michael Da Costa (South), Ron Pember (Landlord), Jonathan Elsom (Interviewer), Betty Wolfe (Mrs Berry), Seymour Mathews (Doctor), Don Henderson (Strip Club Heavy), Del Baker (Detective Sergeant Cowley), Nancy Gabrielle (Johnno's wife)

PRODUCTION TEAM: **Producer** Ted Childs, **Executive Producers** Lloyd Shirley, George Taylor, **Associate Producer** Mary Morgan, **Production Manager** Nicholas Gillott, **Lighting Cameraman** John Keeling, **Camera Operator** John Maskall, **Editor** Chris Burt, **Art Director** Jack Robinson, **Sound Mixer** Tony Dawe, **Dubbing Mixer** Hugh Strain, **Dubbing Editor** Ian Toynton, **Assistant Director** Stuart Freeman, **Second Assistant Director** Bill Westley*, **Stunt Arranger** Peter Brayham*, **Casting Director** Lesley de Pettitt, **Technical Consultant** Jack Quarrie BEM*

* uncredited on screen

ON THE PLOT: As a result of a serious beating, a young Flying Squad detective, DS Cowley, dies in hospital. Feeling responsible, and intent on getting revenge on the killers, his superior, Detective Inspector Jack Regan begins to investigate. He recruits Detective Sergeant George Carter back into the Squad from divisional duties, hoping his local knowledge of South London will come in useful. Carter is worried to see Regan driving his own car; Regan explains he's not meant to be on the case.

Ignoring orders from Detective Chief Inspector Haskins, Regan takes Carter to visit the pub where Cowley was last seen. Carter recalls that the pub is frequented by the Tusser gang and is regarded as their territory. When Regan hears that their rivals, the

Mallory mob, were also drinking in the pub, he suspects that something has happened to Mallory, who is believed to be abroad.

Mallory's girlfriend, an American jazz singer called Miriam, shows Regan a photograph of Mallory that she thinks was taken recently in Spain, but when Regan interviews George South, a forger and photographer, he finds the photograph might not have been taken abroad after all. Regan and Carter break into Mallory's farmhouse in Tring and find a medallion in the kitchen, a gift to Mallory from his mother, which he was wearing in Miriam's photograph. This convinces Regan that Mallory has, in fact, been murdered. He visits Tusser, who is serving a 13-year prison sentence for armed robbery, and forces him to admit the name of Mallory's killer: Arthur Dale.

Regan's methods, meanwhile, have upset several of his colleagues, especially Haskins and Detective Inspector Laker of the Serious Crime Squad, who believes that investigations into the Tusser and Mallory gangs are his province. Superintendent Maynon decides to suspend Regan on hearing that he disobeyed orders, but also agrees to a request from Regan to have Mallory's farm searched. Laker is present when the search results in Mallory's corpse being discovered.

Posing as a petty blackmailer, Regan arranges to meet with Arthur Dale and several other members of the Mallory gang who have changed allegiance. Minor villain Andy Morton is mistakenly identified by Dale as having talked about Mallory's murder: he has his hand smashed with an ice skate. Meeting Regan in a warehouse, Dale confirms that he had Cowley silenced, and threatens Regan as well. Carter emerges from hiding, having listened to Dale's admission. After an armed standoff, Dale's men desert him, not wanting to risk a 30-year prison sentence for killing a police officer. Dale is arrested. Back at the Yard, Regan is commended by Maynon for finding the killer but is also warned never to show such insubordination again; he has made enemies of Haskins and Laker. However, Regan feels he got the 'result'– that's all that matters.

NEVER MIND THE DIALOGUE: Jack's first line on screen is delivered after bursting into a sleeping villain's bedroom – 'Get your trousers on, you're nicked.'

Regan and Carter order large Scotches in the pub, and Regan later has a glass with his wife Kate, saying he's already had a 'couple of drinks'.

INSIDE INFORMATION: Jack Quarrie , an ex-Flying Squad Sergeant, was brought in to act as *The Sweeney's* 'official' adviser – the unofficial one being Kennedy Martin's friend in the police: '[My mate] was not a happy camper at the Squad. I'd known him for a long time and he was very happy to assist us. It's interesting, because Jack Quarrie *loathed* it. My friend was an active Flying Squad officer, and Jack Quarrie had just retired from the Squad. My friend said, "Look, they're going to know that somebody is helping you, so hire Jack Quarrie, he's just retired and he's an amiable cove and he knows what's going on." So we did. Jack Quarrie knew the identity of my mate and he was fine about it, but my mate didn't want the connection known.' Dennis Waterman confirms that the series had the benefit of advice from two sources: 'We had an official police adviser and an unofficial one. The official one would say, "If you want a gun you sign three pieces of paper and go and see the armourer", and the unofficial one would say, "Fuck off, you've got a gun in your safe in the office, and if you need it you use it"'.

The drive for authenticity by the production team extended to the stunt team put together by Peter Brayham, who was keen that they should look and behave like real London villains. 'I decided that I would get as many of the faces among the stuntmen –*real* faces – because they looked the business. So I got in a guy called Dinny Powell, British European Light Heavyweight: to me, he was gold dust. I also got a young guy called Mark McBride. Another guy was a pal of mine, who wasn't really a face, but had just come out of the forces, Del Baker. Real people, if you know what I mean. There was another guy called Frank Henson. All wised-up guys who knew how to have a real row. I discussed the script with Tom, and he said, "What would happen if they caught someone in a warehouse?" And I said, "They'd throw him out the window," which is how 'Regan' starts.'

Location filming was carried out at Butler's Wharf, Tower Bridge, and in Richmond, the latter causing further friction between Ian Kennedy Martin and Ted Childs. 'The idea was that it would be located in the East End – always fix the geography of the series, if you do nothing else, because people will turn on always knowing it's going to be the East End of London. And I said, "Now you're telling me you're going to spend half a day in *Richmond!*"

In his autobiography *Reminder*, Dennis Waterman recalls several amusing incidents during the filming of this story, in particular the need for a remount at the end of his exacting boxing sequence, which was shot in the Thomas a Becket gym in Clapham. 'We were to do three three-minute rounds, shot from different angles. I started like a young champ, remembering all the old footwork, jabbing with a good fast straight left followed by the occasional right hook and upper-cut. First round, so far so good. Second round, I was finding my arms were feeling rather heavy. Third round, I was finding my legs weren't actually doing what I was telling them. In three rounds I had gone from Cassius Clay to Sonny Liston, but without his ponderous speed. Then I heard the words all actors fear most: "Hair in the gate!" This means that a piece of foreign matter has been found in the lens and there is a chance it may be on the negative itself. More importantly, it means that you have to shoot the sequence or at least part of the sequence again. I was now well and truly knackered. We were both bleeding, although no real damage had been done, and just the act of lifting my arms up was a real test. But the show must go on, and we started again. Luckily, most of the earlier footage was usable and it turned out to be quite an impressive scene. But I beg you, the next time you are jeering at a boxer on the telly, just try it yourself. Those guys, even the lesser names, are seriously fit. Even we got a round of applause from the crew and bystanders. And there can't be many boxers whose prize for a good (or in my case, adequate) performance is a large vodka and tonic given to them in the ring. That's showbiz!'

NAMES AND FACES: Lee Montague had previously appeared with John Thaw in Roger Marshall's thriller *Five to One* in 1963. Montague and comic actress Maureen Lipman both reappeared together later in *The Sweeney*, in series three's 'Selected Target'. David Daker partnered Michael Elphick – himself a future *Sweeney* guest star – in *Boon*. Stephen Yardley and Don Henderson appeared together in *The XYY Man* as cat burglar Spyder Scott and Detective Sergeant George Bulman (later to become one of ITV's longest-serving policeman) respectively.

Morris Perry, who would appear as Maynon in several *Sweeney* episodes and the first feature film, guested in *Callan*, *Doctor Who*, *The Avengers*, *The Protectors*, *Poirot*, and *The Professionals*. One of his most memorable appearances was in the apocalypse drama *Survivors*, in which he played a rabies-infected philosophy lecturer.

POLICE AND THIEVES: *'People like you can kill each other and I don't give a damn. But when you kill one of us, there are no rules at all.'* Just as Troy Kennedy Martin and John McGrath revitalised the police series in the 1960s in *Z-Cars*, Ian Kennedy Martin did the same in the early 1970s with 'Regan'. In doing so, the play takes hold of a hackneyed plot device – the (then shocking) death of a copper in the line of duty – and turns it completely on its head.

In 'Regan', hardly anyone wants to know about Cowley's murder. Haskins and Laker seem more bothered by the fact that procedures are not being adhered to than by a colleague's death. The characters are either emotionless, like them, or dysfunctional 'loners' like Cowley and Jack. There are no happy family men in sight. The cynical atmosphere increases throughout – Cowley didn't just die from the kicking Dale's men gave him, but from being run over by a car, meaning that the villains' conviction is not at all certain. As it lashes with rain, Regan reflects that the villains have effectively ended the lives of two people – not just Cowley, but his elderly, dependent grandmother as well: 'She's got no reason to go on living now.' Rather than solving their case through system, method, painstaking observation and persistent questioning, Regan and Carter find the killers by threats and intimidation.

Just as *Z-Cars* once depicted fallible coppers – a feature of that series that was later toned down – Regan's personal life, in contrast to Carter's, is in a mess. His health isn't brilliant: 'It would be a good idea if you ate regular meals and drank less. You're 35 and you look 45,' his ex-wife Kate tells him when he calls to visit. In this scene it's also made clear that Regan only sees Susie, his young daughter, once in a blue moon. Regan has meanwhile formed a relationship with a married woman, Annie, who later tells him affectionately that he has to find someone to look after him, before leaving him to go back to her husband.

Perhaps because of the necessity to get background information across in the programme's debut story, the pacing is a little slow in places, but the script retains an air of naturalistic believability that was arguably lost in the subsequent series.

Ironically, as Regan gets nearer and nearer to nailing the villains, Laker and Haskins get closer to throwing him out of the force. Finally having made the capture, Regan starts to beat Dale up before pulling himself back from the brink: Carter just looks on and says nothing. Such displays – temper, brutality and rule-bending – would never have been tolerated in the London of *Dixon of Dock Green*. George Dixon's debut in the feature film *The Blue Lamp* (1949), incidentally, features a similar cop-killing plot.

Regan, Maynon and Cowley can be seen as a trio, with Cowley, who 'thought he could go it alone', as a younger version of Regan, and Maynon as an older one who is now adapting to the new system. (One scene has Maynon readying himself for a TV appearance, indicating that presentation skills – which Regan lacks – are becoming important.) The play opens with a static shot of Cowley's body lying by the river (reminiscent of the end of *Get Carter*), accompanied by downbeat and melancholic music; very different from the up-tempo theme and action-orientated titles adopted for the subsequent series. Viewed with the benefit of hindsight, this is a strong story that establishes the world of *The Sweeney* with confidence and knocks several sacred cows into the bargain. Despite their short-lived collaboration, both Ian Kennedy Martin and Childs can feel justifiably proud of the end result.

🚗 CHAPTER 5 🚗

SERIES ONE: A WORKING CLASS HERO?

AN OFFICE IN SCOTLAND YARD. A MEETING WITH THE COMMANDER of the Flying Squad. Raised voices. DI Jack Regan has obtained information about a plan to spring a criminal from captivity. DCI Haskins, his superior, is delivering a cold and angry reprimand: Regan has not been keeping him informed. In typically coarse terms, Regan angrily defends his methods. Haskins, an educated middle class man, is more intent on humiliating him in front of the Squad Commander than getting on with the job: 'Why don't you stop showing him your profile and get things moving?', Regan explodes. Finally the Commander – gruff, pragmatic, the voice of experience and common sense – throws them both out, telling them not to come back until they've caught the villains.

This is one of the key scenes from 'Ringer', the opening episode in the first series of *The Sweeney*. Screened some six months after the pilot show 'Regan', 'Ringer' follows on from where the pilot left off, reintroducing the characters. Regan is still at loggerheads with his superiors. Carter, now back in the Flying Squad, is more of a background figure, recruited for his local knowledge. Haskins is still trying to keep Regan in check. Trevor Preston, who had previously worked for Ted Childs on *Special Branch* and knew both Ian Kennedy Martin and his brother Troy, provided the script. As Ian had left the programme, Childs was looking out for a number of new writers who could provide stories for the series quickly.

Preston studied at Slade Art College and once worked as a minder for David Hockney. Among his other interests, he had plenty of experience as a television writer, having contributed scripts for *Callan*, *Special Branch*, *Public Eye* and the Gerry Anderson series *The Protectors*. Unusually for an author who has focused on crime, Preston also wrote several series for children; he adapted the *Professor Branestawm* books and *The Lion, the Witch and the Wardrobe* for television prior to concentrating on material for older children. He scripted a story for *Freewheelers* and created the superior drama series *Ace of Wands* featuring the magician/detective Tarot. 'I love writing for children,' he recalled, 'and except for *The Sweeney* – which was the happiest time I had at writing for TV – I loved writing for kids. I used to get these wonderful letters – much more intelligent than any letters I got from adults!'

'Ringer' can essentially be seen as a second pilot for *The Sweeney*, carrying over elements from 'Regan' but moving the series in a subtly different direction. The dialogue became imbued with cockney slang, and there was an increase in the quota of action scenes, including a mass fight between the police and villains and a chase in and around Peckham Rye station.

Preston's take on Regan was also slightly different to Ian Kennedy Martin's. Once himself on the receiving end of a beating from the police, Preston pushes the character to more of an extreme. Regan threatens minor crook Billy Martin with a 'kicking'; then he threatens to charge him with 'assault with a deadly weapon' after finding a closed penknife in the lad's pocket. In addition to Regan's methods, the characterisation is subtly redefined. Regan drinks – heavily, according to Len, his driver. In the first sight of him on screen, he's late and hung-over. He is seen virtually throwing his clothes on, still wearing his girlfriend's dressing gown, while the relatively smartly dressed Carter and Len are seen arriving for work on time.

The scene that ensues when Haskins discovers Carter and Len waiting for Regan is another important indicator of the attitude forming within the series. While the pair do not exactly lie about Regan's whereabouts, they refuse to implicate him in any disciplinary situation, showing solidarity in the face of an interfering manager. Haskins is initially depicted as pedantic, manipulative in his attempt to separate Carter from Regan, and overly conscious of his Squad's public image. 'The people you're seen with… Sooner or later you'll end up in the Sunday papers,' he complains to Regan, possibly foreshadowing the later episode 'Cover Story', which features Regan as the subject of a journalistic exposé.

A third element of the revised character of the programme is the juxtaposition of intellectual and earthy elements. Haskins's scene with Carter contains an exchange where he uses his (public school) education to attest his cerebral superiority over the others. He likens waiting for Regan to *Waiting for Godot*, the Samuel Beckett play in which two tramps wait endlessly for a character who never arrives. The wisecrack is seemingly lost on Len but Carter knows full well what he means, and his later suggestion to the driver that Godot 'plays full back for QPR' is a joke. This is part of the *The Sweeney*'s ethos that is often overlooked – that it drew on both popular and high culture, enriching the ongoing police drama.

Significantly, the narrative in 'Ringer' shifts the focus away from the police, concentrating instead on a hierarchy of villains, a characteristic of many future stories. Frank Kemble, the 'only one the Twins never bothered', is fastidious, well-dressed and well-spoken. Coming from a similar background to Carter, he too is self-educated, although the implication is that he is 'flash', betraying his roots through his receipt of elocution lessons. In a sense, however, Kemble has been trapped; he has no choice but to go through with plans to spring an even more influential criminal, Ray Lindsay, despite his awareness that the Sweeney are on his manor.

Prosser, the bent upper-middle class solicitor who represents Lindsay's interests, typically suggests bribery as a means of solving the problem. Merrick, a younger hard man brought in by Kemble, is trying to claw his way up by emulating the other man in manner and apparel. Unlike Kemble, he is prepared to use a gun, which has ironic and unpleasant consequences for Kemble at the climax of the story. Dave Brooker, meanwhile, is the muscle; a bit backward but fiercely loyal to Kemble and intolerant towards Merrick. At the bottom of the grouping of crooks seen in the episode are 'Stupid' and Billy Martin, who, like Kemble and Brooker on their childhood raid, are just starting out on their own criminal career by 'ringing' cars; breaking them down for parts or respraying them and selling them on.

This rich array of characters occupies much of the episode's screen time. This focus on the villains, their psychology, their loyalty to each other and their relationships, would continue to be an integral part of Preston's work, both on *The Sweeney* and on his other drama series. In 'The Placer', Harry Poole is devoted to his girlfriend and flips completely on discovering her infidelity with a gang member; bisexual Faye in 'Abduction' becomes a kidnapper to help out her boyfriend.

A final new characteristic within 'Ringer' is the way the climax is handled. Two scenes are intercut, rapidly, the contrast between them being used to heighten the tension. Haskins arrests Prosser, talking quietly on the bent brief's back lawn. Regan's team meanwhile intercept Kemble's raid on a prison van. Methodical, logical police work is compared directly with Regan's more direct and often violent approach. The clash between these two systems continues as a theme throughout several of the early *Sweeney* stories.

Trevor Preston's early scripts evidently had a far-reaching influence on the style and structure of the series, as did those by Ian Kennedy Martin's brother Troy. Brought into the series at his brother Ian's request, he had made several diverse contributions to television and film. At home in a variety of genres, Troy had contributed television scripts for the anthology series *Out of the Unknown*, his comedy *If It Moves, File It* and the military drama *Redcap*. He was best known at the time for his film screenplays for *The Italian Job* and *Kelly's Heroes*, and for the creation of the series that changed British television's perception of the police, *Z-Cars*.

Wary of depicting the police as heroic figures, Troy decided to inject humour into the equation. Regan borrows a prototype electronic tracking device to bug a villain's car in the third episode 'Thin Ice', irritating Haskins, who had previously installed it on the tea trolley to ensure the prompt arrival of his morning cuppa. This humourous approach is counterbalanced by more disturbing elements within Troy's scripts; there are also subtle but insistent hints at the presence of corruption in the Squad, and one villain complains that Regan has 'manufactured cases' in the past. In a subversion of the norm, crime is also seen to pay; the crook Gerald Bishop owns at least two large houses and has invested in the City. Another Kennedy Martin script, 'Night Out', features a publicity-obsessed detective, Grant; his Sergeant, Jellineck, regards his boss as 'one of the best guvnors in the Met'. But Regan can't stand him: Grant is the type to put his officers at risk if there is the possibility of good press. He is blasé about what is going on during the bank robbery he asks Regan to investigate, advising him and Iris to hide in the cellars until Regan points out that that's where the robbers are.

By accident or by design, and through comic or dramatic forms of storytelling, in virtually every early *Sweeney* story Regan's superiors in the police hierarchy are treated with suspicion, often with good reason. Regan's behaviour towards them consists of defying them, ignoring them or insulting them, either openly or behind their backs.

Other writers seemed to latch onto these viewpoints. Ranald Graham – who, like Preston and Troy Kennedy Martin, remained throughout all four series of the programme – caught this mood in his first script, 'Queen's Pawn'. Regan's methods, temporarily sanctioned from above, become progressively more risky. Haskins is less prepared than Maynon to sanction Regan's behaviour and protests bitterly that his subordinate is 'going mad'. Even Carter is dubious when Regan organises the temporary kidnapping of one of the main villains: 'Guvnor, I think you're going out of your mind.'

The plot of 'Stoppo Driver' involves Regan setting up Cooney, an apparently corrupt police driver, with a line on a possible wages snatch; Haskins is put out by Regan's premature action. In 'The Placer', another Preston script, Regan allows a robbery to go ahead to ingratiate himself with villain Harry Poole. In several early stories, Regan's way of doing business proves to be correct, while the attitude of his superiors turns out to be wrong. Significantly, *The Sweeney* was also among the first police series to show that the protagonists didn't always get their men (or women), making the series unpredictable and more believable than its predecessors. Ranald Graham's 'Cover Story' is the first instalment in which the villains get away with their plan, and other writers would subsequently build on this approach.

'Cover Story' deals almost exclusively with the character of Regan and his fallibility, and Graham would later script several stories that mined the same territory. In analysing Regan's cynicism and his obsessive dedication to his job, 'Cover Story' shows the destructive effect these qualities have on his relationship with journalist Sandy Williams. Her liberal sensibilities soon become offended by his attitude; in one scene she insists two criminals, Myles and Ward, are innocent until proven guilty, while Regan snarls, 'They've both got records as long as your arm.' The couple's relationship begins on a heady note but soon turns rotten, like the case itself, when their different careers come into conflict. She is reluctantly prepared to risk her journalistic integrity to help Regan; in return he suspects wrongly that she's involved with the criminals, orders her arrest for questioning, and then refuses to meet her face-to-face in the interview room.

These strong, creative, radical scripts were coupled with a range of directorial styles that was very new in contemporary television, with Ted Childs keen to develop a gritty, cinematic style of story-telling. Significantly, Terry Green's handling of 'Ringer' has a more kinetic directorial style than 'Regan'. Striking imagery, such as the interior of Soldier's militaria shop, is included along with visual in-jokes such as the edit from Brooker straight to a shot of a dog's behind. Other directors latched onto this sense of energy. The opening of 'Jigsaw' uses a hand-held camera, a characteristic of documentary film-making which adds to the sense of realism. In 'Queen's Pawn', Viktors Ritelis used a street level take on the type of British visual quirkiness previously seen in *The Avengers*; kidnappers wear pig masks as they grab a villain who was previously seen reading the tale of the Big Bad Wolf to his kids.

Trevor Preston's 'Abduction', screened last in the run of episodes, consolidated many of the series' early themes: Regan's personal life and his job collide, as it becomes clear that the villains of the piece have kidnapped Regan's daughter to force him to back away from investigating their forthcoming jewel robbery. Sworn to silence, Regan still carries on looking into the case, deceiving his ex-wife Kate, Haskins and Knowles, the methodical officer assigned to investigate the kidnap. Conflicts break out about Regan's methods, his dedication to the job and his inability to relate to women, in particular Kate. Significantly, however, as the case is resolved, the Haskins/Regan parting at the denouement is not nearly as hostile as their confrontation in 'Ringer', and Carter is instrumental in the story: Regan turns to him as the only person he can really trust.

The first series of *The Sweeney* was one where the programme found its feet, experimenting with different approaches. The writers retained by the production team dictated the style and content of its next three series, where it became equal parts Troy Kennedy Martin's comedic anarchy, Ranald Graham's study of Regan's character and Trevor Preston's authentic depiction of relationships in London's working class underworld. An extended supporting cast of characters in the first series – the morose Len the driver, the ambitious DS Matthews, a possible rival for Carter, and the comedy relief figure of DS Thorpe – were gradually phased out, with the scripts honed to concentrate on the trio of Regan, Carter and Haskins.

SERIES 1 REGULAR CAST

John Thaw (Detective Inspector Jack Regan)
Dennis Waterman (Detective Sergeant George Carter)
Garfield Morgan (Detective Chief Inspector Frank Haskins) (1, 3-5, 7, 8, 10-13)

SERIES 2 RECURRING CAST

Morris Perry (Detective Chief Superintendent Maynon) (2-4)
Janet Key (Kate Regan) (13)
Carl Rigg (Detective Sergeant Kent) (7)
John Flanagan (Detective Sergeant Matthews) (2-4)
Martin Reed (Detective Constable Thorpe) (2-4, 9)
Nick Brimble (Detective Constable Burtonshaw) (6)
Dennis Du Marne (Fred) (5,9)
Mark McKenzie (Len) (1,2)
Tony Allen (Bill) (3-13)*
Colin Douglas (Commander) (1, 12)

Stephanie Turner (Alison Carter) (5, 13)
Jennifer Thanisch (Susie Regan)** (13)

* uncredited on screen
** also spelt Thamisch and Thanish in the programme titles

PRODUCTION TEAM: **Producer** Ted Childs, **Executive Producers** Lloyd Shirley, George Taylor, **Associate Producer** Mary Morgan, **Art Directors** Jack Robinson (1,2,5,9,11,12) William Alexander (3,4,6,7,8,10,13), **Assistant Art Directors** Martin Atkinson (1,2,5,9,11,12), Roger Bowles (3,4,6,7,8,10,13), **Assistant Directors** Stuart Freeman (1,5) Eamon Duffy (2, 11), Derek Whitehurst (3, 4, 7, 8, 9, 10, 12), Bill Westley (6,13), **Boom Operator** Mike Silverlock, **Camera Operator** John Maskall, **Casting Director** Lesley de Pettit, **Continuity** Marjorie Lavelly, **Dubbing Editors** Ian Toynton, (1,2,5,7,8,10,11,12,13) Peter Compton (3,6,9), **Dubbing Mixer** Hugh Strain, **Editors** Chris Burt (1,3,5,7,8,9,10), John S. Smith (2,6,11,12,13), Ian Toynton (4), **Hairdresser** Stephanie Kaye, **Lighting Cameramen** Dusty Miller (1,3,5,7,8,9,10) Norman Langley (2,6,12,11,13) Mike Davis (4), **Location Managers** Lindsay Vickers (4,7,10,13) Stuart Freeman (6,8) Eamon Duffy (9,12), **Make-up** Michael Morris **Production Manager** Nicholas Gillott, **Sound Mixer** Tony Dawe, **Stills Photographer** Doug Webb, **Stunt Arranger** Peter Brayham*, **Wardrobe Supervisor** David Murphy, **Technical Consultant** Jack Quarrie BEM**, **Theme music** Harry South

* uncredited on screen, apart from 'Stoppo Driver'
** uncredited on screen

1.1 RINGER

Writer : Trevor Preston
Director : Terry Green
First UK transmission : 2/1/1975 9.00-10.00 pm

CAST: Brian Blessed (Frank Kemble), Ian Hendry (Dave Brooker), Jill Townsend (Jenny Peters), Alan Lake (John Merrick), June Brown (Mrs Martin), Steve Gardner (Billy Martin), Colin Prockter ('Stupid Hawes'), Toni Palmer (Edi), Ray Mort (Driscoll), Angus Mackay (Prosser), Leslie Sarony (Soldier)

ON THE PLOT: Regan is keeping tabs on Frank Kemble, photographing everyone who comes and goes from the criminal's garage while, inside, Kemble and his right-hand men, Merrick and Brooker, plan a raid. As Regan stops to telephone the Yard, two young tearaways, Billy Martin and 'Stupid' Hawes, suddenly steal the white mini that he borrowed from his girlfriend.

At their lockup, the two lads find a set of photographs from Regan's observation. Billy recognises a snap of Kemble, visits him and tells him about the mini. Kemble sends Brooker and Merrick to see the owner, Regan's girlfriend, Jenny Peters. She sees through the pair as they pose unconvincingly as coppers. Brooker threatens to burn her with an electric iron unless she tells them who she lent her car to. Meanwhile, helped by Carter's local knowledge, Regan has tracked down the car thieves. Seeing Jenny, Regan reasons that Kemble wouldn't send heavies round unless he was planning a job somewhere, soon. Several of Kemble's associates have disappeared.

Back in Scotland Yard, Regan and Carter get an unexpected lead – from Billy Martin's mother. In return for Regan promising to put in a good word for Billy and 'Stupid', she tells him about a conversation she overheard between Kemble and Prosser concerning a face called Lindsey, a dangerous convict. Kemble has evidently agreed to spring him from captivity as he is transported across London that afternoon.

Haskins and several uniformed officers arrest Prosser while Kemble's team ambush the prison truck, only to find the Squad in the back. As a confused brawl breaks out, Brooker seizes a double-barrelled shotgun and discharges it – but instead of hitting Regan, he accidentally kills Kemble.

NEVER MIND THE DIALOGUE: Regan and Carter introduce themselves to Billy Martin: 'We're the Sweeney, son, and we haven't had any dinner!'

'No shooters!' Kemble orders Merrick and Brooker, stating that he doesn't want to see any bulges in people's trousers. 'I'd better tell Fancy to wear his loose strides then!' Merrick quips, an in-joke about Brian Blessed's role as Fancy Smith in *Z-Cars*.

Len the driver on Regan's drinking: 'His kidneys must be waving a white flag.'

INSIDE INFORMATION: 'Ringer' was one of several scripts that had to be written quickly when Ian Kennedy Martin withdrew the storylines that he had been working on. 'I had to write that in six days,' author Trevor Preston recalls. 'I had to get it out fast, so it really was speed, cigarettes and whack it out. I think that really is the best way to write. You sit down at a typewriter and you just do it. The lovely thing about *The Sweeney* was that it got going, got on its feet, got crewed up, they were shooting them, and we were all writing the stuff within the time it now takes a fucking producer to read the script!'

'Ringer' was also the first episode of *The Sweeney* to be filmed, during the June local elections in 1974. Director Terry Green, who had been a graphic designer at ABC Television, devised the striking title sequence of still images, edited together by head of post-production Chris Burt. Ironically, they were only used due to budgetary constraints, a factor that also dictated the first choice of title music.

'When they started shooting the episodes, the title music hadn't been settled on,' film editor John S Smith remembers. 'I was then getting music from libraries. I picked a couple of pieces and I put them on the titles. I showed them to Lloyd Shirley and said, "What do you think of that?" He was horrified. He said, "Oh no, it's too American." I realised then that he was thinking 'not America' and that he wanted to make this a London-based show. Terry Green knew Harry South, and that's when they got him in to do the music.' South's opening and closing music, brash and melancholic respectively, perfectly matched the beginning and end sequences of Regan, Haskins and Carter arresting two villains after a car chase and taking their leave of the Squad Office set, based at the Colet Court production office.

South's music was the only piece of commissioned music used in *The Sweeney.* 'You'd get the pictures together, and the style, then you'd go off to music libraries like De Wolfe and Zomba,' John S Smith explains. 'It was the same system on *Special Branch.* In the end, we exhausted all the libraries, and we were fishing around trying to find libraries with fresher music. There was one piece of music ['Hideout'] that had a bit of suspense and tension and we wore that out.'

The opening title sequence took a day to shoot and required a special car stunt for Regan's Ford Consul. 'The 180-degree turn was done by Les Crawford [Roger Moore's stuntman on *The Saint*],' stunt arranger Peter Brayham explains. 'I got him in to do that, although I did most of the car stunts myself. There was a driver, Tony Allen, who fell in love with that car. He said, "I suppose you're gonna give me it back all smashed up!"'

According to Dennis Waterman's autobiography *Reminder,* filming this episode was particularly eventful. 'Our location was bang in the middle of two housing estates, so all the young tearaways came sauntering around, making our lives hell... Finally I was driven to say, "Oh, sod this, let's go to the pub." John looked at his watch. "It's only half past eleven in the morning," he said cautiously. "Not to drink!" I exclaimed. "Just to get away from all this crap. Just to have a half and a bit of comfort and quiet for a few minutes." We piled into the nearest pub, and lo and behold, Ian Hendry and Alan Lake had beaten us to it. They were sitting comfortably with their halves in their hands. I ordered two halves of bitter and asked if they'd like another themselves. "Piss off," said Lake. "This isn't beer, it's brandy." This could turn out to be an interesting day, I thought.'

Waterman was proved right, as stunt arranger Peter Brayham remembers. 'Alan Lake used to get pissed and he'd go in strong. He hit John, and I pulled him to one side and said, "Do it with me, Alan. If you hit me I'm gonna break your jaw." He hit me, and I didn't hit him on the chin, but I gave him a good dig, because he was wild. He hit John over the head, I think. The next day [Lake] went in to Ted and showed him the bruises where I'd hit him in the ribs; I'd done it deliberately, because he was uncontrollable. I thought I was going to get the sack. Ted called me in and asked me what it was all about, and I told him. And he went, "Well, stuff him, he deserves it!"'

When *The Sweeney* premiered on 2 January 1975, the production team were invited to a special screening (bar Thaw and Waterman, who watched the 'Ringer' at the leading man's house). 'Lloyd Shirley and George Taylor took us all to the green room at Thames Television the night it was first transmitted,' John S Smith remembers fondly, 'and we all had drinks. As the ratings progressed people got excited, and there were more and more parties!'

Most of the episode was filmed in and around Peckham, including a chase sequence through Peckham Rye railway station. Additional footage was filmed at Charlton Athletic's football ground, the Valley. Perhaps nervous of *The Sweeney*'s promotion of cockney rhyming slang, *TV Times* ran an explanation of the patois to accompany the first episode. Viewers were also invited to write in join in a competition to create a new phrase for the London lingo.

NAMES AND FACES: Ian Hendry was familiar to viewers of sixties and seventies television from his regular roles in *The Avengers* and *The Lotus Eaters*; he also made guest appearances in *The New Avengers, Return of the Saint* and *The Chinese Detective* and was a semi-regular in *Brookside* until his death in 1984. He also appeared in *Get Carter* as Carter's nemesis, Eric Paice. Brian Blessed played Fancy Smith in *Z-Cars* and has since played numerous dramatic and melodramatic roles, from Augustus in *I, Claudius* to the ear-splitting King in *The Black Adder*.

Leslie Sarony first appeared on the stage in 1911 and was a comedian, dancer and songwriter, one half of 'The Two Leslies'. Alan Lake appeared in several films with British porn star Mary Millington; he was married to Diana Dors. June Brown appears as Dot in *EastEnders*.

Terry Green had a background in commercials prior to direction, and was recruited by Ted Childs for the last film series of *Special Branch*. He went on to direct numerous episodes of *Minder* and *The Bill*, and later worked on the film *Cold Justice*, which starred Dennis Waterman and Ron Dean.

POLICE AND THIEVES: *'The bloody Sweeney. That's all we need, innit?'* 'Ringer' is a bold statement of intent. In the pre-titles sequence, working class villains unload guns and gas masks from a disguised ambulance, in an urgently directed film sequence of hand-held camerawork and fast edits, accompanied by jazz/rock incidental music reminiscent of Lalo Schifrin's influential score for *Dirty Harry*. The change of emphasis from the understated, downbeat feel of 'Regan' is immediately apparent and the uncompromising stance is reinforced by the series' name and episode title – the first use on British television of underworld slang as the title of a drama.

Trevor Preston's convincing representation of the trio of villains is aided by strong performances from Brian Blessed, Ian Hendry and Alan Lake, strong opposition for Regan and Carter in their first hour-long case.

Another example of Preston's use of contemporary cultural references, one of many changes in style from 'Regan', is the scene where 'Stupid' plays with Regan's camera while enthusing about the 1966 film *Blow Up* ('He strips off these two little birds, they don't half like it, phwooarr!').

Overall, this is a fast and furious first night for the series. 'Ringer' roars with a new streetwise style that almost overnight changed the perception of both the police and criminals in British popular culture.

1.2 JACKPOT

Writer : Tony Marsh [Troy Kennedy Martin]
Director : Tom Clegg
First UK transmission : 9/1/1975 9.00-10.00 pm

CAST: Ed Devereaux (Biggleswade) Richard Davies (Doctor), Morgan Sheppard (Morrison), Bernard Gallagher (Desk Sgt), Carolyn Jones (Irene), Murray Brown (Mo Simmonds), Sally Faulkner (WPC Bond), Natalie Kent (Doris), Bart Allison (Wilf)

ON THE PLOT: Men are slammed into fences; bank notes lie scattered on the ground. The aftermath of a wages snatch foiled by the Squad. Despite the success of the ambush and the apparent arrest of the gang, a sour note is struck when Regan learns one bag of money – containing £35,000 – has disappeared.

Back at the local station, Carter begins questioning gang leader Harry Biggleswade while Regan's team go through aspects of the case again. When interviewed, Biggleswade's parents stay schtumm while his sister Irene looks on from another flat. Searches reveal nothing and the interrogation goes nowhere. Convinced that one of Regan's team has nicked the money, Maynon warns him that he'd better find it. He later calls in Morrison, another officer, to start looking through the Squad's bank accounts.

Viewing film footage of the robbery, the Squad men see that Biggleswade threw a bag of money out of shot, and it landed close to impoverished bookie and failed entrepreneur Charlie Quigley. Quigley's flat is empty and, as evidence comes in that the money's being spent, Regan believes he has solved the case. He anonymously briefs a member of the press on these lines, but his efforts to clear the Squad's name backfire. Maynon later berates Regan for the appearance of a newspaper with the headline 'Can The Yard Count?'

WPC Bond, sent to talk to the locals on Biggleswade's estate, reports back that Harry's daughter Sheba is terminal ill with a kidney disorder; Irene and her boyfriend, Tony Wirral, have been looking after her, but Wirral has disappeared. Studying more film footage, Regan realises that Wirral was driving an unauthorised hot dog van which was at the crime scene; he is a missing member of the gang. Regan predicts that once Biggleswade hears that Wirral's fled with the money, meant for his daughter, he will tell all.

NEVER MIND THE DIALOGUE: 'Biggles' gets a lot of good lines – misquoting Hiawatha on the whereabouts of the cash: 'All of a sudden a dirty great puddin' went flying through the air. It came to Earth I know not where.'

On hearing the police have searched his flat, he says, 'I bet you left it in a right mess.' Regan agrees: 'We left it how we found it – a right mess.'

According to Carter, Big Tel maintains he was just taking his dog for a walk when the fraças started, carrying a heavy duty chain ('It's a big dog') and wearing an ex-army flak jacket ('The weather turned nasty'). So how come the dog was found back in the kitchen in Tel's home – did it lock itself in? 'He used to be a circus dog, he knows a lot of tricks!'

Carter, on hearing that Biggleswade intended the money to be spent on Sheba's operation, admits to a grudging respect for him, saying he can't help but take his hat off to him. 'If he'd had a gun that day, he'd have taken your hat off, and your head with it,' Regan retorts cynically. 'He's just another bastard with a bit of bottle.'

INSIDE INFORMATION: Credited to Tony Marsh, 'Jackpot' was actually scripted by Troy Kennedy Martin. 'I was trying to make a point,' he says. 'I think Ted or Mary Morgan tried to fuck around with the script so I took my name off. [There] was another scene I was told that I couldn't use because they haven't got a search warrant. So I put in the line, "Oh, we must have forgotten it."' All other episodes by Kennedy Martin were made as written.

'Jackpot' also began a fruitful partnership between the writer and the director. 'Tom Clegg was one of the best directors I've ever worked with on scripts,' Kennedy Martin says. 'Tom's not worried about the action, he knows he can do it. Other directors would come in and say, "Christ, what happens when we do this...", and zero in on a fire or a crash and leave the actors. Tom would concentrate on the actors.'

However, 'Jackpot' bore all the hallmarks of the elder Kennedy Martin's elliptical approach to plotting: 'I just thought wouldn't it be great if you could do [a story] about this guy throwing this bag of money, and then sort of build on it.' Significantly, the episode was also the first to show the series could handle comedy as well as hard-hitting drama. 'The humour was a very important part of it,' Tom Clegg explains. 'You felt it was essential because it was such a seedy world. We wanted to be the first series to say that the villains and the Flying Squad were just about the same. They were on different sides but they could easily swap.'

The economic feel of *The Sweeney*'s production is evident in the scene where Regan and Carter review film of the robbery. The scene was shot in Euston Films' own editing room at the top of the Colet Court production office.

NAMES AND FACES: Australian actor Ed Devereaux was best known to UK viewers for his role as the ranger in *Skippy the Bush Kangaroo*. An experienced actor who divided his time between Britain and Australia, he had previously appeared in *Smithy* and *Journey Out of Darkness*. He can also be spotted in an episode of *The Professionals* – 'Runner'. Welsh character actor Richard Davies appeared in *Please, Sir!* and *Fawlty Towers*. Sally Faulkner and Murray Brown had recently appeared in the cult horror picture *Vampyres*, while Bernard Gallagher went on to appear in early episodes of *Casualty*.

Prior to *The Sweeney*, Tom Clegg had directed episodes of *Special Branch*. More recently he directed *Bravo Two Zero*, a film adaptation of Andy McNab's account of a failed SAS incursion into Iraq during the Gulf War; Troy Kennedy Martin worked on the script. Clegg was also brought on board by Chris Burt to direct the BAFTA-winning *Sharpe* series. A prolific and experienced television director, Clegg has worked on many TV series, including both the original and the revived *Van der Valk*, *Return of the Saint*, *Space: 1999*, *Boon*, *The Professionals*, *Minder* and *Between the Lines*. His one-off projects included *Mountbatten: The Last Viceroy* and the film *McVicar* starring Roger Daltrey.

POLICE AND THIEVES: *'You'd better find that money, Jack. And all of it.'* Very unlike 'Ringer' in both its direction and its flashback structure, 'Jackpot' is another prominent early *Sweeney* story that establishes another of the main characteristics of the series – deploying comic set pieces to make a cynical, pessimistic story more palatable. There is a lot of humour on display, from Matthews whistling the *Laurel and Hardy* theme when told he's to search Charlie Quigley's house without a warrant, to the slow handclap Thorpe receives on realising that Quigley has left.

One particularly surreal sequence sees the Squad watching film footage of themselves fighting the bigggers and commenting on the action, while the chase for the bag of money is transformed into a deranged game of rugby. (Their comments include 'Did your mum teach you to fight?' and, on witnessing a cop kicking a blagger in the face, 'Self defence, that one.') The violence is also shown to hurt; several cops, including Regan, sport black eyes or wear plasters throughout the rest of the episode.

'Jackpot' also explores the Squad's ambivalent relationship with the press. The police were under watchful media observation in the seventies for corruption, and the press scrutiny of the Squad's activities features throughout *The Sweeney* – particularly in the first series – added to the sense of *realpolitik*.

1.3 THIN ICE

Writer : Troy Kennedy Martin
Director : Tom Clegg
First UK transmission : 16/1/1975 9.00-10.00 pm

CAST: Alfred Marks (Bishop), Peter Jeffrey (Pringle), Brian Glover (Moose), Bill Dean (Charlie Norton), Brian Wilde (Stanley), Maurice O'Connell (Morgan), Margaret Nolan (Betty), Ivan Beavis (Sergeant), Robert Gillespie (Steward), Tony Aitken (Shipping Clerk), Bridget Brice (Secretary)

ON THE PLOT: Gang boss Gerald Bishop flees Britain on a private cruise ship. This is a cause of annoyance for Regan, who claims that he was on the point of putting a case together to nail the man. He complains officially about the recent involvement of Superintendent Pringle from the Fraud Squad; Pringle's investigations into Bishop's activities in the City were responsible for the crook's tactical retreat. At a meeting with Maynon, however, Regan is assigned to another case in Norfolk.

Before complying with this, Regan sees the Moose, Bishop's intellectually challenged gofer. He convinces the man that he's on Bishop's payroll, which enables him to obtain details about Bishop's dog – the man's only real love in the world. Later, acting on Bishop's instructions, the Moose breaks the dog out of kennels. Thorpe, left on surveillance and complaining of exposure, reports this theft; Pringle is furious when he realises that Regan is still on the case and warns him to back off.

The Moose takes the dog to Bishop's residence in France, but it is the wrong animal. Bishop subsequently goes berserk, beating up the Moose and killing the dog. Regan meets the Moose as he returns to Britain; for his own safety, the man is prepared to turn Queen's evidence on his former employer. It turns out that Regan was responsible for switching the dogs; he now has the animal in the Police pound, as Bishop originally imported it to Britain illegally. Pringle complains to Maynon about Regan's conduct, but is forced to back down. Bishop, worried for the animal's safety, and also aware that various financial dealings are collapsing around him, makes anxious calls to his accountant and solicitor. A phone tap intercepts them, and the Squad soon become aware that he has decided to fly home. As they set off to arrest him, Pringle concedes defeat – but warns Regan that it's only the end of a battle, not the war.

NEVER MIND THE DIALOGUE: Carter tells the Moose he's in demand. 'Yes,' Moose agrees. 'Like a toilet roll.'

Regan, Carter and Matthews sit in a drawn-out interview with publicity-mad shotgun murderer Charlie Norton. Norton shot his wife and her lover and is now over-elaborating every detail 'like a 19th century novel – 300 boring pages,' according to Regan.

Bishop on his four-legged friend: 'As far as I'm concerned the world's major source of solar radiation shines out of that dogs ar-' His last word is drowned out by the sound of the ship's funnel blowing off as if he were in *Carry On Cruising*.

He later worries: 'There are diseases dogs can catch just by smelling each other.'

INSIDE INFORMATION: By 'Thin Ice', Dennis Waterman had already decided who his two favourite writers were: 'Troy Kennedy Martin's scripts was always quite quirky and difficult to work out, and a bit jaundiced – which was always nice – and Trevor came from Brixton, was London based, quite a hard man himself and knew about the people who were out there! They were so real and easy to do, you didn't really have to change anything. Once it was apparent how easily John and I worked together, it was easy for them to write for us.'

The Sweeney production team's desire for authenticity extended to naturalistic scenes of characters driving and conversing in their cars. Apparently simple sequences were complex to shoot, as Tom Clegg remembers. 'Often I would end up driving if we were trying to get a certain shot. You'd have big lights on the bonnet, plus the camera, so to actually see where you were going was quite tricky. More often, the sound guy would be in the boot, I would be lying on the floor of the car, and everybody would muck in with the [sound] board and the microphones. Sometimes we would put the cars on low-loaders with one of our cars in front and another behind; it was quite tricky for the drivers. But everybody was so fed up with scenes where the actor was supposed to be driving but just ended up looking at the passenger the whole time. You knew they weren't really driving.'

Thames chose this episode for a press screening in advance of the first series' transmission. It was felt that higher violence content in 'Ringer' might create bad publicity for the show.

NAMES AND FACES: Alfred Marks had played a cantankerous copper in the horror film *Scream and Scream Again*; he later appeared in *Virtual Murder* and an Alexei Sayle spoof of *The Time Tunnel*, *Drunk In Time*. Brian Glover was a teacher, then a wrestler, before becoming a distinguished classical actor. For many years he was the voice of the Tetley Tea folk in a series of long-running adverts, and played numerous straight and funny 'northerner' roles, including Heslop in *Porridge*, Mr Rottweiler in *Bottom* and a prison governor who ends up as the monster's lunch in *Alien*[3]. Peter Jeffrey played the headmaster in Lindsay Anderson's film *If...* and made countless television appearances, including a police commissioner in *Our Friends in the North*.

Brian Wilde was a stalwart of *Last of the Summer Wine* and *Porridge*. Bill Dean played another whinging scouser, Harry Cross, in *Brookside*. Margaret Nolan had been a glamour model in the late 1950s and early 1960s, was the golden body behind the credits of *Goldfinger* and had her bottom slapped by Sean Connery in the film proper. She was also a mainstay of the later *Carry On* films.

POLICE AND THIEVES: '*Oh, come on, Moose, don't waste my time. I know you know, you know I know you know, so tell us where he's gone.*' This is a slightly fragmented piece, packed with satiric comedy in the vein of 'Jackpot' as Bishop throws the content of a flower vase out of a window and leaves a note at his house saying 'No More Milk'. However, preposterous scenes such as his watching out for the dog's arrival and even pouring it champagne are contrasted with his grotesque off-screen actions – hospitalising the Moose and, according to Regan, killing an ex-girlfriend. Troy Kennedy Martin was evidently enjoying the creative freedom afforded by the series and tapping a vein of dark comedy drama which he had previously explored in his initial script for *The Italian Job*; Bishop certainly wouldn't have been out of place in the company of Mr Bridger and Camp Freddy. The prevailing mood of comic anarchy is underlined by the over-enthusiastic dubbing of screeching tyres on to every police car.

There is some muted political comment on the increasing influx of accountants into the police force, and the implication that interest in prosecuting Bishop has only been stepped up since large sums of money became involved on the stock exchange. Haskins also seems more co-operative than in 'Ringer'. However, while warning Regan of a committee of accountants 'constantly regenerating itself' as it takes over the police, he's totting up his own expenses, as if, in the style of *Invasion of the Body Snatchers*, he's already been got at!

1.4 QUEEN'S PAWN

Writer : Ranald Graham
Director : Viktors Ritelis
First UK transmission : 23/1/1975 9.00-10.00 pm

CAST: Tony Selby (Lyon), Julian Glover (Bernard Stone), Lynn Dearth (Sheila), Tony Caunter (Clarke), Christopher Ellison (Budd), Ben Howard (Ronnie), Malou Cartwright (Angie), Keith Washington (Reporter), Gertan Klauber (Emilio), Judy Monahan (Mrs Budd), Malcolm Knight (Dodger), Jonathan Blake (the Army man), Louis Raynes (Publican)

ON THE PLOT: Three villains, Lyon, Clarke and Budd, are all acquitted of a robbery charge and walk cockily out of court; the resulting media coverage is a source of humiliation to the police. Maynon gives Regan four days to use any method he likes to get the trio convicted. Regan and Carter confront the villains at Emilio's, a high-class restaurant where the champagne flows freely. Lyon is troubled by the meeting and consults his solicitor, Bernie Stone, who advises him not to react. Regan and Carter then pay visits to Budd and Clarke, putting pressure on each man in turn to grass on Lyon. Matthews, on surveillance outside Budd's house, spots a stressed Mrs Budd posting a pregnancy test application.

Regan subsequently decides that Budd, under pressure from his wife to go straight, is the weak link in the firm. Digging out some old cases of accidental death of people Lyon knew, Regan starts making out the gang boss had them killed. Rattled, Lyon phones Budd and Clarke to reassure them that he wasn't responsible, which has the opposite effect. Regan then ups the stakes further by coercing Dodger, a small-time crook and kitchen appliance salesman, into kidnapping Clarke. Recalling that Budd's house has no telephone, he sends Matthews to 'reassure' the Budds that Lyon is not responsible for this kidnap. Budd is far from reassured, and his wife, whose pregnancy test is positive, is also beginning to crack under the pressure.

Having already lost the services of Bernie Stone, Lyon and his wife call on the Budds. Unable to convince Budd that he hasn't killed Clarke, Lyon is sure Budd is about to grass on him for all their past jobs. He calls in a hit man. Clarke, meanwhile, escapes from his inept kidnappers; Regan's tactics appear to have backfired disastrously. Budd, meanwhile, is drinking with his wife in their local pub when Lyon's hired killer shoots him down. News of this death reaches Clarke and he turns himself in, making a full statement to Haskins and Maynon. In front of all his friends, Lyon is arrested for murder.

NEVER MIND THE DIALOGUE: Lyon's rant at his departing solicitor: 'I paid you good money and you bottled out on me when I needed you most!'

Regan finds Clarke telling fairy tales to his kids and interrupts. 'All right, Hans Christian Andersen.' 'You're perverting their education!' Clarke protests.

'Christ. That Sheila's got some lunch on her,' George observes as Lyon's missus struts her stuff on the dance floor. Her 'chest hanging out won't exactly inspire confidence in her fellow suffragettes,' Regan observes. Sheila's realisation of Jane Budd's condition is priceless – 'Oh, are they 'aving a baby?' Mrs Budd, meanwhile, is 'neurotic', screaming 'I can't go on!' – a lot.

The morning after the night before, Angie, Clarke's bird, is looking the worse for wear. Carter's advice? 'Next time, take more water with it.'

NAMES AND FACES: Ranald Graham later scripted several episodes of *The Professionals*, including the memorable 'Wild Justice' in which Bodie appears to be becoming (more?) mentally unstable. He worked with the *Professionals* producer Raymond Menmuir and script editor Gerry O'Hara again on *Special Squad*, an Australian crime fighting series screened in 1984.

Graham went on to oversee *Dempsey and Makepeace*, another television film series set in London, working from a format devised by Jesse Carr-Martindale. This series concerned the adventures of Magnum-wielding NYPD cop Dempsey, who was transferred to Scotland Yard to work with aristocratic blonde Harriet Makepeace in a *Professionals*-style outfit known as SI10. *Sweeney* writers Roger Marshall and Murray Smith also worked on the series.

In 1990, Graham produced *Yellowthread Street*, starring Ray Lonnen and Mark McGann; this drama series covered the cases investigated by a group of cops stationed in Hong Kong. The 13-part film series was shot on location for Yorkshire Television.

Viktors Ritelis worked for both the BBC and ITV, directing episodes of *Counterstrike*, *Blake's 7* and *Colditz*, in addition to the cultish horror movie *The Corpse*.

Tony Selby is renowned for his chirpy cockney characters (often villains), cropping up in *Up the Junction*, *Get Some In!*, *Ace of Wands*, the 1971 film *Villain*, *Minder* and *Callan*. The latter also featured Julian Glover as a suave KGB interrogator. Having once been rejected for the part of James Bond for being 'too cold', Glover settled for being the villain of the piece, Kristatos, in *For Your Eyes Only*. Christopher Ellison became popular as DI Burnside in *The Bill* and the spin-off *Burnside*. Tony Caunter now plays car salesman Roy Evans in *EastEnders*. Gertan Klauber played a number of roles as 'heavy' Germans and was also the galley-master in *Carry On Cleo*.

POLICE AND THIEVES: *'Tempo, George. You should play chess. The person who makes the first move and always keeps attacking is always going to be one move ahead.'* Regan plays Iago to Lyon's Othello, needling his insecurity about the other members of his gang, Budd and Clarke. From its title onwards, this story returns again and again to the metaphor of chess; Bernie Stone, Lyon's solicitor – another untrustworthy member of the educated middle class – is seen beating Lyon with Fool's Mate, and he can obviously see through Regan's attempts to manufacture a case against his client.

Regan's psychological approach, and eccentricities like Clarke's kidnapper, Ronnie, cradling a black poodle, contrast with the grim and cynical nature of the story itself.

The chain of events which leads to Budd's murder is precipitated by Maynon's concern about how bad Lyon's acquittal will look in the press for his promotion prospects. Haskins's concern about his own career sees him agree with his superior's plan to give Regan carte blanche and see 'revenge harnessed to justice,' a volte face from his position in earlier stories.

'Queen's Pawn' was the closest *The Sweeney* came to portraying the police as openly ruthless, with Regan organising a kidnapping and being indirectly responsible for murder, behaviour excused by his superiors' desire to get a result. Regan's actions are only legitimised by Lyon being an unpleasant, calculating killer, for all his humourous veneer. The shockingly cynical mood is reinforced in the final moments by Maynon being quite happy for Regan to take the blame for arranging Clarke's kidnapping if it comes out in court. Tough stuff indeed, and a million miles from *Dixon of Dock Green*. As Regan tells a troubled Carter, 'This isn't the boy scouts.'

1.5 JIGSAW

Writer : Tudor Gates
Director : Bill Brayne
First UK transmission : 30/1/1975 9.00-10.00 pm

CAST: Del Henney (Eddie), Sheila Gish (June), Ken Parry (Fat Eric), Jack Woolgar (Nightwatchman), Richard Hampton (Hilary Elkin), Joan Scott (Headmistress), Evie Garrett (Nightwatchman's daughter), Valerie Bell (Barmaid), Alan Collins (Charlie)

ON THE PLOT: Regan is having a fruitless meeting with an informant in a pub when he sees Eddie Boyse, a con recently released from the nick, singing to the clientele. A few minutes later, the news comes in that a safe has been emptied only a few streets way and a nightwatchman has been clobbered. 'Don't look at me, Mr Regan, I was with you,' Boyse smirks. However, Regan is immediately convinced that Boyse did it.

He and Carter try tapping all their usual informants for information, roughing up various faces in the West End. They also turn over Fat Eric, a barber who has form and has worked with Boyse before. However, Regan's pursuit of these two is seen as 'spite' and harassment; Haskins intervenes in the case as does Eddie's MP, Hilary Elkin. Warned off, Regan continues to tail Boyse, turning up at a school parents' evening to do a talk about crime prevention while Eddie and his woman June are there.

There seems to be no real evidence against Boyse, but, visiting the pub again with Carter, Regan spots a photograph on the pub wall showing the nightwatchman holding a darts cup. Apparently, before he was injured he used to pop in every night to play for half an hour. Regan visits the injured man, pretending to have collected a whip-round for him. This enables him to establish that the safe was robbed half an hour earlier than everyone thought; the nightwatchman kept quiet about this to avoid losing his job.

The Squad nick Boyse, and as he runs away he injures June's child. Haskins later orders Carter to turn Boyse loose, fearing more political interference. Regan is furious but is then confronted by June, who gives him an additional statement. As Eddie is arrested and humiliated while addressing the local school, Regan notes there are more criminals doing time because their partners informed on them than for any other reason.

NEVER MIND THE DIALOGUE: Never mind the singing either – Eddie's crooning 'I found you just in time,' on stage. Heavy irony, as Regan notices.
Another villain on Eddie's team is barber Fat Eric, who says that at the time of the robbery he was seeing a vicar to sort out his son's wedding. Regan can't believe it: 'The only time he went to church was to steal the collection box.'

Eddie addresses the local, middle class Parent Teacher Association in villain patois, referring to 'being hassled by the Old Bill – er, I mean the police.'

Regan offers to take Carter off to an after-hours drinking club; Carter declines, saying he got food poisoning there last time.

INSIDE INFORMATION: The filming of 'Jigsaw' featured one of many pranks at the expense of a member of the production team. 'Stephanie Kaye, the hairdresser, loved shopping, and they were out one day filming at this block of flats in Battersea,' first assistant director Bill Westley remembers. 'She went out at lunchtime and bought all these new clothes. She didn't think they could see her, but [camera operator] John Maskall was up in the flats, overlooking the back of the equipment truck, which was where she thought no one could see her trying on her new togs. Of course, old John's got the camera with 'im and films the lot – knockers out, everything! When we did the out-takes reel for the Christmas party, there she was up on the screen, large as life. Brought the house down, that one did.'

Well known London landmark Battersea Power Station appears in the background when Carter and several other Squad men chase Boyse through this tower block.

At the conclusion of its first month, *The Sweeney* was the sixth most popular show on British television, averaging 7.2 million viewers per episode.

NAMES AND FACES: An active trade unionist, writer Tudor Gates co-created *Vendetta* for the BBC; screened from 1966 to 1968, this series concerned a pair of international agents travelling the world and tracking down members of the Mafia and starred Stelio Candelli, Neil McCallum and Kieron Moore.

Gates also wrote episodes of *Ghost Squad* and *Strange Report*, the plays *Oscar X, Who Saw Him Die?* and *Ladies who Lunch*, the screenplays for *The Vampire Lovers, Lust for a Vampire* and *Twins of Evil*, together with co-scripting credits on two Dino De Laurentiis comic book capers made in 1967: Roger Vadim's *Barbarella* and Mario Bava's *Diabolik*. In 1978, Gates and Anthony Burgess each adapted Conan Doyle stories for a short-lived series of Sherlock Holmes television plays. Starring Geoffrey Whitehead, they were filmed in Warsaw with American funding.

Canadian director Bill Brayne went on to direct episodes of *The Bill*, *Making News*, *The Professionals* and *Lovejoy*. He also worked on the feature films *A Flame to the Phoenix*, *Cold War Killers* and *Deadly Recruits*.

Del Henney appeared in *The Professionals* episodes 'Where the Jungle Ends' and 'A Man Called Quinn'; in the latter he portrayed another suited-and-booted character capable of mixing it. He often plays hard cases or worldly-wise coppers in programmes such as *Jonathan Creek*, *Midsomer Murders* and *A Touch of Frost*. Sheila Gish appeared with John Thaw in *Stanley and the Women* and *Inspector Morse*. Stephanie Turner had the lead role in the early series of *Juliet Bravo* as Inspector Jean Darblay; previously she had been cast with Dennis Waterman in the *Special Branch* episode 'Stand and Deliver'. Ken Parry often played camp cameos in a variety of 1970s series and also popped up in the saucy feature film *Come Play with Me*. Jack Woolgar appeared in the film *Death Line* and was a regular in *Crossroads*.

POLICE AND THIEVES: *'You could be making a good career for yourself in the force, but no, you had to team up with good old Jack back in the Sweeney.'* This is another slick early episode. A poster for *Dirty Harry* – a film in which a suspect complains to the local Mayor that he's being harassed by a rogue cop – is seen in the background, an example of the series openly acknowledging some of its influences. (Carter also mentions Clint Eastwood.) Regan's single-minded pursuit of Boyse is contrasted with the attitudes of Alison Carter and the MP Elkin, educated liberal characters concerned about Regan's brutalising effect on George and the DI's harassment of a suspect.

Haskins is again almost openly defied by Regan, and at one point tells him, 'I'd take you off this case but frankly there's no one else I can put on it at the moment!' The implication is that the DI is pursuing a vendetta against Boyse and doesn't care if other characters like the nightwatchman suffer. The safe blagger has deliberately flaunted his relationship and adopted child in public, provoking Regan, who in his own personal life has a failed marriage and estranged daughter.

1.6 NIGHT OUT
Writer : Troy Kennedy Martin
Director : David Wickes
First UK transmission : 6/2/1975 9.00-10.00 pm

CAST: Mitzi Rogers (Iris Long), T P McKenna (Grant), David Hargreaves (Jellineck), Peter Childs (Jim), Christopher Beeney (Photographer), Derrick O'Connor (Eagle), Weslie Murphy (Dukes), John Oxley (Uniformed Policeman), Tony Sympson (The Old Man), Brian Coburn (The Scotsman), Michael Middleton (The Van Driver), Jeffrey Segal (The Reporter)

ON THE PLOT: Regan is 'volunteered' to help out on a stakeout with Grant, a publicity-seeking Robbery Squad DCI with a reputation for endangering his workforce. The National Anglian Bank in Walstone Gardens is currently in the process of being robbed, the aim being to obtain something secret in one of the safety deposit boxes. Safecrackers entered the premises via the upstairs window of the pub next door. The upstairs room is rented by Iris Long, whom Regan once had an affair with, so he has the ideal excuse to gain access and keep an eye on the bank. The thieves in the vault and a lookout on the roof are both in radio contact with the robbery's organiser, 'Control'; Grant wants to let the robbery continue until this man has been tracked down.

Regan reluctantly visits Iris, who has apparently turned to prostitution. Dukes, the pub landlord, who has let the robbers use the cellar of his pub to tunnel into the bank, warns 'Control' about Regan's visit. Grant's squad realise that 'Control' is mobile and will be hard to track down.

Iris tells Regan that she has little involvement in the robbery and he nearly bumps into Jim, one of the safecrackers, while investigating a possible intruder on the pub roof. Stationed downstairs in the bar, Carter and Burtonshaw keep watch; they become involved in a pub brawl and Carter is beaten senseless outside by some men from Grant's squad. Regan gets the local police to arrest Dukes.

The following morning, Dick, the lookout on the roof, notices that no one has collected the Sunday paper. 'Control' suspects the publican has become unreliable and orders Jim and Dick to go into the pub and silence him. Regan barricades the cellar door and a gunfight breaks out as Dick and another robber enter the pub thorough the bedroom while Jim enters through the cellar. Regan succeeds in shooting them all but is hit in the leg himself. He then has to endure the final indignity – a photo call in hospital with Grant.

NEVER MIND THE DIALOGUE: Plenty of interplay between Regan and Iris; she's convinced he's only after one thing. He asserts: 'The world does not revolve around your body, this bloke Galileo proved it – it goes round the sun.' He then adds that he doesn't need sex every afternoon any more, to which Iris retorts, 'You don't get it, either!'

Getting a soaking, Regan finds Iris has put his gun in the dishwasher to clean it. 'That's government property!' he protests indignantly. Later, after sex, he informs her, 'You've ruined my pistol, you know that?'

The villains meanwhile are a bit worried by the fact that there's been a big scrap in the pub. Then they shrug it off as having nothing to do with them. 'Well, I suppose it *is* Saturday night, innit?'

INSIDE INFORMATION: The production of 'Night Out' was memorable for several reasons. 'It was the one they used to sell the show, because it had humour in it as well,' David Wickes remembers. Stunt arranger Peter Brayham recalls that he was specifically asked to provide something out of the ordinary. 'Wicksey said he'd had a memo from Al Burnett, one of the top brass – the Lew Grade of his day – saying that he wanted something really special, as he was going to try and push [*The Sweeney*] for America'.

The set piece that resulted was a fight that included Scottish football fans, shot in The

Warrington pub in Hammersmith. 'That was a difficult one,' Wickes says, 'because I didn't want this silly fight with the Scottish fans – it was like a saloon fight in a Western – to be confused with the real stuff that was going on outside with Dennis being beaten up against the wall. That was nasty. In those days the Tartan Army was very dangerous – they were like Millwall – so it was topical. I wanted to keep it amusing, so I had to do things like mirrors breaking and Western saloon bar music.'

Wickes also disagreed with Troy Kennedy Martin over the depiction of the villains, whom the writer originally wanted to be masked. 'I fought for that, and said "I really want these guys to be seen." And he went away and wrote that with less than enthusiasm, shall we say. But I will say that in the end, when he saw the rough cut, he leaned over in the Steenbeck [editing] room and said "You were right."'

The night filming on the pub roof in this episode was filmed at the The Red Cow in Hammersmith, the Euston crew's regular watering hole, which was virtually opposite Colet Court, the company's base. The pub's cellars were also used for the scenes of the robbery. The Red Cow was used throughout the series as various boozers. 'We used the bar, we used the kitchens, we used everything, and we painted it different colours,' Wickes recalls with a laugh. 'The publican made a fortune out of it: "Green? I dunno, that's another £500…"'

The shoot for 'Night Out' also required the director to bond in a typical *Sweeney* manner with his two stars. 'One day, I remember David Wickes was a little bit nervous with John and Dennis,' Peter Brayham recalls. 'He said, "Peter, I have to go and loosen up with the boys." The next morning, he came in, and I knew what had happened: they'd got him well pissed. With David Wickes that's almost unknown – you don't see that very often. He came to me and said, "Peter, do you know what we're doing today?" "Yes I do, David." "Is it all planned?" "Yes it is, David." So he said, "Could you do it without me? I'm going for a lie down!" So I did the morning shoot, and by lunchtime he was fine. After that, Dennis and David had gelled.'

NAMES AND FACES: David Wickes was born on tour with his father's theatre company; his father was the magician 'Chang', a lifelong friend of Charlie Chaplin. David spent several years in the army before moving into television and becoming the first director on *World of Sport*. He later crossed over to drama and worked extensively on *Public Eye*. After directing an episode of *Special Branch* and several commercials, he was asked by Ted Childs to direct 'Regan', an assignment for which he proved unavailable. Following his stint on *The Sweeney*, including the first feature film, he assisted the BBC in setting up their answer to the *Sweeney*, *Target*, and also directed several episodes of *The Professionals*. He now runs David Wickes Television, which produced *The New Professionals*.

Irish character actor T P McKenna was a 'colleague' of Richard Burton's *Villain* and played *Callan*'s arch-enemy, Richmond. Peter Childs appeared as Marker's temporary partner Ron Gash in *Public Eye* and as the intellectually challenged DI Rycott in *Minder*. Nick Brimble was in subsequent episodes of *The Sweeney* and the film

Sweeney! and has supported as a 'heavy' on numerous other occasions, including the SAS film *Who Dares Wins* and the role of sinister security man Corder in Alan Plater's *To Play the King* and *The Final Cut.* Christopher Beeney was a former child star from the same generation as Dennis Waterman and found fame in *Upstairs, Downstairs.* David Hargreaves later appeared in the other police shows *Juliet Bravo* and *Merseybeat.*

POLICE AND THIEVES: *'You wouldn't cross the road to see me if you saw me lying naked on a zebra crossing!'* Memorable for Regan falling in a puddle during a quick sortie on the pub roof, this story is another subversive comedy with some serious comment concerning the politicisation of the police. One of the most amusing moments concerns the bar-room brawl triggered off by Carter. The sequence borders on farce as bottles, furniture and stuntmen fly about. The scene contrasts well with what follows, where Carter gets a serious beating from some Robbery Squad lads who don't realise he's a cop until afterwards.

It's also interesting to see Kennedy Martin flouting conventional storytelling disciplines; having posed the question, the script refuses to reveal what was so important about the 'government documents' everyone's looking for. We learn little about the robbers or their mysterious draftsman; the men in the vault are prepared to kill, they seem to be well organised but not in themselves political, and are helping themselves to various other trinkets in the bank in addition to the papers. The presence of the media is again felt: Grant, a publicity-seeking careerist, only drops the charges against Iris after Regan threatens him with negative press coverage. The story again ends on a cynical note, with both men adopting a false pose of camaraderie for the police magazine *Badge of Courage.*

1.7 THE PLACER

Writer : Trevor Preston
Director : Ted Childs
First UK transmission : 13/2/1975 9.00-10.00 pm

CAST: Stanley Meadows (Harry Poole), Susan Tracy (Fran), Tony Steedman (Andrew Barkiss), Marjie Lawrance (Mrs Harris), John Forgeham (Dennis Rawlins), Robert Russell (Arni), Jeremy Young (Wren), Terry Cowling (Kesey), William Moore (Det Sgt Bowyer), Mollie Maureen (Old Woman)

ON THE PLOT: Regan goes undercover as a trucker to investigate a number of lorry hijacks. He picks up a hitchhiker, Fran, and gives her his cover story – he has criminal 'form' and is interested in making some cash. She takes his phone number and he drops her off in a pub carpark. As she then drives away in her own car, Carter and DS Kent follow. Carter later illicitly searches Fran's flat while she's out, but is surprised when another face, Rawlins, turns up; Carter legs it.

Fran introduces Regan to Harry Poole, the man who's masterminding the thefts. Poole makes Regan an offer to 'lose' his lorryload of boiled sweets. This robbery goes ahead as planned; Regan is given some money, and a kicking, to make the robbery look convincing. Thus initiated into the firm, Regan is able to get closer to Poole; when the Squad nick Harry's chauffeur on a trumped-up charge, he gives Regan the job instead. Regan discovers that Poole regularly plays golf. With Haskins's help, the Squad observe a game with businessman Andrew Barkiss. Barkiss is obviously involved in the robberies, but thinks the operation needs to cool off for a while due to rising police interest.

Rawlins, who has taken a dislike to Poole's new recruit, tails him and sees him talking to Carter; the latter is recognised, Regan is snatched and given another beating. Fran isn't sure if Regan's a cop or not, and she, Rawlins, and another thug, Arni, take him to see Poole and Barkiss at Barkiss' chemical plant. This is where Barkiss has been selling the goods from the robberies. Regan turns the tables on Rawlins, accusing him of having an affair with Fran and trying to take over Harry's firm. Finding an incriminating bunch of keys on Regan, Poole goes berserk with a gun, killing Rawlins and trying to kill Fran before Regan shoots him.

NEVER MIND THE DIALOGUE: Regan entertains Harry and Fran with his jokes, of which we only hear the punchlines. We are treated, however, to a gem in the warehouse: Regan: 'I knew a feller once. He was so mean when he caught crabs he wouldn't kill 'em: he thought they were money spiders.'

Regan on Haskins: 'He's doing for the Squad what the Boston Strangler did for door to door salesmen.'

On realising Fran has been carrying on with Rawlinson, Harry goes mental with a shooter. 'I was gonna marry 'er!'

NAMES AND FACES: Tony Steedman also appeared in *Citizen Smith*. John Forgeham has played a variety of villains and wideboys in (among others) *The Italian Job*, *Shoestring* and *Nice Work*. Susan Tracy's many television appearances include *Poirot*, *Minder*, *Boon* and *The Gentle Touch*. Stanley Meadows appeared as a professional Londoner in movies like *The Ipcress File* and the original series of *Randall and Hopkirk (Deceased)*. William Moore was Ronnie Corbett's dad in *Sorry*. Carl Rigg later defected to the BBC's *Target* as another copper, DC Dukes, and also appeared in *Emmerdale*.

Ted Childs, who switched from producing to direct this episode, left advertising to work in TV, training as a programme director with ABC Television before moving on to producing the factual programmes *This Week* and *The World at War*. He took over production of *Special Branch* from Geoffrey Gilbert and oversaw the final series before being appointed producer on *The Sweeney*. After overseeing Euston's *Quatermass* film he moved to Claridge Films, part of Tyne Tees Television. In the mid-1980s Childs was appointed Managing Director of Central Films, acting as executive producer on a wide range of films and series for ITV, including *Soldier Soldier*, *Peak Practice*, *Sharpe*,

Cadfael, Chancer, Gone to the Dogs, Thief Takers and *Heat of the Sun*. He oversaw several of John Thaw's series, including *Inspector Morse, Kavanagh QC, Goodnight Mr Tom* and *The Waiting Time*. The Guild of Film Production Executives honoured Ted with its annual Award of Merit in 1991 and he later received an OBE for his services to television.

POLICE AND THIEVES: *'I've got to get close to Harry Poole, really close. He's the placer, he's the grey matter.'* A story about infidelity. Harry's firm seems destined for a bad end even before Regan begins his espionage. In Preston's underworld, loyalty is all-important and once it's compromised, the villains' gang self-destructs. The authentic detail concerning the lorry-driving background is reminiscent of the 1957 Stanley Baker film *Hell Drivers*.

The characterisation of Regan undercover also has interesting facets to it, as he seems to be going 'native' and developing a friendship with Harry Poole. There is plenty of pathos on display when the invalid boss of the haulage company complains of the job losses that may be incurred among honest drivers due to Regan's apparent corruption. Haskins's conflict with Regan is toned down for this episode; he agrees to go sick to avoid a meeting in which he knows he'll be instructed to take Regan off the case.

1.8 COVER STORY

Writer : Ranald Graham
Director : Ted Childs
First UK transmission : 20/2/1975 9.00-10.00 pm

CAST: Prunella Gee (Sandy Williams), Bernadette Milnes (Maureen Whittle), Michael McStay (Nightclub Manager), Timothy Carlton (Justin), Mike Savage (Ward), James Marcus (Myles), Thalia Kouri (Maid), Los Gitanos (Flamenco Artistes)

ON THE PLOT: The Squad are trying to track down some stolen money, hoping this will enable them to send down two unconvicted criminals, Myles and Ward. Whittle, the third member of the gang, is already behind bars. Regan is perturbed to find that an ambitious photo-journalist, Sandy Williams, has written an article about the trio containing information the police weren't aware of. He questions her and the pair hit it off; they begin an affair, despite Carter reminding Regan that Sandy is the prime suspect for ferrying instructions between Whittle and the others.

When Sandy leaves Regan in her house to meet with Whittle's wife and then with a courier for the gang, Regan reluctantly begins to suspect that she is implicated. As a tip-off comes in that the stolen money is hidden at Whittle's house, and the Squad learn that Sandy has seen Whittle in prison, Regan confronts her. She refuses to reveal what she has been discussing with the gang, claiming journalistic confidentiality.

Regan points out that, despite their relationship, he will have no alternative but to arrest her – his career is at stake. Reluctantly she passes on what she's been told.

Acting on this information, Regan realises he's been duped and the cash has gone. Interviewed by Carter, Sandy claims to have been misled. Regan doesn't believe her and refuses to see her. She is released due to lack of evidence; the Squad have totally messed up the case. Regan, sent on leave by Haskins, begins drinking and shooting his mouth off in the pub. Carter visits Myles and Ward, angrily demanding to know if they set Sandy up. They admit they did – after giving the DS a kicking. Carter tells Regan and they drive to Sandy's home, but she's left to work in America.

NEVER MIND THE DIALOGUE: Ward, on seeing Carter entering the ghastly, Formica-tabled villains' drinker: 'Terrible smell in here all of a sudden!'

Sandy has a go at Regan about the 'machinery of justice'; he suddenly decides to take her out to dinner 'out of the kindness of my mechanical heart.'

On finding Sandy's left him, Regan emerges from her house. Is she OK, Carter wants to know. 'She's fine,' says Regan curtly, chucking her last message to him in the bin.

INSIDE INFORMATION: 'Tony Allen became John's dresser, and he started out as his stand in *The Sweeney*, before we cast him as Bill the driver,' Ted Childs remembers. 'John wanted the people he trusted to work with him and television enabled him to work that way.' Allen became a close friend of Thaw's and worked on all his major TV projects, including *Inspector Morse* and *Kavangah QC*.

The scenes in which Sandy has a meeting with one of the Whittle gang were filmed on the South Bank in London.

NAMES AND FACES: Mike Savage had similar parts as a heavy in *Minder* and *The Professionals*. He played PC Jumbo Dickinson in the sitcom *The Fuzz* and Roland Browning's dad in *Grange Hill*. James Marcus was a violent Droog in *A Clockwork Orange*. Prunella Gee appeared in *Hammer House of Horror*: 'Witching Time', the Nigel Kneale sitcom *Kinvig* and more recently as Maxine's mum in *Coronation Street*.

Having started as a production assistant, Douglas Camfield was promoted to a director in the mid-1960s, working on *Doctor Who* and *Paul Temple*. By the early 1970s the intense quality of his work and his ability to handle action sequences ensured he was much in demand as a director. Persuaded to return to *Doctor Who* by producer Philip Hinchcliffe, who later also employed him on *Target*, Camfield directed 'The Seeds of Doom', arguably one of the series' most controversial and violent instalments. For Euston Films, he worked on *Special Branch*, *Van Der Valk* and *Danger UXB* in addition to *The Sweeney*; he also handled several episodes of *The Professionals*. Later he directed a prestigious adaptation of Sir Walter Scott's *Ivanhoe*, which starred Anthony Andrews, James Mason, Lysette Anthony and Julian Glover. Camfield's early death, due to a heart condition, deprived British television of a gifted director who would undoubtedly have gone on to greater things.

POLICE AND THIEVES: *'I don't think you can love unless you put your love before your work. I was prepared to do that for you. But were you prepared to do that for me?'* This is an interesting character-driven story, dealing with a clash of values; feminism versus masculinity and idealism versus cynicism. Personal integrity is a recurring theme: villains never grass and always kick the law if they have the chance, and journalists don't reveal their sources, but Regan is the exception. At one point Sandy asks him, 'Don't you bloody policemen have any personal code?' Regan seems out of his depth with this confident, assertive woman, and he won't accept the fact that she can earn enough money for the pair of them to live on; his job will always take precedence.

The alcoholism on display in the story adds an extra dimension, as the couple's relationship begins with plenty of hedonistic boozing; later, when the pair have split, Regan morosely downs a skinful in a pub and looks fairly certain to get in a fight. The occasional lapses in logic are ably glossed over by Douglas Camfield's direction, which maintains an intense atmosphere and employs numerous tricks to keep the viewer hooked, including fading dialogue in and out of the soundtrack and interspersing monochrome flashbacks as Regan reflects on what he has lost.

The trappings of the conventional detective story are used to explore the impact Regan's work has on his private life; the villains are only in one scene, and the final car chase is an attempt to salvage a personal relationship rather than to catch the villains. The rain-sodden London streets make the story exceptionally melancholy, and the stake-out at the rubbish dump implies that, like Sandy's farewell tape, Regan's latest relationship is destined for the bin.

1.9 GOLDEN BOY

Writer : Martin Hall
Director : Tom Clegg
First UK transmission : 27/2/1975 9.00-10.00 pm

CAST: Dudley Sutton (Max Deller), John Nolan (Bernard Conway), Anthony Morton (Harry Fuller), Colin Campbell (Terry Potter), Tony Jay (Lambourne), Anne Zelda (Joanna Drummond), Peter Miles (Mr Bradshaw), Tim Wylton (Customs Man), Michael Segal (Reporter), Helli Louise, Fran Fullenwider (Girls in pub)

ON THE PLOT: Meeting his backer, Lambourne, at a cricket match, Max Deller agrees to go ahead with a plan to rob gold bullion from a city bank. He intends to blackmail Bernard Conway, née Peters, a fellow ex-borstal boy who's made good, into helping him.

Regan's team are bogged down with Bradshaw, a civil servant conducting a time-and-motion study into the Squad's procedures. Regan takes him to the pub to keep him out of the way, and there he sees impoverished con Fuller. The man is flush with money and drunk, having helped Max to track Conway down. A suspicious Regan and Carter pull Fuller in, then release him so Carter can tail him and see how he came by his cash. Fuller and Max give Carter the slip; the former later dies accidentally. Max, having made contact with Conway, forces the latter to dispose of Fuller's body. Conway does so, but knocks down a gamekeeper; he reports his car as stolen to cover his tracks. Regan and Carter, following up Fuller's death, interview Conway and his affluent girlfriend Jo about the car, and are puzzled over the man's evasiveness concerning his past.

Max goes ahead with the robbery. Posing as a cleaning outfit, he and his team gain access to the firm, feeding video footage of a deserted vault into the closed circuit TV to fool the security guards while they clear the place out. Over £1 million in gold bullion is taken.

Regan finds out Conway is a manager of Jo's father's company, which manufactures sporting equipment. Conway seems to be going along with Max's plan to smuggle the gold – melted down and disguised as iron weights – out to Beirut. However, Conway has changed sides: he switches the weights back, and Max is nicked.

NEVER MIND THE DIALOGUE: 'Your stomach must be lined with double gloss emulsion!' There is plenty of comedy in the scenes between Regan, Carter and a drunken Harry Fuller. The charges the cops threaten to unload on him include 'unlawful possession of money', 'being a public nuisance' and ruining Carter's jacket. They finally advise him to put the nation first by having a bath.

INSIDE INFORMATION: The pre-title sequence of this episode was shot in the Long Room of the pavilion at Lords cricket ground in St John's Wood.

NAMES AND FACES: Martin Hall had previously written for *Softly Softly* and *Strange Report*.

Dudley Sutton's comic touch featured in *Shine On Harvey Moon* and *Up the Workers*. His best known role is Tinker in *Lovejoy*. He also combined comedy with menace in the film *The Devils*. Also in the cast is Colin Campbell, with whom Sutton played the title roles in Sidney J Furie's *The Leather Boys* back in 1963.

Ironically, the dreaded time-and-motion man, Peter Miles, was frequently cast as sinister types, including Nazis and mad scientists, in the 1970s.

POLICE AND THIEVES: *'That's right, it's a blag. And a bloody big one!'* In the tradition of comics like Frankie Howerd and Kenneth Williams, Dudley Sutton plays a seemingly camp upper class figure who can suddenly make the switch to being a proletarian spiv, depending on the company he keeps. Anthony Morton's Harry Fuller is another great character in the *Sweeney* gallery of grotesques, with the rheumy eyes, dozy look and soiled dignity of the complete alcoholic.

This story has several interesting twists, including Conway being straighter than he seems. The plot has its roots in caper movies such as *The Italian Job* and in Sean Connery's attempts to evade video surveillance in *The Anderson Tapes*. The 'rigged camera' scam has been imitated several times since, and was the first instance of hi-tech crime appearing in *The Sweeney*. The idea of Regan taking Bradshaw down the pub to put him out of action for the afternoon is another enjoyable example of the anti-authoritarian attitude behind the series.

1.10 STOPPO DRIVER

Writers : Allan Prior, Peter Brayham* and Sandra Chapman*
Director : Terry Green
First UK transmission : 6/3/1975 9.00-10.00 pm
* uncredited on screen

CAST: Nicola Pagett (Sara Prince), Billy Murray (Brian Cooney), Wolfe Morris (Greg Prince), Aubrey Morris (Card Player), Paul Angelis (Barney Prince), Paul Henry (Morris Brass), Carrie Lee Baker (Marie), Hugh Futcher (Porter)

ON THE PLOT: Barney Prince and Morris Brass carry out a blagging, but their driver, Charlie Spencer, is killed following a car chase with the Squad. This mishap causes problems for the Prince family – Barney, his father Greg and sister Sarah – as they need a driver for their considerably bigger follow-up job. On reading the papers they see that Brian Cooney, the Squad driver in the aforementioned chase, is getting married.

The couple celebrate their wedding day in the company of Regan, Carter and Haskins; they later retire to a hotel ready to fly to Paris, but their privacy is rudely interrupted as the Princes kidnap Marie Cooney. Her husband is coerced into driving for the firm as they pull off their planned job – robbing the big pot at a high-stakes illicit card game. Marie is later released.

Investigating the robbery in their capacity as Duty Squad, Regan and Carter realise that a highly professional driver was involved in the job. They are told by Haskins to hand the case over to CID but press on regardless when they hear that a police-issue ballpoint pen was found on the floor of the abandoned getaway car. Carter finds a bank statement which shows that £10,000 has been paid into Cooney's account. Regan sees that the driver's wife is behaving oddly following her ordeal; he believes Cooney is corrupt. The DI sets him up by pointing out an ideal target for a robbery – a van carrying old banknotes.

Barney and Morris go with Cooney's offer to put some work their way. With the Squad in hot pursuit, the driver deliberately crashes the getaway car into some petrol drums, bailing out before the car explodes. Badly injured, Cooney explains to Haskins that he was blackmailed by the Prince firm and wanted revenge – an act that means the end of his police career.

NEVER MIND THE DIALOGUE: Carter to Cooney, shaken, after the first car chase of the day: 'Who taught you to drive? Evel Knievel?'

The influence of the American cop show is felt as Regan and Carter discuss

Cooney's possible guilt. 'It does happen, you know.' 'Yeah, on *Hawaii Five-O!* Also: 'Book him, Danno!'

Further contemporary references creep in as Haskins advises Regan to go home and watch *Match of the Day*.

Irritated, Greg Prince tells Morris to 'Go and play with the traffic.' He also warns his family, 'That morgue'll be knee deep in cozzers.'

Celebrating the Princes' financial gain, Maurice gets so pissed he falls down the stairs. Off screen, sadly.

INSIDE INFORMATION: Although credited to Allan Prior, the script was initiated by stunt arranger Peter Brayham, explaining the story's higher than normal amount of car stunts. 'I wrote one called 'Stoppo Driver'. I came into Ted and said, "I've got an idea." It was two stories, actually. One was about illegal gambling in this country: it used to happen in boats and hotel rooms, all over the place. The other story was about a bent cozzer who had his wife kidnapped. But they got a writer to put his name on it, and I was a little bit upset. I wrote the whole thing with a girl called Sandra Chapman and Ted paid me for it, but in those days you could never be a stunt man and a writer. Ted said, "What you've done is good, but the dialogue needs working on and I need to get a writer to do it." And I said, "OK." I just didn't care, because I wanted to do a really big action car chase, and it's since gone down as one of the best.'

'Stoppo Driver' was the only story of the first *Sweeney* series to credit Brayham on the closing titles. It was a recognition of the episode's high car chase quota, as well as a possible nod to his hand in the origination of the script.

NAMES AND FACES: Allan Prior started writing for television in the early 1950s, contributing scripts to *Z-Cars*, *Coronation Street* and *Dr Finlay's Casebook*. In 1966 he received a Silver Dagger Special Merit Award for his work on *Z-Cars*. He later dramatised *Hawkeye, the Pathfinder* with Alistair Bell and created the 1980s drama serial *The Charmer*. He co-created the soap *Howard's Way* and also penned over 20 novels, two of them autobiographical. His most recent play, *Führer*, was adapted for Radio 4.

Nicola Pagett was well known for her role in *Upstairs Downstairs* and had the title role in *Anna Karenina*. Aubrey Morris, specialising in psychotic types, appeared in *A Clockwork Orange*, *The Wicker Man* and *The Prisoner*. Paul Henry was familiar to viewers with his tea cosy hat as Benny in *Crossroads*. Billy Murray was later in *The Bill* as corrupt copper – and cop killer – Don Beech.

POLICE AND THIEVES: *'If he can't take a joke he shouldn't have joined.'* This story is a fairly straightforward runaround after the varied approaches of the previous stories, although the unpleasant treatment of Cooney's wife lends it some psychological depth. The sequence in which Cooney finds her missing, with her hair left on the bathroom floor and a warning smeared on the mirror, is particularly cinematic, complete with the

Hitchcock touch of an aircraft roaring overhead.

Cooney, a middle class character, who seems arrogant and has not formed close friendships with many people, is a victim of hubris, and his failure to relate to Regan and Carter is the fundamental cause of his later undoing. It's interesting to note that, like Conway in the preceding story, Cooney makes an effort to face up to and rectify his predicament.

There is little insight into the Prince family, but Nicola Paget's performance as Sara, the gangland Lady Macbeth, is particularly worthy of praise; her coldly matter-of-fact threat to 'stripe' Maria's face is chilling. Angelis and Henry are rather less at ease in their opening scene. The Regan-Haskins conflict returns in this episode, in a subtle scene where Haskins seems to be making a jibe about Regan's failed marriage.

1.11 BIG SPENDER

Writer : Allan Prior
Director : Viktors Ritelis
First UK Transmission : 13/3/1975 9.00-10.00 pm

CAST: Warren Mitchell (William Wardle), Catherine Schell (Stella Goodman), Godfrey James (Charlie Smith), Julian Holloway (John Smith), Billy Hamon (Barry Smith), Maureen Pryor (Enid Wardle), Peter Armitage (Jacko), Peter Glaze (Joe Spratt), Sally Knyvette (Angela)

ON THE PLOT: Haskins orders blanket surveillance of the three Brothers Smith: 'Barry Smith – the pretty one, the youngest brother. John Smith – the brains. Charlie Smith – the muscle.' The gang are behind a string of blags, but Barry reports to his brothers that he has found an easier way of making money. He is later seen collecting it off a carpark manager, Wardle. Regan and Carter tail him to the races but lose him when Regan goes to place a bet. Carter tails Barry to a health club where Charlie Smith later warns Stella Goodman, an attractive gold-digger and ex-prostitute, to 'keep Wardle sweet' when the manager arrives to see her.

Barry Smith notices Regan and Carter following him and drives off at high speed, crashing his car and sustaining serious injuries. £10,000 is found in the wreck. Regan talks to the other two brothers but fails to get any evidence that the money came from criminal activity. At the Smiths' car-breaking yard he spots Wardle; later, Carter is recognised as a cop at the racecourse. Jacko, an accomplice of Wardle's, is drunk and frightened – he has access to a fortune and can't spend it. Charlie Smith, acting on John's orders, and aware the police are closing in, silences the man with a knife in the back.

Searching Wardle's house, Regan works out that the manager is working a huge fiddle, claiming to his company that he's selling fewer tickets than he actually is and then creaming off the difference. Having tumbled this, the Smiths have been taking half this money but have now decided to have Wardle killed too. The carpark manager realises their intentions and borrows some women's clothes from Stella to make his way home, where Regan and Carter arrest him. The cops later go to nick the Smith brothers, but Charlie opens fire on them, and is then crushed to death under a pile of rusted cars. Haskins is angry – Wardle will undoubtedly be too scared to testify against John Smith. As he sees it, the operation is a failure.

NEVER MIND THE DIALOGUE: Regan offers Carter a meat pie but he refuses on health grounds. 'My Mum used to work in a pie factory. The stories she used to tell us. One year there was this cat…'

John's criteria for regarding Jacko as a weak link are simply that 'He's always on the sauce, and he's stopped pulling birds.'

Regan and Carter greet Wardle after he has escaped from the Smiths disguised as a woman: 'Hello, Mr Wardle, you *do* look nice!'

The whole scene that follows is a rich mix of comedy and pathos, in which Wardle is full of self pity and remorse while the cops simply cannot take him seriously owing to his attire. 'Why not cut and run?' Regan wonders. Carter, cracking up laughing, can't resist interjecting 'What – in those shoes?'

NAMES AND FACES: Warren Mitchell is best known for playing the bigoted Alf Garnett in *Till Death Us Do Part* and *In Sickness and In Health*. Julian Holloway, son of Stanley, appeared in various *Carry On*s. Tubby comic Peter Glaze was frequently the butt of jokes about his girth in *Crackerjack*. Sally Knyvette had regular parts in both *Blake's 7*, as Jenna, and *Emmerdale*, as Joe Sugden's wife. Godfrey James spent part of the 1970s and 1980s puffing and panting his way round various Mediterranean islands in the Michael J Bird thrillers *The Lotus Eaters*, *The Aphrodite Inheritance* and *The Dark Side of the Sun*. Catherine Schell (originally Catherina von Schell) previously appeared as a crook's wife in the film *Return of the Pink Panther* and later became a regular on *Space: 1999*.

POLICE AND THIEVES: *'I want them away, Jack. We're going to hound those three musketeers until we've got a case no brief can break down.'* This is another plain and uncomplicated story of a character on the perimeter of the underworld. Warren Mitchell's portrayal of Wardle, the 'menopausal spendthrift' out of his depth with Stella and the Smith brothers, is by turns hilarious and moving.

The Smiths are evidently partly based on the Richardson brothers, who were rivals to the Krays in 1960s London, ran scrap-yards south of the Thames and, in addition to organising 'long firm' rackets, operated the Heathrow Airport carpark fiddle which is very similar to Wardle's scheme. While falling short of the high standard set by Trevor Preston, there are some interesting aspects to the Smiths' characterisation, in particular the older brother's reverence for their late father: 'The old man … He was the best, the hardest.' Regan and Haskins are in conflict again; Haskins is trying to promote Regan to move him out of the Squad.

1.12 CONTACT BREAKER

Writer : Robert Banks Stewart
Director : Bill Brayne
First UK transmission : 20/3/1975 9.00-10.00 pm

CAST: Warren Clarke (Danny Keever), Coral Atkins (Brenda Keever), Tony Anholt (Mark Colebrook), John Collin (Parish), Jim Norton (Harrister), Kenneth Gardiner (Arthur), Cheryl Hall (Jenny), Jill Balcon (Miss Hepple), Sydney Arnold (Tilly), Ivor Roberts (Sale), David Jackson (Eddy Cory), Frank Jarvis (Prison Officer), Patrick Durkin (Foreman Decorator)

ON THE PLOT: Over £200,000 is stolen from a bank. The gang responsible have drilled their way in through a neighbouring antiques shop. The noise of the drilling is drowned out by nearby stock-car racing. The elderly antique shop owner overheard one of the gang saying, 'Nice work with the electrics, Danny,' which leads Regan and Carter to look for a wireman of that name. They begin to suspect Danny Keever, who was once nicked by Haskins and used to be in Eddie Corey's gang.

Keever is currently doing bird but as part of his rehabilitation he works in an electronics factory, and was allowed out to see his wife Brenda on the weekend of the robbery. A multi-tester, stolen from this factory and ostensibly used on the job, is later found with Keever's prints on it. Keever's probation officer, an architect called Colebrook, believes this proves Danny's guilt. Keever himself maintains he intends to go straight, and insists he was at the stock car race. Video footage of this is analysed but proves inconclusive. Regan tries to retrieve the suit Keever wore on the day, but Brenda has burnt it.

Haskins is convinced of Keever's guilt, but Regan has started to suspect that Keever is being stitched up, particularly when he hears the multi-tester was faulty. He is given 24 hours by the Commander to prove his theory.

The gang, headed by Peters, have meanwhile assembled and divided up the loot. One face, Harrister, is put out to find he's only getting a fifth of the money rather than a quarter; the fifth share is paying for fitting up Keever, which will serve as the gang's alibi. Harrister tails Peters as he pays off Brenda Keever. Carter later nicks both men. Regan, aware that the bank robbers had information about the building's layout, finds that Colebrook designed the building. Brenda and Colebrook, who are in it together, run for it when Regan arrives. Colebrook abandons his lover, but both of them end up nicked.

NEVER MIND THE DIALOGUE: Regan and Carter wait sceptically for a robbery to happen: 'No one's gonna blag that bank. Haskins's informants were always rubbish.'

There's a running gag concerning the fact that Haskins had his jaw broken by Danny during their previous escapade.

According to Regan, Brenda's family is so bent that 'If it had a coat of arms it would have crossed jemmies on it.'

One of the robbers grabs a painting on his way out of the antiques shop: 'It'll make a nice Christmas present.'

INSIDE INFORMATION: The gang's bank raid was again filmed in the cellars of Colet Court.

NAMES AND FACES: Robert Banks Stewart scripted episodes of *The Avengers*, *Adam Adamant Lives!* and *Doctor Who*; he also created and wrote several parts of the science fiction thriller serial *Undermind*. In addition to working on fantasy series he was one of the first writers called on by *Callan*'s first associate producer, Terence Feely, to share the workload with series creator James Mitchell. Stewart went on to co-create *Shoestring*, which starred Trevor Eve as a West Country private eye. When Eve decided against doing a third series, the writer opted to relocate the thriller format to Jersey, resulting in the long-running show *Bergerac*. Stewart later produced the phenomenally popular *The Darling Buds of May*, an adaptation of the novels by H E Bates featuring the Larkin family. He also created and produced *Moon and Son*, a 1991 comedy drama concerning a psychic investigator which pre-empted the later, more commercially successful *Jonathan Creek*.

Cheryl Hall is more familiar as Wolfie's girlfriend in *Citizen Smith*. David Jackson was a regular as Gan in *Blake's 7* and was the first of the crew to come to an ignominious end, squashed by falling polystyrene. Warren Clarke played one of the Droogs who became a copper in *A Clockwork Orange*, a friend of Waterman's, he went on to find fame in the detective series *Dalziel and Pascoe*. The late Tony Anholt was a regular in *The Protectors*, *Space:1999* and *Howard's Way*. Jim Norton more recently played Bishop Len Brennan in *Father Ted*.

POLICE AND THIEVES: '*You've just got a thing about him because he busted your jaw. I'm trying to make sure we don't charge the wrong man.*' This story is almost the opposite of 'Jigsaw' as Regan is convinced of a man's innocence rather than his guilt, and goes against his superiors to prove it. The details concerning the robbery are well researched and the revelation of the real villains' identities – the apparently do-gooding probation officer and the apparently long-suffering villain's wife – is a well-executed plot twist. Coral Atkins delivers a suitably self-centred and duplicitous performance as Brenda.

Danny Keever is a rare thing in *The Sweeney*: a criminal who's done his time and is attempting to go straight. For once, we see the Squad's prejudices proved wrong, and see an unsympathetic side to Carter, when he doesn't care that his visit to the factory where Keever works will reveal him as a reformed criminal in front of his colleagues.

1.13 ABDUCTION

Writer : Trevor Preston
Director : Tom Clegg
First UK transmission : 20/3/1975 9.10-10.10 pm

CAST: Stewart Wilson (Inspector Knowles), Wanda Ventham (Brenda), Patricia Maynard (Miss Alexander), Joe Gladwin (Stanley Proctor), Reginald Marsh (Foss), Arnold Diamond (Dr Cohen), Naomi Chance (Miss Mayhew) [Faye], Eric Mason (Kenny Jarvis), Michael McVey (Paul), Jonathan Dennis (Alan Foss)

ON THE PLOT: Kate Regan turns up to collect daughter Susie from her school, only to find she has gone missing, while Regan, out meeting an informant, Stan Procter, is unaware he is being watched...

A CID detective, Knowles, is assigned to investigate Susie's disappearance; he interviews both Regan and Kate, and it becomes clear that a blonde woman has taken their child. Knowles notes that a woman abducting a grown child does not fit the usual psychological profile for such crimes. Later, Regan receives a parcel containing one of Susie's shoes, plus a threatening phone call. Keeping this to himself, Regan goes to the only person he can trust, George Carter. He reveals that he is being warned away from investigating one of his cases connected with Stan Procter – but he hasn't got a clue which one.

Carter warily agrees to go through Regan's caseload, investigating various jewellery importers, one of which, Procter believes, is shortly to be robbed. The DS pretends to be giving crime prevention information as he revisits the importers. A short time later, Procter, trying to phone Regan, is beaten to death. Searching his wallet, Regan and Carter find some paperwork from Arnold Foss & Sons, one of the companies on Regan's list. Carter stakes out Foss's premises. Meanwhile, Knowles questions Regan again, wondering why Susie's kidnappers have not got in touch; Kate begins to crack up under the strain.

Carter sees a blonde woman, Faye, with Arnold Foss's son Alan. He follows her, which leads to him and Regan rescuing Susie from bisexual Faye and her companion Brenda. Faye reveals she was talked into the kidnapping by Alan Foss. To protect Brenda, Faye tells Regan and Carter all she knows about Alan's forthcoming job. Regan defends his actions in withholding the information from Knowles, and then leads a team to catch the gang in the act of robbing a safe. The gang is led by Kenny Jarvis, whom Regan furiously drags into a lift and nearly beats to death before Carter intervenes.

NEVER MIND THE DIALOGUE: A script full of nail-bitingly angry confrontations. At one point Regan accuses Kate of being a useless mother; later, thinking the kidnapping could be revenge against Regan by someone he's put away, she says, 'Why couldn't they just pay to have you beaten up or something?'

Regan gripes to his driver: 'I sometimes hate this bastard place, it's a holiday camp for thieves and weidos. All the rubbish. You age prematurely trying to sort some of them out. Try to protect the public and all they do is call you fascist. You nail a villain and some ponced-up pin-striped Hampstead barrister screws it up like an old fag packet on a point of procedure, then pops off for a game of squash and a glass of Madeira. He's taking home about 30 grand a year, while we can just about afford two weeks in Eastbourne and a second-hand car. Nah, it's all bloody wrong, my son.'

Faye insists she would never have hurt Regan's daughter: 'The three of us played monopoly together.' 'What, Uncle Brenda, Auntie Faye and Susie?' Carter sneers nastily. Regan: 'Have you any idea what you've done to her mother? She could end up in a mental hospital because of you. If you were Alan Foss I'd take you somewhere quiet and make sure you never walked straight again.'

Cracking up, Kate starts hitting the Scotch. 'That won't help', Regan tells her. 'It hasn't been helping you for years!' she replies. Later, having found the bottles dead, Regan starts on the beers in the fridge.

INSIDE INFORMATION: The examination of Regan's character and personality in this episode reflected writer Trevor Preston's own feelings towards the police. 'I'm very ambivalent about policemen. My father used to say, "If you see one, cross the road." I knew several that really were quite altruistic towards people, particularly one of my brothers. I don't think all coppers are bastards. I always felt that Regan was a man slightly trapped in himself. ['Abduction'] was always one of John's favourites because it allowed him to do a bit more acting other than just be a policeman.'

The filming of 'Abduction' required a villain's point-of-view shot from inside a car, a simple sequence complicated by the production team's legendarily unhelpful mechanic. 'We used this fella called Bernie Barnsley,' Tom Clegg says. 'Bernie had this amazing ability to ignore or overlook why you wanted a particular car. I said to him, "I want a Jaguar or an equivalent status car, but the one essential thing is, it must have electric windows, it's essential for the scene." So he turns up with a Jaguar with electric windows that don't work! He said, "I didn't know you wanted them to work," all innocence. He didn't have a spare battery, so we had to take a battery out of one of the crew's cars and put it in to get the windows to operate!'

By this stage of *The Sweeney*'s production, it was apparent to the cast and crew that the series would be recommissioned, as Dennis Waterman remembers: 'After the first [series], they said, "It looks very, very likely – due to the reaction – that we're gonna do another one." So, it was on the cards, but we never knew until the phone calls, and we were always on a contract for just one series. Or, we used to learn that we were doing some more *Sweeney* when we bumped into one of the caterers. They'd say, "Oh yes, we're starting in September, didn't you know?" "No, nobody's talked to me!"'

Screening of this episode was delayed for ten minutes, due to a party political broadcast by the Labour Party. 'Abduction' was subjected to an extensive Freudian analysis in the book *Euston Films – Made For Television*.

NAMES AND FACES: A regular as Colonel Lake in *UFO*, Wanda Ventham also appeared in horror films such as *The Blood Beast Terror* and *Captain Kronos – Vampire Hunter*. She starred in the TV series *The Lotus Eaters* as Ian Hendry's wife and also took a fancy to Arthur Daley in *Minder*. Arnold Diamond was the continually frustrated Inspector Latignant in *The Saint*. Reginald Marsh played various starchy company men in 1970s sitcoms, including Paul Eddington's boss 'Sir' in *The Good Life*. Joe Gladwyn was one of many *Sweeney* actors who was subsequently reused in the BBC's *Target*, playing another informer in the first series episode 'Lady Luck.' He later became a regular on *Last of the Summer Wine* as Wally Batty. Patricia Maynard appeared in *Coronation Street*, *Doomwatch*, *Minder* and *Doctor Who*, and was married to Dennis Waterman.

POLICE AND THIEVES: *'You let these animals get away with it once, just once, and every copper'll be living on a knife-edge, scared to let their kids out of their sight.'* A story with plenty of strong character conflict, which tackles the archetypal parental nightmare of child abduction head on. The characterisation of the lesbian and bisexual criminals in this story might seem outmoded by today's standards; however, it is made clear that Faye's criminality is not related to her sexual orientation.

None of the characters emerges from this story in a particularly favourable light. Regan takes a dangerous risk in charging into the kidnappers' house without back-up. Appropriately for a nightmare, there is a bogeyman – the kid-threatening, OAP-murdering Kenny Jarvis – and restricting him to an appearance in one scene increases the sense of menace surrounding the character. Again, there is a spineless middle class character, as Alan Foss, an ineffectual man drawn into the jewel gang out of greed, vomits in fright when the police arrest him.

'Abduction' is in many ways the high-point of the first series, and through Kate Regan, we get to see how other people view her ex-husband. It's a bleak view: an intolerant, incomplete man in a love/hate relationship with his job. *'Anyone would think Regan was the only copper in London!'*

CHAPTER 6

SERIES TWO: STREET FIGHTING MEN

BY ACCIDENT OF TRANSMISSION ORDER OR BY DESIGN, SERIES one of *The Sweeney* revolved very much around Jack Regan, rogue cop. George Carter, periodically relegated to the background, was viewed, like Haskins, as a member of the supporting cast. In series two this format was to change; Regan's questionable methods and his uncomfortable relationship with authority were softened in the majority of the episodes, while the characters of both George Carter and Frank Haskins were given more room to develop.

For a variety of reasons, from the situation with individual actors to a desire to make this new focus clear, the various supporting characters seen in the first series, such as the Commander and Carter's wife, were phased out or not reintroduced.

Roger Marshall, a new arrival on the writing team, wrote several important scripts that helped to remove all but the smallest traces of the edginess in the relationship between Jack Regan and George Carter as originally conceived by Ian Kennedy Martin, and established the renewed emphasis on a team. One sequence in his script 'Golden Fleece' shows the private lives of the three remaining central *Sweeney* characters all being interrupted by a phone call. (Carter sits and reads, Regan wonders how to entertain Susie all day, while Frank Haskins, the only character in a steady relationship at this point, does the washing-up with his wife.) Marshall's early television career included writing episodes for *Sea Hunt*, *Emergency Ward 10*, *No Hiding Place*, *Knight Errant* and *The Avengers*. Significantly, he then went on to co-create and write many episodes of the downbeat Thames Television crime series *Public Eye*.

While no scripts from Troy Kennedy Martin were included in the second transmitted series, Trevor Preston contributed several, and in hindsight believes that he, Kennedy Martin and Marshall all began to use the series as a vehicle for their own respective brands of social commentary. 'I think what was good about *The Sweeney* was that you had three basic writers who were all very different people and all totally committed to what they were doing. We all fenced off a little area that we used and they fitted beautifully; if you had 13 of the four that I had written it would get so fucking boring and the same for the others, but the way they interlaced was perfect. One week it would be this, one week it would be that; it was very cleverly put together. I give Ted a lot of credit for that.'

'Chalk And Cheese', the series opener from Preston, concerns two villains from contrasting class backgrounds, one of whom, Tommy Garrett, grew up alongside Carter: 'People thought we were brothers.' This brings Carter to the foreground by exploring his London roots and asserts the point in the Writer's Guide [see Appendix 1] that Carter could easily have gone over to the wrong side of the law. Ranald Graham's 'Supersnout', the third story, develops the friendship between Carter and Regan, contrasting this relationship with Regan's shady association with his informant Stickley. Stickley frequents seedy dives – toilets, strip clubs, snooker halls – while Carter has dinner round Regan's flat. Despite being off-duty they are still discussing work as Regan descends into drunken melancholia.

The friendship between the two characters deepens in 'Hit And Run', the first of three scripts by Marshall, which killed off Alison Carter. Carter grieves; Regan gives him emotional support, calling round his house with a bottle of Scotch and offering to keep him company. The case is soon resolved by the DS, who exhibits sufficient self-control in doing this to keep his job (contrasting with Regan's beating of Kenny Jarvis in 'Abduction'). Carter tells Regan afterwards that he can 'do more damage' where he is, in the police. This story is really a turning point in the whole series, bringing the two characters together by giving them something in common – both having 'lost' their wives because of their jobs. This also provides Carter with plausible motivation for spending screen time out socialising, boozing and wenching with Regan, setting the tone for the future relationship between the pair.

The character of Haskins is further developed in several stories in the second series. He is shown in a more sympathetic light, and the running conflict with Regan, so evident in the early episodes of the first series, continues to be toned down. In Trevor Preston's 'Big Brother', Regan is accused of beating up a suspect. Haskins 'doesn't know what to believe' when Regan denies the allegations. 'By now, I thought there was at least a mutual trust, an understanding,' Regan protests. Haskins speaks his mind: 'You're a violent man Jack... a broken marriage, drinking, deliberate flouting of authority... the whole damn thing is symptomatic... of a man who is heading for a fall.' Despite this, and a threat that he will 'personally bury' Regan if the accusations are borne out, Haskins is surprisingly vociferous in his support for Regan. Scenes of him adopting an innocent-until-proven-guilty line, telling the journalist Frewin to put up or shut up, are a far cry from the 'grey flannel' character of 'Regan' and 'Ringer'.

'Golden Fleece' reverses this situation: Haskins is now in trouble and Regan, instinctively knowing him not to be corrupt, disobeys orders in order to prove him innocent. The story also offers a new insight into Haskins's character by showing that *his* personal life isn't immune to the pressures of the job either. Doreen Haskins seems on edge even before her husband is arrested, fussing about her dishwasher and money for the church collection while Haskins tries to keep her and himself calm. She wants Haskins out of the police, and is scared that he'll crack up under the strain (perhaps foreshadowing her own mental illness in Roger Marshall's series four story 'Victims'). Haskins's wish to retire, and his depression about being suspended from his position, allows the audience to feel sympathy for him rather than empathising with Regan's usual anti-authority attitude.

'Faces' and 'Stay Lucky, Eh?' both show that Haskins can be one of the lads, getting stuck in to punch-ups and shoot-outs. In the latter he is also left to question the upper class, sloshed and struck-off physician 'Doc' Clair, as one 'intellectual' to another, ringing to tell Doreen that he'll be home late. 'Stay Lucky, Eh?' is also significant because, like many other stories in the second series, it continues to expand on Preston's theme concerning the relationships and lives of the criminal characters and the way they operate in their own hierarchy. In this story, Tony Kirby is the 'big man' at the top, the draughtsman who finances a semi-successful robbery: he employs and exploits two 'craftsmen', Jenner and Tyson, to rob a safe, just as gunman Vincent Vaughan uses Herbie Mew, an 'earwig', to get information about robberies.

Two stories by newcomer Ray Jenkins explore the relationships between villains from a psychological angle, using manipulation as their theme. 'Trap' features a 'police-bashing' news journalist as in 'Big Brother', but in this instance the villains are exploiting the press desire to root out corruption, while simultaneously leaning on a former partner for money. Jenkins' second script, 'I Want the Man', has the small-time crook Frankie Little and Popeye, a snout, being used by main man Maynard.

As in the first series, a number of 'guest' actors cropped up to play the criminals; frequently dangerous, flamboyant characters, such as Tober (Colin Welland) and Tony Kirby (Peter Vaughan). Also memorable are Aussie criminals Col (Patrick Mower) and Ray (George Layton), who were granted two episodes of screen time in 'Golden Fleece' and 'Trojan Bus'.

Other episodes in series two attempted to break new ground. Murray Smith's script 'Faces' delves into the espionage game, a concept he would return to in his own creations, *Strangers* and *Bulman*. The security services – political agents of the state – form an uneasy alliance with the 'apolitical' police in order to destroy a similar uneasy alliance of terrorists and 'apolitical' villains. Andrew Wilson's 'Country Boy', meanwhile, explores the impact of technology on crime, showing technically minded villains at work instead of the usual pick-handle merchants. As well as a clash between technology and Regan's more Luddite tendencies, the story also deals with the tension between Regan and the new, well-educated cop Keel, whom he initially fears will replace him. Keel enjoys 'the theatre, art and literature'. Regan, whose university was obviously the one of life, dismisses him as 'useless... a fifth floor wonderboy'. However, in a reversal of the usual mistrust of the educated middle classes in the series, Keel later shows he is a competent detective. Nevertheless, it's implied that he isn't fully accepted as 'one of the lads' by Regan until he's proved himself in a ruck and got himself shot in the process. In the end it is a combination of their respective skills (Regan intuitive, Keel logical), rather than constant rivalry, that sees the police win the day.

Significantly, however, due to a change in scheduling, the second series conclusion was not an upbeat story like 'Trojan Bus' (villains nicked, no deaths and a comedy ending) but the downbeat 'Thou Shalt Not Kill!' Ranald Graham's script concerns a failed bank robbery that turns into a hostage situation. When they hear that Regan's in charge, Haskins's superior orders him to take over instead, restating the theme that Regan isn't held in very high esteem at the Yard. Haskins goes for the psychological approach and it goes horribly wrong. The final scenes of bloodshed, with Regan blaming Haskins for allowing the situation to get out of hand, served to conclude the series on a sour note. While the programme had moved even further away from Ian Kennedy Martin's original conception, it retained the power to shock and provoke.

SERIES 2 REGULAR CAST

John Thaw (Detective Inspector Jack Regan)
Dennis Waterman (Detective Sergeant George Carter)
Garfield Morgan (Detective Chief Inspector Frank Haskins) (2, 4-7, 9-13)
Tony Allen (Bill)*

SERIES 2 RECURRING CAST

Martin Reed (Detective Constable Thorpe) (2)
Nick Brimble (Detective Constable. Burtonshaw) (13)
John Alkin (Detective Sergeant Tom Daniels) (8,11)
Stephanie Turner (Alison Carter) (5)
Jennifer Thanisch (Susie Regan) (7)

* uncredited on screen

PRODUCTION TEAM: **Producer** Ted Childs, **Executive Producers** Lloyd Shirley, George Taylor, **Associate Producer** Mary Morgan, **Art Director** William Alexander, **Assistant Art Director** Roger Bowles, **Assistant Directors** Ray Corbett (1,6,8,9,11) Derek Whitehurst (2,4,5,7) Bill Westley (3,10,12,13), **Boom operator** Mike Silverlock, **Camera Operator** John Maskall, **Casting Director** Lesley de Pettitt, **Continuity** Doreen Soan, **Dubbing Editors** Ian Toynton (1-6, 8-13) Peter Compton (7), **Dubbing Mixer** Hugh Strain, **Editors** Chris Burt (2,4,5,7,9,10,12) John S Smth (1,3,6,8,11,13), **Hairdressers** Stephanie Kaye (1,2,4,5,7,8,11) Stephanie K Gillot (3,6,9,10,12,13), **Lighting Cameramen** Dusty Miller (2,4,5,7,9,10,12) Norman Langley (1,3,6,8,11,13), **Make up** Michael Morris, **Production Manager** Nicholas Gillott, **Location Manager** Laurie Greenwood **Sound Mixer** Tony Dawe, **Stills Photographer** Doug Webb **Stunt Arranger** Peter Brayham* **Wardrobe Supervisor** David Murphy, **Technical Consultant** Jack Quarrie BEM*, **Theme music** Harry South

* uncredited on screen

2.1 CHALK AND CHEESE

Writer : Trevor Preston
Director : Terry Green
First UK transmission : 1/9/1975 9.00-10.00 pm

CAST: Shane Briant (Giles Nunn), Lesley-Anne Down (Caroline Selhurst), Paul Jones (Thomas Garrett), David Lodge (Pop Garrett), Peter Howell (Alan Sevier), Ken Wynn (Alby Fenner), Jeremy Child (Elphick), Raymond Adamson (Tolman), Terrence Sewards (Prees), Eric Dodson (Mr De Courcey), Stephen Bent (Scouler), Maggie Maxwell (Mrs De Courcey), Betty England (Mrs Tolman), Ivor Salter (Ibbit)

ON THE PLOT: Tommy Garrett, a promising young ex-boxer, and Giles Nunn, a 'Chelsea headcase' with gambling debts, are systematically robbing the wealthy. Regan and Carter are looking into these thefts, and have found that one of the robbers drinks at a 'Hooray Henry' joint, the Caliban Club. They lean on petty crook Alby Fenner for help.

Another robbery takes place; Tolman, the victim, tries to fight back and is punched. He knows his boxing and tells the Squad that a professional hit him. This prompts Carter to look up his old sports coach, 'Pop' Garrett – Tommy's father. Carter also sees Tommy, an old mate – and later learns from Pop that Tommy has given up his day job but is managing to run a flash car. Reluctantly Carter starts to wonder if Tommy is one of the robbers, but keeps his suspicions from Pop.

Regan meanwhile tracks down Nunn through the Caliban Club. He and Carter realise that the two men were brought together by the upper class Caroline Selhurst; she is supplying the addresses to rob. It also becomes clear that she is having sex with both Garrett and Nunn. Tommy, besotted with her, is unaware of this. Carter feels some sympathy for his old friend's position, but Regan is convinced someone will end up dead if they don't find the pair quickly. They arrest Caroline but she won't admit anything.

Nunn and Garrett decide to do one further job; this goes wrong as their victim runs Nunn over and Tommy accidentally shoots the man dead. Hearing of this, the cops angrily round on Caroline – they could have prevented this if she'd told them in time. Regan nicks Nunn at his flat. Carter confides in Pop and they find Tommy in Pop's gym. The pair try to talk to the distraught young man, but he commits suicide.

NEVER MIND THE DIALOGUE: 'You're a thief – you've been laying your grubby Germans on everything that wasn't nailed down since your voice broke,' Regan tells Alby Fenner. Fenner has only worked at the Caliban Club for a few weeks but already a few things have 'walked'.

Seeing Caroline's sexual to-ing and fro-ing between Nunn and Garret, Regan wonders: 'Perhaps they have an arrangement; you know, he sees her Mondays, Wednesdays and Fridays.' 'Leave off, [Tommy] wants to marry her,' says Carter, genuinely upset at the way his old mate's being taken for a ride. He loses his rag with Caroline completely when they meet up, calling her 'rubbish!'

Garrett to Nunn: 'It's all a big game to you, isn't it? Carryin' shooters, driving stolen cars, putting the fear of Christ up someone you was having dinner with last week. Like those sick sods in Hampstead who dine out on stories of how they met villains.'

Does Nunn work, Regan wonders? 'Don't be silly, Jack!' is the reply.

Regan finds that Nunn has stashed his cannabis inside a false book: 'I prefer cocoa'.

INSIDE INFORMATION: Some location footage for this episode was executed on Willets Lane near Rush Green in Buckinghamshire, a stretch of road that was also used as a location in episodes of *The Avengers* and *The New Avengers*.

NAMES AND FACES: Shane Briant was groomed for stardom by Hammer Film Productions in the early 1970s but now lives and acts in Australia; he recently appeared in the sci-fi drama *Farscape*. Lesley-Anne Down was in *Upstairs Downstairs* and went on to a successful film career, appearing on the wrong side of the law again with Sean Connery in the Michael Crichton drama *The First Great Train Robbery*. Paul Jones was the singer in Manfred Mann and later a Radio 2 DJ. David Lodge was a stalwart of Spike Milligan's *Q* series. Jeremy Child has played a variety of comic 'silly asses' – for example in *Fairly Secret Army* – and upper class types in *First Among Equals*, *Bird of Prey* and the senior cop in *Fool's Gold*, LWT's story of the Brinks Mat bullion robbery.

POLICE AND THIEVES: *'One son. What a waste.'* One of Trevor Preston's angriest stories, 'Chalk and Cheese' is a modern-day tragedy with a strong undercurrent of class tension. The informant Elphick implies that the upper classes are riddled with decadence; they are depicted as promiscuous, deceitful and lazy. By contrast, Pop is a respected pillar of the working class community, honest and hard working but poor. Tommy remarks that one of Pop's arms is longer than the other owing to a lifetime of 'gut-wrenching graft' in the shipyards. Caroline 'spends more getting her Barnet done' than Pop earns in a week. Tommy, though one of the crooks, still has a strong moral code, hating guns and, one suspects, hating what he's doing. By comparison with Caroline, Carter still has strong loyalties to his old friend.

David Lodge is excellent in the role of Pop, powerless to help his son, and Terry Green's direction is at its best, using haunting wine glass music, characters photographed in silhouette and a thunder storm to emphasise the tension and bleak inevitability of the story. A strong and emotionally draining start to the second series.

2.2 FACES

Writer : Murray Smith
Director : William Brayne
First UK transmission : 8/9/1975 9.00-10.00 pm

CAST Colin Welland (Tober), Barry Stanton (the German), Jeffrey Wickham (the Major), Keith Buckley (Jake), John Cording (Evil Willie), Grahame Mallard (Ingram), John Vyvyan (Albert), John Bardon (Doc Boyd)

ON THE PLOT: Five men have carried out three wages snatches in London in as many days. At the third robbery a security guard is shot in the leg, increasing media pressure on the Yard to find the culprits. Carter gets a tip-off from his informant, 'the Dwarf', that a wanted ex-Marine, Tober, is responsible, and that he's holed up in a junk shop. McConbie meets at the premises with another blagger, 'Doc' Boyd, and it becomes clear the pair are doing the robberies with a terrorist cell, whose members comprise a German called Schmidt, student agitator 'Evil Willie' Saunders, and another man 'done out like a first class anarchist', Jake. The Squad begin photographic surveillance of the shop. DS Thorpe thinks he recognises one of the pictures but isn't sure.

After Carter is nearly caught by Tober while on an illicit search of the premises, Tober decides to pull out of the gang, well aware that the heat is on. However, Schmidt coerces him to stay by threatening to have his daughter in Manchester killed.

The Squad, having had a further tip from 'the Dwarf', stake out a chemical plant – the gang's next target. However, Regan's preparations are disrupted by the presence of Major Carver from the intelligence services, who earlier told Carter he had no interest in the case. Carver reveals to Haskins that he has an agent in the gang. This turns out to be Jake, who's really a discredited ex-copper, Jenkins. Aware that there is a leak, Schmidt decides the blag will be a dummy run to identify the infiltrator; the Squad is ordered to stay out of sight to avoid blowing Jenkins' cover.

As the robbers watch wages being unloaded from a security van, DC Thorpe is recognised by Saunders, whom he once arrested on drugs charges. Regan orders his team to arrest the gang, which they do following a firefight and a car chase. In return for Regan allowing him to arrange protection for his daughter, Tober agrees to grass on the rest of the gang. Jenkins escapes from the hospital to continue his undercover mission.

NEVER MIND THE DIALOGUE: Regan speculates on Tober's desertion from the Marines: 'Maybe he wanted some excitement.'

Tober, asked for directions to a street close to the cemetery: 'We're all close to that, aren't we?'

Tober doesn't mention the war but otherwise does Basil Fawlty proud, referring to 'Krauts', the bunker, and 'Wagnerian funerals'.

Regan states: 'Violent robbery is always down to us... I don't care who the villains vote for,' and fittingly we're never told what the LPP's politics are – only that they're 'extreme'.

'I've just been with the assistant commissioner,' Haskins says. 'Not, I trust, in the biblical sense,' is Regan's inevitable reply.

Carter picks a fight with Tober purely for the hell of it. 'They tell me you're a hard man, McCombie.' 'I am, kid, I am.' 'Yeah?' Cue punches.

INSIDE INFORMATION: Southall Gas Works in Middlesex was used as a location for the blag and car chase at the episode's conclusion. In its closed-down state the works was often used as a TV location in the 1970s, featuring in *Doctor Who*, *The New Avengers* and *The Professionals*. Euston's *Quatermass* serial also featured the site, which has now been demolished.

A clip from the climactic blagging sequence in 'Faces' featured in a retrospective chat show, *The Trouble with the Seventies*, in 1996 in which comedian Tony Slattery nominated *The Sweeney* as his favourite TV programme from that decade. Garfield Morgan and Dennis Waterman were guests on the show and talked about their 1970s crime-fighting days. The clip used on *The Trouble with the Seventies* showed Haskins involved in the closing fight sequence, an aspect of the series Morgan always treated enthusiastically: '[I] always enjoyed the action sequences. I had done a number of my own stunts in films and TV films and so was always happy working with guys like Peter Brayham.'

'We were famous for our car chases – that was our stock in trade,' film editor John S Smith remembers. 'From an editing point of view, a film crew could go out and film all day and come back with as many as 50 set-ups on a car chase. When you edit the whole thing together, it only lasts a minute or a minute and a half. It was an awful lot of work for an editor and sound man. Lots of skids; Fullers Earth was put on the road so there was a bit of power to it when they went round a corner. I used to say on a car chase, "Never let a car exit the frame if it's coming towards you – because your eye will always complete the movement – then you can cut to the next one," so it was keeping the energy going all the time.'

Security firm Group 4, often the butt of jokes in the mid-1990s, lent Euston one of their vans for this episode.

NAMES AND FACES: Murray Smith was a paratrooper and Special Forces officer before retiring and deciding to write for television. He first rose to prominence by adapting Kenneth Royce's books featuring burglar Spider Scott for *The XYY Man* series. It was Smith's subsequent series *Strangers* that cemented his reputation. Softening Kenneth Royce's image of the detective, Smith and actor Don Henderson between them created a memorable 1980s character in Detective Sergeant (later Chief Inspector) Bulman, an unorthodox, Shakespeare-quoting Inner City squad investigator.

Two years after *Strangers* concluded, the character returned as a private investigator and horologist, paired with Lucy McGinty (Siobhan Redmond) in *Bulman*, which ran for two series. Smith ended this programme on a memorably tense note, with the lead characters apparently being cut down by machine-gun fire. He went on to write a second vehicle for Henderson and *EastEnders* star Leslie Grantham, *The Paradise Club*, which was not so successful. Smith switched to novels after this series, his 1993 work *The Devil's Juggler* drawing critical acclaim for its realistic depiction of a Colombian drugs cartel.

Like Brian Blessed, Colin Welland is another *Z-Cars* veteran who changed sides in *The Sweeney*. An award-winning writer, he also appeared with Roy Kinnear in a largely forgotten 1970s comedy about incompetent builders, *Cowboys*. Actor and theatre director Barry Stanton has appeared in *The Old Men at the Zoo*, *The Glam Metal Detectives* and the films *Robbery* and *The Madness of King George*. Jeffrey Wickham has done much classical theatre, his television appearances including *Yes, Prime Minister*, *Mother Love* and *Clarissa* (which starred his daughter Saskia in the title role). John Bardon later appeared in *East is East* and as Jim in *EastEnders*.

POLICE AND THIEVES: *'Jenkins might even have appeared at the Old Bailey with some cock-and-bull story about working for the government. But who'd have believed a discredited ex-policeman, eh?'* This is one of the most exciting episodes of the series, featuring a stunning car chase and very well-directed fight sequences, an example of small screen cinema that stands up well in comparison to big screen thrillers of the period like *Magnum Force* and *The Gauntlet*. Fittingly, there are several memorable villains. 'Mancunian psychopath' Tober, one of the gang, is a powerful ex-marine wanted for court-martial for breaking the back of his Master at Arms, and provides an interesting contrast to the quietly spoken, politically motivated game players Carver and Schmidt.

Regan has more in common with Tober, owing to the situation with his daughter, than he has with the 'spooks' and 'funnies' in their ivory tower in Whitehall. He reacts to Major Carver's disowning of his own agent, an ex-policeman who's putting his life on the line, with resigned disgust.

This tale of spies, terrorists, cops and robbers is peppered with quirky irony, including the revelations that the terrorist organisation is called 'Liberty and Peace for the People' and that Evil Willie and Tober unwittingly fought on opposite sides in Northern Ireland. 'Faces' was one of the few instances where the show directly alluded to 1970s terrorist groups like the Angry Brigade and the IRA, which both carried out campaigns of violence against Britain in the 1970s.

2.3 SUPERSNOUT

Writer : Ranald Graham
Director : Tom Clegg
First UK transmission : 15/9/1975 9.00-10.00 pm

CAST: Bill Maynard (Quirk), John Tordoff (Stickley), Vernon Dobtcheff (Kretchmar), Carl Duering (Dantziz), Rosemarie Dunham (the Dowager), Christopher Coll (Shop Owner), George Silver (Yannos), Vincent Wong (Japanese Tourist), Geoffrey Drew (Stooge), Brandy di Frank (Stripper)

ON THE PLOT: DCI Quirk, temporarily standing in while Haskins is on a case in Toronto, orders a sceptical Regan to look for the 'post office gang'. Regan talks this through with Carter, and both believe the gang is a figment of Quirk's imagination. Regan is more preoccupied with paying off top informant, Joey Stickley. The pair work together secretly and even Carter has been led to believe that Regan would like to nick the man. Regan is perturbed to hear from Quirk that the DCI has learnt the mythical gang are being drafted. This is down to Yannos, a Dutch target criminal whom the Serious Crime Squad have an interest in. When Regan sees Stickley, however, he's told there is no such gang and no forthcoming job.

Carter, sent undercover to join the gang as a bent cab driver, reports back to Regan that Stickley seems to be involved and that a robbery is imminent at a jeweller's shop. Recalling that Quirk himself nicked Stickley years ago, Regan suspects Stickley may have started working for the DCI instead, which will leave Regan without his top snout.

Quirk instructs that his informant be allowed to leave the scene unimpeded. He is eager to make the foiling of the robbery the pinnacle of his previously undistinguished career. He plans the Squad's response to the robbery down to the last detail, using a scaled plan of the jeweler's shop with figurines representing everyone present; he also orders the whole operation to be videotaped and invites two observers over from the German police.

When the actual robbery occurs, it becomes a farce, as Serious Crime Squad men, also at the shop, begin fighting with people from the Squad. Quirk's snout, who is not Stickley, is caught, while Yannos casually strolls away with the swag. Observing the chaos, Quirk cracks up. Regan realises that Stickley has arranged much of this farce to humiliate Quirk in revenge for being nicked by him. He angrily beats him up, but realises he cannot dispense with his services. Carter, now aware of the relationship between the pair, accompanies his self-disgusted boss for a drink.

NEVER MIND THE DIALOGUE: Regan thinks Quirk has a Captain Ahab-like obsession with a non-existent gang. 'Whales, buffalo, Eldorado… they're all dreams, like a happy marriage. You've got to enjoy the good life down here.'

Regan to Stickley, early on : 'Who else have you been meeting in your stinking toilets?'

Regan meets Stickley in a strip club. Stickley (still with flecks of fruit sticking to his face) comments on the stripper's assets: 'Do you think those are real?'

Stickley finally admits he's deliberately made fools of Quirk and his snout, and the Regional Crime Squad, who 'done my mate up'. Regan snaps: 'Mates? You haven't got any mates, you put them all inside!'

Carter catches Regan drunkenly trying to light the wrong end of his fag. Later Regan offers his to a stressed-out jewellery store man who accepts, then realises: 'I don't actually smoke.'

INSIDE INFORMATION: 'Supersnout' was another episode where aspects of real-life policing were incorporated into the script. 'There was a Ranald Graham script about a jewellery raid where the radios didn't work,' says Ted Childs. 'Somebody from the Home Office rather preciously said, "I don't think this is a good idea." You talked to the policemen themselves and they said, "Every bloody day something stops working." It happened all the time. It's probably a lot better today.'

'Supersnout' was also the first script where Tom Clegg made perhaps unexpected casting choices, here in the roles of the repulsive Stickley and control freak Quirk. 'I liked the reptilian quality John Tordoff brought to that part and Bill Maynard had done a brilliant play for Granada. They were both known as comedians, but comedians have a great gift for timing and a great sense of tragedy about them.'

Several scenes involving Carter's taxi were filmed at Gloucester Road tube station, and other location filming was carried out near Westbourne Park.

NAMES AND FACES: After *Oh No – It's Selwyn Froggit*, ITV were looking for another comedy vehicle for Bill Maynard, which led to the title role in *The Gaffer*, with Russell Hunter (previously the seedy Lonely in *Callan*) as the shop steward. Maynard is now better known for playing the rough diamond Greengrass in *Heartbeat*. John Tordoff reprised his role as a sleazebag in the *Minder* episode 'Rembrandt Doesn't Live Here Any More', where he played a strip club barman. Rosemarie Dunham played a dubious landlady in *Get Carter* (Carter mentions the film in an in-joke.) Vincent Wong was one of a limited number of Chinese actors working consistently through the 1970s.

POLICE AND THIEVES: *'Some things about this job are great, and some things stink.'* Quirk is a 'theoretical' cop, rather like Haskins, and in this instance his overplanning is his undoing: real people rarely act like chess pieces. It's appropriate that viewers gain little insight into the arch criminal Yannos himself, given the illusory nature of the planned robbery. Assisted by Tom Clegg's direction, this episode is a riotous chronicle of Regan's inevitable dealings with the seamier and more hedonistic side of life. Taking in toilets and strip clubs on the way, almost every scene has something controversial in it, from Regan and Carter's cholesterol-and booze-filled evening meal to the shot of a robber apparently about to have a piss on the side of the lorry he's planning to steal.

Stickley himself is revolting, like a darker and filthier version of *Callan*'s snout and confidant Lonely. Regan is completely caught up in his informant's mind games – ironic in that the double bluffs and deceptions being perpetrated are not that different in principle to those Regan himself carried out in 'Queen's Pawn'. Regan is forced to exhibit more and more duplicity. 'Get out of here, you two-faced little bastard,' he yells at Stickley early on, putting on an act himself in front of other police. 'Don't touch him, you'll get contaminated,' he warns a colleague. It's already too late for him.

2.4 BIG BROTHER

Writer : Trevor Preston
Director : Tom Clegg
First UK transmission : 22/9/1975 9.00-10.00 pm

CAST: Michael Robbins (Lee), Gwen Taylor (Ann Knightly), Maurice Roëves (Phil

Deacon), David Dixon (Andy Deacon), John Clive (Frewin), Roy Boyd (Stan Traynor), John Halstead (Betty), Keith Bell (Swan), Mardelle Jordine (Angela), Doyle Richmond (Rea)

ON THE PLOT: Kevin Walter Lee and Andy Deacon are brought in for questioning about a wages snatch in which a security guard was blinded with ammonia. Regan loses his temper with Deacon at one point and is seen by Carter to nearly hit him. Minutes later, Deacon collapses and a subsequent medical report shows he has injuries consistent with a severe beating.

Carter and Haskins are both sceptical when they hear Regan protesting his innocence. Haskins confronts Regan, telling him if there is any proof of Regan's guilt he will be personally 'bury him'. Deacon remains comatose in hospital. John Frewin, a reporter, thinks that this is a flagrant case of police brutality and, after accosting Carter during his lunch break, makes allegations against the Squad in his paper. Meanwhile, Phil Deacon, a considerably more professional criminal than his young brother, furiously sends for a hitman to terminate Regan. Glasgow headcase Eddie Swann arrives in the Smoke, collects photographs and a rifle, and is told to wait for the word.

Haskins sees Frewin's headline – 'A Step Beyond the Law' – and calls the reporter in for a chat, while Regan enlists Carter's help to clear his name. With help from a snout and Regan's girlfriend, a probation officer, the cops start to retrace Andy Deacon's movements. Deacon was seeing a black girl, Angela Bailley, who has form as a prostitute. The cops talk to Angela and she is evasive; it turns out that Angela's ex-pimp, Rea, gave Deacon a beating, and the youth later took painkillers and Scotch prior to going to bed. His kidney ruptured the next day when Regan nicked him in a dawn raid.

Carter and Regan chase Rea and arrest him after he pulls a knife on the pair. He later admits his guilt, saying Deacon had insulted him. Deacon meanwhile recovers in hospital and tells his brother what happened. The older brother calls off the planned hit.

NEVER MIND THE DIALOGUE: Lee accuses Regan of being the cause of Deacon's condition: 'You gave him a toeing.' 'That's not my game.' 'Word is, you're an evil bastard, even the other Old Bill think so,' Lee asserts. 'Charge him,' Regan says and walks off.

Lee sparks up in the interview room – and Carter takes the fag out of his mouth and stamps on it. 'Oi!' Lee protests. 'That's my last one!' 'I didn't say you could smoke,' Carter replies. Lee is thick as they come, particularly in the exchange where Carter tricks him into admitting his involvement in the blag. Carter: 'There were witnesses: a tallyman in a parked Rover.' Lee: 'There weren't no parked Rov-'

INSIDE INFORMATION: Andy Deacon's injuries were inspired by an unpleasant incident early in writer Trevor Preston's life. 'I got that kicking from the police, and my Dad came to pick me up from the police station. We got the trolley bus home. I was sitting there and got up to go and the whole seat was covered in blood – I was shitting blood.'

NAMES AND FACES: Michael Robbins played Arthur in *On the Buses* and numerous other comic cockney parts. Maurice Roëves was in Jimmy McGovern's drama *Hillsborough* and memorably played an impotent rocker who set fire to himself in the Scottish comedy drama *Tutti Frutti*. John Clive was the voice of the 'Nowhere Man', Jeremy, in The Beatles' cartoon film *Yellow Submarine*. David Dixon was Ford Prefect in the television version of *The Hitchhiker's Guide to the Galaxy*.

POLICE AND THIEVES: *'You made a rick there, my son. He's Phil Deacon's brother, and when he finds out he'll cut your legs orf!'* The title is double-edged: 'Big Brother' refers both to the character of Phil Deacon and George Orwell's *Nineteen Eighty-Four*, with its theme of state-sanctioned police brutality. In hindsight, the episode is marred by the inclusion of two stereotyped black criminals, a hooker and a pimp/dealer. However, there is also a distaste for bigotry in the script, as it is Andy Deacon's racist jibe that provoked Rea into assaulting him. Stan Traynor, Deacon senior's right-hand man, is a minor but believable figure in his defence of Regan. In Preston's scripts these lieutenant figures – like Carter – often prove to be the voice of reason: 'At least you know where you are with Regan, he's not like some of these other bastards.'

The conclusion of the story, in which the hitman simply packs his bags and goes home, is anticlimactic but has a sense of reality about it. Swann may be a psychopath, but he's a controlled professional, in contrast to Regan being too ready to use his fists on criminals, and Rea being jealous of white men who associate with his girls.

2.5 HIT AND RUN

Writer : Roger Marshall
Director : Mike Vardy
First UK transmission : 29/9/1975 9.00-10.00 pm

CAST: Gary Waldhorn (Fowler), Sheila Ruskin (Judy), Patrick Troughton (Crofts), Margaret Whiting ('The Fladge'), Michael Sheard (Mr Penketh), James Snell (Johnny Moxom), Liz Smith (Landlady), Terry Bale (Minicab Operator), Katherine Parr (Mrs Carter)

ON THE PLOT: Judy, a colleague of Alison Carter's on the teaching staff at St. Bartholomew's, has carried several shipments of stolen diamonds to France, unaware of their true value. Her boyfriend, Fowler, talked her into this but now she wants out. He makes an unsuccessful attempt to talk her into another shipment.

Carter misses his sister-in-law's 21st birthday and, to make it up to Alison, meets her for lunch before she returns to the school. Reg Crofts, Fowler's boss, has meanwhile decided to have Judy killed. He hires Moxom, a young tearaway, to run her down. At the school, Alison borrows Judy's overcoat to go out and post George's football pools coupon. Spotting her in the coat, Moxom runs her over and she later dies in hospital.

A grief-stricken George Carter is given time off to deal with this bereavement and

Regan gives him emotional support. Trying to return the borrowed overcoat, Carter talks to Penketh, the school headmaster, and learns that Judy has disappeared from the school. She has also moved out of her flat. Hearing that Judy used to run regular trips to France, and recalling that Alison once told him of a colleague in trouble, Carter starts to guess the truth. He takes his suspicions to Regan. The cops talk to a local taxi firm and find out where Judy is now living – and going around in disguise.

However, Fowler has also tracked her down, and suggests the pair of them leave London – Crofts has threatened to kill him as well. The pair are caught by Regan and Carter and admit the truth. Regan is disgusted with Judy for not reporting her predicament to the police. He tells Carter to take the pair in, but Carter leaves and goes after Crofts. Regan is worried that Carter might exact revenge on the villain, but on arriving at Croft's place in Fulham, finds Carter has just had the man arrested. Carter tells Regan that he intends to do more damage where he is – by staying in the force.

NEVER MIND THE DIALOGUE: Carter's grim speech about his wife's murder: 'A sudden death, a body on a slab. That's all. You can't relate to them all, can you? Only this time it isn't just a body, it's my wife's body. My wife's sudden death... A report on the death of Alison Mary Carter, aged 29. Just 29. If this world runs for another million years she'll still be 29.'

On a lighter note, Regan's informant, The Fladge, says her Welsh ex-boyfriend has stolen a lorryload of tinned carrots and is now trying to sell them as tinned pears instead. Regan does Max Boyce: 'That go lovely with a drop of cream, boy!'

INSIDE INFORMATION: Dennis Waterman recalls how how Stephanie Turner's dramatic exit came about: 'It was one of those situations where Steph might have been in some episodes but we didn't really know, and her agent kept saying, "You've gotta put her on a retainer, then" and Ted said, "Well, we can't do that because we don't know what the scripts are gonna be yet". So, we had a story where she was killed – easier and cheaper than a retainer!' Roger Marshall had a reputation for convincing family centred drama, and his first brief for the series was simple: 'Bump off Dennis's wife!'

Regan's second scene with 'The Fladge' was filmed at Chiswick Mall on the Thames.

NAMES AND FACES: Mike Vardy initially came to Euston Films to work on *Special Branch*, having previously directed several Thames series including *Callan* and *Armchair Theatre*. He went on to handle instalments of *The Bill*, *Hazell*, *Rumpole of the Bailey*, *Van Der Valk*, *Minder* and *Stay Lucky*. He directed the 1973 Hammer film *Man At The Top*, the BBC adaptation of A J Cronin's novel *The Citadel* and, more recently, *The Final Cut*, the conclusion to the *House of Cards* trilogy starring Ian Richardson as the duplicitous politician Francis Urqhart.

Well-known as the second *Doctor Who*, Patrick Troughton played a diverse range of parts, including a sleazy blackmailing neighbour in the first *Inspector Morse*. Michael Sheard played another schoolmaster, the infamous Mr Bronson, in *Grange Hill* and various Nazis, including Hitler in the film *Indiana Jones and the Last Crusade*. Liz Smith specialises in garrulous old women, such as in *I Didn't Know You Cared*, *Karaoke* and *The Royle Family*. Gary Waldhorn appeared regularly in *The Vicar of Dibley*.

POLICE AND THIEVES: *'Oh Christ, I'm so sorry, mate…'* Unexpectedly, the series has a change of pace, showing the impact of one awful crime on the life of George Carter. An accurate analysis of the way men handle bereavement, the script allows both Thaw and Waterman to display their range. The scene where the pair pour out the Scotch and Carter pours out his anguish is particularly impressive, with Waterman arguably giving his best performance.

The construction of Marshall's script, honed by years of experience on *Public Eye*, is also worthy of note. In a few scenes in the first act, Marshall sketches a close if fractious relationship between Carter and Alison. As a result, her death is remarkably shocking, considering this is only the third time the character has appeared in the series. The second act constantly telegraphs reminders to Carter and the audience that Alison is no longer there through heartbreaking domestic details: the now cold cup of tea that she made for Carter and put by the bed, the half-written letter to her sister. The final irony, left unexplored, is that she was run over trying to post Carter's football pool entry, which he didn't post the previous night because he was out with Regan.

The only false note in the story comes from (the normally dependable but here miscast) Patrick Troughton, who seems unable to convey sufficient menace in his portrayal of Reg Crofts. Although he looks the part of the sleazy villain, complete with fur coat and greasy hair, he seems uncomfortable with the cockney slang and hard man talk. Proof, perhaps, that Euston's read-through-and-shoot filming technique didn't always suit an actor used to extensive rehearsal.

2.6 TRAP
Writer : Ray Jenkins
Director : James Goddard
First UK transmission : 6/10/1975 9.00-10.00 pm

CAST: Sydney Tafler (Manny Bellow), Liz Begley (Mrs Riley), Kenneth Colley (Noah Riley), Bernard Kay (Thomas), Geoffrey Whitehead (Mills), Brian Hall (Davies), Harry Jones (Hooter), James Valentine (Woods), Sean Clark (Danny), Polly Perkins (Singer)

ON THE PLOT: Several years ago Regan nicked two villains, Woods and Davies, while they were robbing a dairy. A third man got away. Now, one of Regan's snouts, Noah Riley, has gone to Mills, a news editor, claiming he was the third man and that Regan was bribed into letting him off. Mills accosts Regan, intending to print allegations of corruption. Soon the press are following Regan's every move, photographing him. Woods and Davies, just released from jail, are also on his tail and watching intently.

Woods is also leaning on another associate from the robbery, Manny Bellow, who has invested the blag money in a legitimate taxi firm.

Regan knows for certain that Noah is being leaned on, forced to lie to the press by Woods and Davies. The crooks' objective is to get Regan thrown out of the police: 'If I'm out of the force, I'm open to invitations down dark alleys.' He and Carter visit the pub where the two men are having their coming-out party, but the cops end up on the receiving end of a kicking rather than information.

Haskins has heard hints from the press that a story is about to break against Regan. He gives Regan till 9.00 pm the following day to come clean about what's happening. Regan talks to Mrs Riley, who passes on a clue from her son that he's staying in four star comfort. Carter searches nearby four star hotels until he finds the one housing Noah and a journalist, Thomas. Noah, who has been getting more and more unstable, agrees to drop the story if Regan can ensure his mother if safe – the crooks have threatened to kill her if he doesn't cooperate with their scheme.

The pair snatch Mrs Riley and take her to Bellow's minicab office. This dismays Bellow, and as they vent their frustration on him, his son throws away the keys to his dad's car. This delays their departure long enough for the Squad, called in by Regan, to arrive en masse. Regan and Carter sit it out while Woods and Davies are nicked and Mrs Riley is recovered safely.

Regan and Mills are both reprimanded for withholding information, and Regan is told afer a meeting with A10 that he will never be promoted again.

NEVER MIND THE DIALOGUE: Some excellent, venomous remarks. Davis describes Regan as a cyst while Regan calls him a cannibal. Several times, Mills asks his underlings for the facts, declaring: 'These are the nails we need for running through [Regan's] hands and feet.' Earlier he gleefully comments, 'I think we've got a very worried Mister Plod.'

On entering a villains' drinker, Regan and Carter are confronted by Woods and Davis, who enquire, 'What's your poison?' Carter: 'You are!' Result – instant fighting.

Bellow loses his toupée in a tussle with Davis, prompting Bellows' son to cry out: 'You pulled 'is hair off!'

INSIDE INFORMATION: A police friend of writer Ray Jenkins who, despite long service in the force, never rose above the rank of sergeant, inspired Regan's final comment that he'll never rise above the rank of DI. 'Something happened and he was held back,' Jenkins says. 'If he had been a mason he would have been OK. A10, the police complaints body, was full of masons at that time.'

Brian Hall's casting as the vicious Davies was another example of *The Sweeney* imitating life, as director Tom Clegg recalls. 'I loved Brian Hall. He used to run with the Krays. He would do little jobs and knew them all the people from that scene. He was a bit of a wideboy, so he could get away with it.'

NAMES AND FACES: Ray Jenkins scripted numerous drama serials between the 1960s and 1980s, including *Z-Cars*, and his work often covered psychological themes, notably in the claustrophobic *Armchair Thriller* instalment, 'The Girl who Walked Quickly'. A memorable writer for *Callan*, his scripts were the most politically censored on that series; 'Amos Green Must Live', a thinly veiled critique of the right wing politician Enoch Powell, was postponed until after the 1970 general election. Jenkins also scripted the play *Five Green Bottles*, contributed several episodes to *The Gentle Touch*, and adapted Wilkie Collins' *The Woman in White* for the BBC in 1981.

Starting out as a designer on *The Avengers*, 'Big' Jim Goddard switched to directing and worked on *Callan* and *Armchair Theatre*. A friend of Trevor Preston's, he directed *Out* and *Fox*, returning to Euston Films to handle some episodes of *Reilly – Ace of Spies*. He later moved into feature films, including *The Four Minute Mile* and *The Impossible Spy* (as well as the disastrous Madonna vehicle *Shanghai Surprise*), as well as directing several instalments of *Inspector Morse*.

Kenneth Colley was Jesus in *Monty Python's Life of Brian* and has been in *Pennies From Heaven, Inspector Morse* and *Between the Lines*. Geoffrey Whitehead's many TV appearances include *Z-Cars, The Cleopatras* and *Alas Smith and Jones*. Brian Hall was on Bob Hoskins' firm in *The Long Good Friday* and played Terry the dodgy chef in *Fawlty Towers*. Sydney Tafler, one of Britain's best-loved Jewish character actors, was in the film version of *The Birthday Party* and sitcoms *Alexander the Greatest* and *Citizen James* (with Sid James). He came to prominence in the 'spiv' cycle of late 1940s British cinema, and is affectionately namechecked in the Ian Dury and the Blockheads song 'Common as Muck'.

POLICE AND THIEVES: *'I'm gonna hit that filth like an air raid!'* This is a complex story concerning obsession and, like Jenkins' work on *Callan*, needs more than one viewing for all the nuances to become clear. Again, the threat to the established order is personal, hingeing on the attempt to destroy Regan's career. Ernie Davies and the mother-fixated Noah are both mentally unbalanced, and the story is enlivened by the unsettling performances of Brian Hall and Kenneth Colley respectively. Noah goes more and more out of his mind, worrying about his Mum, and is last seen sitting on the kerb with his head in his hands.

James Goddard's distinctive direction – with closely cropped shots of faces and the recurring use of freeze-framed black and white images, showing Regan being systematically stalked and photographed by the press – add to the sense of pressure the characters are under.

As in the preceding story, the humour is very much under restraint, mostly confined to a couple of scenes where Woods, out of touch with modern cars due to a long period of incarceration, has trouble finding reverse gear in Bellows' Maxi and, later, hotwiring a Jag.

2.7 GOLDEN FLEECE

Writer : Roger Marshall
Director : David Wickes
First UK transmission : 13/10/1975 9.00-10.00 pm

CAST: Patrick Mower (Colin), George Leyton (Ray), Philip Madoc (Pettiford), Madhav Sharma (Earle), Cheryl Kennedy (Judy Collier), Anne Stallybrass (Doreen Haskins), Michael Latimer (Jackman), Nicholas Smith (Simpkins), Peter Godfrey (Wally Vince), Martin Wyldeck (Cowley), Damaris Hayman (Mrs Cowley), Allyson Rees (Au Pair)

ON THE PLOT: Two Australians, Colin McGruder and Ray Stagpole, have recently been behind a string of robberies; they surprise Cowley, their latest victim, by blowing apart his dressing table with a shotgun. At Warburtons, a City bank, secretary Judy Collier is supplying the pair with the addresses of the firm's wealthy clients.

When Haskins, who is contemplating retiring from the police, applies for a job at Warburtons, the Aussies mistakenly think he's onto them. They employ the dubious services of snout Wally Vince, who stitches Haskins up by telling A10 (the police's internal complaints didvision) that the detective has been demanding money and threatening to fit up his brother-in-law. Haskins is 'caught' receiving a bung from Vince at a football ground; Pettiford from A10 tells him he is suspended. Regan and Carter's phones were both temporarily disabled by Vince, but Pettiford won't believe Haskins's assertion that he didn't want to go to the pitch on his own.

Regan, who has previously found money planted in his coat pocket that may have been intended for Haskins, starts to suspect that his boss is being stitched up. Haskins's house is searched, and a bank account that he keeps for informants is investigated. He himself is depressed, and his wife reaffirms to Regan that she wants him to leave the police. The Squad's new Commander is unwilling to put his head over the parapet and help, so Regan looks over Haskins's recent cases again and soon ends up at Warburtons. Warned off by Judy, who does a bunk to Rio, the Aussies decide to cut their losses and follow her. They leave the sports complex where they've been working, the Squad only just missing them. As a result, Haskins is told by the Commander that he's in the clear, but Regan is furious that the villains have got away.

NEVER MIND THE DIALOGUE: Wally Vince, pointing out he'll be persona non grata after fitting up Haskins: 'Well, they're not likely to give me an MBE and send me home in a taxi, are they?'

Col keeps delivering insults to pool manager Simpkins and covering them by breaking into song. 'Poof! – The Magic Dragon, lived by the sea...' Ray's been given a shiner by a Sheila and Col keeps reminding him to hide it – 'Put your glasses on.' They watch an au pair girl: 'Tasty, very tasty,' Col says as he eats his ice cream. Leery, more like.

Money is planted on Regan to make him suspicious of Haskins; Carter points out at the end that the pair can't just keep it. 'Yeah, nice thought, though,' Regan says, and stuffs the cash in his pocket.

Regan finds lollipops in the boot of the Euston motor: 'Who loves ya, baby!'

There's a nice piece of comic timing as Mrs Haskins offers Regan a beer from the fridge; about to drink straight out of the can, he's taken aback by her offer of a glass. In a blackly funny – and nasty – opening sequence, Col and Ray rob Mr Cowley, in his 17th century-style bedroom, blowing in the dressing table with a shotgun. 'Stand and deliver, your money or your wife!' they demand; said woman understandably screams her head off. 'On second thoughts, we'll just take the money!'

INSIDE INFORMATION: Writer Roger Marshall's second script saw a reappraisal of the Haskins character, for a very simple reason. 'In my background, which is really live television, when you go to the read-through and see these dozen people round the table, you often have an uneasy feeling if there's someone there you haven't given an innings to,' he says. 'Garfield was a good actor and I wanted to give him something meaty. Haskins was so often the part that no one wanted to explore.' For his part, Morgan was impressed with Marshall's treatment of the DCI: '[It was] always interesting to develop other sides of a character. Roger Marshall wrote really good scripts that were a joy to play.'

David Wickes returned to direct *The Sweeney* at a point where the double-act between Regan and Carter had become firmly established. 'It's because [the actors] got on so well. Ted's partly responsible for this, for directing the writers into this area. It became *Butch Cassidy and the Sundance Kid*, and you got the younger sergeant with the older inspector who won't admit he's getting on.' Wickes also recalls that the other 'Golden Fleece' double-act, Col and Ray, left a lasting impression on the viewing public. 'Pat [Mower] said to me, only a few years ago, that people still come up to him and say, "Why wasn't that a series?" Apparently his accent was spot on.'

The impressive black eye George Layton sports in the story was real and written into the script at short notice. 'I was being driven home when a car flashed us from behind,' Layton recalls. 'The car cut in front and forced us to stop. I got out – and this bloke punched me in the face, knocked me down and drove off at high speed!'

'We had a running gag with Dennis,' stunt arranger Peter Brayham remembers of the fight at the supermarket in this episode. 'I always used to give him one on the nose, and he ad-libbed the line "Why is it always me hooter?", which they kept in.'

Haskins's arrest was filmed at Griffin Park, Brentford. The Sports Centre was the Bank of England Recreational Club in Roehampton, with Haskins's home close to Colet Court's Hammersmith base. This story was the first *Sweeney* episode to make it to number one in the viewers' TV charts, clocking up 8.1 million viewers.

NAMES AND FACES: Multilingual Philip Madoc has played a diversity of roles, from Lloyd George to one of the loopiest of *Doctor Who*'s mad scientists in the memorable story

'The Brain of Morbius'. Both he and Patrick Mower were in *Target*, where Madoc played Tate (the Haskins figure). Madoc later appeared as Inspector Noel Bain in the Wales-based series *A Mind to Kill*. Patrick Mower appeared as a public school villain in *The Avengers*, moved on via the Hammer classic *The Devil Rides Out* to star regularly in *Callan* and *Special Branch* before being cast by David Wickes as Chief Superintendent Steve Hackett in *Target*, the BBC's (misguided) answer to *The Sweeney*. He now appears in *Emmerdale*.

George Layton wrote for *On the Buses* and appeared in *Doctor in Charge*, *Doctor at Large* and *Doctor in the House* (as Dr Paul Collier) and as a regular in *Minder* (Des). Anne Stallybrass was the third wife of *Henry VIII* and James Onedin's *first* wife. Nicholas Smith is more familiar as Mr Rumbold in *Are You Being Served?*, another ineffectual manager. Cheryl Kennedy had part of a secret formula tattooed on her bottom in the Dick Emery film *Ooh, You Are Awful*. She was also married off to a walking corpse in the very spooky omnibus special, *Schalcken the Painter*.

POLICE AND THIEVES: *'She could force my rhubarb anytime.'* A welcome change of pace after the intensity of the previous two stories, with a comic take on the harrowing plot of 'Chalk and Cheese'– robbery of the upper classes and a girl supplying the information.

This is effectively the first instalment of a two-part story, serving to introduce the cheerfully amoral anti-heroes Col and Ray; charming, humorous, innuendo-spouting, slightly sexually ambivalent practical-joke-playing sociopaths. The story is again a little reminiscent of a caper movie, but the comic set pieces are offset by the pair's violence in the opening sequence and the threat facing Haskins. Significantly, Col and Ray don't meet the opposing duo of Regan and Carter and they escape, another example of the realistic 'win some, lose some' attitude of the series.

2.8 POPPY

Writer : Trevor Preston
Director : Tom Clegg
First UK transmission : 20/10/1975 9.00-10.00 pm

CAST: James Booth (Vic Labbett), John Rhys Davies (Ron Brett), Veronica Lang (Sally Labbett), Helen Gill (Kay Nolan), Frank Middlemass (Sterndale), John D Collins (Stephen Vane), Patsy Smart (Alice), Virginia Moore (Veronica)

ON THE PLOT: Three years ago Vic Labbett stole £410,000 but, when he fled the country, he couldn't take the 'poppy' with him. Now he's back in London to collect. He is spotted by one of Regan's informants. The DI starts trying to track him down, visiting the robber's wife, Sally, and Sterndale, the banker from whom the money was originally stolen.

Sterndale gets another visitor – insurance man Steven Vane, who is brokering a secret deal between Sterndale and Labbett. Labbett has agreed to give the stolen cash back to Sterndale – which was not insured – in return for £100,000 of uncut diamonds instead, which he can then easily get abroad. Sterndale contemplates informing Regan, but Vane warns him off.

Sally Labbett, under surveillance, loses the Squad car that is tailing her and meets with Ron Brett, who helped Labbett pull off the original job. She tells him Vic is back. He gets in touch with Labbett through Labbett's mistress, Kay Nolan. Labbett promises Brett his overdue share of the money, and later retrieves the 'poppy' from its hiding place in a waterproof trunk in the Thames.

Regan has now worked out that Vane is a go-between. They trail him to an abandoned warehouse where he hands Labbett the diamonds. Labbett sees the Squad coming into the building and mistakenly thinks Vane has stitched him up. He pumps three shots into him before doing a runner.

Regan and Carter track down Kay (Labbett was using her car) and later speak to Sally. Once she finds out about Labbett's bit on the side she gives Regan the location of the private airfield which Labbett used to escape three years ago. Following a mud-spattered car chase in which Brett's Jag is written off, Labbett and Brett are nicked. Regan realises that Labbett was planning to keep the diamonds for himself, stringing Brett along and not telling him about the deal.

NEVER MIND THE DIALOGUE: The Squad lose Labbett, leading Regan to growl: 'We could have done better with half a dozen old age pensioners!' He then sees Daniels, the new boy, trying to tend to a wounded squad man instead of joining in the chase: 'What are you doing poncing round with him for? He's not dying, is he?'

Finally, when Vic is nicked he scowls, 'I think you London policeman are wonderful.'

Best of all is Regan's brilliantly unkind summary of a conversation with Haskins: 'It's like talking to half a hundredweight of condemned veal!'

INSIDE INFORMATION: Trevor Preston's sixth script was symptomatic of *The Sweeney*'s punishing production schedule. 'We were poking them out every ten to fourteen days,' Preston says. 'I had to write 'Poppy' in *three*. It just came out.'

By 'Poppy', Thaw and Waterman were relaxed enough in their roles to embellish the dialogue they were given. 'We didn't make a lot of script suggestions ourselves, but if we were walking into or out of the Squad office, we'd be having a conversation about what we did last night, which wasn't in the script. We were aware that in a lot of police and film shows, all they ever talked about was police work, which must be cobblers. So, we built these other lives around the scripts that we had, and we were given total freedom with slight changes to the dialogue, and threw in quite a lot of gags and stuff.'

John Alkin would regularly play Daniels in *The Sweeney* from 'Poppy' onwards and also appeared in the two feature films. Director David Wickes remembers him as 'a damn good actor, very natural and believable. The idea was to give the impression that the Squad was bigger than just Garfield, John and Dennis. There were one or two others but the main one was Daniels.'

Some central London filming took place at Farringdon tube station and Tower Bridge, with additional location work (at Vane's flat) being executed at Ennismore Gardens off the Brompton Road.

NAMES AND FACES: John Alkin had previously appeared in the intelligent children's SF series *Timeslip* and the Yorkshire Television comedy *Hackett*. He went on to be a semi-regular in *The Sandbaggers* as Len Shepherd and also appeared in *To Serve Them All My Days*, *Space: 1999* and the colour remake of *The Lady Vanishes*.

John Rhys Davies gave a characteristically florid performance in *I, Claudius* as Macro. His film roles include *Raiders of the Lost Ark* and *The Living Daylights* and more recently he appeared in the US series *Sliders*. Frank Middlemass specialised in playing genial old buffers in series such as *To Serve Them All My Days*, and a reactionary old buffer in *Ripping Yarns* – 'What that boy needs is a damn good thrashing!'

James Booth, among many other Jack the Lad parts, was in *Zulu* and the original *Auf Wiedersehen, Pet*. John D Collins was one of the perpetually stranded British airmen in the *Secret Army* spoof *'Allo, 'Allo*. Patsy Smart routinely played septuagenarian cameos in the 1970s, and had her throat slashed by Linda Hayden in the 1975 sex shocker *Exposé*.

POLICE AND THIEVES: *'Kay's right. The poppy's brought us bad luck.'* A story with greed as its theme. The structure is almost a prototype for Preston's *Out*, featuring a character returning to London after being absent for some time and encountering all his old contacts. Labbett (a dangerous performance from James Booth) is not averse to slapping his mistress about or betraying his friends; he is convinced Vane will in turn betray him. Brett, another loyal and sensible 'lieutenant' figure, can't really take in the fact that Labbett has lied to him. Once again, the money, either in banknote or diamond form, is seen to be the root of the problem, the curse of mammon bringing nothing but unhappiness, and in one case death, to the antagonists.

The episode ends with an excellent car chase in which the Squad pursue Brett's car – another outing for the Euston Jaguar – across a field before causing it to crash. 'I hope you're bloody insured', a morose Brett tells Regan.

2.9 STAY LUCKY, EH?

Writer : Trevor Preston
Director : Douglas Camfield
First UK transmission : 27/10/1975 9.00-10.00 pm

CAST: Peter Vaughan (Kirby), Ken Hutchison (Vincent Vaughan), Alun Armstrong (Peter Jenner), Paul Moriarty (Barry Tyson), Sandy Ratcliff (Liz Jenner), Brian

McDermott (Ken Algar), Michael Ripper (Herbie Mew), John Woodnutt ('Doc' Clare), John Challis (Skef Warren), Donald Webster (Tommy Llewellyn), Ray Barron (Bobby Haigh), Gloria Walker (Kirby's girl)

ON THE PLOT: Two 'craftsmen', Barry Tyson and Peter Jenner, blow a safe and are dividing the proceeds – £8000 each for themselves, plus £11,000 for their banker, Tony Kirby – when they are accosted by a stranger who snatches the readies and shoots Jenner in the leg.

Investigating the robbery, Haskins wonders if one of his old customers, Tony Kirby – also known as Wembley's 'Mr Fix it' – could have planned the job. This theory is correct; Kirby is meanwhile none too pleased to hear from Tyson that the money's been nicked. Regan pays Jenner a visit as he is one of several faces in the area who has form; he initially believes Jenner's wife, Liz, who says that she was out for a meal with Peter and that he is ill with food poisoning. However, Regan and Carter later pull in Tyson, and start to find evidence of the pair's guilt.

Kirby and his minder, Skef Warren, warn Peter Jenner's wife Liz not to talk to the police. However, Peter's leg wound haemorrhages after being fixed up by the struck-off army surgeon 'Doc' Clare. Talking to Liz, Regan realises she is the daughter of one of his old informants, Herbie Mew. She is too scared to tell him what's been happening, however.

Regan pays a visit to Mew, who works as a theatre caretaker. It is he who provided details of Tyson and Jennifer's job to the face who robbed them – Slough hard man Vincent Vaughn – to take his son-in-law down a peg or two. He didn't intend for anyone to be hurt, and now Vaughn is pressurising him for further jobs.

On Regan's instructions, Mew lures Kirby and Skef to the theatre for a confrontation with Vaughn. The Squad men stake the place out and, in the ensuing struggle, Vaughn shoots Skef and wounds Kirby, before being shot by Regan and Haskins.

NEVER MIND THE DIALOGUE: Regan bemoans the disappearance of all the 'honest' villains. They've gone 'like the White Whale and cheap housing'. He describes Jenner as having a face 'the colour of a cheap envelope'– an excellent piece of earthy imagery.

Vaughn pumps several rounds into a new radio bought by 'no shooters' Herbie. Regan remarks later, 'It's not working, Herbie – you think these bullet holes have got anything to do with it?'

Also, in an edgy scene he tells Liz Jenner, 'I want to help, I want to put people like Kirby away so they can't mess up people's lives.' She replies, 'It's a bit bloody late for that!'

Regan says, 'Somebody put something in my drink last night.' Carter: 'What?' Regan: 'Alcohol.' Regan also suggests that pouring a bottle of Napoleon brandy down boozy Doc Clare would get him to talk.

Thomas Rhys Llewellyn – another great character – threatens Carter. 'If you weren't official, I'd tear your face off!' 'You mean you'd try,' Carter corrects him.

Kirby finds that Vaughn wears a wig. 'Looks like we've got ourselves a bit of an actor, Skef – a thespian.'

INSIDE INFORMATION: *The Sweeney* production team had a real-life run in with another objectionable character who wore a wig, as first assistant director Bill Westley remembers. 'This journalist had rubbished Dennis's family and I was determined to get him back. He was at Colet Court one day doing a story and had nodded off. Now, he had this dodgy syrup [syrup of fig = wig] and he was a very vain man. He was bit like Frankie Howerd – he thought that no one could tell, but of course the world and his wife knew. So, I put this big industrial fan behind him and let rip. This syrup flies across the room and lands on the desk at the other end of the room between Dennis and John, who are reading through a scene! Well, we're all falling about, Dennis is on the floor, and John picks it up and goes, "What the bloody hell's this?" Never saw anyone move so fast: that bloke was across the room, grabbed the wig off John and was out the door! We never saw him again.'

NAMES AND FACES: Peter Vaughan might as well have been Tony Kirby on the inside in his role as Harry Grout in *Porridge*. He also appeared in *Citizen Smith* and as Clapham patriarch Billy Fox in Trevor Preston's *Fox*. More recently, he won a BAFTA award for his performance as the increasingly senile father of Christopher Eccleston's character in *Our Friends in the North*, which also featured Alun Armstrong. Armstrong played numerous Geordie roles, notably in *Get Carter*. John Challis continued as a wideboy, becoming the second-hand car dealer Boycie in *Only Fools and Horses*. Michael Ripper was a superstitious barman/policeman/gravedigger in numerous Hammer horrors, and towards the end of his career became a regular in the sitcom *Butterflies*. Paul Moriarty and Sandy Ratcliff later went into *EastEnders*. Before her transfer to Albert Square, Ratcliff appeared in the second epiosde of *Target*, 'Blow Out', directed by Douglas Camfield. Ken Hutchison returned in *Sweeney 2* and played Heathcliff in *Wuthering Heights*.

POLICE AND THIEVES: *'He's been the entrepreneur behind too many of the big jobs we've had through here.'* This is another story in which money proves to be the cause of a character's downfall. Herbie is an 'old school' villain with whom it's easy to sympathise. Liz has married a man like her father, and, regretting his own past mistakes, Herbie is trying to force his son-in-law to treat his daughter better, a clever twist kept back until the third act. Regan admits to having 'a grudging regard' for Jenner and Tyson's 'craftsmanship' and is more interested in stopping Kirby's kind 'mucking up people's lives.'

These characters are contrasted with the likes of Kirby and Vaughn, who threaten the social order by manipulation and intimidation. One of the less cynical *Sweeney* stories, with Regan interceding on behalf of the characters caught in the middle, and eschewing wealth and promotion in order to do it. Didacticism is thankfully avoided by the humour in the script, an example being Regan's definition of promotion as being in possession of 'the key to the executive khazi'.

2.10 TROJAN BUS

Writer : Roger Marshall
Director : Ted Childs
First UK transmission : 3/11/1975 9.00-10.00 pm

CAST: Patrick Mower (Col), George Layton (Ray), Lynda Bellingham (Nancy), Robert Dorning (Geisler), Frederick Jaeger (Goldman), Leslie Dwyer (Ted Greenhead), Roger Sloman (Cosby), Carol Macready (Kath), Frederick Schiller (Austrian Tourist), Gillian Duxbury (Goldman's girlfriend)

ON THE PLOT: 'Nice and easy does it…' Avaricious Antipodeans Col and Ray from 'Golden Fleece' are back in the Smoke. Once again a woman is helping them out, this time Nancy King, an art expert. An unfinished self-portrait by Goya is being held in the safe at the gallery where she works, which is run by the gullible and cost-conscious Leonard Geisler. The pair suss that Geisler will shortly be taking the painting, wrapped up, to be valued by a Spanish expert, catching the number 52 bus as he always does. The duo then go to ground on a boat, on which they're running tours of the Thames.

Regan and Carter hear that the two Aussies are back in the country. After foiling an unconnected wages snatch at a supermarket, they start making inquiries. Regan learns from a bartender that Col has recently been seen reading up about art. He is too late, however, to prevent Col and Ray stealing a bus, picking up Geisler, then clobbering him and absconding with the painting. A confused tourist who was the bus's only other passenger proves to be no help. Regan despairingly wonders if the 'flash monkeys' have escaped him again.

Col and Ray hand the painting over to Goldman, an art dealer who plans to fence it for them. They then make their preparations to leave London. Regan and Carter discover Lucy's part in the robbery, and by convincing her that Geisler's dead, they get her to tell them about the boat. A chase up the river ensues before the Aussies' boat runs out of fuel at Traitor's Gate. Col and Ray engage in a vicious firefight with the Squad, using grenades, a rifle and a pump action shotgun. Both Aussies are wounded, and Col finally comes face to face with and is arrested by Regan.

NEVER MIND THE DIALOGUE: At a supermarket blag, Regan KOs Cosby, a blagger, then tries slapping him awake. 'Come on, you slaaag!' Cosby wakes up, grins at him and passes out again.

Cosby to an increasingly paranoid Regan: 'I swear you've got a thing about Australia!' He thinks Regan's pissed off about the cricket!

Col looks over Goldman's boat and his girlfriend sunbathing topless on deck – 'All shipshape and Bristol fashion.' He's still looking at the girl as he tries a cocktail: 'It's a bit tart for my taste!'

Where does all their money go, Ray wonders despairingly. 'I dunno, Ray, it's like asking where do flies go in the winter,' Col replies.

Regan and Carter, talking Scotch: 'There should be a couple of inches left.' 'As the actress said to the bishop.'

Other comic exchanges include the appearance of Ted Greenhead spouting John Masefield quotations, and Regan fretting about someone borrowing his phone and raiding his supply of Scotch. He dusts both items with fuschine powder to catch the culprit – and Haskins later uses the phone. Regan and Carter come back to the office to find an angry Haskins with purple dye all over his ear.

INSIDE INFORMATION: 'The sequel came up because they liked the characters,' Roger Marshall says of the return of wise-cracking Aussie gunmen Col and Ray, 'but the second one Ted directed I thought went over the top. A third one was planned but a directive came down from Thaw and Waterman that, if we did did it, they weren't coming in! They said, quite rightly, "Come on, it's our show!"'

The popularity of the Aussie duo did not go unnoticed by others, however. 'Somebody rang from the BBC who'd worked at Thames,' Marshall goes on, 'and said, "There's a helluva good idea for a series there, have you thought about it? Would you be interested if I punt it around?" I said yes and of course never heard another thing.'

Ray's (real) black eye in 'Golden Fleece' was followed up with a (fake) cut nose, part of the running joke that the character was always on the receiving end of physical abuse from his girlfriends.

This episode was originally intended to close the second series but was brought forward in the schedule. (See 'Thou Shalt Not Kill!') Notable location filming took place on the Thames beside Hammersmith Bridge, Tower Bridge and around St Katherine's Dock.

NAMES AND FACES: A film and TV veteran, Leslie Dwyer was later well-known as the pissed-up, children-hating Punch-and-Judy-Man Mr Partridge in *Hi-De-Hi*. *General Hospital* star Lynda Bellingham returned in the film *Sweeney!* and featured in *All Creatures Great and Small* before embarking on a long career advertising gravy powder. Robert Dorning assisted Spike Milligan in the *Q* series. Roger Sloman appeared as a violent vegetarian in *Nuts in May* and is also memorable for his brief cameo as 'Mr Bastard', a TV detector van man in *The Young Ones*. In 2001 he joined the cast of the revived *Crossroads*.

POLICE AND THIEVES: *'This never happened to Paul Newman.'* Including the hijacking of a London bus and an Austrian tourist complete with lederhosen, this was the most outrageous the series got. A parody of *Butch Cassidy and the Sundance Kid* that also satirises the way that cinema can glamorise such characters, the episode is packed with comedy and action. Like 'Golden Fleece', 'Trojan Bus' reprises the plot of 'Chalk and Cheese'– shotgun-carrying blaggers carrying out robberies through privileged inside information, with inevitable results, as Regan notes: 'I don't like the way they give the impression they're lovable jokers, colonial clowns. They're not, they're vicious. They carry a shotgun … If you carry a gun you're gonna end up using it.' Nancy King, like Judy Collier, is an affluent middle class woman who seems to be turned on by mixing with criminals.

The incidental music is used very evocatively in both 'Aussie' stories. A lighthearted piece like the theme from *The Sting* keeps cropping up to more and more melancholic effect as the joke wears thinner and thinner.

2.11 I WANT THE MAN

Writer : Ray Jenkins
Director : Tom Clegg
First UK transmission : 10/11/1975 9.00-10.00 pm

CAST: Roy Kinnear (Frankie Little), Michael Coles (Maynard), Russell Hunter (Popeye), Elizabeth Cassidy (Sandy Little), Peter Halliday (Chief Inspector Gordon), Patsy Dermott (Christine), Henry Woolf (Jimmy Dancer), Walter McMonagle (Bell), John Gleeson (Flying Squad Officer)

ON THE PLOT: Retired boxer Maynard is planning a job, using the money from a jewellery snatch to finance it, passed from small-time villain Frankie Little to Maynard's girlfriend Christine in a restaurant. Regan is tipped off by Popeye, an informant, but when he gets there the girl has scarpered with the jewellery and Popeye has been abducted by one of Maynard's men.

Taking Frankie Little to the local nick, Regan forces him into a deal. He will drop the charge of conspiracy against Little in return for information. He wants details of the forthcoming job and the identity of 'The Man' behind it. Before releasing Little he turns his flat over, looking for the jewellery, and meets Little's daughter, a young single mother. Little is desperate to avoid a further prison sentence so he can help her bring up the baby. Regan tells Little to claim he bribed Regan if Maynard asks why he was freed.

The villain is, however, suspicious of Little, and when they meet, orders him to stay at his house the night before the job. He also has Popeye's companion Jimmy Dancer beaten up after Regan interviews him at a football ground. The Squad also try to find the woman that Little met – Maynard's girlfriend Christine – but fail to narrow down which flat she lives in within an expensive block. Eventually it becomes clear from records of a dinner-dance at the football club that Maynard is the man they want. Meanwhile Popeye, locked in Maynard's garage, smashes his way out with a gas cylinder before being caught again and silenced.

Sandy Little gives Regan a cryptic message from Frankie – 'Old readies'. Regan realises that the gang are out to steal a consignment of old bank notes scheduled for destruction, and he and the Squad nick them all in the act. Little, having been out of jail only eight months, ends up being put away again.

NEVER MIND THE DIALOGUE: 'That does something for you Frankie,' quips Maynard as Frankie tries on his gas mask.

Popeye is starving: 'How about a tin of spinach?' Bell suggests.

More chilling Jenkins dialogue: 'I can't tolerate a grass, you know what I mean, I feel like running a knife up and down his arm,' Maynard says.

The Squad try to guess what the villains' plans are. 'Hijack?' Haskins suggests. 'Hello guv,' Regan replies, straightfaced.

INSIDE INFORMATION: *The Sweeney* production team were keen to secure the services of actor Russell Hunter, asking him more or less to reprise his most famous role as *Callan*'s scrofulous little friend Lonely from the Thames series. Ray Jenkins was well acquainted with the Lonely character due to his work on *Callan*, and was asked to write the script for 'I Want the Man' when Hunter was cast.

Guest actor Roy Kinnear was particularly memorable in the role of the put-upon Frankie Little. 'Roy Kinnear was wonderful. He was such a delight,' writer Ray Jenkins remembers. 'He looked one thing, which of course he wasn't. John Thaw was an extremely generous guy to those he really liked – I'm not saying he wasn't to other people, he was a very kind man – but he would perk up when guest actors came in who were as good as he was. He would flick into something that he knew was really good, and Roy Kinnear was one of the examples.'

Originally, Little was held on a very different charge to the one of corruption. 'I wanted something that would hold a guy for a long time,' Jenkins says. 'I went to my police friend and asked him what I could use, and he said, "I'll tell you, but you'll never get it through. There's a thing called Rainy Day Cellophane." In the glove compartment of the police car they would have pristine hundred dollar American bills with cellophane round. The police would take this with them, drop it on the floor, tell the guy they wanted him to pick it up, his fingers would go on the thing and that way they had his prints. They could then hold him, because it was the most difficult thing to get any quick response to something like forgery, particularly with American money.

'So I used it, and it was getting nearer and nearer the thing being made, and I had a phone call from Ted two or three days before the start of principal photography: "Hello, Ray. We can't use this cellophane stuff." "Why not?" "Well, our advisers have seen the script and they say we can't." I said, "Look, there's a dual argument here. If this is true, they have no defence. If it's untrue, it doesn't matter, does it? Both ways you can get away with it." Ted just said, "You're – not – using – it.' The script was duly rewritten.

Regan's scenes with Jimmy Dancer were filmed at Stamford Brook, Chelsea's football ground.

NAMES AND FACES: Roy Kinnear, a much underrated straight actor, is best remembered for his comedy roles in *That Was the Week That Was*, *Till Death Us Do Part*, *Hardwick House* and *The Dick Emery Show*. Michael Coles had previously played Inspector

Murray of Scotland Yard in the Hammer films *Dracula A.D. 1972* and *The Satanic Rites of Dracula*. Russell Hunter's TV appearances include *Ace of Wands*, *Doctor Who*, *Lovejoy*, *A Touch of Frost* and *The Ruth Rendell Mysteries*. He is best remembered for his portrayal of 'Lonely' in the long-running drama series *Callan*. Henry Woolf, a longtime associate of playwright Harold Pinter, was in *Rutland Weekend Television* and *Words and Pictures*. Elizabeth Cassidy had a regular part in Philip Martin's surreal BBC drama *Gangsters*. Peter Halliday starred in *A for Andromeda* and *The Andromeda Breakthrough*.

POLICE AND THIEVES: *'I don't like little men.'* This is another unsettling tale in which both villains and police manipulate the little, ineffectual and, in some cases, vulnerable and dysfunctional people around them. In their own way, both Regan and Maynard put pressure on Little through his daughter Sandy. The ending is downbeat: Little is nicked, Popeye, who 'didn't get away with it either', is missing presumed dead, and Popeye's friend Jimmy Dancer 'might as well be.' The details in this latter relationship are underplayed but it is hinted that the two men are gay, paralleling a plotline Jenkins once wrote for *Callan*.

Once again, an upper middle class woman, Christine, has been attracted by the glamour of the underworld, even though she has no stomach for the violence dealt out to unfortunates caught in the crossfire like Popeye. Roy Kinnear is excellent in a controlled and intense performance as the used and abused Little, more than holding his own against the Thaw and Waterman team, which was by now at the top of its game.

2.12 COUNTRY BOY

Writer : Andrew Wilson
Director : James Goddard
First UK transmission : 17/11/1975 9.10-10.10 pm

CAST: Robert Swann (David Keel), Myra Frances (Liz Keel), Christine Shaw (Kathy Peters), Antonia Katsaros (Anne Clark), Leslie Schofield (Ian Ross), David Belcher (Police Inspector), Shaun Curry (Peters), Malcolm Kaye (Brian Slater), Alan Brown (Consultant), Roy Sampson (Uniformed Constable), Bobby Collins (Young Boy)

ON THE PLOT: In the Vine Hill district, 20 or more burglar alarms are all being set off simultaneously, resulting in chaos as the local police try to track down the premises' owners. The local Superintendent rightly thinks some criminals have found a way to trigger off the alarm system through the phone lines and are going to use this confusion as cover for a big robbery. As Peters, the area's phone engineer, has gone missing, Haskins – despite protests from Regan – calls in a technical expert, David Keel, from Bristol Regional Crime Squad.

Keel studies technical plans of the local GPO system and is convinced that the alarm system can only have been tampered with from one particular street. However, when Regan searches under the street he finds nothing. Gang member Slater, overlooking the situation from a nearby roof, keeps his boss informed of the situation. Later the Squad men realise that someone has been up there, firing off ammunition to add to the confusion. Annoyed that he has been let down by a 'wet behind the ears academic', Regan throws Keel out of the office.

Mrs Peters receives a visitor asking for some steroid pills that her husband needs, and it becomes clear that the gang have kidnapped the engineer. Keel, visiting the search site again, talks to a local kid who has found a bottle of these pills, and realises the gang is holed up in a deserted house. As the gang congregate and set off the alarms again, the Squad men move in and catch them. Keel rips out their alarm-generating equipment, leaving only one alarm ringing – in a local bank. The rest of the gang bar one are subsequently caught. In a final shoot-out in the local generating plant, Keel is wounded but shoots down the last member of the gang. Regan is rather perplexed to find Keel's 'friend' Liz, whom he asked out, is actually the copper's wife.

NEVER MIND THE DIALOGUE: Slater to his boss, gleefully surveying the alarm panic: 'It's like bloody Armageddon. They're wetting themselves down there!'

On being told there's a 'good team' in Bristol, Carter says: 'City or Rovers?'

Keel arrives in the Smoke in a tux and cravat, having been whisked out of the opera he was watching. 'Hope we didn't spoil your last movement,' Regan says.

The DI interjects as Keel starts talking electronics: 'Look, I'm no good with pretty pictures. No guff – where are the villains?'

A sozzled Mrs Peters, seeing Regan and Carter: 'You'll never guess who's walked in, two great He-Men, standing there lusting after my body!'

INSIDE INFORMATION: Transmission of 'Country Boy' was put back by ten minutes because of a party political broadcast by the Labour Party.

NAMES AND FACES: Robert Swann played the whip Rowntree in *If...*, in which he gleefully admonished Malcolm McDowell. Shaun Curry was Vince's dad in *Just Good Friends*. Leslie Schofield played Tom in the third series of *The Fall and Rise of Reginald Perrin*, later joining *EastEnders*. Myra Frances was in the BBC's gritty ecological disaster series *Survivors*, and at the other end of the science fiction scale played the memorably over-the-top Lady Adrasta in the *Doctor Who* story 'The Creature from the Pit'.

POLICE AND THIEVES: *'He's another fifth floor wonderboy – useless!'* Like the villains in 'Night Out', the criminals in this story are clever and methodical, and the police have to adopt similar technical methods to catch them. A cinematic reference to *Dirty Harry* is included in the character of Brian Slater, packing an M16 with a telescopic sight. The theme here is technology (which Regan can't cope with) and its increasing relevance to crime. This leads to a personality clash between Regan and Keel, but the conflict is resolved amicably; Keel is capable of working as a copper and is one of the few middle class, well-educated characters in the series to emerge with honours.

However, a note of ambiguity is included in the character of Liz, Keel's wife, as neither she nor her husband tell Regan they're married at first, going along with his assumption that they've got a 'brother and sister' friendship. The implication is that underneath his intellectual exterior, Keel actually has similar personal problems to Regan; either that or the Keels have a one-sided open marriage, consistent with the series' perception of the middle classes as decadent.

James Goddard's direction is again distinctive. Just as he depicted psychological turmoil so effectively in 'Trap', the opening scene of 'Country Boy' has technological meltdown effectively shorthanded by an edit of confused faces, blinking alarm signals and an unintelligible babble of voices.

2.13 THOU SHALT NOT KILL!

Writer : Ranald Graham
Director : Douglas Camfield
First UK transmission : 24/11/1975 9.00-10.00 pm

CAST: Ronald Lacey (Barry Monk), Dean Harris (Jimmy Wands), Harriet Philpin (Julia Coulson), Barrie Cookson (Assistant Commissioner), Olive McFarland (Mrs Dowland), Nicholas McArdle (Inspector Wilson), Iris Russell (Miss Jennifer Lewis), Hubert Rees (Reginald Dowland), Christopher Crooks (Frank Gough), Mike Lewin (Johnson), Stuart McGugan (Hicks), Sally Lahee (Bank Clerk), David Masterman (Greg)

ON THE PLOT: A bank raid goes off at the Faraday University campus. The Squad, having had a tip-off, are there to block the blaggers' escape route and, in a firefight and chase, all but two men are caught. The remaining duo, Wands and Monk, have holed up inside the branch. The pair release the majority of their hostages, bar three – Dowland, the bank manager, lecturer Jennifer Lewis and Julia Coulson, a student with debts. Outside the bank Regan organises marksmen, wanting them to pick off the two robbers once both are in plain sight. Haskins hears news of the siege and is ordered by the Assistant Commissioner to take over managing the siege.

In the bank, tension grows between the robbers and the hostages. Wands forces Dowland to give Julia some money after hearing about her late grant cheque. Monk is fixated on the lecturer, while both the robbers have it in for Dowland himself. The situation is exacerbated by a phone call from Dowland's wife, engineered by Gough, a journalist after a scoop.

Haskins has the chance to order both robbers to be taken out while this call is in progress, but fatally he hesitates, and the opportunity is missed. He decides to give in to the robbers' demands for a car and then tail them. Leaving Mrs Lewis behind, the robbers leave the campus in the car, then run over the police motorcyclist who is tailing them and briefly escape from the pursuing Squad. They return to their hideout near Slough, ready to switch vehicles and make their way to the airport. They plan to kill Dowland and release Julia, but Dowland breaks free and kills Wands, before Monk kills him and smashes Julia's face into the side of the car.

As the Squad arrives on the scene, Regan furiously turns on Haskins. 'If you'd have ordered us to fire when we had the chance, Dowland would still be alive, that girl wouldn't have been scarred for life, that policeman wouldn't have been smashed up and, more importantly, the chances of a villain ever taking hostages again would be a lot less than they're gonna be now.'

NEVER MIND THE DIALOGUE: Regan on the siege: 'This is gonna be a right *bastard*.'

It is claimed that Wands has 'psychopathic tendencies.' 'We could have told him that without laying him on a couch,' Carter says exasperatedly.

'Your missus wants a word with you,' Wands tells Dowland, perhaps thinking he's in a sitcom.

Wands paraphrases The Beatles: 'Freedom is a warm Jag.'

INSIDE INFORMATION: This episode was originally scheduled for transmission on 3 November, but after an armed bank robbery took place that day the IBA replaced it with 'Trojan Bus'. Location filming for the campus took place at Brunel University near Uxbridge, which was later used in *The New Avengers* episode 'Sleeper'.

Ted Childs remembers that Douglas Camfield's precise planning of the location filming met with a typical response from *The Sweeney* crew. 'He had this thing about holding people's attention and we were filming at what was the new campus of Brunel University. They would allow us on this campus for two days and Dougie worked it all out. His idea was that when the cameras were in position he would do all the shots required for that scene. He had all the crew lined up for the briefing; it was like a military operation. He gave all of us pieces of paper with the schedule and he said, "Now, this is my position A, we will shoot here scenes 41, 32 and 74." And one of the crew at the back of the crowd shouted out, "HOUSE!" We all collapsed with laughter.'

NAMES AND FACES: Ronald Lacey played many slimy characters in films such as *Raiders of the Lost Ark* and Robert Fuest's adaptation of *The Final Programme*. He was also the regular 'man from the ministry' in *Jason King* and played Harris in *Porridge*. Iris Russell played 'Father' in *The Avengers*. Nicholas McArdle was a regular in *Colditz*. Stuart McGugan played Gunner Macintosh in the long running forces comedy *It Ain't Half Hot, Mum* before joining Maurice Roëves in the gloomy rock 'n' roll comedy drama *Tutti Frutti*.

POLICE AND THIEVES: *'This guy Wands was always gonna take a piece of the world with him.'* This is an intolerant and angry story in which Haskins does a deal with the Devil and later faces the consequences. Wands are Monk are shown to have no redeeming features – Wands flaunts his outlaw status by being the only criminal to wear a highwayman-style mask – and the other blaggers show no compunction in casually shooting down a man to show they mean business.

Fittingly for such a strong series climax, the press return to circle like vultures around the Squad's activities, offering Wands a radio interview which potentially further complicates the case due to the sightseers the publicity will attract. Wands' comment that Julia will be able to solve her financial problems by selling the story of her involvement in the robbery further illustrates one of the ironic consequences of the public's fascination with high-profile crime. The identification of hostages with their captors is also hinted at: Julia is seduced into Monk and Wands' world, partly through fear, but turns on them when they become murderers.

Using every angle afforded by the oddly futuristic location that is a stark contrast to *The Sweeney*'s usual imagery of urban dereliction, Douglas Camfield's direction emphasises the seriousness of the story. Elements such as a robotic police marksman grunting 'Monk still on target', his finger itching to squeeze the trigger, and the echoed cries of Julia as Monk beats Dowland at the end, screw the tension to an unbearable pitch.

Regan is several times framed in a tight close-up, the expression in his eyes nothing short of murderous. Owing a debt to the movies *Dog Day Afternoon* and *The Wild Bunch*, with double-act humour conspicuous by its absence, this is a tightly directed, hard and uncompromising finale to arguably the best series of *The Sweeney*. Merciless.

⛐ CHAPTER 7 ⛐

SERIES THREE: LAW AND DISORDER

OPENING TOWARDS THE END OF THE LONG HOT SUMMER OF 1976, the third series of *The Sweeney* was one of consolidation. The programme had found its identity and become an institution; it could afford both to relax and to take a few risks with viewers' expectations. Interviewed in 1978, Dennis Waterman said, 'What I'd really like to do is comedy... I hate images and I don't want to be lumbered with one as a cockney policeman.' In the third series, the ever-present comic seam in the series began to be mined more and more, perhaps inspired by the two leads' predilection for it. Thaw and Waterman had previously appeared in the comedy *Thick as Thieves* and on *The Les Dawson Show* respectively.

'Visiting Fireman' has the pair (pissed, naturally) performing a full song and dance routine. A number of episodes began to have comic subplots, such as 'Loving Arms', where the Squad caseload includes investigating stolen toilet roll holders. The norm was for plenty of quick-fire comic exchanges like the following, where Carter tells Regan he's wanted by his superior.

Carter: 'The headmaster's been looking for you.'
Regan: 'Right, I'd better go and get my bottom smacked, then.'
Carter: 'It hurts him more than it hurts you.'
Regan: 'Ah, shuddup...'

Andrew Wilson's script 'Tomorrow Man' emphasised the way the series was changing. Both this and Wilson's series two story 'Country Boy' hypothesise that crime is becoming more and more technologically orientated, and that both sides of the law are becoming specialists in this field. Just as 'Country Boy' shows the cop of the future (Keel), 'Tomorrow Man' shows his villainous alter-ego in proto-hacker Tony Grey. To complete the parallel with that earlier story, again the Squad draft in an expert to help them. However, this time, rather than being introduced as a potential rival to Regan, computer scientist Jenny Smart is the comical target for his and Carter's chat-up lines, and straight woman to their attempts to understand computers. ('What's a cursor?' 'Someone we nick for obscene language...') The inclusion of seasoned comic character actor George Cole in this story, playing dubious businessman Dennis Longfield, served to bolster the comic atmosphere, as well as no doubt inspiring the casting director of a future Euston series.

In series three, the comedy and the steady influx of blossoming British character actors (John Hurt, Hywel Bennett, Ronald Fraser, Lee Montague, Arthur English, George Sweeney (!), Karl Howman, Geraldine James and Maureen Lipman) were nevertheless being used to sweeten some fairly bitter pills. As the banter in the stories got lighter, the subject matter became progressively more cynical, reflecting external events. The political violence in Northern Ireland, Baader-Meinhof urban guerrillas and the fall from grace of public figures like Jeremy Thorpe and John Stonehouse were all mirrored by the series, an example being Roger Marshall's linked stories featuring the psychopathic ex-squaddie Tim Cook – known as 'the Leopard', a nickname based on Donald Neilson, so-called 'Black Panther' and kidnapper of Leslie Whittle.

An increasingly frequent tendency in the third series was for the authorities to be outwitted by the criminals – such as in Troy Kennedy Martin's 'Selected Target'. In Trevor Preston's sole contribution to this series, 'May', Regan is powerless to prevent villains beating their victim senseless; likewise in Tony Hoare's grim debut 'In From the Cold', a murder remains unsolved at the denouement. Tony Grey, the 'Tomorrow Man', runs rings around cops, villains and rival computer designers alike. The intellectual son of mobster Joe Castle provokes gang war, wheels and deals left, right and centre and similarly gets off scot free in newcomer Peter Hill's 'Sweet Smell of Succession'.

As well as depicting the police occasionally losing control in the fight against crime, series three showed the police losing control of themselves. Roger Marshall's 'Taste of Fear' features a bully/coward Squad recruit brutally laying into an ageing thief and subsequently cracking up (an interesting contrast to the assured professionalism of Keel in series two's 'Country Boy'), and 'Bad Apple' features a cynical group of bent cops on the take. Preston's 'May' features cops beating up a suspect in the local nick, while Troy Kennedy Martin's 'Visiting Fireman' implies that one of Regan's informants is being detained on trumped-up charges while the British government silences the witnesses to a plan to sell plutonium abroad secretly.

On the character front, the Haskins/Regan feud continued the series two trend of cooling off, with Regan's boss becoming more accustomed to and tolerant of Regan's foibles:

Haskins: 'Ah Jack, I wanted you earlier, rather urgently as it happened...'
Regan: 'Yeah guv, I... ah... I was... er... you know.'

This revised relationship is illustrated in several 'character-based' stories which focus on the two leads. Ranald Graham's 'Lady Luck' has similar themes to his earlier stories 'Cover Story' and 'Supersnout', concentrating on Regan, under suspicion for fitting-up a suspect. Crucially, while Haskins insists Regan must clear his name, it's made clear he doesn't believe the accusations; Carter, meanwhile, actually does seem to think Regan is guilty but hints that he's prepared to fiddle the evidence to help him out. 'May' emphasises that Regan's acquaintances are all connected to his job; in an early scene he reminds his old friend (possibly more than that) May that 'When Kate left me, if it wasn't for you I'd be lying in the gutter with a bottle and a brown paper bag.' Richard Harris contributed 'Down to You, Brother', another Regan-based character story with a subtext about parental responsibility. Both Regan and Meadows (the retired villain) have a shared concern for their daughters; Meadows, another manipulative character, manoeuvres Regan into nicking his daughter's 'flash' criminal boyfriend in order to bring about the end of their liaison.

Carter's character also got his share of stories, such as 'Sweet Smell of Succession', where he loses out on promotion, a house and the prospect of a steady girlfriend, all in one day. The Peter J Hammond story 'Pay Off', a second Carter vehicle, sees George's personal life also becoming mixed up with his work via his affair with Shirley Glass. In both these stories, Carter and Regan have words; in the latter, they're on the point of coming to blows before Haskins intervenes. However, by the end of both stories matters are resolved and the pair head off to the pub to drown their sorrows (less explicitly in 'Pay Off', where Carter is still visibly angry).

Despite these disputes and their differences in character (Carter often being more tolerant than Regan, initially defending the new recruit Hargreaves – 'You've got to give everyone a chance haven't you, guv?'), the closeness in the friendship between the duo continued to grow over the stories. Roger Marshall commented in 1987: 'The chemistry between John and Dennis was marvellous. There was no sort of "He's hogging the limelight this week, I'll have to have a good one next week."'

Overall, this series saw the programme walking a knife edge, with comedy, camaraderie, action and serious drama all having equal proportions in the mix. When *The Sweeney* returned for its final series two years later, it was to be in a very different form.

SERIES 3 REGULAR CAST

John Thaw (Detective Inspector Jack Regan)
Dennis Waterman (Detective Sergeant George Carter)
Garfield Morgan (Detective Chief Inspector Frank Haskins) (2,4-6,8-13)
Tony Allen (Bill)*

SERIES 3 RECURRING CAST

Morris Perry (Detective Chief Superintendent Maynon) (3)
John Alkin (Detective Sergeant Tom Daniels) (2,4-6,10)
Jennifer Thanisch (Susie Regan) (9)

* uncredited on screen

PRODUCTION TEAM: Producer Ted Childs, **Executive Producers** Lloyd Shirley, George Taylor, **Associate Producer** Mary Morgan, **Art Directors** William Alexander (1-5, 7-13), Terry Parr (6), **Assistant Art Director** Roger Bowles (1-4,5,10,13), **Assistant**

Directors Bill Westley (1,2,4,6,7,9,13), David Bracknell (3,5,8,11,12), Michael Murphy (10), **Boom operator** Mike Silverlock, **Camera Operator** John Maskall, **Casting Directors** Marilyn Johnson (1,2,6,7,9,13), Lesley de Pettitt (3,4,5,8,11,12), Patsy Pollock (10), **Continuity** Phyllis Townsend, **Dubbing Editors** Peter Compton (1,2,6,7,9,10,11,13), Ian Toynton (3,4,5,8,12), **Dubbing Mixer** Hugh Strain, **Editors** Chris Burt (3,5,12), John S Smith (1,2,4,7,8,10,11), Ian Toynton (6,9,13), **Hairdresser** Mary Sturges, **Lighting Cameramen** Dusty Miller (1,2,3,5,7,10,12), Norman Langley (4,6,8,9,11,13), **Make-up** Michael Morris, **Production Manager** Laurie Greenwood (1,2,6,7,9,10,13), Nicholas Gillott (3,4,5,8,11,12), **Location Managers** Laurie Greenwood (3,4,5,8,11,12), Stephen Pushkin (1,2,6,7,9,10,13), **Sound Mixer** Tony Dawe, **Stills Photographer** Doug Webb, **Stunt Arrangers** Peter Brayham (1-5, 8-13), Romo Gorraro (6,7), **Wardrobe Supervisor** David Murphy, **Technical Consultant** Jack Quarrie BEM*, **Theme Music** Harry South

* uncredited on screen

3.1 SELECTED TARGET

Writer : Troy Kennedy Martin
Director : Tom Clegg
First UK transmission : 6/9/1976 9.00-10.00 pm

CAST: Lee Montague (Colley Kibber), Ronald Fraser (Titus Oates), James Aubrey (Reynes), Peter Schofield (Boothroyd), Maureen Lipman (Mrs Smedley), Jonathan Elsom (Mr Bradshaw), Basil Dignam (Moberly), Deidre Costello (Gwen Kibber), Roger Hammond (Finch), Judy Matheson (Kibber's girlfriend), Bill Treacher (Tom), Hugh Martin (Murray), Annie Lambert (Air Hostess), Frederick Marks (Detective), Roger Putt (Prison Officer), James Fagin (Receptionist), Miles Elles (Porter), David Barnham (Toby Bradshaw), Tracy Strand (Anne Kibber)

ON THE PLOT: Oates and Kibber, two heavyweight crooks, are released from jail. Some incriminating notes were previously found on Kibber during a search by the screws; he is promptly designated a 'target criminal' by the Yard. The Squad begins a major surveillance operation supervised by Carter. Regan, however, is more interested in Oates, who initially grassed to the authorities about Kibber's notebook. Regan is suspicious of him and interrogates him at his hotel. Regan also takes time out to visit an air hostess, and when he returns Oates has vanished in the company of Reynes – one of Kibber's men.

Carter believes that Kibber may have had Oates killed for grassing on him. Regan, however, thinks the pair are actually working together; he is proven right when Kibber throws off his tail and meets Oates. Kibber's activities – including being serviced by two callgirls – have all been to get the police looking the wrong way. Oates informs him that he's now completed setting up the job. However, the apprehensive Reynes needs a pep talk.

The Squad surveillance team, holed up in a flat opposite Kibber's house, are attacked by three thugs. As a massive fight breaks out in the block of flats, Kibber slips away and persuades Reynes to carry on as planned.

Working with a further set of written notes found in the prison and using a process of elimination, Carter works out that the job involves pressurising a banker, Bradshaw. Regan visits Bradshaw's bank, while Carter visits his home to find a stolen car parked in the driveway. Mrs Bradshaw won't answer the telephone so the DS reasons she's being held hostage. At the bank, Regan finds that Bradshaw has already transferred £2 million to the USA, where it's just been collected by Oates. The gang has also left the Bradshaws' house. Unlike the villains, the Squad leaves the scene empty-handed.

NEVER MIND THE DIALOGUE: Fresh out of the nick, Kibber asks his ten-year-old daughter: 'What do you want to be when you grow up?' 'A social worker,' she replies. In a scene that plays with audience expectation and mood, the child's mother is visibly upset that Kibber is rejecting her.

Boothroyd, Regan's boss in this story, asserts that 'an unnecessarily large amount of film' is being used to cover Kibber's activities with the callgirls.

Regan interviews Oates early on in his hotel suite, Oates pointing out that it won't look good, being seen with the police while he's out on parole. Regan calls him a 'cheeky sod.'

The 'blag' is a simple computer transfer of money. 'Is it that easy?' Regan asks despairingly.

INSIDE INFORMATION: 'I met a few of the villains and they made me feel a bit nauseous – they were a bit dangerous,' Troy Kennedy Martin remembers. 'For me it's just characters. I attempted to make the episodes a bit more comic and view them as exercises in style, working in names – Kibber, Titus Oates. I put in a character called Reynes just so I could have Oates say "Reyne's stopped play!"'

Ronald Fraser was another actor who joined the Euston Films' drinking club. 'I worked out a way to get him out of the pub,' assistant director Bill Westley recalls. 'We fitted him out with a radio speaker, which looked like a hearing aid. We'd call him up, he'd immediately say, "Must go, old boy," in the middle of a conversation, join us for a scene and, like the true pro he was, he'd be spot-on and word perfect.'

Filming occurred at the exterior of the Copthorne Tara Hotel in Kensington and in and around Waterloo station. The fight sequence was filmed at Pinter Tower (named after the playwright Harold Pinter) in Stockwell.

NAMES AND FACES: Ronald Fraser appeared in many sitcoms throughout the 1970s, including a *Comedy Playhouse* instalment, 'Born Every Minute', where he played a con-man. He was also Inspector Spooner in the first series of the Galton and Speight sitcom *Spooner's Patch*. Among his many film appearances were *The Punch and Judy Man* and

Ooh, You Are Awful. Fraser also played straight roles, such as a villainous Scotsman in the Michael Caine film *Too Late the Hero.* Bill Treacher later became a household name as Arthur Fowler in *EastEnders.* As a child actor, James Aubrey starred in Peter Brook's 1963 film of *Lord of the Flies,* acquiring adult notoriety over ten years later in *A Bouquet of Barbed Wire.*

POLICE AND THIEVES: *'I want an accountant, a brief and some sort of female companionship, in that order.'* This is another mini 'caper movie' from the pen of Troy Kennedy Martin, with plenty of sardonic wit in the dialogue. The irony even extends to the title, as the police have selected the *wrong* target. The usual mistrust within the hierarchy of the police exists, as exhibited when Regan breaks into Haskins's office to find out what's been written on his annual appraisal. Philosophising villain Oates is able to exploit this lack of co-operation to good effect, turning the police bureaucracies against each other while ruminating on Kung Fu – 'Its aim is to use the strength of your opponent to break him.'

As in 'Night Out', the massive fight sequence in the second act, involving police photographers, the Squad, three heavies wearing crash helmets, and a man in a string vest who's having his tea, seems to be lampooning the action-orientated brief of the programme. Veteran comic actor Ronald Fraser enjoys himself as Oates; Lee Montague and Maureen Lipman (notable as a bored suburban housewife) reappear from earlier episodes. More comedy involves the running joke of Regan trying to get *his* oats in a hotel room with yet another air hostess, while periodically rushing back to interview Titus.

A tongue-in-cheek, leisurely start to the third series, with Regan oddly absent for most of the running time. Most of the entertainment value comes from seeing how Oates and Kibber run rings around the police.

3.2 IN FROM THE COLD

Writer : Tony Hoare
Director : Terry Green
First UK transmission : 13/9/1976 9.00-10.00 pm

CAST: Anthony Heaton (Billy Medhurst), Maureen Sweeney (Mrs Medhurst), Lewis Fiander (Ashby-Jones), Martin Fisk (Eddie Jackson), Johnny Shannon (Mason), James Beckett (Stan), Paul Kember (Micky), Peter Clapham (Inspector), James Taylor (Gregory), Miranda Bell (Mrs Jackson)

ON THE PLOT: 'I'd know that bastard anywhere!' Billy Medhurst, member of a team responsible for shooting and crippling a young Flying Squad officer two years previously, is spotted and nicked on the street by Regan.

Regan is determined that Medhurst should come up with the name of the man who fired the shot, but his attempts to put pressure on Medhurst are thwarted by the arrival of the crook's lawyer, Ashby-Jones. The injured officer, Jackson, picks Medhurst out in an ID parade. After talking to his wife, Medhurst seems to agree to shop the rest of the gang in return for a reduced sentence. But as he is taken to court to be charged, the prison van is ambushed, and Regan and Carter, escorting it, are overpowered. Medhurst is sprung, apparently unwillingly.

Regan and Carter wonder if Ashby-Jones, who's known to be a sharp operator, may have organised this breakout. Later a headless body is found in the Thames. Medhurst's wife identifies the corpse as her husband after discussions concerning a birthmark.

However, this is all a set-up; Medhurst, very much alive, is intent on going through with his scam to nick a lorry-load of frozen meat. This job goes off, and Regan, talking to the owner of the depot, realises the man is involved. Ashby-Jones is also in on the robbery, having a relative in the trade who can dispose of the meat. The hand-over is accidentally delayed, and Haskins catches the solicitor red-handed, discussing the job on the phone. Jones leads the Squad to where Medhurst has parked the lorry. Medhurst's two accomplices are found unconscious in the freezer, while Medhurst makes a break for it, injuring himself in a fall. Regan is left to reflect that he never caught the man responsible for Jackson's almost identical injury.

NEVER MIND THE DIALOGUE: 'A lot of porridge, 16 years,' Regan tells Medhurst, and later remarks straightfaced to Haskins about the body in the river: 'Having his head cut off hasn't helped identification.'

The villains aren't impressed with the media coverage of the body – 'It didn't even make the bloody headlines!'

Medhurst has to leave his mates out of sight in the back of the lorry freezer: 'I'll nip into a sports shop and get 'em a fur-lined jockstrap apiece.'

'It's a long way down, Billy,' Regan warns Medhurst at the edge of a 40-foot drop. 'Too far for you, cozzer!' Medhurst agrees before jumping.

Medhurst's wife is naked in the bathtub when Regan and Carter visit her: 'Have a bloody good look, you pair of blimpers!' she shouts.

Billy Medhurst is a nasty character but with a ready wit. On being reminded about crippled, wheelchair-bound copper Eddie Jackson, he quips: 'Well, if Ironside can do it...', nearly provoking Regan into taking a swing at him.

Medhurst is outside the chip shop when Carter first confronts him: 'Oi, Billy – giz a chip!' Medhurst obligingly chucks the whole bag over Carter before legging it.

NAMES AND FACES: A reformed criminal who had been in prison, Tony Hoare would go on to become a principal writer on *Minder*. He contributed episodes such as 'Caught in the Act, Fact', 'Whose Wife is it Anyway?', 'Come in T-64, Your Time is Ticking Away' (which featured George Layton and a minicab war) and the feature-length Christmas special 'An Officer and a Car Salesman'. Hoare also wrote the 90-minute Brighton-based drama *Palmer*, which starred Ray Winstone and, more recently, episodes of *City Central*. The tabloid press noted his presence at Ronnie Biggs' 70th birthday party in Rio.

Anthony Heaton had fisticuffs with Dennis Waterman in the *Minder* episode 'Monday Night Fever'. Lewis Fiander returned in *Sweeney 2* and appeared in Johnny Speight's play *If There Weren't Any Blacks You'd Have to Invent Them* alongside Richard Beckinsale and Leonard Rossiter.

INSIDE INFORMATION: London Bridge – prior to its purchase and transportation to America – can be seen in the background during the scene with Johnny Shannon.

Heaton's line about the job having 'gone reels' (reels of cotton = rotten) may have been an in-joke, inspired by the comment assistant director Bill Westley used whenever something went wrong during production.

Big Vern, *Viz* magazine's cockney villain comic strip, paid homage to this story, 'Taste of Fear' and the Richard Burton gangster film *Villain* in the early 1990s.

POLICE AND THIEVES: *'They're gonna see you go down, and they're talking telephone numbers.'* Violent and serious in contrast to the almost sedate 'Selected Target', 'In From the Cold' would perhaps have made a better series opener; the reliable Terry Green's direction grips from the opening sequence. Regan's recollections of Jackson's shooting, using slow motion and freeze-frame techniques accompanied by stark electronic music, give this episode a memorably unsettling atmosphere, further enhanced by being filmed during the sweltering drought of 1976.

Having fully absorbed the trappings of the series, Hoare presents another duplicitous middle class character plus some excellent gallows humour concerning the Burke and Hare activities of Micky and Stan: 'Your husband's handling a different kind of cold meat now, isn't he, Mrs Medhurst?' The title appears to have been inspired by the John Le Carré novel *The Spy who Came In from the Cold*, in which Alec Leamas, the protagonist, having been hunted by the authorities, leaps to his death on the wrong side of the Berlin Wall.

3.3 VISITING FIREMAN

Writer : Troy Kennedy Martin
Director : Tom Clegg
First UK transmission : 20/9/1976 9.00-10.00 pm

CAST: Nadim Sawalha (Captain Shebbeq), Valentine Palmer (Carew), Jim McManus (Ollie Parsons), Frederick Treves (Beemax), Michael Cronin (Sgt Chivers), Ian Thompson (DI Thompson), Ronnie Brody (Mechanic), Anthony Langdon (Bill Shand), Katya Wyeth (Helga), Lawrence Harrington (Carew's Lawyer), Richard Felgate (McFarland), Pauline Cunningham (Typist), Joe Griffiths (Pianist), Durra (Belly Dancer)

ON THE PLOT: Regan is told to go home and stay out of trouble for 48 hours by Maynon.

This unofficial suspension has arisen from Regan's night on the tiles with one Victor Anthony Carew, a known criminal whom the DI was pressing for information on an impending robbery.

At a loose end, he helps out Captain Shebbeq, an old friend from the Turkish police who's just arrived in London. One of Shebbeq's cases involves investigating the theft of a British lorry in Turkey. Shebbeq's enquires have run into resistance abroad so he is now continuing them in Britain. He intends to interview Parsons, the driver of the lorry who was wrongfully imprisoned for the theft before being released and sent home. Regan finds that the records of the trip have been burnt in a fire. Beemax, the military type who owns the haulage firm that employed Parsons, is holding back information. Someone, it seems, is also trying to kill Shebbeq – he borrows Regan's car for a time and Regan later finds a bomb wired to the ignition.

Shebbeq initially had a theory that the lorry was carrying gold, but later realises the load comprised plutonium. A potentially illegal sale has been made to a group in Turkey intent on the manufacture of a nuclear weapon. The plutonium was also the cause of Parsons' cancer.

Parson's house is emptied out when Regan and Shebbeq next visit, and the same story greets them at Beemax's company, where various incriminating papers have been incinerated. A helicopter roars overhead and MacFarland, an undercover agent, orders both cops off his patch. It seems that they have intruded upon a British Intelligence operation, and Regan is told by Maynon not to make waves. He returns home, but finds that he has at least been vindicated in the Carew case – as a huge blag goes off in town.

NEVER MIND THE DIALOGUE: Carew whinges about 'walking around without shoelaces': Regan buys him a porn mag.

On seeing that a bomb's been wired to his car, Regan throws it into a garden centre next to a garage. After the explosion, a mechanic asks, 'Any oil and water?' And exactly what was destroyed in the greenhouses – was it £1000-worth of cucumbers, or raspberries? Or rhubarb?

Lots of Regan/Shebbeq interplay: Regan wonders if the cop got his gun from an antique shop on the Portobello road. Shebbeq wishes he could emulate the determination of his football idol, Nobby Styles. 'Yeah, where are you now, Nobby, when we most need you?' Regan laments.

'I can see you now on your prayer mat, facing east, praising Allah,' Regan wisecracks to Shebbeq, and later, he jests about him having three pensions, one for each wife.

Regan admits he was 'too smashed' to remember details about his chats with his informant. Maynon tells Regan, 'There's enough people in this building trying to bury you, don't do it yourself.'

Regan and Carter sing a drunken duet together – 'As Long As It Comes from the Heart' – and fall in a heap.

INSIDE INFORMATION: This is the first screened story to refer to Regan's predilection for women in a particular German steel helmet. A scene featuring Helga sporting this contraption was cut after the initial transmission of the story: she comes out of Regan's bedroom and asks, 'Do I have to wear zis bloody thing all night?' Although the scene didn't involve nudity, it must have touched a nerve somewhere.

A keen member of the production team was the victim of another practical joke based around the German helmet, concocted by Kennedy Martin and first assistant director Bill Westley. 'There was a bright Oxbridge girl ... she had a double-barreled name and she wanted to get on,' Ted Childs remembers. 'We wanted some photographs. It was Troy's thing to get this bird wearing pyjamas and this helmet, which we persuaded her to do. She insisted that the photos would be destroyed afterwards. Billy was a bit of a sergeant major but he was a great laugh and, of course, the photographs went everywhere. Weren't used in the episode, of course!'

Regan and Carter's song and dance routine in 'Visiting Fireman' is one of the highlights of the entire series. 'That kind of thing cheers the actors up,' Kennedy Martin says. 'It was so completely different from most series where you've got the script editor saying, "Oh no, you can't do that." The actors dive on it.' The cut to the next scene, in which Jack is suspended, is a brilliant example of the series' effortless mixture of the comic and the dramatic. 'That was [*The Sweeney*'s] great strength,' concurs Kennedy Martin. 'You could see someone getting a belting in a lift and the next minute they'd be making jokes about yoghurt or Haskins's cactus.'

NAMES AND FACES: Nadim Sawalha was frequently cast as an Arabic character on TV. His daughters Julia and Nadia have become regulars in a variety of series, such as *Absolutely Fabulous* and *EastEnders* respectively. Michael Cronin played 'Bullet' Baxter, the gym teacher in *Grange Hill*, another man with no sense of humour. He was also a senior member of a BNP-type organisation in *Between the Lines*. Katya Wyeth stood in for Carol Cleveland on occasions in *Monty Python's Flying Circus*, played a vampire Countess in *Twins of Evil* and posed for *Mayfair*. Frederick Treves specialises in playing aristocratic types and is a descendant of the Victorian physician of the same name who treated the Elephant Man. Joe Griffiths was previously the pianist in 'Regan'.

POLICE AND THIEVES: *'That's par for Heathrow, isn't it? Fortress England. If Hitler was alive they'd give him a job out there.'* This story sees the series turning its ire on another part of the British establishment, namely the security services. Alongside the trademark Kennedy Martin comedy there is plenty of anger on display, such as in the scene where Parsons defends Beemax, quite unaware of what the British secret state has done to him. There are two distinct plots and the 'firemen' of the title arrive to clear up the mess in both. Troy Kennedy Martin returned to the nuclear theme in much more detail in his seminal 1980s work *Edge of Darkness*.

An interesting feature of the story is the inclusion of Shebbeq, an unorthodox cop in the Regan mould. There is some witty subversion of the stereotyping of Arabic characters when it turns out Shebbeq's a football fan, and sly digs are made at the 1970s anti-immigration lobby.

3.4 TOMORROW MAN

Writer : Angus Wilson
Director : David Wickes
First UK transmission : 27/9/1976 9.00-10.00 pm

CAST: John Hurt (Anthony Grey), George Cole (Longfield), Peter Bayliss (Burnham), Ann Curthoys (Dr Jennifer Smart), Nina Thomas (Caroline), Lawrence James (Desk Sgt), Keith Ashton (Massey), Jason James (Police Sgt), Dennis Blanch (CID Detective), Frank Maher (gang leader)*

* uncredited on screen

ON THE PLOT: Recently released from prison for killing a woman in a motor accident, computer expert Tony Grey visits his old business partner, the pompous Dennis Longfield, at DataTask Computing, a firm that advises on 'high security' shipments. Grey wants his old job back but Longfield refuses and Grey begins an ingenious scheme to get even, teaming up with Burnham, a 'respectable' villain. This brings him to the attention of Regan and Carter, who have Burnham down as a target criminal.

A lookalike of Grey has started terrorising Longfield, and when Regan hears of Grey's computing background he calls in technical help in the form of Home Office expert Dr Jennifer Smart. She studies the Datatask computer. Longfield, anxious to claim credit, denies that Grey played a large part in designing the system, so she concludes that he poses no real risk. The Squad and Jennifer keep Grey under surveillance while he starts up a computer studies course with Burnham's backing. The course is a front, as Grey, helped by an ex-marine, later gains access to the roof of DataTask and plants a radio link to his own system, knocking out a security guard in the process.

Regan questions Grey about the break-in but cannot prove anything. He returns to DataTask, where Daniels finds evidence of Grey's tampering. At this point Grey uses the radio link to hack into the DataTask system and divert the route of a van carrying gold bullion. Wiping out the computer's memory completes his revenge on Longfield, and he collects half of his pay-off from Burnham prior to leaving.

The bullion van is raided, but Regan and Carter have successfully intercepted it and the blaggers in Burnham's employ are rounded up. Haskins is pleased when Burnham himself is also nicked, having kept an incriminating plan of the van's route. However, the Squad men are disappointed that Grey himself gets clean away, the only person being arrested – and later mistakenly released – being Grey's lookalike.

NEVER MIND THE DIALOGUE: Regan is distinctly unimpressed by the pompous Dennis Longfield's complaints of victimisation, pointing out that 'So far all that's actually happened is that a whiskey bottle has been smashed, you've been insulted and an alarm clock has been planted in your car.' Nevertheless, Regan he bursts into Grey's hotel room only to find him with his girlfriend, looking sweaty and out of breath. 'You look hot, Mr Grey, have you been having a bad dream?' 'We don't all go to bed to sleep,' Grey retorts.

Regan and Carter's computer illiteracy leads to a computer expert, Dr Jennifer Smart, being brought in. She lives up to her name, avoiding Regan and Carter's advances, leading to a feud over who'll give her a lift home. Needless to say, she's too sensible to go with either of them.

INSIDE INFORMATION: Night filming took place in the same office block near Chelsea Bridge director David Wickes had used in 'Golden Fleece': 'We often used the same locations for different episodes, trying to shoot from different angles and dressing them differently to disguise them. As always, time was the enemy and, with up to 15 locations per episode to discover every fortnight, we tended to return to places where we knew we would be welcome.'

NAMES AND FACES: John Hurt delivered an outstanding performance as Caligula in *I, Claudius* and later developed a successful film career; he was famous for being the first victim of the *Alien* and for his moving portrayal of John Merrick, *The Elephant Man*. Before becoming the embodiment of Thatcherism as Arthur Daley, George Cole played Flash Harry in the 1950s *St Trinians* films and was privy to further dodgy dealings in the sitcom *The Bounder*. Dennis Blanch was George Bulman's long-suffering sidekick Derek Willis in *The XYY Man* and *Strangers*.

POLICE AND THIEVES: *'It's all science fiction as far as I'm concerned.'* Stories of hackers and computer viruses may be a cliché nowadays but in 1976 this story was very much ahead of its time. Today, the DataTask computer system would probably fit into a palmtop. A well-researched tale of revenge in which Longfield's greed is the cause of his undoing, 'Tomorrow Man' has a number of parallels with Andrew Wilson's earlier 'Country Boy'. Significantly, Regan's intuition stops the bullion robbery, despite his lack of technological understanding.

3.5 TASTE OF FEAR

Writer : Roger Marshall
Director : David Wickes
First UK transmission : 4/10/1976 9.00-10.00 pm

CAST: Norman Eshley (Robert Hargreaves), Arthur English (Tug Wilson), George Sweeney (Cook), Bernard Spear (Benny), Leslie Dunlop (Eileen Shaw), Ralph Arliss (Ames), Norma Streader (Helen Hargreaves), Anne-Louise Wakefield (Susie Farmer), Shay Gorman (Shaw)

ON THE PLOT: A bookie's house is violently robbed by Cook and Ames. The unbalanced Cook 'kneecaps' the Irish occupier, Pat Shaw, on hearing his accent. As the Squad investigate, they are joined by a new recruit – DS Robert Hargreaves, fresh out of the Fraud Squad and a high fliers' course. Carter and Hargreaves interview Shaw's daughter and start to wonder if the robbers are runaways from the army, and Carter later shows her some photos of deserters. She recognises a photograph of Ames. Overhearing this conversation in the local pub, 'Tug' Wilson, the ageing tealeaf who is planning the pair's robbery spree, goes to the caravan site where the pair are holed up. He warns them that the police are onto them, and, already upset by the unnecessary shooting of Pat Shaw, tells them he is going to ground.

Cook has torn his long leather jacket and put it in to be repaired. This leads to the Squad trailing him back to the caravan site. They storm the squaddies' caravan, at which point Hargreaves freezes in a panic attack and the pair are able to escape on a motorbike. Hargreaves conceals his error by claiming he misunderstood his orders.

Regan, thinking Hargreaves must be corrupt, tries unofficially through Haskins to remove him from his team, but Haskins blocks this. The Squad start surveillance on Wilton Avenue, working from a name that Ames let slip, while Cook and Ames hide in the shop run by Ames's sister, who lives in the same street. Hargreaves recognises Tug Wilson paying a visit to the shop, and Regan sends the DS to redeem himself by questioning Wilson. This he spectacularly fails to do, beating the truth out of the older man as soon as he's alone with him. Regan agrees to drop the charges against Wilson to prevent a complaint being made against his Squad and warns Hargreaves that he's on borrowed time. The Squad raid the shop and, in a gun battle, Ames perishes and Cook is arrested, but Hargreaves cracks and runs away. Regan and Carter later find him whimpering in a phone box, his usefulness to the Squad at an end.

NEVER MIND THE DIALOGUE: Regan grumbles about Hargreaves: 'I don't know, he doesn't swear, he doesn't smoke … when he *does* drink, it's cider, in halves … and ten to one he's a God botherer.'

He also gets some good shouting in about 'half-arsed bloody amateurs'. Tug Wilson reinterprets his beating up by the police. He tells Regan he 'fell down the stairs'.

Cookie's catchphrase : 'Poxy filth!'

Regan wonders whether to write his report and then get drunk, or the other way round – 'Why not just get drunk?' Carter suggests. Despite being full of tetanus jabs, Carter gets pissed on whiskey, then wonders if his leg will drop off.

'Cookie' was burned in an IRA ambush where his mates were killed, hence his mental instability: 'There's two things I like, *really* like. One's kicking Micks and the other's thumping birds.'

Carter compliments Regan's suit – priced £40 – and offers to buy it. But only because his Mum wants something for the dog to sleep on.

'It's a hard world, guv,' Carter says at the end. 'Yeah, but keep it to yourself, George. No one else wants to know,' Regan replies morosely.

INSIDE INFORMATION: George Sweeney's performance as Cook impressed director David Wickes with its realism. 'I had to hold him back because he was going too far a couple of times… When I asked him to put his fist through the mirror, he didn't hesitate: "I'll do that! I'll do that!" We had a nurse standing by on the set, but Jesus Christ… !'

Wickes's handling of 'Taste of Fear' impressed author Roger Marshall. 'I thought David did it extremely well. The violence and the anti-Irish angle was very frightening. Again, they must have thought I'd come up with a great character because Ted asked me to do another one about Cook. One of my favourite scenes was where Regan and Carter were getting a bit pie-eyed in the Squad room: Dennis had had some injections because he'd stood on a fork. David Wickes shot it in one take and I remember it as something very special.'

The travel agent Ames's sister runs was in the Fulham Palace Road, the caravan site was near Pinewood and Wilson's doss house was near Colet Court.

NAMES AND FACES: Arthur English first became famous for his character of Tosh the spiv in the 1940s. He later appeared in *Are You Being Served?* and as a longstanding drinking pal of Alf Garnett's in *In Sickness and In Health*. George Sweeney played another mad squaddy in an episode of *The New Avengers*, and as semi-regular Speed in *Citizen Smith* he helped Wolfie steal a tank to storm Parliament. Norman Eshley was in *Warship* and played the long-suffering Geoffrey Fourmile in *George and Mildred*. Shay Gorman was Malone in *Boys from the Blackstuff*. Leslie Dunlop appeared in *Angels* and the sitcom *May to December*. She currently appears in the district nurse drama *Where The Heart Is*.

POLICE AND THIEVES: *'Police baiting's a national sport now, or didn't you notice?'* Featuring an appropriately frightening performance by George Sweeney, this story has dated a little due to one plot point being dependent on fashion: Cook and Ames are identified as being army runaways simply on the grounds that the military were the only profession at the time to have short haircuts. Academic, blazer-sporting and initially decidedly smug, Hargreaves is a coward in public school bully clothing: he gives Wilson a beating and potentially invites more accusations of police brutality against the Squad. At the end, in one of the series' most downbeat and affecting scenes, he's also a figure to be pitied. Married to an ambitious Judge's daughter who has high hopes for him, Hargreaves is subject to the pressures of his own class, and is simply not up to coping with them.

3.6 BAD APPLE

Writer : Roger Marshall
Director : Douglas Camfield
First UK transmission : 11/10/1976 9.00-10.00 pm

CAST: Norman Jones (Det Insp Perrant), John Lyons (Det Sgt Huke), Sheila Brennan (Marge Proctor), Brian Poyser (Ash), Rod Culbertson (Grigg), Colin Rix (Letts), David

Miller (Hudson), Kenneth Gilbert (Supt Reynolds), Patricia Franklyn (Mrs Perrant), Ellis Dale (Bank Manager), Maggie McCarthy (WPC Collins), Billy James (Drag Sripper), Steven Hatton (Johnny Peters)

ON THE PLOT: Regan and Carter are seconded by Haskins to investigate possible corruption among a group of officers in a small town outside London. Two bent cops, DS Huke and DI Perrant, are at work in the town, and are seen going about their business; pocketing stolen money, fitting up a minor crook for unsolved robberies, watering down charges on a fraudster in return for cash. They also release an armed robber, Ronnie Grigg, on bail providing he does a bank job for them. Huke is also receiving protection money from Marge Procter, the hardboiled owner of the Blue Parrot pub; in return he's turning a blind eye to the pub's unusual interpretation of licensing hours and its peddling of stolen booze.

Carter and Haskins install themselves in the local station, where the local commander isn't happy about their presence. Meanwhile, Regan poses as an ex-con to get a job as a barman in Marge's pub. Ronnie Grigg is nicked in Southampton on another job and Carter interrogates him, pretending to be one of the forthcoming police recipients of Grigg's bung. Taken in by this ruse, Grigg tells Carter to assure Perrant that he will get his money.

The net begins to close. Regan dyes some banknotes with fuchsine powder which Huke later collects from the pub. Meanwhile, Perrant, wondering if there is a third cop besides Carter and Haskins, phones Daniels in London and learns of Regan's presence. He clears out his bent bank accounts and goes on the run. Huke is nicked with incriminating dye on his hands, and admits that Perrant was thinking of buying a boat. Regan and Carter chase the corrupt DI along the river, finally cornering him. After a furious struggle, Perrant is nicked – face to face with Regan at last.

NEVER MIND THE DIALOGUE: Regan and Carter ask Johns about a third bent cop. He reveals the miscreant died of natural causes – '…if eating yourself, drinking yourself and whoring yourself to death can be considered natural.'

The bent cops pocket stolen money off a villain they've nicked: 'Who'd have thought he'd have spent so much, so soon?'

Regan on the Blue Parrot's stolen booze: 'Every time I close my eyes I see Shaw Taylor.'

'Four years. That's a lot of porridge,' Perrant says.

'I've met some cack-handed villains…' is Perrant's verdict on Ronnie Grigg's attempt to stick up a garage with the aid of a water pistol.

The rather conservative ex-cop Johns on Regan and Carter's apparel: 'Thank God I wore uniform.'

On seeing a drunk, Huke wonders how people can get stoned so early in the day; Carter says he'll show him. Marge appears in shades, stating she had 'too much of the tiddly last night'. Early on it's mentioned that a DI got drunk in the station's annual knees-up. 'It's been known,' Regan says solemnly.

INSIDE INFORMATION: The story was relocated to a non-metropolitan setting for reasons of credibility. 'I felt that Regan going undercover in London wouldn't work as he was such a well-known officer,' Roger Marshall reasons. 'He'd been in the papers and the idea of him being unknown to these other officers would have been a bit daft. That's why we went provincial with 'Bad Apple'.'

NAMES AND FACES: Norman Jones featured in episodes of *The Adventures of Sherlock Holmes* and *Inspector Morse*. John Lyons appeared in *Sweeney 2* and was DS Toolan in *A Touch of Frost*. Kenneth Gilbert was one of Douglas Camfield's unofficial repertory company and was again employed by the director in 1976, as the duplicitous Dunbar in the *Doctor Who* story 'The Seeds of Doom.'

POLICE AND THIEVES: *'Every copper on every beat has to pay for what you are, has to live you down.'* This was one of the first stories on television to handle police corruption with a degree of intelligence. Arguably, given G F Newman's later series *Law and Order*, 'Bad Apple' could perhaps have gone further. However, *The Sweeney* production team's sensitivity to corruption in the real Flying Squad meant this was one instance where the series' authenticity had to be diluted in the interests of public relations with Scotland Yard. The location of the action in a small town outside London also helped deflect any awkward questions from the Met.

The bent cops Perrant and Huke are malign versions of Regan and Carter, casually going about their corrupt daily business. They've hidden their assets well: even Perrant's wife is unaware of his secret bank accounts. Welcome hints of cynicism include Perrant's reference to a third accomplice, 'the man upstairs', who is never caught or heard from again. Whether or not this is the local Superintendent, who claims he's been 'sitting up there in blissful bloody ignorance', is left to the viewer's imagination. The only scene that grates slightly is Carter's early line, 'Not a bent copper?' – as if such a thing was inconceivable. It's not often the series has this *Dixon of Dock Green*-style naiveté.

Camfield's direction is impressive throughout, particularly in the scene where *Avengers*-style mayhem meets street-fighting as Perrant and Regan duel with a big stick and a rubbish bin at the denouement.

3.7 MAY

Writer : Trevor Preston
Director : Tom Clegg
First UK transmission : 25/10/1976 9.00-10.00 pm
NB : 'Night Out' was repeated on 19/10/1976

CAST: Marjorie Yates (May), Karl Howman (Davey Holmes), Geraldine Moffatt (Sheila Martin), Brian Gwaspari (Cree), Frank Mills (Len), Tim Hardy (Francis), Jeremy Sinden (Det Con Feast), Roger Booth (Ashcroft), Tim Meats (Jessop), Adrian Shergold

(Don Edwards), Kathleen St John (Miss Finch), Cyril Shaps (Turner)

ON THE PLOT: Nobody likes a moneylender, certainly not one like Turner. 'That old Shylock' – that's how he's normally referred to – or 'That old bastard!' One night, working late in his office, he's beaten senseless and his takings are snatched.

Regan receives a visit from May Holmes, wife of a late villain Regan knew. Davey, her son, is being questioned about the Turner break-in by two detectives, DS Cree and DC Feast. Davey was seen leaving the shop on the night of the attack; he had £500 hidden on his bike; and, worst of all, when the detectives tried to arrest him, he hit Cree and ran for it. May is convinced that Davey is innocent, and that he legally borrowed the £500 off Turner before the robbery. Regan promises that he'll help, and with Carter in tow, tracks Davey to a block of flats. Davey refuses to say what he really needed the £500 for, and tries to leg it. Having reluctantly delivered the lad to the local nick, Regan continues to look into the case.

At the station, Cree and Feast start grilling Davey. It appears they're about to beat a confession out of him when they get a phone call from the hospital. Turner has recovered and cleared Davey's name, so he is released. Meanwhile, Regan and Carter have searched a flat that Davey had a key to and found out that he's been having it away with Sheila, the wife of Rick Martin, a vicious blagger currently in prison. Davey needed the money as Jessop, an estate agent who's threatening to tell Martin about his relationship with his wife, is blackmailing him. After seeing her, he goes to pay Jessop off, but the blackmailer, out to make more money, has tipped off Rick Martin's minder, Ashcroft.

Having scoured London looking for Davey, Regan and Carter return to May's house. Soon afterwards, Davey is delivered back to the house having had a severe beating. He still has the money – the villains weren't interested in it. Regan slams his fist angrily into the wall.

NEVER MIND THE DIALOGUE: Davey's mate, on being asked whether he was seeing anyone special: 'Well, they're all special on the night, aren't they?'
'You're in bother, son. Big bother,' Regan tells Davey.

Carter sits bored and bemused as Regan and May reminisce about a wild party some years before at which Jack and May's husband Bobby were apparently 'dressed up like a couple of tarts'. 'I've always fancied him myself,' Carter admits.

Regan, on finding some fag ends, one with lipstick and one without: 'Cigarettes. His and hers. Young Davey's been practising his postural variations with someone.'

Regan's flat is displayed in all its bachelor glory;: unwashed clothing, chip papers and dirty plates used as ashtrays. Grumbling that there's never any clean glasses in the place, Regan starts drinking Vodka out of a milk jug.

How close Regan and May have been in the past in unclear. 'We was lonely, Jack,' May says, and they value each other's friendship very highly. Regan becomes angry at Davey causing May so much upset, telling him: 'If you weren't who you were, I'd kick your arse up to your shoulder blades.'

NAMES AND FACES: Karl Howman later carved out a career as cockney 'lad' in numerous shows from *Get Some In!* to the 1980s comedy *Brush Strokes*. Cyril Shaps, one of the most familiar Jewish actors on television, has been in *The Liver Birds* and *Paul Merton – The Series*. Brian Gwaspari returned as a villain in *Sweeney 2* and later appeared in *Between the Lines*. Jeremy Sinden, who has since died, was the son of Sir Donald and appeared in *Brideshead Revisited*. Geraldine Moffat played a similar character as a villain's moll in *Get Carter*.

INSIDE INFORMATION: 'May' contains one of *The Sweeney*'s most chilling villains, the courteous, well-dressed and softly spoken Ashcroft: 'Mr Jessop sends his apologies. Not feeling well. Something to do with his legs.' The threat implied by this character – he never acts violently on screen – again came from Trevor Preston's real-life experience. 'All this silly stuff you see in the most recent films – these guys like fucking gorillas, with bald heads and necks like cocks – they're not the frightening sort,' Preston says. 'The most frightening guy I ever met would go into a pub and he would check every single door. Then he would find a corner opposite the entrance, and if anyone was sitting there he would buy them a really big drink or give them a fiver to move, so he had two walls behind him. A really, really hard man who would be quiet and have what my old man would call 'seagull eyes'– completely dead. He'd just look at someone and softly say, "You'll do."'

Director Tom Clegg remembers the effect the young Karl Howman had on *The Sweeney* team. 'Very nearly his first part. A cheeky little kid, full of himself. Everybody loved him. At the end of the shoot, the crew picked him up and dumped him head first in a bucket of water. It was all in good fun, of course.'

Trevor Preston also recalls one of the crew's practical jokes. 'I wasn't there, but during filming John had to rush in and grab the telephone to order an ambulance because somebody had had a really good kicking outside. They had taken this fucking table apart and stuck it back together with blu-tak and stuck the phone on the top and when he grabbed the phone the whole lot fell apart. All the legs went out; the cameraman fell off his seat from laughing so much.'

POLICE AND THIEVES: *'Jack, he's only a kid.'* A depressing urban tragedy, with excellent performances from Karl Howman and Marjorie Yates. 'May' is a change of pace after the undercover runaround that precedes it, an absorbing human drama that has a bleak inevitability. Davey is intimidated by Cree, out of his depth with Sheila Martin, blackmailed by Jessop and nearly beaten to death by Ashcroft. It's doubly ironic that Davey's involvement with a 'scrubber' is the same situation that led his father Bobby into crime and ultimately imprisonment. The idea that Davey could be following in his father's footsteps is an interesting concept that recurs in other Preston scripts, such as *Fox*. In this case it turns out to be a piece of misdirection.

The friendship and support that Regan and May offer each other is contrasted with the duplicitous behaviour of the largely unseen estate agent, Jessop. The characters are all too believable, from Ashcroft to the amoral cops Cree and Feast, who seem quite happy beating confessions out of people.

After a 1987 repeat of this story, an HTV announcer stammered: 'I'm sorry ... I feel very moved by *The Sweeney* this evening.'

3.8 SWEET SMELL OF SUCCESSION

Writer : Peter Hill
Director : William Brayne
First UK transmission : 8/11/1976 9.00-10.00 pm
NB : 'Jackpot' was repeated on 1/11/1976

CAST: Hywel Bennett (Steven Castle), Peter Dyneley (Pat Tarley), Sue Lloyd (Arleen Baker), Willoughby Goddard (Daniel Kitter), Maxwell Shaw (Colin Raleigh), Alan Tilvern (Charlie Walters), David Stern (Ted Parkin), Gail Granger (Jill), Geoffrey Todd (Phil Nairn), Jack Allen (the Vicar), Peter Brayham (Johnno)

ON THE PLOT: Joe Castle, gangland boss, is dead. Regan anticipates a turf war is now about to break out between Castle's former minder, Pat Tarley, and Charlie Walters, head of a rival 'firm'. However, to Regan's surprise an unknown face turns up at the funeral – Steven Castle, Joe's son, an academic from Manchester, who has previously had no contact with his father. Regan decides to use Steven's presence as an opportunity to escalate matters, despite a warning from Haskins not to get a potentially innocent party hurt.

Tarley, alerted by Regan to Castle Jr's presence, pays the young man a visit and sees he has already shacked up with Arleen Baker, his father's mistress. Tarley lays it on the line, announcing he will be taking over the Castle business. However, after he leaves, Steven announces that he has plans of his own in that direction.

Colin Raleigh, a flashy jewel thief, arrives on the scene. He left some jewellery with Joe to be fenced and now wants his money. Castle finds that has the gems. Tarley, having also seen Raleigh, comes searching for the jewellery, but Castle misdirects him to Raleigh. Holding a knife to Raleigh's throat, Tarley realises he's been conned. Meanwhile, Castle meets with Ted Parkin, who works for Charlie Walters.

Regan, trying to turn Castle against the two warring firms, hands the man a list of the illegitimate outlets belonging to his father's organisation. Castle passes this list to Walters' firm, and also tells them about the jewellery, saying that Tarley will be collecting it from Raleigh at a disused warehouse. Walters and hard man Johnno Smith ambush the other gang and shoot Tarley. The Squad, tipped off by Castle, then move in and arrest everyone. Castle, who is in receipt not only of his father's legal businesses and an insurance reward from the police, gets off scot free, as does his secret partner, Parkin, who has deposed his boss.

NEVER MIND THE DIALOGUE: Tarley, on first seeing Castle with Arleen Baker, sneers, 'Your old man barely cold yet and here you are giving his bird one. Quite like old times.' Tarley to Regan: 'Get stuffed, Kojak.'

Regan and Carter ask Kitter, the lardy lawyer, what will happen to Castle's brothels and protection rackets. Kitter replies, 'I'd have thought you should know that. You *are* supposed to be the police around here!'

Col Raleigh, the flash villain, says he wants to go straight and set up a restaurant. Regan reminds him that he likes porridge...

After one of Tarley's visits, Castle tries to tell Regan that he and Arleen were having a row. 'Got a good left hook, has she?' Regan retorts.

While menacing Castle, Tarley swigs at booze purloined from Castle's drinks cabinet. He then gives the bottle back and leaves. Phil Nairn obviously has a taste for the stuff as he grabs the bottle off Castle again before walking out of the house with it.

When Pat Tarley threatens to 'sort out the old boiler', it's clear he's referring to Arleen Baker, rather than the central heating.

NAMES AND FACES: Peter Hill had previously written for *Callan*, *Hunter's Walk* and *Special Branch*. Hywel Bennett went on to play another educated man who didn't fancy working for a living, in the long-running comedy *Shelley*. Peter Dyneley previously voiced the somewhat more environmentally friendly figure of Jeff Tracey in *Thunderbirds*. David Stern played the boss in *Thief Takers*. Sue Lloyd was a regular in *The Baron* and *Crossroads*, and also appeared in *The Ipcress File*. Willoughby Goddard munched his way through many chicken legs as overweight William Gessler in the 1950s adventure series *William Tell*. Alan Tilvern was one of the voices in *Who Framed Roger Rabbit?*

INSIDE INFORMATION: 'Sweet Smell of Succession' saw *Sweeney* stunt arranger Peter Brayham in his only credited role, as the tough guy (what else?) Johnno Smith. During filming of the third series, something happened to Brayham that drove home how popular *The Sweeney* had become.

'I'm coming home one night after working on the show, and I used to drive real quick in those days,' he says. 'I used to drive big sports cars and a big Merc. Tearing through the streets, and I came through the West End – we were working in Islington or somewhere like that – through Hyde Park, screeching round the corner into Chelsea, and all of a sudden – boom boom boom – the police'd got me, hadn't they?

'And these are the very words the geezer said: "Who do you think you are? The Sweeney?" I laughed! And he said, "You think it's funny, do yer?" "I do actually, and I'll tell you why." I pulled some scripts over and said "Look," but they told me to get out of the car because they thought I was at it. "I'm the stunt co-ordinator on *The Sweeney*," I said, "and we've been doing a night shoot." And he went, "*The Sweeney?* The geezer does *The Sweeney!*" And he *knew my name!* He said, "Peter Brayham, that's right! I've seen your name up on the screen!" We were having this conversation, and he went, "All right, son, go on, but be careful..."'

The sequence in which the cops pursue Raleigh was filmed near the Westway flyover in Hammersmith.

POLICE AND THIEVES: *'Look at me – can't get promoted, can't get a mortgage, can't even hold on to a bird.'* This is a further story about manipulation, in which Castle – middle class and educated – ruthlessly gets his own way. By comparison, Carter, pursuing a middle class lifestyle (mortgage, promotion, steady girlfriend), fails in his aspirations. His attempts at armchair psychology prove to be a failure when he invites Jill, a temporary secretary from the Squad office, to his flat for dinner; he likes her, but also wants to find out about his promotion prospects. Feeling used, she runs 'home to mum and the cup of cocoa', although, significantly, he's already abandoned the idea. The anti-materialist values of the series are reinforced again at the conclusion; considering that Castle will be 'up west' drinking champagne and getting his leg over, Carter is still able to laugh at his predicament. 'Do you know what *my* old man left me? Bleedin' gas bill!' Some of the gangland dialogue feels a little more forced than usual, but the stylised monochrome flashbacks in the pre-titles sequence compensate impressively.

3.9 DOWN TO YOU, BROTHER

Writer : Richard Harris
Director : Chris Menaul
First UK transmission : 22/11/1976 9.00-10.00 pm
NB : The film *McKenna's Gold* was shown on 15 /11/1976

CAST: Derek Francis (Meadows), Terrance Budd (Douglas Owen), Tina Heath (Deborah Meadows), Kenny Lynch (Holder), Malcolm Tierney (Miller), Ron Pember (Apps), John Barrard (Chauffeur), Simon Callow (Det Sgt), Michael Logan (Joke teller), Jenny Cryst (Girl at hotel)

ON THE PLOT: As a result of Haskins's social diary being double-booked, Regan is asked to stand in for him at a 'stag do' at the Cunard Hotel. Amid plenty of prosperous businessmen chomping on fat cigars, Regan encounters a familiar face, Raymond Meadows, a wealthy, retired villain. Meadows invites Regan back for a drink in his luxurious home and, apparently the worse for wear, tells Regan that his current wealth was all down to the last job he did, which Regan failed to nick him for: 'It's all down to you, brother.'

Later, seemingly mortified by this slip, Meadows phones Regan at home and asks him to forget what he said. Regan, stirred up by this admission, instead begins surveillance of Meadows, wondering if the crook really has retired after all. As this operation goes on, his path crosses with Meadows again, when the latter buys an expensive doll for Susie. Regan angrily returns it and then has to buy his daughter another one.

Regan and Carter realise Meadows' own daughter, Debbie, is 'seeing' Dougie Owen, a flash young villain whom Meadows dislikes. Regan discerns that Meadows wants to break this relationship up and has manipulated him into keeping watch, aware that Owen is bound to be currently planning a job. Debbie works in a shop, and it becomes clear to Regan that Owen is planning to blag the safe in the neighboring premises, having made impressions of Debbie's keys. Unknown to Carter, Regan resolves to teach Meadows a lesson.

As Owen and his associates are arrested, Regan lets the young crook beat him up and leave. As predicted, Owen storms round to Meadows' house and gives the old man a pasting. He then gives himself up as Regan and Carter arrive, announcing 'It's all settled.' A battered Meadows is reunited with his daughter. When he accuses Regan of letting Dougie go, Regan corrects him; he let Meadows go, several years ago.

NEVER MIND THE DIALOGUE: Regan on Dougie: 'Look, he's a working villain, so he's either planning or doing.'

Regan also gets an irate phone call from his ex-wife because he bought his daughter Susie a doll. When Carter expresses his sympathy, Regan just says 'Shut up.'

Carter makes an awful joke. 'Put the rolls [Rolls] in the garage, James – I'll butter them later.'

INSIDE INFORMATION: 'I was pleased with the result of my scripts. The standard was always high and John Thaw and Dennis Waterman were always good to watch,' author Richard Harris says of the production team's treatment of his material. 'Was Regan heroic? Not particularly. He was a working copper who knew his game.'

During shooting for the story, assistant director Bill Westley carried out another prank on a member of the production team. 'Mickey Morris was our make-up man. Lovely grey hair, distinguished, but he could never get over the fact that he had gone grey, so he used to dye it black,' Westley says with a sly grin. 'What he used to use, I don't know, but it was like soot, it was horrible. At the end of the day his shirt would be caked in it. Anyway, we were doing this shoot in a house in Chelsea that had an indoor pool, and he had his box, and when I say, "Wrap," Mickey picks his box up and runs off. This time, however, the idea is that when he picks his box up, all his stuff spills out of it; a mean trick, I know. Then somebody else comes to help him, or so he thinks, and 'accidentally' pushes him in the pool. Poor sod, all this black starts coming out of his hair. It filled the bloody pool! There was hell to pay.'

NAMES AND FACES: Richard Harris adapted the *Hazell* series books for television and wrote several stage plays, including *In Two Minds,* which Garfield Morgan appeared in. He also wrote scripts for *Redcap, Public Eye* and *Hunter's Walk.*

Chris Menaul later directed *The Professionals* and penned the story outline for 'Need to Know', which was scripted by Brian Clemens. He directed the David Lodge drama *Nice Work* and the feature film *Fatherland,* adapted from Robert Harris's story of an alternative Britain in which Hitler won the Second World War. More recently he has directed *Homicide: Life on the Street* and the television film *The Passion of Ayn Rand* starring Helen Mirren and Peter Fonda.

Simon Callow later appeared as a disturbed MI5 operator in Howard Brenton's psychological drama *Dead Head*. Character actor Derek Francis, among many other roles, played Wackford Squeers in the BBC's *Nicholas Nickleby*. *Lizzy Dripping* star Tina Heath, meanwhile, joined the inmates of *Blue Peter*. Malcolm Tierney played a recurring villain in *Lovejoy*.

POLICE AND THIEVES: *'All in all, Jack, you boobed. It was all down to me. A hundred and fifty grand I pulled on that little number.'* A psychological drama in which villains and coppers play mind games with each other. Meadows and Regan identify with each other, both having 'lost' their wives (Meadows' wife committed suicide) and both having protective feelings towards their daughters. Regan remarks to Haskins: 'Worry the life out of you sometimes, don't they, kids, guv.' In a possible allusion to 'Abduction', Regan panics when he momentarily loses sight of Susie when they're walking in the park. While the audience can sympathise with Regan's parental pride being hurt by Meadows flaunting his wealth, Regan's engineering of an explicit beating for the old villain reminds the viewer of the unpleasant side of his character. Ironically, the beating achieves what Meadows wanted: the scene ends with him being comforted by his daughter Deborah.

The direction by newcomer Chris Menaul is striking, and he is another *Sweeney* helmsman to incorporate cinematic references into the series. Dougie beats Meadows up to the accompaniment of Vivaldi's *Four Seasons*, a sequence obviously influenced by Stanley Kubrick's scenes of violence set to classical music in *A Clockwork Orange*.

3.10 PAY OFF

Writer : Peter J Hammond
Director : Douglas Camfield
First UK transmission : 29/11/1976 9.00-10.00 pm

CAST: Dave King (Albert Drake), Geraldine James (Shirley Glass), Ken Kitson (Killick), George Harris (Zachariah Franklyn), William Armour (Murdoch), Anthony Douse (Ernie Millan), James Warrior (Taffy), David Elison (Vaughton)

ON THE PLOT: George Carter begins an affair with Shirley Glass, a croupier at Drake's Casino. She has anonymously been sent a newspaper cutting showing a picture of a quarry, with the words 'RIP Eddie Glass' – her ex-lover's name – scrawled on it. Carter agrees to help her find out what happened to Glass, finding out he had skills as a wheelsman. Regan warns him against getting personally involved.

At the casino, it becomes clear that Eddie Glass worked for Drake as a getaway driver on a job, during which he drove off in panic and accidentally killed another blagger. Drake had Glass killed in revenge. One of the robbers, Zak, sent Shirley the newspaper as he had a soft spot for her and wanted her to forget about Eddie. Carter realises that Glass was killed as a result of bottling on a job, one of the Squad's previous cases. He takes his suspicions to Haskins but because of prior warnings he is sent to take a holiday and cool off.

Some children playing in a quarry unearth Glass's body. Regan suggests the story is kept out of the papers and that Carter is not informed. He questions Murdoch, one of the men who didn't get away. Regan threatens to have the man's sentence extended and Murdoch gives him a name – that of Drake's casino colleague Gus Killick.

Carter and Shirley's own enquiries provoke Drake into deciding to top them both, and Zak lures the pair to the quarry. Regan decides it's time to let Carter know what's happening but can't find him; the Squad tail Killick to the quarry. Holding Carter and Shirley at gunpoint, Drake is distracted by the sight of Eddie's opened grave, and the pair run for it. When the Squad arrive, the chase turns into a gun battle in which Zak is killed. Despite his protests to the contrary, Shirley is convinced Carter was just using her to nick the gang and she storms off.

NEVER MIND THE DIALOGUE: The whole first scene in the casino is amusing, with Carter chatting up Shirley at the card table ('Do you play any other sort of games?') while Haskins wonders if Carter is coming back to London with him. 'Well, George is a country boy at heart,' Regan says with a leery wink. Haskins then goes home – 'He's not going to be ripping Mum's hairnet off in a fit of passion, is he?' – and Regan butts in on Carter's little scene. 'Have you met my father?' Carter says.

It seems that Carter initially failed to perform satisfactorily with Shirley: 'Blame the brewery.' He even winces when she gives him some Alka Seltzers and he hears them fizzing.

Regan is pissed off when he finds out that Carter has gone over his head and taken the case to Haskins. 'Oh, come on, Jack, you've played the Lone Ranger in your time,' Haskins placates him. 'Yeah, but I don't intend to end up as bloody Tonto,' Regan retorts.

INSIDE INFORMATION: 'I've always preferred writing character-led stories that relied on atmosphere and, if you like, dealt with areas on the edge of crime,' writer P J Hammond says. 'I have never liked writing about guns and fast cars. That's why programmes like *Z-Cars*, *The Gentle Touch*, *Wycliffe*, *Dangerfield* and half-hour episodes of *The Bill* suited me. I was less happy working on shows that depended upon action for action's sake, and my ideas inevitably suffered because of this.' Changes made to 'Pay Off' during production meant this was the only script for *The Sweeney* Hammond wrote. 'It's such a pity that the true version was never made,' he adds.

NAMES AND FACES: Peter J Hammond was a well-established writer by the mid-1970s, script editing *Z-Cars* and writing several episodes. He also worked on *Dixon of Dock Green*, *Hunter's Walk*, *Special Branch*, *Target*, *New Scotland Yard*, *The Bill* and *Spy Trap*.

He is arguably best remembered for his work on fantasy serials. He contributed to Trevor Preston's paranormal series *Ace of Wands* and later created *Sapphire and Steel*. This minimalist drama, starring David McCallum and Joanna Lumley, is still fondly remembered for its mix of everyday characters and bizarre, sometimes terrifying situations.

Geraldine James also starred in *Blott on the Landscape*, *The History Man*, and *Band of Gold*. She worked with John Thaw on several occasions, in *Inspector Morse*, *Stanley and the Women* and *Kavanagh QC*. Formerly a popular comedian, Dave King appeared as a bent cop in *The Long Good Friday*. His TV appearances included *Pennies from Heaven*, *Target*, *Minder* and *Bleak House*. David Ellison later played Sergeant Joe Beck in *Juliet Bravo*. James Warrior was recast as a scruffier Welsh cop, Jellyneck, in *Sweeney 2* and the fourth series of *The Sweeney*.

POLICE AND THIEVES: *'Your word of honour? You're a policeman, aren't you? You don't know the meaning of the word!'* Despite P J Hammond's misgivings about the realisation of his script, this is an absorbing character-driven story in which no one really trusts each other: Carter and Shirley Glass, the gang of villains, the villains and Shirley and even Regan and Carter. A new girlfriend intruding on the friendship between Jack and George again bodes ill, as it does in most other stories where this happens.

A haunting, gloomy air that hangs over Carter's temporary estrangement from the police, together with a carefully structured script and imaginative direction, make a tragic ending seem inevitable. The final scenes, involving a chase through a quarry and a series of blazing rows between all the characters, are heightened by the hot 1976 weather during filming.

3.11 LOVING ARMS
Writer : Robert Wales
Director : Tom Clegg
First UK transmission : 6/12/1976 9.00-10.00 pm

CAST: Roy Stone (Arthur Ward), Clifford Kershaw (Fred Booth), Anne Dyson (Lilly Booth), Alan David (Blakeney), Mona Hammond (Anne Robson), George Tovey (Len Walters), Julian Littman (Jeremy Clark), Steven Pacey (PC McKenna), Max Mason (PC Adler), Angela Phillips (Girl robber), Perry Balfour, Ray Winstone (Youths)

ON THE PLOT: Len Walters, a newsagent whom Regan knows, has been subjected to an unsuccessful robbery at gunpoint. Regan becomes interested when Walters, an ex-serviceman, insists the Colt .45 involved was a real gun, not a toy as the local nick have stated in the press.

Fred Booth, a semi-retired engineer, is meanwhile visited by Artie Ward. Pretending to be a small businessman, Ward asks Booth to make some replica Smith & Wesson .38s. Ward has cottoned on to the market in these guns; his potential customers

John Thaw as Detective Inspector Jack Regan and Dennis Waterman as Detective Sergeant George Carter publicise series four of *The Sweeney* in 1978. *(FremantleMedia)*

Squad regular Tom Daniels (John Alkin), and Robert Hargreaves (Norman Eshley), in 'Taste of Fear'. *(FremantleMedia)*

The Squad arrest the psychopathic Cook (George Sweeney, centre) who appeared in two linked stories, 'Taste of Fear' and 'On the Run'. *(FremantleMedia)*

The Squad arrest Maynard (Michael Coles) and the unfortunate Frankie Little (Roy Kinnear) at the end of 'I Want the Man'. *(FremantleMedia)*

Director Tom Clegg's crew filming the climactic car chase at the end of 'Poppy', which includes (from second left to right) an S-Type Jag, a Triumph and a Ford Consul. *(FremantleMedia)*

Above: Regan takes on more security van blaggers in the first feature film *Sweeney!* (*Canal Plus Image*)

Left: Regan and Bianca (Diane Keen) flee from gunmen in *Sweeney!* (*Canal Plus Image*)

The UK film poster for *Sweeney!* *(Canal Plus Image)*

Filming the Sqaud in action during the security van robbery in *Sweeney!* *(Canal Plus Image)*

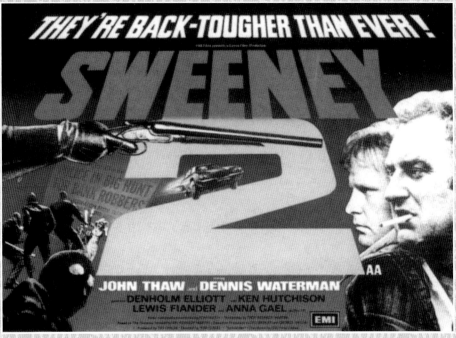

The UK film poster for *Sweeney 2 (Canal Plus Image)*

The villains rob the factory in *Sweeney 2 (Canal Plus Image)*

Above: Carter tackles a
corrupt PC (John Vine)
in *Sweeney 2*
(Canal Plus Image)

Right: Regan and Carter
both pull at the end-of-case
piss-up in *Sweeney 2*
(Canal Plus Image)

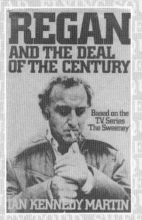

Left: The hardback of one of Ian Kennedy Martin's original novels, from 1977. **Second left to right:** The first *Sweeney* Annual, and the sheet music for the signature tune, both from 1976.

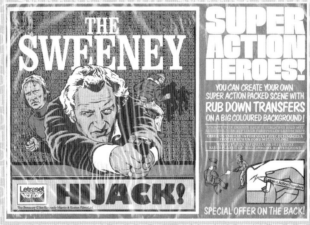

The rub down transfer set from 1976.

The single of *The Sweeney* theme from 1975, and the CD/LP soundtrack released in 2001.

include the lads who have the .45. As Booth's wife is seriously ill, and refusing treatment owing to her religious beliefs, Booth agrees to do the job for cash, pointing out the guns will only be for display.

Two girls stick up a chip shop in Acton with one of Booth's guns, dropping it after firing at a police constable. Regan hears that the gun is made from mild steel and is likely to explode if fired. He also realises there is more than one such gun around. Soon afterwards, McKenna, a keen young constable, is killed when a gun explodes. Regan blames himself for this death, having given one of the PC's colleagues a dressing down earlier for losing the two girl robbers.

A local heavy, Blakeney, has got wind of Ward's dealings, and he beats information out of him. Having obtained Booth's address, and aware the Squad are turning the manor upside down following McKenna's death, Blakeney throws Ward to the wolves. Regan suspects Blakeney's motives are far from altruistic, but cannot prove it. Ward is caught by the Squad, and gives Regan Booth's address.

Mrs Booth finally gives her consent to be taken to hospital as Regan arrests her husband, saying it'll be up to the courts to sort out whether he's guilty or innocent.

NEVER MIND THE DIALOGUE: Newsagent to gun-toting young blagger: 'You got the wrong place son, you want the OK Corral!'

Regan and George are initially on a case involving stolen toilet roll holders: 'Let's get back to the big bad world of bent bog rolls.'

Regan bursts in on Blakeney, telling him to 'Sit down. You look more honest when you're bent.' On being asked about a warrant, Regan says, 'You invited us in.'

Bursting into a prayer meeting around Mrs Booth's bed, convinced he's about to meet a load of gun runners, all Regan can manage is a muted 'Oh…'

The Assistant Commissioner's office phones to complain about Regan. 'What have I done, used their tea urn?' he grumbles.

Blakeney gives Artie Ward a kicking to get Booth's address, and then says to his lads, 'Don't just stand there, get the man an aspirin or something!'

Ward has social pretensions, asking for payment in guineas.

INSIDE INFORMATION: A company called Baptys provided armourers who looked after the guns on *The Sweeney*. Stunt arranger Peter Brayham would liaise with them during production. 'If you're on a shoot and you want the guns for more than three or four days, you have what they call a practical gun – which fires blanks – and a dummy,' he says. 'If we were on location, the armourer would make arrangements to lock them up in a police station overnight. They were declared, put in the station, and picked up the next morning. But we had a lot of times where the guy who gave permission wasn't there and we were held up shooting – the guns were still locked up and they weren't available. Now it's a bit different. Very seldom did John have a gun in his hand. They were a couple of mavericks in the storyline, but would rarely resort to using a weapon. When the occasion arose and they did have to use one, I don't think John was over keen.'

NAMES AND FACES: Robert Wales wrote for *Van Der Valk* and tackled religion again in his play, *The Cell*, concerning a convent's autocratic Reverend Mother in conflict with a young nun.

Billed here as a 'youth', Ray Winstone has since made a career playing cockney heavies, including the leading role in the borstal drama *Scum* and the boxer Kenny in *Fox*. He has since received critical acclaim for his performance as a wife-battering drunk in the film *Nil by Mouth*, and also appeared in the Brit crime films *Face* and *Sexy Beast*. Winstone recently joined the right side as a troubled loner cop in *Lenny Blue*.

George Tovey was crushed by a couple of Egyptian mummies in the *Doctor Who* story 'Pyramids of Mars' and is the father of Roberta Tovey, who played Susan in the first of the Doctor's big screen adventures, *Dr Who and the Daleks*. Steven Pacey became a regular in *Blake's 7*. Alan David's television credits include *Inspector Morse* and *Maigret*. Mona Hammond later appeared in *EastEnders*.

POLICE AND THIEVES: *'If I hadn't bollocked that young copper, his mate wouldn't have had a go on his own.'* A bit of an oddball episode. The motivation of some of the characters, and the question of how guns meant for display can still fire, are a little unclear, despite the writer's evident research. There is some muted criticism of religious fundamentalism, and Booth's plight is movingly portrayed. Alan David's performance as Blakeney enlivens proceedings – perhaps the story should have focused more on this memorably nasty and colourful character.

Documentary-style direction also makes a return in several naturalistic sequences shot at night around the West End. At one point, Carter finds a wad of Artie's money and, although he probably handed it in as evidence later, it looks like he's pocketing it – probably not an intentional allusion to police corruption. This episode is the only one that has not been repeated on terrestrial TV, apparently owing to contractual problems.

3.12 'LADY LUCK'

Writer : Ranald Graham
Director : Mike Vardy
First UK transmission : 13/12/1976 9.00-10.00 pm

CAST: Moira Redmond (Marcia Edmunds), Norman Rodway (Edmunds), James Cossins (Colonel Rosier), Daphne Oxenford (Mrs Rosier), Peggy Bulloch (Old Lady), Carolyn Hudson (Marcia's friend)

ON THE PLOT: A gang rob a betting shop and one of them, Edmunds, collides with an elderly woman and hospitalises her. A few days later, Edmund's wife Marcia, looks up Regan, whom she previously spotted in a pub, and grasses on her husband, but under a false name, Carole. Edmunds is arrested, protesting his innocence. Regan finds Marcia hiding and she apologises for the deception – she is convinced that Edmunds won't find out about her actions.

At the hospital, the old woman picks Edmunds out of the line-up, and a shotgun is subsequently found at his house. However, at this point Edmunds states that at the time of the blag, he and his wife were having lunch with Colonel Rosier. He was out of sight for half an hour, apparently looking for a rare bottle of wine; but when Carter and Bill try to repeat the car journey from Edmunds' house to the betting shop and back, they realise it takes over 45 minutes. Regan joins them and they attempt the trip again, but it still takes too long. Haskins warns Regan that if he can't come up with a better case then he will no longer be regarded as a trustworthy officer: currently it appears that Regan is fitting Edmunds up.

Regan advises Marcia to change her statement to say Edmunds was out of sight for 45 minutes, but she refuses to perjure herself. However, she recalls that Edmunds is a keen motorcyclist and a bike is found hidden in a nearby lockup. Once again, the journey from the Edmunds' house to the betting shop is enacted, with the motorbike hidden by Edmunds, and this time is proven to be possible. Regan is off the hook but the DPP phone with bad news. The old woman has died in hospital and, without her testimony, the charges will be dropped. Marcia is hysterical about her husband's return and Regan asks her why she can't just leave him. She won't. Regan leaves her in disgust.

NEVER MIND THE DIALOGUE: The dinner party is a middle class comedy of manners in which the pompous Colonel Rosier insists that he's had a 'a bloody good bottle of wine!', despite his wife admonishing him for swearing. Edmunds confesses where he obtained it: 'Well, if you must know, Colonel, it fell off the back of a lorry !'

Defending Edmunds, Rosier declares the robbery charges are 'Preposterous, absolutely preposterous!' and is incensed at Regan's ignorance of fine wines: 'Inspector, do you have any idea what a '34 Chateaux d'Yquem is ?'

'You spend months slouching, drinking with social vermin, mortgaging your liver for a pension, and every now and then I feel I really deserve it when something nice, clean and unexpected turns up – like a ripe apple.' Regan's moment of poetry prefigures the moment when the forbidden fruit goes sour.

NAMES AND FACES: A distinguished radio and theatre actor, Norman Rodway appeared in *Reilly – Ace of Spies*, *The Lakes* and played a memorably mentally unbalanced colleague of Patrick McGoohan's John Drake in the *Danger Man* episode 'The Man Who Wouldn't Talk.' He played another menacing role as Bryce, the cop who put villain Frank Ross away in *Out*. James Cossins specialised in pompous military types, from an outboard motor salesman in *Fawlty Towers* to a sleazy MP who met a nasty end in the under-rated horror film *Death Line*.

POLICE AND THIEVES: *'Look, 'Carole', let's not muck about. You're a sexy suburban housewife on the make and I'm a hard-working copper. Now, you might just have some information for me... But I'm not a saint, and I might just fancy you.'* As Ranald Graham's previous scripts 'Cover Story' and 'Supersnout', Regan's personal relationships and his public duty become messily intertwined. Here, having slept with Marcia – one of the few times the series alludes to the Flying Squad having groupies – he becomes belligerent to the point of misogyny when he discovers Edmunds is her husband, and the arguments between the pair are particularly unpleasant. 'As soon as you felt I threatened your precious police purity, you turned off like a tap!', Marcia lambasts him, while he blames her when he's being accused of corruption.

Although at the end Regan regains the confidence of his colleagues, the tone is decidedly downbeat. Edmunds does over the sarcastically named Dead Cert Racing Shop in a false moustache and is one of the most professional villains in the series. He arrives back from the blag calm and collected, as if nothing has happened, and protests his innocence so convincingly even Carter has doubts. It's a nice irony that the Squad prove Edmunds did the robbery, only to have the means of prosecuting him denied them. Like Steven Castle in 'Sweet Smell of Succession', he is another educated and wealthy middle class criminal who gets away.

3.13 ON THE RUN

Writer : Roger Marshall
Director : David Wickes
First UK transmission : 20/12/1976 9.00-10.00 pm

CAST: George Sweeney (Tim Cook), Brendan Price (Pinder), John Sharp (Uncle), Jan Harvey (Pat), Dave Hill (Shayler), Alan Mitchell (Stackman) Keith James (Lakin), Anna Wing (Mrs Haldane), Roger Brierley (Psychiatrist), Malya Woolf (Nurse)

ON THE PLOT: Tim Cook (put away at the end of 'Taste of Fear') is sprung from captivity. The break is organised by Pinder, a gay prisoner who owes Cook after the ex-squaddie poured boiling water over one of his tormentors in prison. Cook has become even more unbalanced since his incarceration, and has developed an obsessive hatred of Regan.

Pinder is now on a rehabilitation programme, spending weekends in jail and living with his male lover, 'Uncle' Woodhouse, a prosperous ex-JP, the rest of the time. While Regan investigates, and subsequently rules out the possibility that Cook has left the country, Cook hides in a flat owned by Woodhouse, until he is spotted by a neighbour. He then squats in a cricket pavilion while Pinder arranges for him to move into Woodhouse's house. 'Uncle', who dotes on Pinder, readily agrees that his 'friend' can stay.

Regan tracks down Woodhouse via his flat, having also deduced the connection with Pinder. He warns the old man that he suspects him of harbouring a dangerous criminal. After Regan leaves, Woodhouse tells Cook to get out of the house. Losing it, Cook gives him a severe pasting and then hides out in the countryside with Pinder. Having been advised of Cook's state by a psychologist and also spoken to a hospitalised Woodhouse, Regan and Carter are alerted to Cook's location when a shotgun is stolen from a manor house and Pinder's jeep is found abandoned.

Pinder falls ill, and Cook forces a passing car to take him to hospital before checking his weaponry and blacking himself up like a commando. As the Squad cordon off the woods and search, he knocks several men, including Carter, unconscious. Finally Cook attacks Regan and nearly strangles him. In the nick of time, Carter recovers and pumps several bullets into the lunatic, killing him.

NEVER MIND THE DIALOGUE: Mrs Haldane, the neighbour who saw Cook, describes him as anthropoid – 'It's stuff you burn on stoves,' Regan explains to Carter afterwards. 'No, that's anthra*cite*.' Carter rejoins. 'Same thing,' Regan maintains.

Woodhouse bathes Pinder's feet, searching for words to describe the pleasure and settling on 'epicurean'. Later on in the same scene the question of Pinder's finances – his 'pocket money' – arises, and 'Uncle', in the manner of Oscar Wilde, drawls: 'There's nothing banal about money. Not having it, that is banal.' Ironically, the action cuts at the end of this scene to a shot of Cook vigorously doing his daily press-ups.

Jack's new girlfriend is called Pat Nightly. 'I knew her sister – Twice!' smirks George.

INSIDE INFORMATION: The third series of *The Sweeney* was filled out to 15 weeks with two repeated episodes and a film. Whether this was because the whole series was running behind schedule is not known, but getting 'On the Run' to meet its showing date was a nightmare for David Wickes. 'I remember delivering it to telecine from the lab an hour before it went on the air. *An hour!* he says. 'And I remember thinking, "Should it be a motorbike or a van? Could the motorbike get through the traffic quicker? What if he falls off? Have we got a back-up?" Oh, my God – *an hour!* And the people waiting at telecine had a hand held out: "Come on! Come on! We haven't rehearsed it yet!" The thing runs for 52 minutes, they have to have time to rewind it, and in the end they were down to five minutes!'

The location filming of Regan's nautical holiday was carried out at Virginia Water, which also had a convenient cricket ground nearby. Uncle's townhouse was in Hampstead, while Cook's escape in the lift was filmed in a closed-down wing of the old Hammersmith Hospital, 200 yards from Colet Court. Cook's guard in this scene was played by Del Baker, who appeared as Cowley in 'Regan'.

NAMES AND FACES: Brendan Price played DS Frank Bonney in the BBC'S *Sweeney* rip-off, *Target*. Dave Hill appears in the cop series *City Central*. Anna Wing went on to play Grandma Beale in *EastEnders*. John Sharp was one of the many Number 2s in *The Prisoner*. Jan Harvey has been a regular in *Howard's Way* and *Bugs*.

POLICE AND THIEVES: *'Cook really got under your skin, didn't he, Jack? He's your Mister Hyde.'* Allowed more screen time, Cook develops into a memorably psychotic creature of some depth, not unlike the villain in the first Dirty Harry film, although with a military twist. His psychotic attacks, aided by Ron Geesin's music 'Frenzy', are genuinely frightening, amplified by another unforgettable performance by George Sweeney.

The script and direction alludes to Cook throughout as a caged animal who has a 'psychopathic hatred of being cooped up' and is relegated to the fringes of a safe, rural England. He is constantly forced out of 'respectable' environments like Uncle's townhouse and the local cricket hut, and it's no surprise that he's shot and killed in open woodland, the only place he feels at home. The implication in 'Taste of Fear' that Cook was a repressed homosexual is made explicit here through his relationship with Pinder, a pretty boy gold-digger. His exploitation of Uncle Woodhouse's infatuation and leeching off his wealth again shows a corrupt underbelly to civilised society. However, Regan and Carter's lines about 'homo sapiens' and being 'fruity' have a dated, homophobic feel to them, although the script was merely reflecting the real attitude of some policemen to homosexuality.

The episode, and the third series, ends with a nasty manhunt with near-fatal consequences for Regan, and he returns to his girlfriend a battered mess. 'You're a rotten long-term risk, Jack,' she tells him as a freeze-frame close-up of his injured face fills the screen. The clear implication is that Regan is living on borrowed time.

With the benefit of hindsight, *The Sweeney* production team believe that it would have been better to have finished the programme after three series. 'On the Run', with drama, action, a memorable villain and an ominous low-key ending, would have been a dramatic and satisfying conclusion.

☙ CHAPTER 8 ☙

SERIES FOUR: LAST ORDERS

'**F**ROM BEING A FULL BLOODED, GRIPPING, CORPSE-BEFORE-THE-
credits thriller, with a real social message, one of our best home grown results,
Thames' *The Sweeney* (ITV Thurs Nov 23; 9.00 pm) has softened and wrinkled into a
squashy tomato.' So wrote critic Hazel Holt in *Stage and Screen* in 1978, commenting on
the marked difference between the fourth and final series of *The Sweeney* and its three
predecessors. Admittedly she was reviewing 'Hearts and Minds', a one-off comedy
episode featuring comedians Eric Morecambe and Ernie Wise, made as a goodbye
present from Thames for John Thaw and Dennis Waterman. However, there is
something to be said for Holt's assertion that in this episode the series had lost some of
its early hard edge.

'Hearts and Minds' was co-written by producer Ted Childs, who contributed several
other stories – 'Jack or Knave', 'Drag Act' and 'Latin Lady'. These stories contained a high
degree of humour mixed in with the drama, building on precedents set by earlier
episodes. However, this was balanced by a new tone of pessimism; for every comedy set
piece there was a miserable downside. There had been over a year's break between the
broadcast of the third series and the final one, and John Thaw looked visibly greyer and
world-wearier. Throughout the final season, Regan's character often seemed to be tired
and fed up, prefiguring developments in the final story 'Jack or Knave'. Overall, there
were various changes of style in this season, with all involved keen to keep the series as
fresh as possible.

The title sequence that accompanied the final stories illustrates how the programme
had changed. The blue-tinted animated car chase that accompanied earlier episodes had
now been replaced by a filmed car chase/punch-up, in effect a harder version of a scene
in the *Starsky And Hutch* titles. These titles ended with an uncalled-for shot of Regan
administering a blow to camera/punching the villain's face; a hint, perhaps, that the
programme had lost some of its subtlety. The closing titles, meanwhile, maintained an air
of poignancy and world-weary exhaustion, depicting Regan and Carter wandering
around the seedier parts of the West End, Regan finally stubbing a cigarette out on the
pavement as the sequence and the title music finished. Both the beginning and end titles
were shot with a mirrored lens, lending them a kaleidoscopic effect.

Haskins, previously shown in the blue-tinted sequence effectively wagging a severe-
looking finger at his subordinates, was instead relegated to the task of climbing out of the

back door of the Squad car at the heels of his colleagues. (Implicitly trailing after Regan, whose methods he no longer questioned.) This clip was sporadically edited in and out of the titles, depending on whether actor Garfield Morgan was appearing in that week's episode or not. For approximately half the episodes he did not appear, owing to other commitments. When absent, his role was filled by various 'guest guvnors' (including Geoffrey Palmer, Richard Wilson and, on several occasions, Benjamin Whitrow), who were mainly included for comic relief. Other guest stars this season included Diana Dors, George Sewell, Joss Ackland, Richard Griffiths and Lynda Marchal aka Lynda La Plante.

The core *Sweeney* writers continued to do the business, with Troy Kennedy Martin scripting the grimly funny 'Hard Men', which featured more incompetence, both the police and the villains raiding the wrong houses in the course of the story. Trevor Preston's opener to the season, the comical 'Messenger of the Gods', feels like a pilot for *Minder* in its presentation of small-time villain Lukie Sparrow's wedding. While he is another character who's caught between the police and other villains, in keeping with the lighter tone of Preston's script he averts the downbeat ending the criminals have in store for him, hitching a lift out of the Smoke in the sports car of a leggy blonde. In a pure *On the Buses*-style coda, Regan and Carter leg it on seeing the cantankerous Mrs Rix approaching.

This comedy is a contrast to Regan's terrifying speech to Lukie's friend Charlie Pearce about life in prison. 'You don't know what it's like in the nick, do yer? You can't breathe for the stink of sweaty bodies, stale food and slop outs... Doors slamming, keys rattling, yard boots on the catwalk... And when they lock you up at night there's some great big hairy con wanting you to be nice to him.' Showing that Preston had indeed retained his hard edge, the other two stories by him in this series, 'Money, Money, Money' and 'Bait', were decidedly more depressing in subject matter. In the latter, it seems to be only a matter of time before the police-hating Vic Tolman's out of jail again and after Regan's blood.

Ranald Graham's sole contribution, 'Nightmare', toned down the writer's usual emphasis on Regan but included another feature of the final series, the sense that Britain in the late-1970s was moving on. Jane, the New Age-type whom Regan shares a bed with in 'Nightmare', the punkettes in 'Messenger of the Gods' and Eddie Monk's vegetarian daughter whom Carter asks out in 'Money, Money, Money', were all indicative of social change. The implication was that Regan was becoming yesterday's man, a point underlined by the world-weariness and disillusionment he shows in several stories, in particular Richard Harris's key script, 'Trust Red'.

As in series three's 'Down to You, Brother', Regan identifies in 'Trust Red' with the villain, Redgrave, and both men poignantly reflect that they're getting too old for their respective lines of work. 'I'm overweight, George, d'you know that?' the tired DI tells Carter. 'I smoke too much, drink too much, most of the time I sit on my arse, and when I'm not doing that I'm chasing some lunatic whose sole intention given half the chance is to smash my bloody head in.' Redgrave, all too aware that he is getting too old for safe breaking, has a young and pregnant girlfriend. He is seen shopping with her by a friend of his ex-wife's, who acidly tells him, 'She thought it was your daughter.' George

Carter, by contrast, seems to be becoming Regan's surrogate son, staying on the DI's sofa after getting pissed at his birthday party. The duo's mates – *married* mates, Regan reminds Carter – have all gone home, and Regan's too 'knackered' to go after the two girls Carter has been eyeing up.

The Carter story of the season was Tony Hoare's 'One of Your Own', which showed George identifying more with villain Jimmy Fleet than with his colleagues, who he feels have let him down. (This was another proto-*Minder* episode, a series on which Hoare would become an important writer.) At the end, Carter gets the villain off the hook by disposing of his gun – the bond he has formed with Fleet is more important to him than the job. By comparison, Regan, the 'clockwork ferret', won't stop putting his role as a policeman first, ironic given that 'the job' is what finally leads him to resign.

Hoare's other script, 'The Bigger They Are', and Roger Marshall's 'Feet of Clay' both deal with people who have hidden pasts. In 'The Bigger They Are', the now wealthy and successful Leonard Gold is blackmailed over an atrocity committed some 20 years earlier during the Malaysian Emergency; police corruption also rears its head again. In 'Feet of Clay', Alan Ember, an old informant of Regan's who has taken on a new identity, is convinced that his son has been kidnapped; in fact, the lad is trying to con money out of his parents, unaware of his father's background. Regan sees through the scam straight away, pointing out that 'In our business you meet too many victims. Road accidents, burglaries, knifings, shootings… There's a look, a smell. You don't look right and you don't smell right.'

Genuine victims also became the theme of Marshall's last story. 'Victims' is the final series' Haskins episode, a grim story that did much to wrap the series up. The police achieve nothing at the end and are despised for the actions they have taken, which have left a small-time villain dead. The other victim is Haskins's wife: his overriding dedication to his police work has pushed his wife into a nervous breakdown. In Ted Childs' finale, 'Jack or Knave', the disillusionment is taken to its final, and totally logical stage. Accused but acquitted of corruption, Regan is finally provoked into resigning, declaring how 'totally and abjectly pissed off' he is before walking away from his colleagues. Based on the developments in the fourth series, if a fifth had been made, it seems reasonable to conclude that the episodes would have comprised 50 per cent situation comedy and 50 per cent outright despair.

Unlike many other series that outlasted their welcome, *The Sweeney* ended its four-year run without losing out to its rivals or compromising on its ability to provoke the viewer; arguably, a feature film every few years might have sustained the concept. However, as a television series, *The Sweeney* certainly quit while it was ahead, having reinvented British crime drama and firmly established itself in the national consciousness.

'The Sweeney's doing ninety 'cos they got the word to go
To get a gang of villains in a shed up at Heathrow…'
Squeeze, 'Cool for Cats', 1979

SERIES 4 REGULAR CAST
John Thaw (Detective Inspector Jack Regan)
Dennis Waterman (Detective Sergeant George Carter)
Garfield Morgan (Detective Chief Inspector Frank Haskins) (4-6, 10,11, 13,14)
Tony Allen (Bill)*

SERIES 4 RECURRING CAST
Benjamin Whitrow (Detective Chief Superintendent Braithwaite)
    (2,3,11[uncredited], 12)
Nick Brimble (Detective Constable Burtonshaw) (8)
James Warrior (Detective Constable Jellineck) (2,12)
Roger Davidson (Major Chapman) (2,12)
John Alkin (Detective Sergeant Daniels) (3,4,5,10,13)

*uncredited on screen

PRODUCTION TEAM: **Producer** Ted Childs, **Executive Producers** Lloyd Shirley, George Taylor, **Associate Producer** Mary Morgan, **Art Director** William Alexander (1,2,3,5-9,12,14), Martin Atkinson (11), Terry Parr (4,10), **Assistant Director** Michael Murray, **Location Manager** Brian Bilgorri, **Boom operator** Mike Silverlock, **Camera Operator** John Maskall (1,3-5,6,9-11,14), Mike Proudfoot (2,7,8,12), **Casting Director** Marilyn Johnson (1-3,5-14), Ann Felden (4), **Continuity** Phyllis Townsend, **Dubbing Mixer** Hugh Strain, **Focus** Mike Proudfoot (3,4,6,9,10, 14), Robin McDonald (1,2,5, 7,8,11,12,13), **Editor** Ian Toynton (3,6,8,10), John S Smth (1,2,4,5,9,11, 12,13,14), Peter Delfgou (7), **Hairdresser** Mary Sturgess, **Director of Photography** Dusty Miller (1,9,14), Norman Langley (2,4,5,11,13), Roy Pointer (3,6,7,8,10,12), **Make-up** Michael Morris (1,3,4,6,9,10,14), Eddie Knight (2,5,7,8,11,12,13), **Production Supervisor** Laurie Greenwood, **Sound Editor** Ian Toynton (1,4), Clive Smith (6,9,10,14), Mike Murr (2,5,7,8,11,12,13), **Sound Mixer** Tony Dawe (1,3,4,6,9,14), Derek Rye (2,5,7,8,11,12,13), John Brommage (10), **Stunt Arranger** Peter Brayham, **Wardrobe Master** David Murphy, **Technical Consultant** Jack Quarrie BEM, **Theme music** Harry South

4.1 MESSENGER OF THE GODS
Writer : Trevor Preston
Director : Terry Green
First UK transmission : 7/9/1978 9.00-10.00 pm

CAST: Diana Dors (Mrs Rix), Malcolm McFee (Lukie), Dawn Perllman (Linda Rix), James Ottaway (Uncle Billy), Richard Adams (Ray), Andrew Mussell (Rick), Rosemary Martin (Mrs Lipman), Fanny Carby (Dot Plummer), Michael Melia (Stan Rudd),

Derek Martin (Spooner), John Judd (Sergeant), Rosie Collins (Gloria), Michael Tarn (Charlie), Timothy Kightly (Vicar), Bernard Stone (Mr Lipman), Helen Keating (Cathy), Patrick Hannaway (Bernie), Cliff Diggins (Olly), Del Baker (Sid), Chris Webb (Arthur)

ON THE PLOT: Lukie Sparrow, petty crook and serial womaniser, is finally about to tie the marital knot with Linda Rix when Regan and Carter nick him for being involved in the theft of £30,000-worth of mercury – 'the messenger of the gods'. Lukie protests his innocence and his friend and housemate Charlie Pearce puts up an alibi – saying he heard Lukie working the toilet in his room – and he is subsequently released. Regan also has to contend with Lukie's prospective mother-in-law, fire-spitting Lilly Rix, who is furious at the disruption to her daughter's wedding.

By pressurising the wife of convict Dave Clayton, Regan and Carter subsequently find out that Lukie did take part in the blag, organised by hard man Albie Spooner. The villain escapes arrest and, mistakenly thinking that Lukie's turned grass, Spooner tells fellow face Stan Rudd to exact retribution.

The Rix brothers, who have found out about Lukie's womanising, are already leaning on him as Stan's group turn up outside the church where the wedding's being rehearsed. A punch-up ensues and Lukie scarpers. Carter finds and nicks Spooner and learns that the heat is on the soon-to-be bridegroom. Soon, everyone – cops, blaggers and the Rix family included – is out combing the streets, looking for 'the Clapham Casanova'.

Lukie tries to arrange a meeting with Linda Rix in a park, but her mother locks her in the khazi. Regan and Carter visit the Rix household, where they have a row with the mother, rescue Linda from being stuck on a window ledge and nick her two brothers. Linda tells the cops where Lukie is, and they race to the scene just in time to save Lukie. In the ensuing scrap, Stan and his associates are nicked but Lukie gets away, given a lift by an obliging leggy blonde.

NEVER MIND THE DIALOGUE: Dorothy Plummer, Lukie's batty landlady – 'Oh, I'm always in… except when I'm out' – going on about watching *Dr Terror's House of Horrors*: 'That Christopher Lee… put me right off me port, it did.'

The Rixes warn Lukie: 'If we catch you playing the Alsatian with any spare rattle, we're gonna chastise you.' However, their raucous, irascible mother steals the show, trying to organise the family from hell's wedding. She even tells the Vicar to shut up!

The highlight is a side-splitting scene where Regan and Carter visit the Rix household. They have a row with the mother, rescue Linda from being stuck on a window ledge and nick the two brothers – which causes Mrs Rix to faint. Stone-deaf Uncle Billy laughs his head off at this sight: 'She's sparked out, silly cow!' Regan's fed up response is: 'Oh, nick him an' all!'

Spooner gives Regan a bloody nose – when Carter points this out, Regan says, 'Must be the altitude.'

At the beginning, Regan sips Scotch and rehearses his after-dinner speech for the

Flying Squad social club, which contains a joke about Alcoholics Unanimous. It looks like this was a lively do, as the following morning Regan's lolling around in the squad car, groaning, 'Do you mind, George, I'm trying to work out what day it is.'

Mrs Rix doesn't like Lukie's hair, telling him to get it cut for the wedding: 'I don't want him looking like a poof in the photographs.'

Regan comes across as being fairly obnoxious – but realistic – in the scene where he threatens to tell convict Dave Clayton about his wife's affairs unless she gives him information.

INSIDE INFORMATION: The production team had reservations about going ahead with a fourth series of *The Sweeney*, as Trevor Preston remembers: 'We had a long meeting one night. We were all terribly protective of it. We knew we'd done three good ones. I'm not just talking about the writers; the directors, the actors, the crew, had stayed with us all the way through. What we were basically worried about was, "Are we going to do something that is going to denigrate what we've done before?" I don't think the fourth series was very good.'

Despite his feelings about the show's final year, Preston was more than happy with his first script for it. 'I loved doing 'Messenger of the Gods' because I wanted a change. It was my attempt to not always do the heavy ones. I got fed up being known as the guy who got people to kick the shit out of each other.' Working with the episode's major guest star also proved memorable. 'When we got Diana Dors to do it, we had a fucking ball. We turned up at this church and this vicar was a right crabby bugger, I thought "Jesus, this is going to be a fucking nightmare!" Everything we wanted to do we couldn't – "Don't sit on the pew, don't do that," and so on. Fucking Di turns up and she's got the full monty on. She gives the vicar a great big hug and he was eating out of her hand from then on. It was absolutely hilarious to do and I couldn't wait to go on location with her.'

The new title sequence, beginning with a car chase through Fulham gas works before Regan and Carter run after and arrest stunt arranger Peter Brayham, was devised by director Terry Green. 'He'd done a commercial using a prism on the lens of the camera, and he brought the idea of using it in,' John S Smith remembers. 'Ted Childs liked it, went for it, so you got this crazy effect. Ted was always open to suggestions and kept [the series] alive with new ideas.' Childs concurs that the new sequence was part of the production team's attempt to give *The Sweeney* a shakedown in style. 'The feeling was that it was getting a bit old and that was the stage where we were all questioning the wisdom of carrying on. Nobody had the courage not to, I suppose. I think we all knew that it was a great time and once it was over the spell would be broken, which it was.'

'Messenger of the Gods' also contains a sly dig at one of the show's critics. 'There was a guy who was Assistant Commissioner of CID – he came from traffic – who said, "We've got policemen wearing leather jackets and abusing the tea-ladies at our police stations because of your programme,"' Childs elaborates. 'Trevor wrote Regan a speech at a police dinner about a policeman wearing a white crash helmet, and this bloke went ballistic!'

Stan's pursuit of Lukie Sparrow was filmed in White City.

NAMES AND FACES: Derek Martin appeared as a bent copper, Fred Pyle, in G F Newman's police corruption drama *Law and Order*, an unpleasant one in *The Chinese Detective* and an ex-bent copper turned debt collector in Ian Kennedy Martin's 1986 series *King and Castle*. Diana Dors' tumultuous career, from wearing a mink bikini at Cannes in the 1950s to losing weight on TV-am in the 1980s, needs no introduction. Michael Melia later joined *EastEnders* as barman Eddie Royle. John Judd played a screw in *Scum*. Peter Craven was a regular in *Please, Sir!* and *The Fenn Street Gang*.

POLICE AND THIEVES: *'You two can just get back in your car and bugger off!'* Trevor Preston's opening story for *The Sweeney*'s final series kicks it off in fine style: a chase thriller with plenty of pace to keep the punters entertained and some very funny comedy. Lukie Sparrow is obviously a cousin of Adam Faith's *Budgie*, with his serial womanising and winning cockney wideboy cheek (although his pre-AIDS Jack-the-Lad promiscuity would doubtless not impress feminists). Like the best *Minder* episodes, which the story seems to prefigure, there is a serious theme mixed in with the comedy set pieces, in this case loyalty: Charlie Pearce, helping his mate Lukie out with an alibi, contrasts with the adulterous Cath Clayton and the paranoid Spooner, who seems jealous of Lukie's sexual conquests – 'That horny little bastard who grassed us...'

Thaw and Waterman are once again given the opportunity to show off their considerable comic gifts, and Diana Dors is hilarious. Judging by this superb opening night, it looked like the series was far from tired out.

4.2 HARD MEN

Writer : Troy Kennedy Martin
Director : Graham Baker
First UK transmission : 14/9/1978 9.00-10.00 pm

CAST: James Cosmo (Freeth), Stewart Preston (Ross), Jonathan Carr (Stronnach), Alex Norton (Gibson), Ronnie Letham (Hodgy Laing), Brian Hoskin (Bramley), Michael Beint (Dubbin), Julian Hough (Guards Officer), Roger Davidson (Major Chapman), Janet Ellis (Regan's girl), Miranda Forbes (Maggie's mother), Norman Lumsden (Sir Henry), Ian Ricketts (Boyd), David Stockton (PC), Natalie Pennington (Maggie), Sara Simmons, David Drummond (Dinner Party guests), Vickie Climas (Sir Henry's wife), Peggy Bullock (Old Lady)

ON THE PLOT: Detective Sergeant Freeth from Strathclyde CID arrives in London to arrest three Scottish 'Hard Men': Stronnach, Ross and Mannion. Regan and Carter are drafted to assist him, but on raiding the flat where the villains are holed up, they just find Stronnach's body – it seems the other two killed him in a row and then left. Freeth finds masking tape and rope in the flat, indicating the villains are in London to carry out a kidnapping. A photograph of some schoolgirls, with one of the faces ringed, is also discovered. Freeth seems to know more about the villains' intentions than he's prepared to let on… Regan, aware the pair were alerted by a phone call originating from Strathclyde nick, has Freeth's calls back to that station tapped.

Freeth approaches a member of a rival Glaswegian gang, Gibson, for information. He discloses the number of a telephone box that Ross uses, and also tells the DS that his associate, Hodgie Laing, is back in Glasgow. In return for the information, Freeth gives Gibson his criminal record. Carter tells the Scottish detective that he suspects Laing was in fact watching the exchange from nearby. Ross does show up at the phone box, but runs away as soon as he sees Freeth there.

A mother and daughter returning home find Ross and Mannion waiting for them. They attempt to kidnap the child but she runs off. The cops turn up in the wake of the attempted snatch and Freeth reveals that the villains visited the wrong address – they were trying to snatch the daughter of Joe Boyd, a big hoodlum in Glasgow, as part of a gang feud. Now Boyd has been alerted, Ross and Mannion will go to ground to avoid reprisals.

Freeth calls Boyd; the gang boss says he will take one of the pair as an example and leave the other to be arrested. Gibson subsequently shoots Ross with a flare pistol and burns to death in a Kings Cross street, while Freeth arrests Mannion. Freeth returns to Glasgow, leaving Carter and Regan aware that he's run rings around them.

NEVER MIND THE DIALOGUE: Freeth sums up by the prejudice directed at him: 'All the wogs start south of Calais and civilisation stops north of Watford.' There is much comical dialogue along these lines: 'I thought they ate porridge,' Carter reflects on seeing Freeth's liquid breakfast. 'They used to – until they found out it was healthy,' Regan rejoins.

The memo to Regan in the Squad office reads '7.00 am draw weapons, 8.00 am meet Scots loonie at Euston Station.' Jellineck defensively tells an irate Freeth that it's just a figure of speech.

There's a running joke about Freeth battering down doors with his head and sustaining injuries. 'Where I come from we don't batter down doors without a warrant,' he complains to Regan. 'Where you come from they batter everything from fried fish to their bleeding grandmothers,' Regan retorts.

More comedy: Freeth refers to cheap Scotch as 'Electric Soup' and Bill the driver gets the trots prior to a raid.

Gibson, the Scottish hit man known as the Preacher, justifies his sadism by spouting religion: 'So Saul died for his transgressions, which he committed against the Lord...' Raiding a flat, Regan, Carter and Freeth burst in on a pukka dinner party. Carter, thinking the guests are foreign art thieves, mistakenly reads the dinner guests their rights in pidgin Italian! The cops depart, and as the family carry on with their meal –

'a bird in the oven' – there's a crash from outside and more dodgy Italian from further down the corridor.

INSIDE INFORMATION: Director Tom Clegg remembers the senior Kennedy Martin's last script with affection: 'Troy could really write and he had a great sense of humour. His scripts would just make us laugh. For instance, the time when John was in bed with the girl with the Nazi helmet on – it was hilarious.'

The scenes of Freeth's arrival and departure were filmed in Euston Station.

NAMES AND FACES: Like several of his *Sweeney* contemporaries, Graham Baker started his directing career in commercials. He went on to direct feature films including *Beowulf, Omen: The Final Conflict* and *Alien Nation*, which was later developed into a TV series.

James Cosmo played another cop who liked a drink in the *Between the Lines* episode 'Manoeuvre 11' and another menacing Scot in *Stormy Monday*. Alex Norton played the lunatic McAngus in the first series of *The Black Adder* before taking over as the DI in the long-running Scottish detective series *Taggart*. Benjamin Whitrow (along with Jeremy Child) was one of Phil Daniels' carping bosses in *Quadrophenia*. Janet Ellis, mother of pop star Sophie Ellis Bextor, followed in Tina Heath's footsteps by presenting *Blue Peter*, while Norman Lumsden later spent much of his time looking for a book, *Fly Fishing* by J R Hartley, in the long-running Yellow Pages advert.

POLICE AND THIEVES: *'I don't want Boyd littering London with dead Scotsmen. If they want to batter each other to death let 'em do it in Glasgow.'* The humour in Troy Kennedy Martin's last television episode is as black as pitch and Graham Baker's direction reflects this, employing some superbly atmospheric lighting in Freeth's quest through the underworld. In an echo of the antipathy towards stereotyping seen in 'Visiting Fireman', it's revealed that Freeth has never eaten haggis, worn a kilt or seen Ben Nevis. He seems to be an old-fashioned lawgiver, not unlike those in various Westerns, discharging justice so rough even Regan would have second thoughts. James Cosmo is excellent as the monolithic DS, easily confounding Jack and George's moronic mickey-taking, and Freeth is such a fully realised character he would have warranted a spin-off series.

The comedy subplot of a painting stolen from the Palace enriches arguably Troy Kennedy Martin's best script for *The Sweeney*, containing another of his trademark subversions of the series. Regan, the nominal hero, contributes nothing towards the plot resolution, heading off instead in search of sexual gratification – again indulging his fetish for German helmets.

4.3 DRAG ACT

Writer : Ted Childs
Director : Tom Clegg
First UK Transmission : 21/9/1978 9.00-10.00 pm

CAST: Katherine Fahy (Julie Kingdom), Albert Welling (Mike Seton), Patrick Malahide (Mason), Peter Kerrigan (Bowyer), Roger Hume (Lockhart), Derek Deadman (Curry), John Rolfe (DCS Brookford), Dave Atkins (Marriot), John Hartley (Chief Inspector), David Foxxe (Cyril), Oliver Smith (Lorry Driver), Vivienne Johnson (Mavis), Rachael Dix (Marriot's girlfriend)

ON THE PLOT: The Squad are tipped off about a lorry theft in Harlington – or possibly Honiton. Carter sends a team of officers to Honiton, but they have a car accident, which causes political flack for the Squad. At a lorry depot in Harlington, Regan and Carter find the theft has occurred, as a lorry container full of brandy has been taken and replaced with an identical one containing an old banger. The cops visit Regan's informant Cyril, and then Carter teams up with Julie Kingdom, an ambitious new WPC in Harlington nick, as he tries to ascertain if the gang are operating in that area. He quickly becomes romantically involved with her.

Soon a second lorry is stolen; the Squad have it staked out but after a car smash, they lose it. The driver is later murdered, and plastic tubing packed with heroin is found in the petrol tank. It's eventually decided that this is an unconnected drug smuggling case. Meanwhile, Julie and another young probationer PC, Mike Seaton, believe a local fence, Marriot, could be involved in Carter's case. They track down the stolen booze at a farm belonging to one of Marriot's associates, a farmer called Curry. Seaton is injured, and Regan is angry with Julie when he realises there isn't any evidence that Marriot handled the booze. She tells him she discussed her observation of Marriot with Carter. The DS agrees and admits he wasn't listening properly at the time.

Braithwaite has meanwhile heard that Carter has been 'over the side' with a WPC, and warns Regan that he wants no more mention of Julie Kingdom's name or Carter will be slung out of the Squad. She meanwhile suggests checking Curry's stash of booze for Marriot's fingerprints, which successfully proves his guilt. However, on Regan's advice, Carter takes the credit for finding the incriminating evidence to save his career. Julie ends the relationship with Carter and is returned to more menial duties.

NEVER MIND THE DIALOGUE: 'He's got the place bugged – don't come in here looking for a bit of quick relief, he'll fit you up for life,' Regan warns Carter on paying a visit to Cyril, the camp massage parlour proprietor who earwigs on his clients.

'You look like you could do with a bit of quick friction,' Cyril tells Carter. Regan promptly threatens to set the VAT inspectors on him.

Braithwaite refers to some gloriously bad driving, leading to an incident involving a minibus full of OAPs, a judge's greenhouse and a 90-year-old ex-nanny making a citizen's arrest of a Squad car. During a later chase, the driver of a stolen lorry is considerate enough to indicate on leaving a roundabout. 'Bloody cheek!', Regan snarls.

Regan has his lighter flame set too high and nearly singes Braithwaite's 'tache with it.

INSIDE INFORMATION: 'Drag Act' was the first story written for *The Sweeney* by Ted Childs following his uncredited editing of the series' scripts. This was partly motivated by the producer having an eye on future work: 'I could see it coming to an end, and I started thinking, "Where do I go next?"'

The episode features one of *The Sweeney's* most spectacular crashes, when one of the Squad's cars swerves to avoid a collision with a lorry and ploughs through a fence, turning over in the process. Such stunts never had the luxury of a retake. 'Everything we did where we turned a car over and crashed it was Take 1,' Peter Brayham says. 'We never, ever had another car. Camera crews – forget it. We only ever had two cameras most of the time and I had to beg for a third one. Even having a second camera was a special day, normally when we worked two extended days a week.'

A clip from 'Drag Act' featured in an episode of the first series of the comedy drama *Cold Feet*, where Adam (James Nesbitt) can be seen enjoying satellite repeats of his favourite seventies cop show. Appropriately enough, *The Sweeney* theme was played over a ruck between police and clubbers later in the same story.

NAMES AND FACES: Dave Atkins has continued to portray a number of iffy geezers, including Gary Oldman's dad in *The Firm* – 'In my day we'd 'ave just gone round there and given 'em a good kicking.' Patrick Malahide plagued Arthur Daley as recurring plod Chisholm in *Minder*, was later mistakenly pursued by *Inspector Morse* in the episode 'Driven to Distraction', and took the lead role in the period piece *The Inspector Alleyn Mysteries*. He also appeared as Mark Binney in the seminal 1980s drama *The Singing Detective*. Peter Kerrigan played dodgy businessman Malone in *Boys from the Blackstuff*.

POLICE AND THIEVES: *'Jack, have they get a loo here?'* Regan's sozzled girlfriend asks at the start, in contrast with the intelligent Julie Kingdom, who effectively solves the case.

'Drag Act' is a good example of Ted Childs' attempt to push *The Sweeney* in different directions in its final year: the episode seems at times to be a feminist critique of the machismo inherent in the series, as the police hierarchy are reluctant to admit that a 'junior femme fatale has stolen a march on us'. It's interesting to note that the uniformed police involved are all young and inexperienced, just starting out and not all coping with the demands of the job.

Aside from a spectacularly staged car crash, this episode has another of the series' comic highlights, which conversely emphasises the boredom, frustration and unpleasantness of police work. Regan, Braithwaite, Daniels and other Squad men sit on obbo in a van, getting on each other's nerves: Daniels accidentally-on-purpose sprays Braithwaite when he opens a can of lager. Braithwaite sits with his legs crossed, dying for a leak, unable to face the indignity of using the milk bottle like the rest of the lads. He finally rushes outside to relieve himself on the side of the van instead, and is promptly taken to task by a disgusted passer-by.

4.4 TRUST RED

Writer : Richard Harris
Director : Douglas Camfield
First UK transmission : 28/9/1978 9.00-10.00 pm

CAST: John Ronane (Red), John J Carney (Eric), Sara Clee (Jo), Gretchen Franklyn (Charlady), Nigel Humphreys (Con), Hilary Crane (Jean), Anthony O'Donnell (Maurice), Tim Thomas (Billy Boy), Alec Linstead (Optician)

ON THE PLOT: A gang led by Con have been committing a string of robberies, utilising the climbing and electronics skills of Redgrave, a 45-year-old ex-para. On their latest job, however, young Billy Boy, who's got an amphetamine habit, slips from a roof and falls to his death. Forced to dump the body in the countryside, Redgrave becomes depressed; as Billy's father is seriously ill in hospital, there is no one to grieve. 'Red' is also becoming aware that he is getting too old for the game, despite fellow crook Eric's assurances that he is the real talent in Con's firm. He finds out that he needs to start wearing glasses and learns that his estranged wife wants a divorce. Relations are also becoming strained with Jo, his young, pregnant girlfriend

Investigating the robberies, Regan starts to suspect that one of the gang was hurt on their last job. After some deliberation, 'Red' anonymously tips off the law about the location of Billy's body. Regan suspects Redgrave's involvement following an interview with him. He is aware the man is a career criminal who up until now has evaded capture. Something tells him Red's time is up.

The Squad get another lead when they see an old cleaning lady passing on information to Con's gang, and realise where the gang next intend to strike. Carter is puzzled by Redgrave's motivation in tipping the Squad off about the body, but Regan recognises that Redgrave is in two minds; part of him wants to be caught and part of him can't resist going on one last job. The Squad move in and nick the gang in the act, and Redgrave, trying to escape, falls through a glass roof. Con is convinced that Redgrave has done a deal with Regan and grassed. Regan assures the injured Redgrave he will sort this misunderstanding out.

NEVER MIND THE DIALOGUE: Regan speculates on self-doubt: 'Good villain, good copper, good soldier even. One thing in common; it's over the top, chaps, get on with the job, to hell with tomorrow, to hell with the consequences. Because once you stop to think, once you stop to consider the ifs, the buts, the maybes... You've blown it.'

Red's girlfriend Jo to Regan: 'You know the first time you came here you scared the life out of me. My God, I didn't know things like you existed.' 'I think they call it lying down with dogs,' he replies.

The charlady supplying inside information on which offices to blag insists: 'Whatever I do, I do for my grandchildren.'

INSIDE INFORMATION: 'Regan's own personality as reflected in those he was after interested me,' writer Richard Harris says of his work on the series. 'It was the nub of my scripts. In 'Trust Red' it's not so much the crime as the fact that the criminal was getting over the hill and, for whatever reasons, couldn't stop. That's where I started. One middle-aged man who smoked too much running after another middle-aged man climbing up walls to support a family.'

NAMES AND FACES: Gretchen Franklyn's batty old lady is very similar to her later role as Ethel Skinner in *EastEnders*. John Ronane played a copper called Singer in *Strangers*, one of Detective Inspector George Bulman's undercover team. Nigel Humphreys played other hard men in *Scum* and *The Long Good Friday*.

POLICE AND THIEVES: *'You never get the job out of your mind, do you?'* A poignant character piece without much action but with plenty to say about age and responsibility, 'Trust Red' is a moody change of pace from the opening three stories, giving the first hints of Regan's dissatisfaction with his lot. Douglas Camfield, in the last story he directed, handles the serious material well, with several night sequences emphasising the bleak tone. The story is particularly memorable for Red's climactic fall through a skylight that ends his career as a criminal.

Redgrave is given a similar role to Meadows in Richard Harris's 'Down to You, Brother': Regan identifies with him, as both men are driven by motives they can no longer explain and are getting too old for their respective careers. Significantly, while Regan's younger confidant, Carter, warns his boss that he's got to switch off, Redgrave's colleagues push him into one last job. The overall melancholia even affects Carter. He gets smashed at his birthday do in the pub and ends up kipping on Regan's sofa, admitting, before passing out, that his promiscuity arises from the fact that he's 'ever so lonely'.

4.5 NIGHTMARE

Writer : Ranald Graham
Director : David Wickes
First UK transmission : 5/10/1978 9.00-10.00 pm

CAST: Paul Antrim (Farrell), Tony Rohr (Flynn), Barry Philips (Keith Wilson), David Gillies (Norman Charles), Lea Brodie (Jane), Kenneth Watson (Horrocks), J G Devlin (Hey), Enid Irvin (Mrs Charles), Alfred Maron (Stirk), Linda Brill (Maire), Ritchie Stewart (Café owner), David Ellison (Dutchman)

ON THE PLOT: Jane, Regan's hippy-ish girlfriend, has a nightmare in which Regan's in danger and is finally blinded. Oddly enough, elements from the dream start to come true when three London villains trying to steal a lorryload of cigars in Harwich get a nasty surprise. The Dutch lorry driver pulls out a shooter, kills one of the gang and wounds another before being shot himself. Two other faces, Farrel and Flynn, then arrive on the scene just as the surviving robbers are fleeing. They are ex-IRA men who were due to rendezvous with the Dutchman. One of the lorry drivers dies in hospital from a gunshot wound, and the sole survivor is soon tracked down and killed by Farrel and Flynn, who repossess their stolen cigars.

Regan and Carter, one step behind the killers, hear that an old soak, Hey, is knocking out cheap cigars in a Kilburn pub. They lean on him until he divulges where he got them from – Farrel and Flynn's dilapidated antiques shop. Regan and Carter meet with the two men at the shop and are warned off touching a particular piano. Outside, the cops are nearly killed when Flynn 'accidentally' reverses a lorry in their direction.

Regan and Carter break into the shop again at night and search the piano, finding the 'cigars' – containing cocaine – hidden inside. The next day the Squad tail Farrel and Flynn as they transport the coke to a farmhouse in the country.

Haskins liaises with Special Branch and organises a raid, but when a plane lands at the farm Regan feels he has no choice but to storm the building with just Carter for back-up. Inside, the coke is being exchanged for laser-sighted rifles that Farrel and Flynn hope to buy their way back into the IRA with. In the mayhem that follows, both Irishmen are shot and Farrel's young daughter snatches up the gun and fires wildly, before being disarmed by Carter. Regan is temporarily blinded by the laser sight but later recovers in hospital.

NEVER MIND THE DIALOGUE: Regan gets his usual share of one-liners from Ranald Graham. Visiting the mortuary to examine the body of one of the blaggers, he says: 'Right, let's have a look at sleeping beauty!'

Jane tells him about her dream – 'There was a huge thing bearing down on you'. 'Sounds like the barmaid of my local.'

Regan is furious after Flynn nearly runs him down in the alley behind the antique shop; the Irishman asks him what he was doing there. 'I was taking a leak, Seamus – and next time I see your face I'll do it on that!'

Regan tries to give up smoking and then finds he's 'spending the whole of his waking life looking for cigars'. Even Haskins has one of his rare smokes – perhaps to wind the DI up. Needless to say, Regan's experiences prompt him to light up in his hospital bed at the end.

Regan claims he is doing the public a service by shacking up with Jane, the precognitive 'health food nymphomaniac.'

INSIDE INFORMATION: 'The lorry café was on the A1. It was a famous one at the time but has, I believe, now closed,' director David Wickes says of the location filming. Even though the episode featured an impressive range of hardware, including articulated trucks and a light plane, 'Nightmare' had to keep to the same budget as other stories. 'There was a kind of ad hoc robbing of Peter to pay Paul,' Wickes goes on.

'Occasionally, one director would say to another: "I've got a wages blag next week. Can you finish with your security van a day early so I can smash it up on Monday?" All very unofficial, of course. In this case, I remember that the location manager, Stephen Pushkin, had just got his pilot's license and, I think, he got the plane for half price. It really was an hour by hour, day by day series of little negotiations, but it seemed to work for us.'

NAMES AND FACES: Paul Antrim portrayed another terrorist discredited by his organisation in the Birmingham-based series *Gangsters*. J G Devlin made a career playing disreputable Irishmen, such as in the *Steptoe and Son* episode 'The Desperate Hours' and in *Z-Cars'* 'Friday Night'. Kenneth Watson played a semi-regular character in *The Brothers*.

POLICE AND THIEVES: *'You are about to sit the final exam for the Chinese Civil Service. There's only one question and no time limit – tell me all you know.'* Jane's precognitive dream gives the episode its title and is an unusual touch, possibly influenced by the bizarre experiments in format going on in other police serials. (*Starsky and Hutch's* later episodes, screened around the same time, featured Voodoo and a vampire.) While this incongruity gives 'Nightmare' a quirky feel – it's the only episode of this tough police series to touch on the paranormal, after all – it's actually unneccessary, as this is a gripping and entertaining story in its own right. The higher than normal quota of action scenes give 'Nightmare' the feel of a superior instalment of *The Professionals* in places. (A very similar weapon to the laser-sighted rifle crops up in the episode 'Hunter/Hunted'.) There's some good, underplayed continuity too: following Jack's middle-aged ennui in the previous episode, he's given up smoking, is drinking herbal tea and is going to the gym. Following his near-blinding in the tense conclusion, it's not surprising that's he's back on the booze and fags by the end of the story.

The episode is also the only *Sweeney* story to deal directly with the Irish Republican Army, however nervously. It's surely no coincidence that Jack's comment that the IRA 'don't push drugs' rings a little hollow.

4.6 MONEY, MONEY, MONEY

Writer : Trevor Preston
Director : Sid Roberson
First UK transmission : 12/10/1978 9.00-10.00 pm

CAST: Edward Judd (Eddie Monk), Vilma Hollingbury (Anne Monk), Tina Martin (Kath), Glyn Owen (Wally Hough), Michael Culver (Dave Leeford), John Cater (Sleman), James Bree (Saxby), William Simons (Pope), Christine Shaw (Mrs Norris), Lionel Haft (Fischer)

ON THE PLOT: Eddie Monk, a villain who's gone straight and is now a mate of Regan's, gets a big win on the football pools. Soon after his windfall is made public, he starts being blackmailed. Eleven years before, with other villains Alec Sleman and the late Ken Norris, Eddie did a robbery in which Norris injured a nightwatchman. Fischer, a blackmailer who has shacked up with Norris's widow, is demanding £10,000 not to tell the police.

Withholding this turn of events from his wife Anne and his daughter Kath, Eddie goes to pay Fischer off, but is well aware it won't stop there. He visits Sleman and warns him of the situation: if they don't sort the blackmailer out, they'll both go down. Eddie is starting to fall apart under the pressure of keeping his secret. He slaps his wife when she asks about the withdrawal from their bank account, and then goes out and gets drunk.

When Fischer demands another £5000, Monk and Sleman set a trap for him but it backfires, and Eddie, struggling to stop Fischer driving away with the cash, dies after falling from his car. Sleman legs it.

Regan and Carter comfort Monk's family. Wally Hough, once Regan's mentor, gives Regan a tip-off about Monk's old firm and the pair pull in Sleman. He tells all about the blackmailing and the third man, Ken Norris. Paying Norris's widow a visit the cops realise that Fischer is Eddie's killer, and when he enters the flat they arrest him. Regan furiously beats up Fischer before Carter steps in.

Anne Monk decides the rest of the pool winnings should go to the family of the dead nightwatchman.

NEVER MIND THE DIALOGUE: Regan on visiting his local bank: 'Every time I walk in they think I'm about to blag the place!'

Carter has a bit of a thing going with Eddie's vegetarian daughter: 'Has he told you he's a practising heterosexual?' Regan warns her. There's also a reference to Carter losing his wife 'a few years back'.

Regan comments on a bent brief: 'If he put his hand down the lav he'd come up with a box of chocolates.'

INSIDE INFORMATION: 'I always used to choose a subject for every *Sweeney* I wrote,' writer Trevor Preston says. 'This one was about remorse. I wanted to write about a man that had never laid a finger on his wife or kids and in one moment of stress he slaps her. That moment is really what it's all about: it wasn't that he'd won the pools and somebody wanted to dob into that, it was that fact that he couldn't forgive himself for striking his wife.'

NAMES AND FACES: Sid Roberson went on to work on Richard Carpenter's adaptation of *Robin of Sherwood* and the off-beat Highland community drama *Hamish Macbeth*, before turning to comedy such as *The Fast Show* and the Simon Nye series *My Wonderful Life*.

Edward Judd is well remembered for his safety adverts – 'Think once, think twice, think Bike!' He was also the lead in two under-rated British science fiction films, *The Day the Earth Caught Fire* and *Invasion*. Glyn Owen was often in demand as a character actor in the 1970s and eventually became a regular in *Howard's Way*. Michael Culver appeared as Brandt in the first two series of *Secret Army* and guested in *The Adventures of Sherlock Holmes* and the Len Deighton movie thriller *Game, Set and Match*. Lionel Haft played Maureen Lipman's son in a long-running series of British Telecom adverts.

POLICE AND THIEVES: *'There's a lot of room at the bottom.'* Downbeat and dramatic, featuring another of Preston's grey characters, cracking up and getting desperately out of his depth. As in 'Stay Lucky, Eh?' and 'May', working class family life is torn apart and the attitudes of the older, largely non-violent generation of villains is contrasted with the amoral new breed. Eddie is guilt-stricken over hitting his wife Anne, while his persecutor Fischer shows no compunction in assaulting women to get what he wants.

The story concentrates on pathetic middle-aged figures who are ruined by events in their past lives. Both Eddie and ex-cop Wally Hough, whose wife died of cancer, hit the bottle and Sleman, who has also tried to put his past behind him by going into legitimate business, is undone by his past association with crime. Money (the curse of mammon again) is once more rejected at the conclusion; it will not bring Eddie back.

In an echo of Preston's earlier script 'Abduction', a furious Regan gives the villain a beating at the conclusion and Carter has to intercede. Fischer, the blackmail man, is one of Preston's most odious villains, having no code of honour at all.

4.7 BAIT

Writer : Trevor Preston
Director : Sid Roberson
First UK transmission : 19/10/1978 9.00-10.00 pm

CAST: George Sewell (Vic Tolman), Barbara Ewing (Joan), Di Trevis (Lynn), Edward Peel (Lennie), Arthur Cox (Roan), Eric Dodson (Mr Dodds), Alan Hunter (Stoddard), Steven Barnes (Dr Marland), Judy Buxton (Salesgirl), Frederick Bennett (Factory Gatekeeper), Alan Leith (Sgt Stern), Diana Rowan (Traffic Warden), Michael Brodie (Guard), Simone Cowdrey (Little Girl)

ON THE PLOT: The notorious Vic Tolman, recently sprung from prison by his girlfriend Lynn Hearst, has pulled off a string of wages snatches. When Lynn crashes her car and runs away from the ambulance that was meant to take her to hospital, Regan and Carter are alerted that the couple are at work in the Smoke. The detectives find that Lynn's car was parked outside a flat inhabited by ex-convict Joan Maskall; Lynne's six-year-old daughter is being looked after by the woman. Regan illicitly searches the flat while Joan is out and finds a doll. Tracing this to a toyshop, he realises it was purchased for the child by Lynn. She is posing as a dowdy clerk in the wages office of a nearby factory and returns to work, claiming her recent absence was due to a cold.

She drugs everyone's coffee, forcing Dodds, the manager, to drink his when he remains conscious. Meanwhile, Tolman and the retarded heavy Lennie gain access to the works posing as new staff. Lennie floors a security guard and the trio make off with over £82,000.

The three crooks hole up in the country and contemplate a break for a few weeks. Lynn is concerned: using Lennie on more jobs is bound to increase their chances of being caught. She wants to spend more time with her daughter. Tolman will have none of it; he hates the police and has more jobs planned.

Regan hears through a telephone intercept that Lynn's daughter is unwell with measles. A doctor informs Joan that complications may set in and the child is taken to hospital. Against Tolman's advice, Lynn returns to Joan's flat intending to visit the child, and, after a fight, Regan and Carter nick both women. The cops wait at the flat. Tolman, realising Lynn isn't answering the phone, decides to return to London and fetch her. In a struggle, Lennie is shot. Tolman nearly escapes with Regan as a hostage before the DI crashes their getaway car. Tolman is dragged away, screaming that he isn't finished yet...

NEVER MIND THE DIALOGUE: Bill finally gets a line: when Carter whinges about Regan's illegal search of the flat, he agrees with George: 'Not many.' (A cockney expression meaning 'a lot')

'I like Jags, they're my favourites!' the intellectually challenged northern villain Lennie reminds everyone every so often. To his disappointment, Tolman gets him a Zodiac instead.

Vic Tolman employs the 'rather obvious' Lennie to make his robberies even more daring, as if it's all a game between him and the police, whom he has it in for. 'I hate 'em. Lying, grafting, thieving lice! They wouldn't know an honest man if he pissed on their boots. I hate 'em!'

Tolman, on finding Lennie's been shot dead: 'You scum! You dirty, filthy, festering scum!'

INSIDE INFORMATION: Sid Roberson was another director to come from a background in television commercials. 'I felt – and I don't know if I was justified in this – that they would give *The Sweeney* a bit of visual flair,' Ted Childs reflects. 'One of the problems you have with commercials directors is that they're used to making 30-second movies so it's a little bit of a learning curve for them. At the end of the day it was still television so you needed close-up interrogation scenes for that dramatic conflict. Sometimes commercials directors found that a bit difficult.'

Group 4 again loaned a security van to *The Sweeney* production team for this episode. The product placement did them no favours, as the script states that Tolman always 'susses out places where the security's weak'!

NAMES AND FACES: George Sewell played Detective Chief Inspector Craven opposite Patrick Mower as DCI Haggerty in *Special Branch*, and numerous other heavy roles on both sides of the law. He was particularly memorable as the thuggish Con in *Get Carter*, Sewell also spoofed his hard man persona with his role in *The Detectives*. Edward Peel changed sides to play a cop in *Out* and *Juliet Bravo*. Barbara Ewing starred with Timothy West in the 'trouble at mill' comedy *Brass*. Arthur Cox's television work includes *The Avengers, Richard III, The House of Elliot* and *She-Wolf of London*, a series made for HTV but unscreened on terrestrial channels owing to its violent content. Di Trevis became a director of the RSC.

POLICE AND THIEVES: *'It's all a bloody great game with you as well, innit?'* This has parallels with the film *Bonnie and Clyde*, which also featured a pair of police-baiting dysfunctional criminal lovers. Preston takes an unusual line on the theme of family loyalty, portraying Tolman, Lynn and Lennie as a surrogate family rather than a gang. It's ironic that Lynn's commitment to her real family, her daughter – the 'bait' of the title – and Vic Tolman's attachment to his adopted one ultimately gets all three of them either caught or killed. Tolman himself is a memorably psychopathic character, submerged in revenge fantasies and lost in a world he sees as chaotic and meaningless. Lynn and Vic are also sophisticated blaggers, working undercover on a vulnerable target and using knock-out drugs rather than strong-arm tactics to effect a robbery.

Despite this novel look at villainy, the usual excitement and tension is missing, and Carter's quips about 'Uncle' Joan's sexual orientation grate more than they did in 'Abduction'. However, the exciting end scenes make up for these deficiencies.

4.8 THE BIGGER THEY ARE

Writer : Tony Hoare
Director : Mike Vardy
First UK transmission : 26/10/1978 9.00-10.00 pm

CAST: Colin Jeavons (Gold), Jenny Runacre (Sharon), Raymond Skipp (Collins), Tony Steedman (Masterson), Donald Burton (Grey), Colin McCormack (Wade), Ian Collier (Logan), Trevor Thomas (Garner), Richard Hampton (Barnes), Richard Wilson (Anderson), John Carlin (Pierce)

ON THE PLOT: Millionaire Sir Leonard Gold hides a secret – 25 years ago in Malaya, his platoon was responsible for massacring a village of civilians. Collins, a crook who is under Squad surveillance, finds out about this from some papers his civil servant brother bequeathed to him in a deposit box. He visits Gold and attempts to blackmail him.

Gold stalls Collins, asking for proof of the existence of the papers. In the meantime he contacts his old CO, Masterson, a mercenary turned security firm owner, for some 'help'. Collins, unaware that Wade and Logan, two mercenaries in Masterson's employ, are tailing him, tries to gain access to the deposit box. He finds he can't without a solicitor's letter, and gets a friend, Garner, to forge the requisite paperwork. Admitted to the National Anglian Bank, Collins uses a miniature camera to photograph the papers. Garner, left to develop the film, is jumped by the two mercenaries and later has a visit from an increasingly curious Regan. The Squad have been warned off watching Collins by another of Masterson's old platoon, Grey, who is now high up in Special Branch, but Regan has decided to ignore this 'security matter'.

Hearing about both Regan and the mercenaries, Collins does a bunk to Brighton. Gold, however, still wants the papers destroyed. Masterson, Logan and Wade execute a commando-style raid on the National Anglian Bank, stealing the deposit box. Wade is caught and shortly afterwards Regan deduces the connection with Collins from his brother's name on the missing box. He intends to confront Grey but the latter, appalled by the bank raid, has already turned himself in. Grey reveals that Masterson has turned on both him and Gold, wanting money off the millionaire and his future co-operation in dealing with the police. Hearing this confession, Regan arrests Masterson; Gold, however, is unable to handle the disgrace and shoots himself.

NEVER MIND THE DIALOGUE: Gold was originally working class himself and resents giving money to Collins: 'Do you think I got where I am by being intimidated by offal like you?' 'Slaughtering helpless women and kids makes you Mister Wonderful, does it?' Collins retorts.

Collins tells Leroy he can't do anything 'with that lawyer breathing down my Gregory.' (Gregory Peck = neck.)

The bank manager asks what evidence Regan's got on Collins: 'He's a villain and I know he's at it.'

NAMES AND FACES: Colin Jeavons regularly played Inspector Lestrade in Granada Television's *Sherlock Holmes* series, and also turned in a memorable performance as Francis Urquhart's slimy ally Stamper in *House of Cards* and *To Play the King*. Jenny Runacre had recently appeared in the punk film *Jubilee* and also starred as the karate-kicking, vampiric Miss Brunner in *The Final Programme*.

Richard Wilson rocketed to fame playing the curmudgeonly Victor Meldrew in *One Foot in the Grave*. Donald Burton played the commander of HMS Hero in the first two series of the BBC's naval drama *Warship*. Colin McCormack's television appearances include *Supply and Demand*, *Pie in the Sky* and *Kavanagh QC*.

POLICE AND THIEVES: *'The rich and powerful are heirs to the sins of the flesh just like the rest of us.'* This story sees the fourth series broaden its range still further, with the cover-up of a military atrocity in high places and more corruption in the police. With only a little adaptation, the plot would have worked as an instalment of the BBC's police internal investigation drama *Between the Lines*. The exposition of the story is well executed and the subject matter is commendably serious.

Oddly for a story that deals so intelligently with a less than glorious episode of Britain's colonial past, 'The Bigger They Are' is marred by the racial stereotyping of Gold and Leroy. The latter's jive talk, crudely copied from Blaxploitation flicks such as *Shaft* ('We're gonna choreograph a real fancy letter to this manager dude'), is amusing but laughably unrealistic, although it's hinted that both Leroy and the 'honkie bitch' he lives with might just be putting it on to look cool.

4.9 FEET OF CLAY

Writer : Roger Marshall
Director : Chris Burt
First UK transmission : 2/11/1978 9.00-10.00 pm

CAST: Joss Ackland (Alan Ember), Thelma Whiteley (Margot Ember), Brian Capron (Colin), David Wilkinson (Paul Ember), Cheryl Campbell (Erica), Geoffrey Palmer (Cdr Watson), Philippa Gale (DCI Barton), Robert Oates (DI Hinxman), John Junkin (Taxi Yard proprietor), Diana Weston (WPC Janet Reynolds), Stuart Blake (Doctor), Marc Zuber (Abdul), Carol Drinkwater (Roz), Richard Mottau (Peck), John G Heller (Casino manager), Lydia Lisle (Mary), Wendy Young (Jo)

ON THE PLOT: Alan Ember, a wealthy ex-villain who turned Queen's Evidence for Regan in the 1960s and changed his identity, is woken by a phone call – his son Paul's been kidnapped and is on the line, screaming. In desperation, Ember contacts Regan.

Regan and Carter are currently working with the Serious Crime Squad, looking into a series of robberies of wealthy Arab tourists outside various casinos. The robbers are operating a fake taxi, taking cash, travellers' cheques and jewellery. Their latest victim, Abdul, is hospitalised and even his hotel room has been robbed. Forced to break off from this case by Ember's call, Regan agrees to help out his old informant and enlists Carter's help.

The men soon rule out the possibility that one of the people Ember's evidence put away is responsible. They tape record the kidnappers' calls and also interview Paul's girlfriend Erica. A call comes through to leave ransom money in a car; Regan and Carter arrest the youth tuning up to collect the motor but he's just a go-between who knows nothing. The Embers receive a further phone call from Colin, Paul's 'kidnapper'. It becomes clear that the lad hasn't been snatched at all and is happily trying to extort money out of his father.

Regan gets a ticking off from Commander Watson about his lack of attention to the casino robberies, and goes along with the plan to plant undercover cops in one of the casinos. A game is fixed so an officer posing as a customer gets a big win. As the robbers grab him, the Squad move in and arrest them. In the meantime, despite Regan's attempts to dissuade him, Ember goes out and pays off Colin.

Paul is subsequently returned home, but his lack of consistency over the details of his captivity, and the fact that he looks remarkably unscathed, mean that Regan and Carter spot his scam a mile off. They arrest him, leaving the Embers heartbroken.

NEVER MIND THE DIALOGUE: Regan refuses to drive the cab in which he and Carter are going undercover: 'It wouldn't be safe, George, I had three large ones back at the Crown.' 'I know, I bleedin' bought two of them,' Carter concurs sourly.

Regan gets impatient with Alan Ember: 'I'm tired, I'm dirty, I've just spent two nights in a motor that smells like a wrestler's jockstrap.'

Carter observes that Regan got promoted to DI due to Ember's information and the subsequent arrests. Regan's sullen reaction is, 'Do you want to stay a Sergeant all your life?'

A go-between Regan arrests is asked what he was doing with an old banger containing Ember's money: 'I was nicking it, wasn't I?'

'It's a delicate bit of machinery, the family unit,' Regan says about the Embers. 'Makes me glad I'm gay,' Carter replies.

Coin quotes a 1970s Mackesons advert when he gets his hands on Ember's money: 'Looks good, smells good and it tastes – terrific!'

Regan answers 'a call of nature' by running off with an old flame. Carter meanwhile is also seen climbing into bed with a girl – only she's gone the next morning and Carter awakes to find Regan touching him up instead. 'Cor, you bastard,' is Carter's response. Regan gets told off for smoking in hospital: 'Quite right, disgusting habit.'

INSIDE INFORMATION: 'Feet of Clay' was one of the few instances where a *Sweeney* director was replaced. Editor and head of post-production Chris Burt stepped in to complete the production, seeing the experience as an opportunity. 'I directed 'Feet of Clay' so that when I became a producer, I would know if directors were giving me what I wanted or not,' he says. 'I thought it came over a bit slow. I got better on *The Professionals*.'

An out-take from the scene where Carter is reprimanded by the female and very stern DCI Barton ends with Dennis Waterman asking, 'I suppose a shag's out of the question?'

NAMES AND FACES: Following his work on *The Sweeney*, Chris Burt became an associate producer on *Van Der Valk*. He took the same role on *The Professionals*, which he also directed. Burt went on to produce Ian Kennedy Martin's comedy drama *King and Castle*, and returned to Euston to produce Troy's scripts for *Reilly – Ace of Spies*. He worked with Ted Childs on production of *Sharpe*, having previously hired Nigel Kneale to adapt the classic ghost story *The Woman in Black*. A close friend of John Thaw, Burt took over production of *Inspector Morse* and also worked as a producer on the actor's other series *The Waiting Time*, *Stanley and the Women* and *Goodnight Mr Tom*.

Geoffrey Palmer's commander is another middle-aged malcontent similar to those he played in *Butterflies*, the various incarnations of *Reggie Perrin* and *Fairly Secret Army*. Brian Capron was later seen as Mr Hopwood in *Grange Hill* and shady financial adviser Richard Hillman in *Coronation Street*. Joss Ackland's colourful career saw him appearing in *Villain*, among many other films. His TV credits include *Z-Cars* and

Granada Television's *Sherlock Holmes*. John Junkin starred regularly with Marty Feldman in *Marty* and later played one of Frank Ross's firm in Trevor Preston's *Out*. Carole Drinkwater was a regular on *All Creatures Great and Small*. Cheryl Campbell came to prominence in Dennis Potter's *Pennies from Heaven* the same year as 'Feet of Clay', which was her first TV role.

POLICE AND THIEVES: *'Kids – they're better than surgeons with the knife.'* Marshall's dual plotline sustains the suspense of the episode well, while the inclusion of some amusing bent policing and the unpleasant twist in the kidnap tale are indicative of the overall direction of the final series. Typically for Marshall, a tense family drama is at the centre of the action, and it's ironic that Paul, following in his father's footsteps, has no idea about Ember's criminal past; he also has nothing but contempt for his parents' nouveau riche lifestyle.

There's contemporary comment about Britain being in hock to OPEC and a fair degree of resentment on show – in particular from a racist cabbie – about how much money Arab visitors to London have got.

As with Trevor Preston's scripts, some subtle self-referencing occurs, with Marshall clearly aware of the forthcoming closure of the series. The line 'You're in bother son – big bother!' makes a welcome reappearance, one of the casinos is called the Golden Fleece, and the (possibly gay) Colin is seen sucking an ice lolly as Ray did in 'Trojan Bus'.

Perhaps reflecting how much of a comfortable British institution *The Sweeney* had become by this stage, Regan and Carter's reprimand by Commander Watson – as the two seventies Jack the Lads are told off by a comical headmaster figure – is a far cry from their early volatile confrontations with authority.

4.10 ONE OF YOUR OWN

Writer : Tony Hoare
Director : Chris Menaul
First UK transmission : 9/11/1978 9.00-10.00 pm

CAST: Michael Elphick (Fleet), Nick Stringer (Kearney), Sion Probert (Phil), Rachel Davies (Tina), Neil Hallett (Morris), John Turner (Taylor), Sheridan Fitzgerald (Jenny), Delena Kidd (Mrs Morris), Iain Blair (Prison Officer), Nicholas Owen (Constable), Jonathan Blake (Stephen), David Corti (Richard Morris), Clare McLellan (Sally Morris)

ON THE PLOT: A neat con. Fleet, posing as a Flying Squad officer, convinces Morris, a businessman, that he is about to be robbed and to give him his diamond jewellery for safety; then he and his oppo, Taylor, make off with it. Fleet is later nicked, however, and serves eight months on remand before a mix-up enables him to apply for release. Haskins hopes Carter can gain the villain's confidence and sends him undercover as a crook with the alias of Mason. Carter spends a night in the cells with Fleet but the crook gives nothing away.

Released together, the men attend Fleet's coming-out drink in a wine bar and meet Fleet's woman, Tina. At the end of the evening, Carter and Fleet are grabbed by another crook, Patsy Kearney and his gang, and taken to a disused factory tower. Kearney is a 'parasite' who 'makes his living thieving off thieves'; he has already terrorised Taylor into betraying Fleet by carving his chest up. He is on the verge of killing Carter when Fleet cracks and gives Kearney the information.

At this point the Squad, having traced Taylor's car, arrive on the scene. Kearney and his boys run off and, thus reprieved, Carter and Fleet are taken back to the nick, where it is decided that Carter's cover should be kept going until the jewellery is found. Fleet tells Carter that his girlfriend now has the stones, and they go to her flat only to find Kearney has trashed it. Unknown to Fleet, Tina has already left, having decided to take the jewellery and elope to Amsterdam with Morris, whom she fell in with at Fleet's trial. Despite Carter attempting delaying tactics, Fleet gets hold of a shooter and storms round to Kearney's yard to do him. Carter is recognised as a cop and a struggle breaks out. Before the Squad arrive, Fleet saves Carter's life. Carter repays him by throwing away the gun so the Squad can't arrest him, and Fleet goes free.

NEVER MIND THE DIALOGUE: Carter is unhappy about going into the nick and annoyed at Regan's complacent attitude. He worries that he might meet some of the faces in the Scrubs whom he put away. Sharing Regan's seemingly slack attitude, Tom quips: 'Don't worry, George – we have the technology, we can rebuild you!', implying the Squad can make George bionic à la *The Six Million Dollar Man*, a popular programme at the time.

Regan gets off with Carter's girlfriend Jenny in his absence. She has ideas about how to spice up their sex life:

Jenny: 'I've got a helmet.'

Regan: 'Lucky you.'

Jenny: 'Tomorrow, d'you think we could… you know… while you're wearing it?'

NAMES AND FACES: Michael Elphick played the dodgy but likable *Private Schultz*, who ended up drilling a hole in a khazi floor to recover more loot in the BBC comedy drama. He later went on to the lead role in *Boon*, in which Rachel Davies was also an early regular. Nick Stringer was in *The Professionals*, *Shoestring*, *The Bill* (as community liaison officer Ron Smollett) and the *Dixon of Dock Green/Sweeney/Bill* spoof *The Black and Blue Lamp*.

INSIDE INFORMATION: After seeing this episode, *Carry On* comedian Kenneth Williams fumed in his diary: 'We saw *The Sweeney* and the morality was appalling. Three policemen slept with the same tart, who asked one: "Would you wear your helmet?" Heaven knows what sort of image they wish to present for our police.'

The scenes at Kearney's scrapyard were filmed behind Kings Cross station.

POLICE AND THIEVES: *'I told ya. They propped me to get you to tell me about all this terrible villainy you've been up to.'* Like a spy going 'native', Carter identifies more with the villain Fleet than he does with his colleagues. The mood is again bleak: this is the closest Regan and Carter ever come to falling out completely, and the DI's middle-aged ennui is back. Regan calls himself 'disgusting' when he fixes Tom up with Carter's girlfriend, whom he had slept with the night before. The desolate atmosphere is heightened by the brutal torture of Fleet and Carter in a derelict building.

With the benefit of hindsight, 'One of Your Own' can perhaps be seen as a dry run at a replacement for the show, as Fleet and Carter's relationship recalls *The Sweeney* Bible's point that the DS could have ended up on the wrong side of the law. Michael Elphick contributes another potential-spin-off-series guest performance, and it's not that hard to envisage Carter being slung out of the force and teaming up with Fleet to do a few jobs.

In an otherwise suspenseful and well-plotted episode, it's unfortunate that the female characters don't come across better. They are portrayed as nagging wives or duplicitous/promiscuous girlfriends, with Tina and Jenny both cuckolding Fleet and Carter. Even Tom Daniels' wife has left him. That said, some of the men don't come out too well either, such as (upper class) Morris, who doesn't have the courage to tell his wife he's leaving her for Tina.

4.11 HEARTS AND MINDS

Writers : Donald Churchill and Ted Childs
Director : Mike Vardy
First UK transmission : 23/11/1978 9.00-10.00 pm
NB: 'Visiting Fireman' was repeated on 16/11/1978

CAST: Eric Morecambe (himself), Ernie Wise (himself), Edward Hardwicke (Bellcourt), Edward de Souza (Busby), George Mikell (Danilov), Caroline Blakiston (Hildegarde), Jenny Quayle (Wendy), Miles Anderson (Hawkins), Jack Klaff (Al Krim), Ronald Forfar (Police observer), Gary McDermott (Police driver), Martyn Whitby (SPG Inspector), Anthony Smee (Army Lieutenant), Simon Brown (Gene), Barbara Grant (Neighbour), John Moreno (Doad), Joseph Grant (Ulysees Grant) Nicholas McArdle (Tridgewell), Paul Freeman, George Irving (Detectives), Alan Bodenham (Henry), Jean Boht (Woman neighbour), James Winston (Sid), John Fielding (Reporter)

ON THE PLOT: Professor Frederick Busby has developed a new wonder drug for heart disease, which is being used to prolong the life of an Arab sheikh. Danilov, a Soviet agent who wants to gain a hold over the Middle East sovereign, orders some Arab sympathisers to steal a supply of the pills from Busby's flat but the job goes wrong. They shoot their accomplice, housebreaker Harry Greave, whom Regan knew. Regan is asked to look into the case. He interviews Busby's wife. She is virtually separated from her husband and she informs Regan that Busby is birdwatchng in Sussex. He has the pills on him, because he plans to sell them to America now the British government have cut his research grant. While Regan and Carter look for him, the intelligence services, led by Bellcourt, watch them and later move in on the case, reluctantly explaining the political machinations involved.

The foreign agents track down Busby and shoot up his Beatlebus; he abandons it and contacts his girlfriend Wendy, who is the glamour-girl assistant to none other than Morecambe and Wise. He asks her to look after the pills for him and accompany him to the States, and she agrees. Regan and Carter see a signed photograph of Wendy with the two comedians and interview them before talking to Wendy at her flat. She thinks they may be after Busby, who's hiding on the premises, and she ushers the detectives out. They return with a warrant but, by then, she's returned to work and the foreign agents have grabbed Busby.

Busby tells Danilov that Wendy has the pills and the revolutionaries take him to the Lakeside Club in Frimley, where Morecambe and Wise are putting on their show. Wendy has hidden the pills in a ventriloquist's dummy, but Eric finds them and he, Ernie and Wendy exit in a fish van, pursued by the spies. The subsequent car chase involving cops, comics and spies of various persuasions culminates in Eric throwing crates of fish all over the road. The Communist agents drive onto a firing range and surrender to the British Army.

NEVER MIND THE DIALOGUE: Eric Morecambe's on fine form – 'What do you think of it so far? Rubbish!', 'This boy's a fool!' etc.

The two double-acts – Eric and Ernie and Jack and George – meet up. 'Knock knock.' 'Who's there?' 'Police.' 'Police come in!' The comedians predict the reaction to Regan and Carter being offered a drink. 'If he's having one, I'm having one.' Carter wears a raincoat; spurred on by Eric, Regan nearly introduces him as 'Detective Sergeant Columbo.'

Carter's voicebox gets stuck on seeing a string of chorus girls. 'I would. I would. I would.'

Bellcourt tells Regan why MI5 should handle the case from now on. 'It's easier for us, we don't have to deal with constitutional legality.'

INSIDE INFORMATION: 'Hearts and Minds' originated when John Thaw and Dennis Waterman made a guest appearance on the *Morecambe and Wise Christmas Show* in 1976. 'They asked us to do their Christmas show, which at that time was the biggest kudos you could get,' Dennis Waterman remembers, 'especially as we were ITV and they were BBC – those sort of crossovers didn't often happen then. While we were doing it, John and I said, "Alright, we've done this, why don't you do one of ours?"' 'I half jokingly said to them that in their side of the business performers regularly appeared on each other's shows. It was Ernie who picked it up immediately. 'What?' he said. 'You mean come on *The Sweeney*?''

Producer Ted Childs was amenable to the idea. '[Morecambe and Wise] were at the height of their success at the time and their agent rang me and said, "They love the show, is there any chance they could be in it?" So we had to think about how we could do it, and thought that the best thing would be to let them play themselves. Don Churchill and I wrote the script. It was a hoot; we were all on the floor with our legs in the air.

'Eric and Ernie had made films but they weren't really actors. They were themselves and they did that very well. You didn't really have to write it, you just had to tell them where they fitted into the story and they did it on their own. Working with them was a riot. John and Dennis were very funny as well and it was difficult to get any work done! We wondered if we were really going to get away with it, but once we started it didn't really matter.' 'Once we got it written and started doing it it was hilarious,' Waterman laughs. 'John and I found it hard to keep straight faces a lot of the time.'

The comedians had worked with Peter Brayham before. 'Eric was like he was on stage in real life,' the stunt arranger remembers. 'I had a scene where he was in the back of a truck. We did that at the MVT centre where all the cars converge. I said to Frank [Henson], "Get Eric rigged up in a safety harness," because there was a scene where he stands up in the back of the truck and starts throwing fish all over the road. Eric says, "I don't need that," and Frank goes, "Peter Brayham said you did," and Eric waggles his glasses and says, "Well, if *Peter Brayham* said I did…" And he put it on.'

The significance of Eric and Ernie's participation wasn't lost on *Sweeney* director David Wickes. '*The Sweeney* was *so* big – it was above Morecambe and Wise – that *they* came to *The Sweeney*, and that was our accolade. That was when Lloyd, and I think Ted probably, if they were honest, would tell you that's when we knew we'd won. These were the great icons of comedy in the country and had been for many years, and you get *them* to come to *you*.'

'Hearts and Minds' features more end of term in-jokes. The fish truck Eric and Ernie escape in has 'Brayham's Fresh Fish' on its side, and in one scene Regan watches an edition of the documentary series *This Week* (which Ted Childs produced). Regan, a fictional character created for Thames Television, also gets to see the Thames logo before the documentary starts.

Eric and Ernie felt that their appearance in *The Sweeney* was probably their most successful foray into film after disappointing cinema outings with *The Magnificent Two*, *That Riviera Touch* and *The Intelligence Men* in the 1960s. They were keen to make more movies, however, and part of the reason they were enticed to Thames from the BBC in 1978 was the prospect of working with Euston Films.

NAMES AND FACES: Donald Churchill was an actor and writer who died in Spain in 1991 while filming *EL C.I.D.* As an actor he appeared in Granada Television's *Sherlock Holmes*, *Stanley and the Women*, *The Sandbaggers* and as the lead in the police comedy *Spooner's Patch*. He also wrote for *The Mind of Mr J G Reeder* and four editions of *Armchair Theatre*. He created the sitcom *Moody and Pegg*, adapted *Our Mutual Friend* and *Mr Pye* for television, and wrote film screenplays including *Victim*, *The Wild Affair* and *My Family and Other Animals.*

Edward Hardwicke was cast as the second Watson in Granada's *Sherlock Holmes* series and as escape officer Pat Grant in *Colditz*. *Troubleshooters* star Edward deSouza had many glamorous roles in the 1960s and later went on to read horror stories as *The Man in Black* on Radio 4. Caroline Blakiston moved on from playing sexy villainesses in *The Avengers* and *The Champions* to become the first western woman to appear in a Chekhov play in the Soviet Union, speaking in Russian. She also played the Margaret Thatcher-like intelligence boss, the Co-ordinator, in *Mr Palfrey of Westminster*. Jack Klaff, Miles Anderson and Paul Freeman appeared in *This is David Lander*, *House of Cards* and *The Final Cut* respectively.

POLICE AND THIEVES: *'That's the best you've worked for months.'* An espionage tale that would have worked equally well as a conventional episode, with a politically literate commentary about the 1970s 'Brain Drain' to America and, once again, the politically expedient amorality of the security services. With the arrival of Eric Morecambe and Ernie Wise, 'Hearts and Minds' quickly becomes outright farce, culminating in a Keystone Kops-style car chase, after which a disgruntled Haskins walks off saying 'Sort this out, Jack' and Eric sets his glasses askew.

Overall, the effort to keep the production realistic and true to the character of *The Sweeney* comes off. Morecambe and Wise fit easily into a series that had already successfully accommodated broad comedy; their roles would still have worked if their parts had been written for two fictional comedians. Getting the biggest comedy stars of the day to appear as themselves, however, really set the seal on *The Sweeney's* status as a British institution.

4.12 LATIN LADY
Writer : Ted Childs
Director : Peter Smith
First UK transmission : 30/11/1978 9.00-10.00 pm

CAST: Meg Davies (Christobel Delgado), Stuart Wilson (Knox), Donald Morley (Delacroix), Stephen Bent (Eddie Hibbard), Jack Carr (Pat Tyler), Sandra Payne (Meryl), Geoffrey Larder (Askew), Elizabeth Bradley (Mrs Hibberd), Janet Armsden (Betty Edwards), Eamonn Jones (O'Connor), Gladys Powell (Pianist)

ON THE PLOT: Dr Delacroix is leaving the private hospital that he owns when some men clobber him and escape with several suitcases. The Squad arrive on the scene but only manage to grab one of the villains, Knox. Delacroix is evasive about the contents of the suitcases, claiming he has a head injury; when questioned he also lies about his destination (Zurich) and changes his story later.

Knox, meanwhile, refuses to talk. As he's been held for over 12 hours the local

Superintendent tells Regan that he has to charge him or let him go by the following morning. Regan has also become enamoured of Knox's woman, the Latin American Christabel Delgado. As a last resort he lets her talk to Knox, and afterwards the distressed young man agrees to grass on the rest of his gang – Pat Tyler and Eddie Hibbard. Packing a gun, Tyler is knocked down while being chased by the Squad. As there is still a lack of serious evidence against the gang, Regan tells Christabel he's decided to let Knox out on bail.

The blaggers' car turns up, dumped, with incriminating prints, so Knox is kept in custody. Regan pays Christabel a visit; they have a few glasses of wine and end up in bed together. Returning to the station the next morning, Regan is told by Carter that he suspects the car was planted. Delacroix' clinic was doing illegal abortions on the quiet and the cases he was carrying were full of currency. After the gang stole the cash one of the members shopped them to avoid having to share the money. The missing gang member turns out to be Christabel, actually Australian con woman Christine Delton, who used to work as a nurse at the clinic. She is arrested trying to get out of the country.

NEVER MIND THE DIALOGUE: Regan, meeting Tyler's resigned Mum again when he goes to nick him, explains: 'He's been a bit naughty again, love.'

Regan tells Carter to hold off on charging Knox: 'Keep bullshitting till I get there.'

Carter has obviously been watching the *Monty Python*-inspired McVities advert, as he offers Christabel a 'suggestive biscuit.'

Later, when being asked what he was doing with Christabel, Regan tells Braithwaite 'something came up' (in the vein of 1970s Bond film humour).

NAMES AND FACES: Peter Smith had been an in-house BBC director and 'Latin Lady' was his first freelance job. He later directed Alan Bleasdale's violent black comedy *No Surrender* and also worked on episodes of *Midsomer Murders*, *Kavanagh QC*, *A Touch Of Frost*, *Resnick*, *A Perfect Spy*, *Shoestring* and *Bergerac*, in addition to several one-off series and plays.

Stuart Wilson played Vronsky in the BBC's adaptation of *Anna Karenina* and starred in the thriller series *The Assassination Run*. He also took the lead in Troy Kennedy Martin's version of Angus Wilson's *The Old Men at the Zoo*. Meg Davies appeared as Arlette in the short-lived early 1990s revival of *Van Der Valk*, produced by Chris Burt.

POLICE AND THIEVES: *'What do you want me to do now, charge Knox or go on the piss with half the micks in Kilburn?'* A further attempt by Childs to redefine the role of women in the series, this episode gives centre stage to one of *The Sweeney*'s best female villains: Christabel/Christine is a stylish, sexy and smart femme fatale. However, the denouement would perhaps have been more convincing if Christabel had escaped and phoned Regan to rub his nose in the fact that he'd been conned.

Despite an innovative female criminal, and the topical inclusion of an illegal abortion clinic, overall this episode doesn't hold together. There is a sense of going through the motions, and some unnecessary jokey humour that isn't organic to the plot creeps in, particularly when Regan goes to Kilburn to look for tip-offs about the IRA. Predictably, he gets pissed with his mates on expenses.

The script's most interesting theme is the realistic, disparaging reaction of the police to the increased rights of suspects. 'The good old days' when the police could hold people for days without charge have gone, as Braithwaite reminds Regan, perhaps adding to Jack's overall disillusionment. Faced with officious bureaucrats like Askew, maybe he simply can't function in the job any more.

4.13 VICTIMS

Writer : Roger Marshall
Director : Ben Bolt
First UK transmission : 14/12/1978 9.00-10.00 pm
NB: 'Tomorrow Man' was repeated on 7/12/1978

CAST: Sheila Reid (Doreen Haskins), Lynda Marchal (Eve Fischer), Peter Wight (Jimmy Park), Elizabeth Burger (Joan), George Innes (Willoughby), Gillian Rhind (WPC Jackson), Katie Allen (Sharon), Stuart Wilde (Richard Haskins), Benny Lee (Tommy Swain), John Biggerstaff (Mr Cully)

ON THE PLOT: DS Taylor, a corrupt Squad officer, has been shot. Regan and Carter look into the case and find that it was Jimmy Park, a grass whom he was blackmailing, who shot him. Park is being sheltered by girlfriend Eve Fisher, who warns him to stay away by positioning a plant in the window of her flat when Regan and Carter come calling. The next time they visit, the cops suss out Eve's system and Regan tells her to advise Park to turn himself in. He also leaves Daniels on surveillance at the flat, but Eve later loses him. She manages to meet with Park and hand him some of her savings to leave the country. Park explains that he felt he had no choice but to shoot Taylor – the cop was threatening to expose him to the criminal Brodie firm as an informant. Both Eve and Park distrust the police.

Haskins, meanwhile, is being distant and unco-operative; his wife Doreen has walked out. It takes a while before he can bring himself to confide in Regan that his wife may have become mentally ill. The pressure of being a policeman's wife, her remorse over not having more children and the recent death of her invalid mother have evidently taken their toll. Carter, meanwhile, receives a report of Doreen acting strangely. Regan tracks her down – she has returned to her old house, which is due to be demolished. Haskins arrives and persuades her to leave with him but she is still evidently disturbed.

Park has in the meantime been located, living rough in an abandoned warehouse. The Squad move in to arrest him. Regan fetches Eve so she can reason with Park, aware he's armed. However, as she addresses him through a loudhailer, Regan and Carter both sneak into the building while the man's attention is distracted. Park panics, opens fire on Regan and is killed. Convinced the police are murderers, Eve is carried away screaming.

NEVER MIND THE DIALOGUE: Regan and Carter visit Eve Fisher, saying they're 'looking for a man.' 'Aren't we all?' she retorts.

Doreen Haskins goes metaphorical, looking around her old, overgrown garden but talking about herself and Frank: 'How did we let it get in such a mess?'

NAMES AND FACES: Ben Bolt subsequently directed *The Turn of the Screw*, *Wilderness* and the first series of the P D James adaptation *An Unsuitable Job for a Woman*.

Lynda Marchal went on to write a number of highly successful TV series under the name Lynda La Plante, including *Widows* for Euston Films and the seminal police series *Prime Suspect*. George Innes was a regular on Euston's *Danger UXB* before going to America where he appeared in *Cagney and Lacy*. Sheila Reid (playing the only *Sweeney* character to be recast) played Regan (no relation) in a production of *King Lear*.

POLICE AND THIEVES '*What's wrong, Frank? You're falling apart, drifting through it.*' In terms of theme, this could have been the last episode of *The Sweeney*, as entertainment is superseded by the grim realities of policing. Things come full circle as the Squad investigate a cop killing like the one in 'Regan', but this time the cop is bent and the cop-killer is a fairly minor villain, way out of his depth. Even the usual bits of Marshall's comic relief – Tom's crack about the 'Irish turkey looking forward to Christmas' – are designed to fall flat.

One can't help sympathising with Eve, who, had circumstances been different, could have been a friend of Regan's like 'the Fladge' in 'Hit and Run'. At the tragic conclusion of the story, in which everyone is pushed to the limit mentally, no lives are saved; Doreen is still unwell and Haskins seems a broken man, having talked earlier about resignation. All the police have done is ruin two more people's lives.

Sheila Reid, Lynda Marchal and Garfield Morgan's performances are particularly worthy of praise, with Morgan giving his best performance, and one-time-only director Ben Bolt handles the depressing subject matter boldly but sympathetically.

The ending self-references another of the series' greats, 'Chalk and Cheese', as Haskins asks a shaken Regan if he's okay. 'Yeah, just great,' he replies morosely.

4.14 JACK OR KNAVE

Writer : Ted Childs
Director : Tom Clegg
First UK transmission : 28/12/1978 9.00-10.00 pm
NB: 'Selected Target' was repeated on 21/12/1978

CAST: Barrie Ingham (Canning), Richard Griffiths (Harries), Jo Warne (Gloria), Ralph Nossek (Duxbury), David Casey (Jackson), Andrew Downie (Bishop), Jane Cussons (Sonia), Dan Gillan (Desk Sgt), Anna Nygh (Jean), Mathew Scurfield (Kennedy), Andrew Paul (Teenager), Peggy Ann Jones (Lady), Frank Lee, Stephen Gordon (Drivers), Linda Hooks (Ivy)

ON THE PLOT: A vicious blagging takes place half a mile outside the Metropolitan Police's jurisdiction. Several security guards are shot. DCS Canning, an old and unloved rival of Regan's, runs the area and refuses to ask the Yard for help. Colin Anderson, a C11 photographer, gives Carter a lead: Ronnie Harries, a fence, has been photographed at a wedding standing next to a man who resembles an identikit picture of one of the blaggers. Sighting a likely lad leaving Harris's motor accessory shop, Regan and Carter nick him and find dodgy numberplates on him – the teenager legs it. As there is no evidence at the shop, Canning is unimpressed and tells an annoyed Regan 'there are no marks for trying.'

Harries is carrying on with several women and, by threatening to tell his wife, Regan forces him to admit he recently had dealings with a gang in the General Wolf pub, disposing of a package for them by throwing it off Kew Bridge. Divers find the parcel: it contains a gun and false plates both used in the blag. Several arrests follow; Keiran Kennedy, the robber who did the shooting, puts up a fight with a rifle before being caught. Angry at having his case hijacked, Canning contemplates putting in a complaint against Regan but later drops it.

Weeks later, Regan is about to collect a commendation for this work when he is arrested by A10. In 1968, several officers in the nick where he worked were taking bribes and the details have recently been coming out in the press. Regan is imprisoned and Canning, who worked with him at the time, takes revenge by refusing to help clear Regan's name. The DI is later bailed and goes on a solo drinking spree. Carter looks up Gloria Berkley, whom Regan was seeing in the typing pool in 1968; she remembers Regan signed some arrest forms in a hurry one night and had no further involvement with the case. Carter clears Regan of the charge, but Jack has reached the end of his tether and tells his DS and Haskins that he is leaving the force.

NEVER MIND THE DIALOGUE: Regan's famous last words: 'I've given the best years of my life to the job… and how does this wonderful police force show its gratitude? It bangs me up in a crabby cell like a cheap little villain. And what do you bunch of bleeding double-dyed hypocrites want me to do now? You want me to crawl back to work and be terribly grateful I didn't get nicked for something I didn't do. Well, you can stuff it!'

Arresting the head villain, Kennedy, in Thames Ditton yacht club, George is shot at and falls in the river. 'Get wet, George?' Haskins enquires. He gets a caustic 'No' in reply.

And let's hear it one last time: Carter finds one of the gang in bed. 'Get yer vest on, Sid, you're nicked.'

NAMES AND FACES: Richard Griffiths went on to play the civil servant on the run in the memorable BBC computer thriller *Bird of Prey* and Withnail's eccentric Uncle Monty in Bruce Robinson's cult classic *Withnail and I*. He later found further fame as the gourmet detective in *Pie in the Sky*. Andrew Paul appeared as the long-running regular character PC Quinnan in *The Bill*.

INSIDE INFORMATION: This episode was the last one to be filmed. Director Tom Clegg had overseen the programme's inception and had mixed feelings about the series finishing. 'I'm so glad I got to do the last one,' he says. 'It was sad in some ways, but it was good to work with them on it and to have been there right from the very beginning. People just accepted that it was coming to an end. Now, if that had been an American series, it would have gone on for at least another five years, it was so popular. They would never let a series so popular die.'

The cab Regan departs in was owned by another eccentric character called Billy the Fish. 'He used to go down to the fish market and get loads of smoked salmon, kippers and God knows what else,' John S Smith remembers. 'When John drove off, they had all this seafood in there which was for the crew's consumption. So when that big, emotional scene was being shot, the cab stank of fish!'

Appropriately, Regan's departure from the job was filmed outside Colet Court itself.

POLICE AND THIEVES: *'He'll be back. He needs the job like an alcoholic needs booze.' 'Yeah?'* Starting out as one story and finishing up as another, in hindsight this could have tied in better with 'Victims', as Haskins has miraculously reverted to his old self. Overall, this is a straightforward police procedural episode – the blagging plot is nothing remarkable – but Regan's arrest brings his dissatisfaction, subtly hinted at all the way through the fourth series, to a head. Several unexpected double-bluffs – Canning *not* turning out to be the bent cop that A10 are looking for, for example – and Regan's final scenes make this a riveting final episode.

For once, the Squad have been getting some positive press coverage: a newspaper headline reads 'Judge praises Flying Squad'. Considering the numerous times Regan and his men have been baited by the media, it makes his arrest for suspected corruption doubly ironic. Regan's last, furiously delivered speech – one of John Thaw's finest moments – is the final act of a police officer who feels utterly let down by a service which, for all its faults, he was proud to serve. The final scene, with Jack saying goodbye to George, is a reversal of the common episode ending – dating back to the first story – where either Regan or Carter is fed up with the job and one is talked round by the other. This time Regan *won't* calm down and he *won't* go for a drink, bringing the series to a logical conclusion.

CHAPTER 9

THE SWEENEY
AT THE MOVIES

'They were all very excited about *The Sweeney* feature films. John Maskall was the camera operator, and of course he was now shooting not for the television ratio but the widescreen ratio, and you had to be very careful about cropping the tops off people's heads. He was quite anxious, but he got by.' *John S Smith, film editor*

'Troy was going on about it being absolutely *essential* that we go away [to Malta] to get the contrast. He went on and on. I was on his side and George and Lloyd said, "Well, we'll have to work out the budget." Troy told them they were penny-pinching bastards, and they had no idea how to make a film! Anyway, we did go to Malta, and we filmed there, and I think it added an awful lot to the film. When it was shown at BAFTA, later, [Troy, Ted Childs, Lloyd Shirley] and myself were on the panel. Troy stood up and said, "The scenes abroad were not really essential, we didn't really need to go out there." Unbelievable!' *Tom Clegg,* Sweeney 2 *director*

'You can get away with a lot more in movies.' *Ted Childs, producer*

* * *

BY THE END OF 1975, *THE SWEENEY* HAD TAKEN THE TV RATINGS BY storm, featuring regularly in the top five, with 'Trap' and 'Golden Fleece' ranking first. In excess of eight million people were tuning in, and the Euston management began to think about diversification. 'At the time, we wondered what we could do about British cinema, and thought maybe there was a future in spin-offs,' Ted Childs explains, reflecting on the decision to make a feature film version of the series. The result – *Sweeney!* – was a British take on the popular 1970s post-Watergate conspiracy thriller genre exemplified by films such as *The Parallax View* and *All the President's Men.* 'The scene in the pub where Jack Regan's saying "We are the patsies here" to Carter – "Some toff with a white collar steals more than that in an afternoon" – dead right,' director David Wickes maintains, elaborating on the paranoia inherent in the story. 'All those lines were very carefully worked out. They *were* [a] political comment... Nobody does that any more.'

Released in January 1977, *Sweeney!* was made for a budget equivalent to little more than two episodes of the television series. According to Childs, the cost was approximately £110,000, the majority of the money being contributed by Thames Television. The film was made in conjunction with EMI to guarantee a British cinema release through the ABC cinema chain. Series creator Ian Kennedy Martin thought about writing the script (he owned the film rights), but didn't feel he could do the project justice on such a low budget.

According to David Wickes, 'It was Lloyd who pushed [for the film].' But, despite the low production costs and the popularity of the parent TV series, the film was still considered a risk. Big-screen spin-offs of British TV shows, together with the mild porn of *The Confessions* films, were the stock-in-trade of the moribund British film industry at the time. This minor genre was mainly inspired by popular comedy series, with *Porridge*, *The Likely Lads*, *Love Thy Neighbour* and *Dad's Army*, among others, all making the transition to feature-length film versions; the nearest equivalent to *The Sweeney* film was a movie version of the spy drama *Callan*, made in 1974. However, despite being a safe bet for the home market, these films rarely did well internationally.

David Wickes recollects that there was a perceived need to make the *Sweeney* movie appeal to the international market. 'They knew that they had to have major overseas sales, otherwise they couldn't support a budget for it, and the budget wasn't great. It was a British TV series, and although we in this country would love to think otherwise, when a Japanese bus driver gets up in the morning, he's not gonna say, "Ah, so! Must go and see British TV series!" He doesn't do that – you have to *win* him and work hard for him – you need to get the ingredients right. There *had* to be overseas sales, otherwise we'd never have made another one, and that would be the end of Euston Films, virtually. Nat Cohen of EMI understood this very well.'

'There was a view that it ought to be different,' agrees Ted Childs. 'Those of us involved shared that view as well, there should be more stunts and [a] grander design. I remember going to see Nat Cohen with Lloyd and George at EMI – they had an interest in Thames at the time – and [Cohen] said, "What are you going to offer? Most people on a Monday night will sit at home and watch your show. Why would they put their coats on on a wet night and walk down to the ABC at Fulham Broadway and see what they can see for nothing on the telly?" Pass!'

Most of the criticism subsequently directed at *Sweeney!* was due to the increased levels of violence – there are several gory machine-gunnings and deaths embellished by slow motion – but this was all part of the plan to cultivate a cinema audience. 'Because everybody had said that no one would pay to see something they could see on TV,' claims David Wickes, 'I said, "Well, you wait to see what we've got in this!" And I told [Euston] how to sell it – *"What they wouldn't let you see on TV."* I said, "It has to have an X certificate, it *has* to. Because without that, it's stone dead."' The changes made to the format paid off and the first film did well financially; Childs also partly attributes its success to being released in the winter directly after the highly rated third series had finished transmission.

Perhaps surprisingly, *Sweeney!* also proved that a film based on a parochial TV series could do well abroad. Ironically, its success was partly due to its low production costs.

'It made more money pound per pound invested than any other film EMI had ever made,' David Wickes affirms. 'On the back of it they were able to afford *The Deer Hunter* … It was their big, big, big thing, and the first western film ever sold to the People's Republic of China, for example. It sold all over the world and made a huge, *huge* amount of money: it made a 1000 per cent profit on every pound invested in it.'

Although the first film has its detractors, Wickes believes that overall it works as a stand-alone film. 'Barry Foster's accent was picked up by my American agent: he said he heard about three or four lapses in it. That was my fault, because I should have had an American dialogue coach on the set and I never did, because I was a cocky little bastard and I thought I could tell the difference – and I missed it, on several occasions; particularly the rhythm. We should have got a dialogue coach for Barry, or we should have had an American actor, and that's my one big regret about the *Sweeney!* feature film. Everything else I can support, but not that.'

Sweeney!'s distribution was linked to one of British cinema's great oddities, *The Wicker Man*. Opening to mixed press in the UK late in 1973, the film is now regarded as one of the best British horror films ever made. In 1976, however, it was seen as a financial millstone around EMI's neck. *Sweeney!* was marketed as a double-feature with this film in an attempt to recoup EMI's previous loss. 'Nat Cohen was in charge of distribution at EMI,' Ian Kennedy Martin recalls. 'He pulled a West End show for a week and we opened with *The Wicker Man*, which EMI had put a lot of money into but hadn't made any. So what they said was, half the profits would be attributed to *The Wicker Man* and half to *Sweeney!* A typical piece of sleazy film business!'

Released two years later, *Sweeney 2* is more 'traditional', featuring the Squad as a group rather than Regan as a lone hero figure. A plot involving a string of violent armed robberies utilising a gold-plated shotgun took Thaw and Waterman to Malta, their first foreign location shoot. The film was written by Troy Kennedy Martin, whom Childs considered the definitive *Sweeney* writer. 'Troy had done *The Italian Job* by then, and he was more experienced with films,' Childs recalled. 'We weren't as inhibited the second time round.' The end result was simultaneously pessimistic, violent and on occasions farcical, like Troy's TV scripts 'Night Out' and 'Hard Men'. As with *Sweeney!*, the movie was directed by one of the TV show's directors, in this case the prolific Tom Clegg. Perhaps because it was released just before the summer, the second film failed to do as well financially as the first, but is fondly remembered and tends to be the favourite of the pair among the Euston cast and crew. 'It had a very different style, it was more glossy,' Chris Burt comments. 'It was done deliberately because these guys were meant to be rich, living in Malta.'

Dennis Waterman, in particular was more enamoured of the second film than the first: 'The films were well received, but we were never thrilled about *Sweeney!* It was, 'We're doing a film,' 'Oh, that's good,' the script was thrown at us and we were never really involved in it until we started shooting. It was fait accompli: 'The boys have agreed to do a film, this is the script and he's the director,' and it was like, 'Oh, fuck!'

And it was all outside our remit: it was all oil barons and sheikhs, and we suddenly had to have pictures of Big Ben and Tower Bridge. It was like when they film a comedy and move it into a totally different place. The second film was an absolute *Sweeney* job through and through. We were chasing blaggers, and they were very, very tough blaggers. We had a fantastic cast, and I thought that movie was infinitely better than the first one. I thought it was terrific.'

Despite the second film's perceived lack of commercial success, *The Sweeney* remains the only British drama series – with the same cast – to have been spun off into the cinema for more than one big-screen outing. The production crew for the TV series also made the feature films, confirming that the techniques of making cinema for the small screen applied equally to the big. As such, *Sweeney!* and *Sweeney 2* stand as a validation of Euston's whole film-making ethos.

Both films have been released on video, available through EMI, and are still occasionally screened on satellite and terrestrial television. No doubt DVD releases are likely in the not too distant future.

SWEENEY! X CERTIFICATE

Writer : Ranald Graham
Director : David Wickes
GB 1976 89 minutes

Filmed: 5 April 1976 for five weeks   **Released:** January 1977

CAST: John Thaw (Regan), Dennis Waterman (Carter), Barry Foster (McQueen), Ian Bannen (Baker), Colin Welland (Chadwick), Diane Keen (Bianca), Michael Coles (Johnson), Joe Melia (Brent), Brian Glover (Mac), Lynda Bellingham (Janice), Morris Perry (Flying Squad Cdr), Paul Angelis (Secret Serviceman), Nick Brimble (Burtonshaw), John Alkin (Daniels), Bernard Kay (Matthews), Anthony Scott (Johnson's henchman), Anthony Brown (Murder Inquiry Supt), John Oxley (Chadwick's Deputy Editor), Peggy Aitchison (Carter's neighbour), Hal Jeayes (Manservant), Sally Osborne (Sally), John Kane (Special Branch Sgt), Chris Dillinger (Johnson's henchman), Peter Childs (Murder Inquiry Insp), Alan Mitchell (Detective Insp), Leonard Kavanagh (Pathologist), Anthony Woodruff (Coroner), Michael Latimer (PPS), Matthew Long (Traffic Police Sgt), Joyce Grant (McQueen's secretary), Johnny Shannon (Scotland Yard Duty Sgt), David Corti (Young Boy), Susan Skipper (Chadwick's secretary), Nadim Sawalha (Chairman of Oil Producers' Conference), Frank Maher (Shot PC)*

* uncredited

PRODUCTION TEAM: Producer Ted Childs, Executive Producers Lloyd Shirley, George

Taylor, **Associate Producer** Mary Morgan, **Director of Photography** Dusty Miller, **Music** Dennis King, **Art Director** Bill Alexander, **Assistant Art Director** Roger Bowles, **First Assistant Director** Bill Westley, **Second Assistant Director** Michael Murray, **Boom Operator** Mike Silverlock, **Camera Operator** John Maskall, **Casting Director** Marilyn Johnson, **Continuity** Phyllis Townshend, **Dubbing Mixer** Hugh Strain, **Editor** Chris Burt, **Follow Focus** Mike Proudfoot, **Hairdresser** Mary Sturgess, **Location Manager** Stephen Pushkin, **Make-up** Michael Morris, **Production Buyer** Bert Gardner, **Production Assistant** Joy Bayley, **Production Manager** Laurie Greenwood, **Production Accountant** Peter Harvey, **Second Unit Cameraman** Norman Langley, **Sound Mixer** Tony Dawe, **Sound Editor** Clive Smith, **Stills Photographer** Doug Webb, **Stunt Arranger** Peter Brayham, **Special Effects** Arthur Beavis, **Supervising Electrician** John O'Donoghue **Unit Publicist** Catherine O'Brien, **Technical Adviser** Jack Quarrie BEM, **Wardrobe Supervisor** David Murphy

ON THE PLOT: Charles Baker MP, is attending an OPEC conference in central London, pressing for a lowering of the price of oil. Baker's American press secretary, McQueen, calls him to a hotel, where they find the body of Janice Wyatt, a call girl the MP was seeing. McQueen promises Baker he will cover up the apparent suicide.

After foiling a wages blag in Fulham, Regan receives a call from his snout Ronnie Brent, who was also seeing Janice. Her body was found in her flat, but at the time of her death, according to the pathologist's report, Brent was there waiting to take her away for the weekend. Convinced she was in fact murdered, Brent starts making waves, angrily questioning Bianca Hamilton, another 'public relations' assistant at Media Incorporated, Janice's workplace. Bianca tells McQueen, her boss, about the harassment, and that Brent mentioned a Flying Squad officer might be reopening inquiries into the death.

Shortly afterwards, Brent and some of his associates are machine-gunned to death by two men dressed as police constables. Regan and Carter retreat to the pub, get drunk and argue. Driving away afterwards, Regan is 'arrested' by two fake PCs, one of whom, Johnson, is a professional killer. A full 75cl bottle of whiskey is forced down Regan's throat, and he subsequently crashes his car. He is suspended from the police.

It becomes clear that McQueen, far from having Baker's best interests at heart, is using Janice's death as a lever against the politician, making him turn down an interview with the influential editor of *The New Democrat* magazine, Frank Chadwick. Regan visits McQueen at Media Incorporated, unaware of the press agent's role in events. McQueen recommends that he question Bianca, and Regan visits her in a hotel. This is a trap; Johnson arrives on the scene with a machine gun and, as he opens fire, Regan and Bianca exit through the fire escape. Chadwick, meanwhile, confronts McQueen, demanding to know why he can't have access to Baker for his interview. Regan and Bianca are pursued through London's streets, and Johnson shoots a PC when Regan approaches him. The pair go to ground in Carter's flat.

Chadwick deduces that Baker is about to perform a volte face at the OPEC conference, campaigning to *increase* oil prices. He realises the MP is being blackmailed by McQueen and starts writing a damning article about it. Posing as a window cleaner, Johnson detonates a bomb in Chadwick's office, killing him.

Regan and Bianca have sex in Carter's flat after she admits she and Janice Wyatt were both high-class prostitutes, working for Media Incorporated. When Carter arrives, the trio piece together what's happening and leave to make their way to the Yard. But Johnson has again tracked them down. Bianca is shot dead and Regan is injured, leaving the DI shaken by her death.

When Regan forces the investigation through to the highest level, Baker resigns. His Parliamentary Private Secretary informs Regan that, to avoid a diplomatic incident, McQueen, an ex-Security Services agent who is apparently now working for 'multinational oil companies', will be shipped out of the country discreetly.

Regan gets the Squad together and the following morning they arrest McQueen on a charge of 'pimping', to the anger of the MI5 officers guarding him. To prevent him talking, his backers order him to be killed and Johnson shoots McQueen down. Carter realises that Regan engineered the American's death and shouts at him furiously, *'They didn't kill him — you did!'*

NEVER MIND THE DIALOGUE: This script has a number of good one-liners. Regan answers Carter's question about how Ronnie Brent has taken the bad news about Janice with a surly 'Fell about laughing, didn't he?' When an irritating Special Branch man asks him who actually did kill Brent, Regan snarls, 'The Dagenham Girl Pipers' before telling the man to 'Sod off!'

The film opens with Regan and Carter in the latter's flat; Carter is asleep on the sofa due to Regan having nicked the bed. All are still fully clothed after the previous evening's excesses. According to Carter, Regan 'got so pissed he couldn't make it back to his gaff', and there's also some contention over who Sally, yet another air hostess, fancied. All three are obviously hung-over; in Regan and Carter's case they cure this condition by having a ruck with a load of villains and then downing Scotch in the office, hiding the bottle when Regan's boss walks in.

Abandoned in the boozer, Regan promptly moves in on the barmaid: 'Ere, Doreen … George saved my life the other night, but I've left him for you.' Her husband's entrance subsequently puts the mockers on his attempt at leery seduction, leaving Regan to stagger off with a muttered, 'Sod it.'

The fake police who pull Regan over get some sardonic dialogue: 'Dull it isn't,' quips one after machine-gunning Brent, quoting the police recruiting motto of the time. On 'arresting' Regan, they tell him 'Your rear light's not working,' before smashing it in.

Prostitute Bianca's reaction to Regan's assertion that Janice was Baker's mistress is an incredulous, 'What sort of books do you read?'

At one point Regan pushes her in the shower and shouts at her till she breaks down in tears. He then apologises with the immortal line, 'I'm a copper, I know a lot of tarts

… You didn't look like one to me.'

Regan tries to scrounge a fag from Carter, who won't let him have one because he only has one left. 'I only want one,' Regan growls, grabbing it. Carter then refuses to give him a light, leading to a muttered 'Bastard…' The scene as written had Regan asking Carter for a light, and a fed-up Carter lighting it. Waterman ad-libbed the rest of the scene as shot with Thaw.

INSIDE INFORMATION: Filming on *Sweeney!* took approximately five weeks, starting on 5 April 1976, and the film was shot on the cinema standard of 35mm as opposed to 16mm. Locations included Holland Park, Barons Court and St James's Park tube stations (as Regan and Carter rush to work), the entrance to Scotland Yard, Trinity Square, Notting Hill, the grounds of the Tower Hotel (near Tower Bridge) and inside the Gloucester Hotel. The latter location was awkward to gain access to, as it was owned by the Rank Organisation. David Wickes: 'It seems absurd now but, in those days, co-operation between rival film companies and big corporations was rare. What a load of twaddle that was.' The exteriors of Carter's flat were shot in South Kensington while Brent's yard was located in Fulham, behind the Christopher Wray Lighting Emporium. Kids watching the filming continued to be rowdy, despite efforts to bribe them to keep quiet with Mars bars.

Exteriors and interiors for the offices of Media Incorporated were shot at Alembic House (containing a flat belonging to James Bond composer John Barry), where the crew encountered problems with the lift breaking down under the weight of their equipment. Other awkward moments occurred during filming at this venue. 'The location manager got the permission of the managing agents, but not the actual residents, and some of them were rather shirty about us being there,' Ted Childs recalls. 'Understandable really; there were loads of cables running up the stairs, empty paper cups everywhere. The residents obtained a legal injunction telling us to get out by the next morning, so we filmed nearly all night. The thing was, we'd already shot two or three days' worth in there. If we suddenly got out we'd have to start again somewhere else. We did deals on the stairs with the boys contrary to the union, and just about managed to keep awake. It worked, though.'

Chadwick's office was built in Colet Court itself so that an explosion could be staged on the premises. 'Arthur Beavis of Effects Associates at Pinewood blew up Colin Welland and did it the old-fashioned way – ie, for real,' says David Wickes. 'There was no digital enhancement in those days and actors just accepted it. All our ears rang for days!'

Although credited to Ranald Graham, the script's late arrival suggests it may have required last-minute revisions. 'My wife will tell you about the weekends I sat writing at the kitchen table,' Ted Childs says. 'I remember once, David Wickes and I were there all night and then went in the following morning and shot it.'

One familiar face missing from the regular cast (in both films) was that of Garfield Morgan. David Wickes: 'I can't remember why, but there was a reason for it. It might have been unavailability, and it might have been money. John and Dennis weren't very happy with what they were paid, and neither was I. We didn't have a lot of money. I finished [the film] at half past four on the Friday as well, because it was expected. I now realise that movies can go *days* over. In those days I thought it had to be done like we did the series.'

Stuntman Frank Maher played the uncredited role of the unfortunate PC shot in the head by Johnson. Ted Childs: 'He had a kind of steel thing on the guy's head like a cap, then the helmet and then they put some explosive material and a blood bag underneath. We did it and I said to Billy Westley, "We're going to have to go again," and he said, "He's gone fucking mutton [deaf], he won't do it again."' Peter Brayham recalls, "After they blew it up, [Maher] said, "Thanks very much. You've just given me the biggest headache I've ever had in my life!"'

NAMES AND FACES: Lynda Bellingham, Peter Childs, Michael Coles, Brian Glover, Norman Kay, Nadim Sawalha and Colin Welland had all appeared in the television series. Barry Foster was best known as Dutch detective Van Der Valk; the third series about the Dutch detective, made by Euston Films, would premiere nine months after *Sweeney!*'s release, in September 1977. Ian Bannen's notable film appearances included the brutal Second World War drama *The Hill* and the psychological thriller *The Offence*. His television work included the highly regarded adaptation of John Le Carré's *Tinker, Tailor, Soldier, Spy*. Diane Keen was a regular in *The Sandbaggers* before being betrayed by her ruthless boss; she also appeared in numerous adverts for a certain brand of coffee, plus sitcoms such as *The Cuckoo Waltz* and *Rings on Their Fingers*.

POLICE AND THIEVES: *'Still tilting at windmills, Jack?'* Appropriately for a film targeted at an international audience, traditional London landmarks, including Tower Bridge and the Houses of Parliament, are seen throughout the film. However, with a political conspiracy going on, it seems that, behind the icons of the establishment, paranoia, corruption and lies are rife. Special Branch have been monitoring events and it's revealed that they, not McQueen's people, are responsible for planting a bug in Carter's flat, but they make no move to help Regan or Baker. Whether this was the usual inability of different police departments to co-operate or a more sinister attempt to interfere in domestic politics is left open. By his vague references to Bobby Kennedy, it seems McQueen's employers are involved with the American security services; the hired assassins, who go by a company name, Johnson & Johnson, have extensive weaponry and resources.

Killings happen in crowded public places, as Johnson & Johnson are seen impersonating everyone from policemen to dustmen, highlighting the atmosphere of conspiracy. Regan's isolation in fighting the intrigue is highlighted by the attitude of the public; as he and Bianca flee from the gunmen, a conductor tries to throw them off his bus, and a 'chicken-livered' cabbie drives off in panic when asked for help. Even the phones are tapped, or vandalised. As Regan says, it's as if 'the whole country's asleep' and people just aren't interested that their government is being swallowed up by a foreign power. At one point Regan emphasises the feeling of violation by outside forces by asserting, 'No *London* team would do this.'

While the film is obviously an attempt to break away from the conventions *The Sweeney* established on television, the quirky elements of the series are still present. In one scene, while Regan, Carter and Bianca argue about the political situation in George's bathroom, a copy of *Private Eye* hangs from the toilet roll holder.

The ending is particularly effective, a nightmarish slow motion shooting (mirroring the death of Janice at the start of the film), accompanied by discordant electronic music. The freeze-frame close-up of Regan over which the credits roll is reminiscent of the 1970 film *Villain* which features a similar use of Richard Burton's face.

Overall, while *Sweeney!* is perhaps not as confident, cerebral or consistent as the television series or its successor *Sweeney 2*, it still stands as a good, straightforward, suspenseful 1970s British thriller. The film had a short-lived theatrical resurrection when it was screened at the Prince Charles Cinema in Leicester Square in 1997, as part of a promotional launch for the Nissan Almera advertising campaign that spoofed *The Sweeney*.

SWEENEY 2 AA CERTIFICATE

Writer : Troy Kennedy Martin
Director : Tom Clegg
GB 1977 108 mins

Filmed: from 7 November 1977 for five weeks   **Released:** April 1978

CAST: John Thaw (Regan), Dennis Waterman (Carter), Barry Stanton (Big John), John Flanagan (Willard), David Casey (Goodyear), Derrick O'Connor (Llewellyn), John Alkin (Daniels), James Warrior (Jellyneck), Guy Standeven (Logan), Ken Hutchison (Hill), Brian Gwaspari (White), John Thaw (Regan), Denholm Elliott (Jupp), Frederick Treves (McKyle), Johnny Shannon (Harry [villain]), Clifford Kershaw (Gloria's father), Nigel Hawthorne (Dilke), Lewis Fiander (Gorran), Anna Nygh (Shirley Hicks), Michael J Jackson (Soames), Anna Gael (Mrs Hill), Lynn Dearth (Mrs White), Fiona Mollison (Mrs Haughton), Sarah Atkinson (Mrs Mead), John Lyons (Mead), Brian Hall (Haughton), Matthew Scurfield (Jefferson), Gareth Milne (Bank teller), Sebastian Witkin (Skateboarder), Hubert Rees (Bank manager), George Innes (Pete Beale), Roddy McMillan (Collie), Michael O'Hagan (Doyle), Arthur Cox (Detective), Georgina Hale (Switchboard girl), Patrick Malahide (Conway), Max Mason (SPG constable), Frank Coda (Commissionaire), Yvon Dova (Mr Mahmoun), James McManus (Barman), John Vine (PC), David Gillies (PC), Seretta Wilson (Girl), Diana Weston (Air hostess), George Mikell (Superintendent), Mark Zuber (Andy), Joe Zammit-Cardona (Customs official), Leon Lissek (Cardona Alexandros), Marilyn

Finlay (Schoolteacher), Seymour Matthews (Harry [fingerprint man]), Stefan Gryff (Nino), Michael Scholes (Boy in bed), Danny Rae (Taxi driver), Rosario Serrano (Mrs Konstantikis), Eamonn Jones (Barman), Alan Ross (Fiddler)

PRODUCTION TEAM: **Producer** Ted Childs, **Executive Producers** Lloyd Shirley, George Taylor, **Associate Producer** Mary Morgan, **Director of Photography** Dusty Miller, **Music** Tony Hatch, **Art Director** Bill Alexander, **Assistant Art Director** Terry Parr, **First Assistant Director** Bill Westley, **SecondAssistant Director** Michael Murray, **Boom Operator** Mike Silverlock, **Camera Operator** John Maskall, **Casting Director** Marilyn Johnson, **Continuity** Phyllis Townshend, **Dubbing Mixer** Hugh Strain, **Editor** Chris Burt, **Follow Focus** Mike Proudfoot, **Hairdresser** Mary Sturgess, **Location Manager** Stephen Pushkin, **Make-up** Eddie Knight, **Production Buyer** Bert Gardner, **Production Assistant** Joy Bayley, **Production Manager** Laurie Greenwood, **Production Accountant** Peter Harvey, **Second Unit Cameraman** Norman Langley, **Sound Mixer** Derek Rye, **Sound Editor** Ian Toynton, **Stills Photographer** Doug Webb, **Stunt Arranger** Peter Brayham, **Special Effects** Arthur Beavis, **Supervising Electrician** John O'Donoghue, **Titles** Geoff Axtell Associates, **Technical Adviser** Jack Quarrie BEM, **Unit Publicist** Lily Poyser, **Wardrobe Supervisor** David Murphy

ON THE PLOT: 'You're privileged to be looking down the barrel of a gold-plated sawn-off Purdey shotgun. Now, as a bank manager, even you will appreciate that anyone capable of cutting a gun like that in half wouldn't think twice about cutting you in half.' The latest in a string of armed blags goes off in London. The Squad, in hot pursuit of the gang responsible, intercept them. Missing out on the action by having to attend the trial of the corrupt former Squad Commander, Jupp, at the Old Bailey, Regan arrives on the scene to find carnage. A blagger and a stoppo driver dead, a hostage terminally injured, a lollipop man callously run over and a Squad driver crippled. Regan visits Gorran, the snout who gave him dubious information about the job. Gorran is shacked up with Shirley Hicks, the prostitute wife of the dead gang driver, and Regan, aware that both know more about the gang than they're letting on, briefs his team to put the woman under 24-hour surveillance.

The surviving bilaggers – Hill, White, Jefferson, Haughton, Mead and Smith – meanwhile sit down for dinner with their photogenic wives and children in their luxury retreat of Pharos on Malta. White points out that there is a crack in the bottom of their swimming pool – they'll have to go back to London…

A few days later, a bank once again reverberates with the sound of a shotgun blast. In the getaway, Hill drops his gold-plated shotgun, but the gang successfully escapes, at one point driving straight through the window of a car showroom. This time, forensic analysis in the bank turns up a set of fingerprints. In the previous jobs, money was found in the gang's getaway car. Carter finds some on this occasion too and works out that the gang are always stealing similar amounts of cash – the poppy always works out to be exactly $100,000 when converted to dollars, and the excess is discarded. For his part, Regan learns that Jupp once put away a villain called Harrison for a similar run of blags. He visits Jupp in the Scrubs and the ex-copper reveals he was payed to fit Harrison up. He tells Regan about the gang.

Regan and Carter fly to Malta to question the criminals but are turned away by both the local police and Alexandros, the Maltese 'businessman' who handles the villains' estate. While there, Carter spots a school photograph of White holding a sports trophy and visits the crook's old school to unearth the cup. The prints on it match those from the bank...

Hill and the others plan to add to their property – and they have to pay off the local villains. They decide to do one more job, Hill sawing the barrel off his second gold-plated shotgun. His wife phones Regan in London to tip him off, deciding enough is enough. Regan is also given a tip-off by Gorran, however, and believes the call from Malta is misinformation. But he soon finds that some getaway cars left on the street are decoys – they don't have enough petrol in them. After the villains have pulled off their blag successfully, their car crashes. Hill and White are the only survivors.

They hole up in a boarding house, where Shirley Hicks pays a visit. She is tailed there by the Squad, who start sneaking into the premises. As Jellyneck slips on the roof he loses his handcuffs. White sees them, grabs his gun and runs out into the road, where a police marksman takes him out. Hill turns angrily on Shirley, shooting her, before turning the gun on himself just as Regan bursts in. Regan is spattered by the man's blood and, in shock, he shuts himself away from everyone, trying to scrub it off. Hearing news of their men's demise, the blaggers' wives sell off their property. Back in London the Squad meet for celebratory piss-up...

NEVER MIND THE DIALOGUE: 'No one breathalysed this morning? Something of a record.' Alcohol use seems rife in the Squad: at one point they nick someone who's threatened to poison the produce of the local brewery. Carter reflects that, given the amount the Squad drank during the visit, it would have been cheaper if the company had paid the ransom.

A bomb scare takes place in the Hexagon Hotel – nothing to do with the plot, of course – and Regan drags the numerous (wrangling) police factions into the hotel bar for a conference. This is described as having 'a piss-up at the taxpayer's expense while we wait for a bomb to go off in the Penthouse Suite.'

Regan also has a soft porn film of Shirley Hicks – allegedly in his 'private collection'– that features her in various stages of undress squirming all over a Panther Deville. ('Everything you say will be taken down.') The film is an advert, of sorts, as a voice advises viewers: 'Rubber is a national resource – conserve rubber.' The screening helps persuade the Squad men to abandon their reservations about maintaining surveillance on her activities.

It is revealed that the German steel helmet (of 'Visiting Fireman' and 'Hard Men') was apparently taken from Nazi regalia collector Mick Gorran's collection. 'If you ask me he gives [Shirley Hicks] one dressed as Adolf Hitler,' is Regan's theory.

Regan chats up the receptionist in the Hexagon Hotel – 'Look, I've never done anything like this before but here is a key to my flat. Why don't you come back? I can promise you a nice bottle of wine, a very nice meal and, when you want to go, I'll have you taken home in a Squad car.' She accepts the invite but finds him slumped in front of the TV in a drunken stupor, and decides to return said key – by putting it down his underpants.

Carter suddenly announces in the middle of a scene, 'I'm just going for a piss.'

In the line of duty the Squad climb through a bedroom window, interrupting a threesome; the owner tells them to go or he'll call the police – provoking the inevitable reply, 'We *are* the police, mate.'

Regan's replacement driver, Soames, is a teetotal, non-smoking vegetarian who keeps fruit in the glove compartment of the (immaculate) car. Regan advises him to 'Bash it up, smash it up, put a 'Vote Tory' sticker on it, and fill the glove compartment with junk food and chocolate. But no potato crisps, they interfere with transmission.'

The bomb scare in the hotel results in Carter being sent upstairs to see a suspected terrorist while Regan moves in on the female receptionist. Carter isn't amused: 'You're down here chatting up the birds while I'm seeing some fucking maniac with a bomb!' (The only *Sweeney* use of the f-word occurs, liberally, in this film.)

INSIDE INFORMATION: Production of *Sweeney 2* began on 7 November 1977 and lasted five weeks. The sensational ram-raiding stunt, in which the villains drive straight through the window of a car showroom while a police car fails to follow, was filmed over one morning in the Arndale Centre, Wandsworth and performed by regular Sweenet stunt driver Frank Henson. Four cameras were used as Euston didn't have the budget to do re-shoots. During the filming, events took an unexpected turn.

An additional shot for this sequence, showing a hand dropping a shotgun, was needed and was filmed later in Wandsworth. Owing to a lack of time, however, the police hadn't been notified. The gun lay abandoned in the road and, once the camera stopped rolling, assistant director Bill Westley went to retrieve it. Tom Clegg recalls, 'There was a tap on his shoulder: "Excuse me, do you have a license for that?" [and] Bill got driven off to the police station. He was there about three hours.'

Bill Westley takes up the story: 'I got nicked! We had just finished shooting and this cadet policeman happened to walk past. He had seen me pick the shotgun up and he played it by the book and arrested me, because I wasn't the one that had the license for it. Bang to rights! I wasn't allowed to pick that gun up – only the man that supplied the gun and the two actors. When we got down to the police station, it was more or less laughed out, but the policeman who was with the cadet couldn't belittle his colleague because legally he was in the right. Of course, that went round the studio and the film industry like wildfire – "Bill Westley's been nicked for carrying a shotgun!"'

Sensing hassles ahead, Peter Brayham had already refused to be seen handling the guns. 'We had two sawn-off shotguns in that. The armourer said to me, "Can you hold them?" and I said, "No, no. Not on this manor." I knew that [the police] knew me and

I thought, "No, stuff it." So, Bill Westley held the guns and they nicked him ... They didn't care that he was a First Assistant Director – what was he doing holding the guns? There was a very heavy estate in Wandsworth.'

During the writing of the script, Troy Kennedy Martin went AWOL to finish the job. 'To pin Troy down was incredibly difficult,' Tom Clegg recalls, 'so they eventually locked him in a room at the top of Colet Court and told him that he wasn't going out until he had finished it. He got out by ringing up the secretary and telling her that he desperately needed a drink and some jelly babies, so he went off to Scotland for five days where no one could get in touch with him!'

The character of Jupp was modeled on disgraced Flying Squad commander Kenneth Drury. Regan avoids being called as a defence witness for Jupp by telling his barrister: 'Your client is so bent it's been impossible to hang the picture on his office wall straight for the past six months.' A flashback scene in Jupp's office shows that the picture is indeed askew, as Jupp quotes Lord Acton: 'Absolute power corrupts absolutely.' Regan responds flippantly, 'It's written on the wall, sir. Of the lavatory.' All this was drawn from Troy Kennedy Martin's own observations: 'I was really worried about how corrupt the CID were. I remember that Inspector Drury said, "Power corrupts. Absolute power corrupts absolutely." Then he took me round his office and there were pictures of all these guys in the Flying Squad, and none of the pictures were straight on his wall!'

Similarly, the cops' trip to Malta is reminiscent of the abortive attempt to arrest Ronnie Biggs in Brazil in 1974. According to Clegg, the villains 'were like *The Magnificent Seven* robbing a bank. They had a sense of injustice about how this country had gone down the drain.' 'All villains are Conservatives,' Troy says, of characters such as Mr Bridger in his 1960s caper movie *The Italian Job* and his *Sweeney* crooks. 'You rarely meet a left-wing villain, although one of the great train robbers was supposed to be a Labour supporter!'

Comparing the bleaker elements in the script to *The Italian Job*, Troy Kennedy Martin reflected, 'In the sixties, when I wrote that, I was younger and more optimistic, as was everyone. People like Michael Caine were around – really confident characters. There was that line in it – 'We can always take it to the Americans' – and that was really what I felt about movie scripts; there was that kind of feeling. And it was meant to be a comedy thriller. By *Sweeney 2* I was a lot more cynical. I was divorced and had children.'

There were more straightforward reasons for the location filming, too. 'Everyone wanted to go to Malta,' Kennedy Martin says. 'I used to take the kids there when they were small. And the crew had worked *so* hard, so the idea was to have a couple of weeks in the sun.' Incidentally, John Thaw would return to Malta some ten years later, for location filming on Granada's Sherlock Holmes centenary special, *The Sign of Four* (broadcast 29 December 1987), in which he played peg-legged Jonathan Small.

NAMES AND FACES: Lewis Fiander, John Flanagan, Brian Gwaspari, Brian Hall, Ken Hutchison, Patrick Malahide, Derrick O'Connor, Johnny Shannon, Barry Stanton and Frederick Treves had all previously appeared in the televised adventures of *The Sweeney*.

Renowned theatrical actor Nigel Hawthorne was perhaps best known for his performance as another bureaucrat, Sir Humphrey, in *Yes Minister* and *Yes, Prime Minister* and for his outstanding performance in *The Madness of King George*.

BAFTA-winning character actor Denholm Elliott appeared in the controversial Dennis Potter TV play *Brimstone and Treacle* and featured in over a hundred films, including *The Cruel Sea*, *The Night They Raided Minsky's*, *Raiders of the Lost Ark*, *A Room with a View*, *Trading Places* and *A Private Function*.

Interviewed in 1978, Elliott recalled that making *Sweeney 2* was 'painfully reminiscent' of the time he had been arrested in Los Angeles for making a wrong left turn 'after a couple of dry sherries. In America they don't differentiate much between someone who's made a wrong left turn at 3.00 am and someone who's just strangled their grandmother.'

POLICE AND THIEVES: *'We the undersigned leave all our worldly goods to the wives and children of all the said persons. We do this in the belief that England as a nation is finished. Its course is run and the order of the day must be to save what you can. We have built up by our own determination, and where necessary at the point of a gun, a structure on this island which will survive. We have passed this on to our wives and children in the belief that they will look after it and expand it in the same spirit as it was built.'* Film critic Leslie Halliwell delivered a typically myopic judgment on *Sweeney 2*, describing it as a 'silly, sluggish and violent extension of thin material, which would scarcely have made a good one-hour TV episode', missing the intelligent and witty features of the film completely. The quirky humour and characters throw the film's bleaker moments into sharp relief. This is a world in which a kid finds an abandoned gun and simply makes off with it. Informants carry out crimes while innocent people are arrested, such as the CIA man who's defusing a bomb rather than assembling one.

The blaggers have emigrated to Pharos (Greek for a lighthouse) in the belief that England is a sinking ship, emphasised by their decision to convert their money into dollars rather than Sterling. They all choose death instead of a prison cell, bequeathing their spoils to their families – who promptly sell them off. There is no grieving and no loyalty here – when Shirley Hicks is told that her husband's dead, she simply says, 'Do I get a grant to bury him?'

Once again, the police forces are seemingly incapable of agreeing how to sort anything out, whether it's domestic (the hotel bomb) or international (the Maltese police not helping out their opposite numbers). Dilke, Regan's bureaucratic new boss, is swift to apportion blame when things go wrong and stays well away when the going gets dangerous – presumably showing up to take the credit later.

Added to this is the theme of increasing corruption, both on the island, where the villains are paying off the locals, and in the police itself. Troy Kennedy Martin was exploring his worries 'about the degree of corruption which appeared to exist at the Yard' more openly than in the TV series. At times it seems as if Regan, Carter and the other men from the Squad represent the last vestiges of honest copperdom. Jupp, the disgraced Squad Commander, refers to his own forthcoming case as 'The Big C' – and indeed the dishonesty seems to spread like a cancer. Jupp took bribes to 'balance the books', and further down the police hierarchy two uniformed constables steal money from the back of one of the getaway cars.

Regan appears tired and miserable throughout the film, throwing himself at every woman in sight. Although these scenes are all amusing, and complement great comedy sequences like the Squad returning pissed from a brewery, the humour is undercut by a the cynical and melancholy undertone. Regan's sickened reaction to Hill's suicide and his earlier comment, 'Let's get there before it's all over', give the film an air of weary finality despite the upbeat final scene.

CHAPTER 10

MORE POLICING

'I'm gonna be calling you guv all day long, it's all I know and it's all you *need* to know!'
'Shouting George' of the Weeney in Detectives on the Edge of a Nervous Breakdown, 1993

THE SWEENEY'S EXTENSIVE IMPACT ON POPULAR CULTURE IS undeniable, as nearly quarter of a century since its first transmission it is still being spoofed and referenced. Arthur Ellis's surreal black comedy *The Black and Blue Lamp* (1988) parodied elements of the programme in its depiction of a trio of cynical coppers, 'The Filth', who threatened suspects with lines like, 'You're gonna put your hands up to this one son, or I'll take your bollocks off with a Stanley knife!' In 1993, Jim Broadbent did an excellent turn as an ersatz Jack Regan in the Comic Strip's 'Detectives on the Edge of a Nervous Breakdown', sending up the hard nut image of the seventies TV copper – fags, guns, marriage problems and handbrake turns. Members of the same team made an accurate *Sweeney*-style spoof ad plugging Nissan's 'new all-action Almera' in 1997. (Ironically, a cut had to be made, deleting Phil Cornwell's Regan lookalike shouting at a passerby because of complaints about how dangerous this behaviour was for road users). Cornwell's memorable John Thaw impersonation made a return appearance amid the residents of *Stella Street* in 1998, and as recently as 2000, in the Channel 4 comedy *Black Books*, Bill Bailey's character became *Sweeney*-obsessed after a night watching old videos in the episode 'The Blackout'.

This chapter, however, looks at the more serious knock-on effects the programme has had, both off screen and on.

TARGETING THE PROFESSIONALS

One major legacy of *The Sweeney* and Euston Films was their impact upon the production methodology of British television film drama. In September 1977 the BBC responded to ITV's ratings threat with their own tough new cop show, *Target*. Based around the activities of the Regional Crime Squad, it starred Patrick Mower as Detective Superintendent Steve Hackett. Also heading the cast were Brendan Price as his sidekick, DS Frank Bonney, Philip Madoc as Chief Superintendent Tate and, in a concession to women's liberation, Vivien Heilbron as DS Louise Colbert. The BBC clearly had high hopes for the series. It was given saturation trailers in the weeks leading up the first episode's broadcast and the cover story in *Radio Times* for 3-9 September. Despite obvious similarities, no mention was made of *The Sweeney* in pre-publicity. The mid-seventies was a time when the BBC and ITV, the only UK broadcasters, rarely acknowledged each other's existence, a point of principle underlined by their TV listing magazines not carrying details of the opposition's programming.

However, the reality behind *Target* made nonsense of this public Cold War between broadcasters. Aside from Mower, Madoc and Price, who had all guest-starred in *The Sweeney*, a glance through the credits for the first series threw up several other familiar names. The first episode, 'Shipment', was co-written and directed by David Wickes; later directors included Douglas Camfield, Mike Vardy, Terry Green, Chris Menaul and Jim Goddard. The recruitment of Euston people also extended to writers: Ray Jenkins contributed two scripts, while the BBC pseudonym of David Agnew concealed both Roger Marshall's identity and that of *Sweeney* producer Ted Childs. The sense of déjà vu didn't stop there; the action sequences were arranged by none other Peter Brayham.

Not long into the *Target*'s development, *Sweeney* director David Wickes received a call. 'I was a traitor!' he laughs. 'I was asked to go to the fourth floor of the BBC with all kinds of flunkies serving wine – most amazing – and I was told that this was a confidential meeting and that what they wanted was their own *Sweeney*.'

The BBC's desire to emulate the opposition's success required the same rethink of industrial practices that Euston had fought long and hard against the ACTT for. 'In that union-bound era, the Beeb's in-house filming operation was colossal – 40 small film crews based at Ealing Studios,' Wickes explains. 'Sclerotic, old-fashioned, over-manned and horribly set in its ways. I had told the Beeb that Euston was successful because we were a bunch of guerillas and gypsies who cut corners, broke all the rules and worked all night.'

To compete with *The Sweeney*, *Target* consequently became the first BBC drama series to be made entirely on film. Up to that point, the BBC's film units had been secondary to a predominantly studio-video production style, supplying film inserts where required. 'The reaction at Ealing to my proposal to cherry-pick a great crew and turn them into a bunch of street-filming ne'er-do-wells was greeted with horrified disbelief,' Wickes goes on. 'It took months of discussions, rows and posturings to change the ethos – but we did it. Sort of, anyway. With nods and winks 30 years of restrictive practices were slowly eroded and the crew that we selected gradually came round to the idea that they were in business to make films. In the end, I think the selected crew had a great time but, of course, the ones who were not selected for *Target* grumbled darkly in corners and were sent off to do inserts for *Blue Peter* and regional news programmes!'

Even though Wickes managed to mould a BBC film unit to the filmmaking techniques Euston had pioneered, aided and abetted by key members of *The Sweeney* production team, *Target*'s production was still hampered by the centralised, institutional nature of the BBC. Film editor John S Smith, who had also been sounded out about Euston's procedures by the BBC, explains: '*Target* was being shot in Bristol, but of course all of the post-production staff were in London, and the crews were having to travel backwards and forwards. They had all sorts of problems: they couldn't maintain the schedules as fast as we could on *The Sweeney*, as we were all freelancers and we just wanted to work. At the BBC on *Target*, they were all full-timers and they kept wanting to take annual leave and things like that.' As a result, only nine episodes were completed in the first series, with the second running to one less. Euston's general view of their self-appointed rival 'was a matter of great amusement,' Wickes remembers. 'They started off thinking "They'll never make it" and the opinion gradually changed to "Not bad, but we're still the best."'

The production ideology Euston had initiated was also being copied elsewhere. LWT set up their own Euston, a film-making subsidiary entitled Mark 1 Productions (which developed from Albert Fennell and Brian Clemens' Avengers Film and TV Enterprises Ltd) to make *The Professionals*. Created by Clemens with the working title *The A Squad*, this series also made its debut in 1977 as another variation on the seventies trend for buddy cops. There was another male double-act, this time the macho pairing of Bodie and Doyle. Together with their superior Cowley, the pair operated under the auspices of the nebulous government security department CI5. The series again employed Euston's all location approach to filmmaking, as well as employing key people who had worked for the company, including Peter Brayham, David Wickes, John S Smith, John Maskall and Chris Burt; the latter brought Roger Marshall on board to write scripts for the second series.

'Originally *The Professionals* was started off at Harefield, and it was awful,' Peter Brayham remembers. 'I got a phone call to ask if I would be available to do the title sequence. I asked who the director was, and they said, "We haven't got him yet but we think it's going to be David Wickes." So I said, "If you've got David, I think he'll probably ask for me." He did, and we did a military assault course for the titles, and I also did one where I drove the car through the glass. That's the way that started, and I was asked to stay, as things hadn't worked out with their stunt guy. All the people who worked on *The Sweeney* were pulled over after it finished. There's the pattern – "How do we do it? Get the guys who did it first!"' Clearly, it was felt that the Euston style could only be replicated accurately by employing the originators of it.

A FAIR COP?

Aside from *The Sweeney*'s effect upon the production side of television, the cultural impact of the programme's themes on the British crime genre was also significant. Series such as *Z-Cars*, *Dixon of Dock Green* and *Hunter's Walk* all began to look quaint and old-fashioned as the tough rebel cop, personified by Regan, became the new archetype to be imitated.

Target, while being a successful attempt to instil Euston production methods into the BBC, backfired in its attempt to emulate *The Sweeney*'s hardboiled but sophisticated approach to storytelling. It was marketed on the cover of *Radio Times* with a mean and moody Patrick Mower glowering beneath the headline 'A Fair Cop?'

The accompanying article made much of Hackett being a tough character: 'He is quite right of left wing … He is angry – he thinks many things are going wrong.'

The protagonist in *Target* was originally meant to be quite different, however. The programme was envisaged as a character-driven drama starring Colin Blakely in the lead. Graham Williams, the former script editor on *Z-Cars* who had initiated the idea for the new BBC series, was swapped with *Doctor Who* producer Philip Hinchcliffe, who had brought a hard-edged, adult style to the BBC's evergreen science fiction series. Ironically, this approach was thought better suited to the drastic reformatting *Target* underwent in the wake of *The Sweeney*'s success. Unhappy with the format changes, Roger Marshall, engaged to write the pilot script, removed his name from the production. The programme's subject matter was deliberately changed behind the scenes in an attempt to duplicate Euston's hard new house-style.

The resulting series was greeted with hostility by public and critics. Unlike *The Sweeney*'s cops, the character of Hackett seemed artificial, lacked gravitas and failed to find favour with the public; dressed as if he had just walked out of a seventies nightclub, he was simply not felt to be authentic. The *Radio Times* letters pages contained much opprobrium on the subject. 'I have never come across a Det-Supt like Hackett and I hope I never do. His kind would not last long in a real police set-up,' J East opined, going on to say, 'I presume you have an ex-police officer as your adviser for the programme and I can only suggest that he or she has given bad advice. The whole programme was full of technical errors, and the scene in the restaurant [in the first episode 'Shipment'] was the final insult to all serving and ex-policemen.'

Target also attempted to go further with its violence than *The Sweeney* did, but without the three-dimensional characters, wit and élan of the original, it merely looked sensationalist, as correspondent N C Duncan noted. '[*Target*'s] competitors, *Starsky and Hutch* and *The Sweeney*, are often criticised for their violence; but at least they show concern for their colleagues and it is possible to accept their behaviour as a response to the criminals. Hackett's violence, both physical and verbal, is indiscriminate and sickening…' Tom Clegg, another *Sweeney* director approached to direct the show, believes that style was definitely put before content: 'I went up to see Philip Hinchcliffe but I didn't fancy it; the scripts were so weak.'

'Yes, it did get a lot of stick in the press for violence but I think that was because it lacked the *Sweeney*'s propensity for humour,' David Wickes concedes. 'Somehow, its quips never seemed to work. It was like getting an elephant to run in a horse race. It *is* a big thing, and it *can* run, but it's not gonna win. It didn't work too badly, but we never got the right characterisation and we didn't get the right stories. '

By contrast, *The Professionals* was a slicker, more comic-strip refinement of the Euston style, with one eye clearly on the American market: there was a minimum of slang and no regional accents. The threat to the social order in this programme frequently came from foreign agents, in an externalisation of the fears concerning the state of 1970s Britain.

'You can't divorce it from what was going on at the time,' David Wickes says of the series' perceived political slant. 'It was a very different philosophy [to *The Sweeney*], a very different template. Anybody that didn't live through the seventies doesn't know what a dangerous time it was... The whole of Leicester Square was piled up to the second floor with rubbish bags, and London was running with rats. We were in real trouble. Dennis Healey going to the IMF – International Monetary Fund – to bail Britain out with a loan. In those days, people were saying, "Will the last person to leave Britain please switch out the light." There were a lot of really bad, nasty dangers coming from the Soviet Union and its satellites: ghastly people with thumbscrews, and all the horrors that existed behind the Iron Curtain. We had terrible fellow travellers in this country; people blowing things up, threats of anthrax in the water – it was a horrible time. And *The Professionals* reflected that. Two guys have to come along to put it right, and Brian Clemens said to me before we started at Pinewood: "I'll tell you what I want the audience to say: Thank God they're out there."'

With a lesson clearly learnt from *Target*, Wickes was careful that the series should not appear so uncompromising that it alienated the viewer. '[Bodie and Doyle] could have been very unsympathetic. They had something in common with a bouncer outside a club – not your friend, not your friend at all – whereas Regan and Carter *were*. You had to get [the balance] dead right.' The end result resonated with the country's mood, particularly when the Iranian Embassy was stormed by the SAS.

Like *Target*, the programme was not without its critics, some saying it lacked the complexity, the characterisation, and the 'pungency and the fun' of *The Sweeney*. Chris Burt, who, like Wickes, worked on both series, maintains that the big difference was that '*The Sweeney* had real characters that people could immediately latch on to.' However, *The Professionals'* development of the Euston Films' style was a success this time and the series ran for five years. Like *The Sweeney*, *The Professionals* also retains a cult following via satellite TV and video and DVD releases, partly fostered by the appropriation of both shows by 1990s 'lad' culture.

With this new form of TV film-making established, the content of the series moved away from *The Sweeney/Professionals* blueprint. *Shoestring*, the next film series the BBC attempted in Bristol, was a change of pace with a laid back, cerebral private detective in a non metropolitan location; this time, the programme's post-production facilities were also located in the area the series was made. This further, successful diversification in filmed crime shows consequently bred another sub-genre, the provincial detective series, a form that ranges through shows such as *Taggart*, *Spender*, *Frost* and *Dalziel and Pascoe*. Significantly, the most successful example, *Inspector Morse*, starred John Thaw and involved both Ted Childs and Chris Burt.

BAD APPLES

Interviewed in1978, *Sweeney* writer Troy Kennedy Martin observed the way the public gravitated towards individualistic characters like those in *The Professionals*, commenting in particular on the idolisation of the figure of Barlow in *Z-Cars* and linking it to 'the psychological roots of British fascism.' In the hands of writers mindful of real police corruption, *The Sweeney's* intention was always to avoid transforming

Regan into a similarly idolised figure.

G F Newman, a friend of Troy Kennedy Martin's, had also become concerned about the degree of corruption within the police in the 1970s, and also about the way television was avoiding the issue. In the mid-1970s he wrote a trilogy of novels, *You Flash Bastard, Sir You Bastard* and *You Nice Bastard*, concerning the rise to power of Terry Sneed, a totally immoral policeman at Scotland Yard. These were hard, uncompromising books, taking an extremely dim view of the police. Despite his friendship with the Kennedy Martin brothers, Newman was not happy with the arrival of *The Sweeney*, feeling that it would cover similar (unacknowledged) ground to his Sneed books. 'We met at Troy's one night and I very nearly got hooked over,' Trevor Preston laughs. 'Gordon steamed in – you should see him when he's furious – and I can remember, he looked at us and said, "Don't you dare steal my stars!" Apparently he'd written this series of books, which I've still never read, and he thought we were going to rip him off. I didn't even know who this geezer was! I gave him an evil look, and he nipped out pretty quick.'

While *The Sweeney* did break new ground by showing that police corruption was going on in the episode 'Bad Apple', it was simplistically dealt with in the same way as other crimes – by punching out the villains and nicking them. Additionally, despite Regan's rule-bending in order to secure convictions, he was never seen to take bribes. In the real world, Operation Countryman was taking place – which saw many corrupt officers arrested – and Newman consequently wrote *Law and Order* as a reaction against what he perceived as *The Sweeney*'s naïveté on the issue, intending to show that a whole barrel of apples had gone sour. However, to Newman's further annoyance, a few critics missed the point, as Troy Kennedy Martin recalls: 'What was funny was when [*Law and Order*] came on they said it was just like *The Sweeney!*'

Screened in 1978, the series consisted of four connected plays about the criminal justice system, made by the BBC and produced by Tony Garnett. To date, this is the most radical series about the police ever made; John McVicar described it as 'so stunningly good and real it shocked'. Although looking at the law from different perspectives (the Policeman, the Villain, the Brief and the Prisoner), the plays were linked by the common characters of blagger Jack Lynn and Fred Pyle, the corrupt detective who frames him. Filmed in a matter-of-fact documentary style, the series was the total antithesis of the usual heroic portrayal of the police. The series was a necessary dose of realpolitik for the viewing public, although the unflattering picture the plays painted of the police provoked outrage and disbelief when they were first broadcast. The BBC initially said they would not repeat them, but later reversed their decision.

It can't be a complete coincidence that after *Law and Order* was screened, both the BBC and ITV steered their portrayals of the police away from the thorny issue of internal politics. Private investigators such as *Shoestring*, police operating in provincial settings such as *Inspector Morse* and *Bergerac*, or quirky investigation units with a specific brief, such as the Inner City Squad in Murray Smith's *Strangers*, became the norm for several years.

However, throughout the 1980s and into the 1990s, an after-image of the ethically dubious copper seen in *The Sweeney* and *Law and Order* continued to be seen in the genre through ITV's long-running police soap *The Bill*. It featured Regan-like characters like the boozing, chain-smoking and scruffy DS Ted Roach and his irascible guvnor DI Burnside, together with the occasional in-joke: one episode saw Burnside telling a villain to 'Get your backside off that mattress, you're nicked.' (There was a genuine *Sweeney* link, too, as the series was initiated by Thames and the early seasons were executive produced by Lloyd Shirley.) The recent return of the Burnside character in his own spin-off series attests to the enduring popularity of the rebel figure who arrives to 'sort it out' and restore social order. The appeal of this police archetype was also reflected in *The Bill* again in 2002, with the arrival of DS Phil Hunter, another rule-bending, is-he-or-isn't-he bent? copper.

SWEENEY 2.0

Given the impact *The Sweeney* has had on popular television – the attempts to imitate its characters and the efforts to put forward counter-dramas – it's not surprising that to date there have been at least two formal attempts to revive the series, one dating back to 1983.

'I thought it would have been terrific fun. Hong Kong was a place I knew very well, and it was in the period leading up to the British handover,' remembers Roger Marshall, the writer behind the first attempted revival. 'I thought there was a lot of potential in a no-nonsense copper like Regan being seconded to the Hong Kong police. It wouldn't be the Flying Squad against the Krays, it would have been the Hong Kong police against the Triads, and there was also a lot of illegal immigration and smuggling going on. Put this together with the cultural clashes you'd have got with someone of Regan's background working in the Far East... John was keen, and I had Ian Kennedy Martin's blessing. I got David Stirling, a major shareholder in Hong Kong television, interested, but ultimately nothing came of it.'

The series creator, Ian Kennedy Martin, made a second attempt to revive the show in 1998. 'What happened was that Pearson [now Fremantle] thought it could be done again. It has an iconic status and Dennis is looking great. I was commissioned and duly delivered a script which was worked on by Thames Pearson [the late 1990s corporate incarnation of Thames]. But it didn't occur to us that Pearson had a drama policy which was "If it's any good, somebody else will pay for it." So when it went to Pearson, Chris Bye, then head of drama, had to apologise and say, "I've been to the top and they've said we don't do remakes of programmes." Carter would have come back as a Commander, having had a slight problem on the way and been suspended for a couple of years. Then we have two young guys and a girl. When I was writing it I was tied down a bit by audience expectations of what *The Sweeney* looks like, but things have come on quite a bit since then with cops.'

Dennis Waterman himself was intrigued by the possibilities of updating the series for a new audience. '[Ian] had written an outline and it all seemed to work. People were having a go at why Regan had gone – there was speculation that he was bent – but Ian was also talking a lot to a guy who had left the present day Sweeney.' According to Kennedy Martin's source, it seemed that the position of a Flying Squad officer in the 1990s was open to just as much abuse as it had been in the 1970s. 'This guy was saying, "There's so much corruption in and around the place now, it's a totally different world to when you guys were doing it." It would have been quite interesting to have done it, but these people in suits in their wisdom...'

COP OUT

As this book has shown, there was a lot more to *The Sweeney* than angry men in flares and a Mark 1 transit van. Attempts to revitalise the British gangland genre in recent years have invariably proved disappointing or unconvincing. *Sweeney* stunt arranger Peter Brayham is not alone in being dismissive of efforts such as *Lock, Stock and Two Smoking Barrels*, which trade on the superficial macho qualities of a genre *The Sweeney* helped define: 'Absolute crap. [Film director] Guy Ritchie's not exactly the most popular guy amongst the chaps.'

The real spirit of *The Sweeney* lives on, not in these posturing attempts at retro, faux-seventies gangsterism, but in new television shows that continue to push the fictional interpretation of the police forward. *Cracker*, Jimmy McGovern's drama about a criminal profiler, was one example of an attempt to hold a mirror up to society; *Between the Lines*, tackling similar themes to that of Tony Garnett's previous production *Law and Order*, was another. Both series featured strong, well-realised characters and thought-provoking scripts tackling emotive and difficult issues: rape, serial killing, racism, and an examination of the society that creates the perpetrators of such crimes.

Like the first two *Prime Suspect* dramas, *The Chinese Detective*, and some episodes of *The Cops* (Garnett again), these series all have a view of the police and policing that is downbeat, unglamorous and, at times, uncomfortably realistic. However, these shows' darker moments are lightened by the ability of the characters to laugh at both the job and life's absurdities, bringing the flavour of real life to the situations they inhabit.

These qualities are *The Sweeney*'s real legacy.

'In its own context *The Sweeney* was truthful. Real men, and women with no make-up. I think that's why people still talk about it today with *enormous* feeling, because you took them in as pals. People felt involved in it. I think there are about six or seven really *great* episodes – all different stories – and there are moments in them that are razor-sharp and are what policing in this country is like... I think *The Sweeney* has said more about our society than any play. We didn't talk down to people. The trouble with all of the *Wednesday Plays* was that they either wagged their finger at you or had Dennis Potter going off on one. *The Sweeney* was about story-telling and not trying to fucking con people.'
Trevor Preston

APPENDIX 1

THE SWEENEY FORMAT

This appendix contains the Sweeney *'bible' originally written by Ted Childs to brief new writers on aspects of the series. Not all writers can recall seeing this document, so verbal discussions along similar lines may have taken place instead.*

Month not known, 1974

This is a series of one-hour films featuring two detectives who work in the Flying Squad, the elite crime investigation unit of the Metropolitan Police.

The title *The Sweeney* is derived from cockney rhyming slang 'The Sweeney Todd' ie, The Flying Squad. It is a vernacular term used by both criminals and police.

The Flying Squad came into being during the 20s when criminals began to use motor cars. Then, as now, the majority of all crime detection within the Metropolitan Police district was handled by CID units at divisional level. The Flying Squad was formed to transcend divisional boundaries in the effective pursuit of mobile criminals. At present the Flying Squad consists of some 150 detectives, headed by a Senior Officer of Commander rank. The operation element of the Squad consists of four units each commanded by a Detective Chief Inspector. Within each unit there are two Detective Inspectors each commanding two Detective Sergeants and a varying number of Detective Constables. A small number of women detectives work within the Squad.

The Squad's main task is to prevent major crime by establishing very thorough networks of intelligence within the criminal fraternity. The Flying Squad hope that if they cannot prevent a crime their specialist knowledge will enable them to arrest the people who perpetrated it fairly quickly. The Squad itself relates with the other senior crime detection units which have subsequently been formed within Scotland Yard, eg. Serious Crime Squad, the Regional Crime Squad, the Robbery Squad, the Fraud Squad, the Drug Squad and latterly, the Bomb Squad.

The candidates for the Flying Squad are normally selected from CID personnel at Divisional level who have shown particular prowess. Of course, it is possible for a detective to be selected from a Division, to serve in the Flying Squad, to return to a Divisional appointment upon promotion and subsequently to rejoin the Flying Squad at a later date. The term Flying Squad derived from the fact that the unit was originally equipped with a fleet of sports cars co-ordinated by wireless telegraphy. This was one of the first attempts in Britain to apply radio control techniques to police work. High mobility is still a feature of Flying Squad operations. The Squad is still equipped with high performance cars, normally within the 21/2/3 litre range.

One interesting feature of the Squad's operations is that its detectives do not normally drive themselves. Each car is driven by a 'driver'. These drivers are not detectives but expert Traffic Division constables. They are seconded to the Flying Squad to work in plain clothes. Drivers do not undertake detective work per se although as police constables they may well assist with arrests, etc.

The overall episode screen time (ex titles) is 48.40. We expect the final draft script to read at about 53 minutes. Each film will open with a teaser of up to three minutes duration which is followed by the opening titles. The story is played across three acts, each of which must be no more than 19 and not less than eight minutes in length.

The two running characters are Detective Inspector Jack Regan and Detective Sergeant Carter. Regan will appear in every episode, Carter will appear in approximately 10 out of 13 episodes. In addition to these running characters, each script should be built around three major speaking parts with up to ten minor speaking parts.

Experience indicates that within this film format, it is better to provide a small number of major parts which attract leading actors and actresses rather than a cycle of cameos which are difficult to cast. Few players of ability are interested in a one-page scene.

Each film is shot over ten days. We must, therefore, shoot an average of five minutes edited screen time a day. This means we have to impose restrictions on the number of locations we use. Normally ten locations, ie. one per shooting day, is enough. By location we mean an area in which a number of scenes can be shot. For example, a school or college (during holidays) affords us a variety of interesting locations – chapels, classrooms, laboratories as well as extensive grounds and does not necessitate the uneconomic use of the film unit"s time. The more time we spend loading and unloading vehicles and driving around London, the less time, within the ten days, we have to actually make a film.

There is one standing composite set at Colet Court, which provides our weather cover option. This is a representation of the Flying Squad offices at Scotland Yard. It consists of a large open plan office, part of which is referred to as 'the Squad office' and contains the desks at which the detective inspectors sit, and another section called the Reserve Room, in which detective sergeants and below congregate when not on outside duty. The set also contains the switchboard and radio transmitter which serves the particular needs of the Flying Squad. In addition, there are two other smaller offices which can serve as offices for more senior officers, as interview rooms, etc. There is also a corridor area adjoining this set with lifts, staircase, entrances, etc.

We normally schedule two days in the ten-week shooting cycle in the office composite set. This means we anticipate ten minutes of any film being set within these Scotland Yard offices. Since we are shooting through the summer months, exterior night shooting is very expensive for us to undertake and we cannot normally anticipate more than three minutes exterior night material in any script. Interior night scenes are not normally difficult to contrive.

The series is set in London and we do not propose to take our unit on journeys of more than one hour's driving time from our base in Hammersmith.

We would point out that some locations that appear to offer attractive possibilities can present difficulties. For example, London Transport, although prepared to allow us to hire buses, will not normally let us film any material which relates to fictitious criminal events on its property or its railway trains. British Rail is more obliging although one is usually restricted to off-peak time in the Greater London area. Although we can obtain film facilities from airports such as Heathrow and Luton, the authorities insist that operational requirements take priority. This means they can cancel a location booking at the last moment and cause us considerable embarrassment. We do not, therefore, usually entertain such locations.

Nor can we obtain facilities from the Metropolitan Police. Under certain circumstances they will allow us to film people and cars leaving and entering police stations and Scotland Yard. However, we must give them considerable notice of any such intention.

Similarly, it is not possible to film interiors of HM Prisons or any other Home Office properties which relate to the police service or the law courts. The police will not normally allow us to stage crime in public thoroughfares. It is best if we plan shootings, hold-ups, etc for staging on private property.

In general writers should not be too specific when delimiting locations. Where names are vital to the plot it is wise to use totally fictitious names which can be quickly approved by our legal representatives before we proceed with filming. A quick glance at the Yellow Pages will often indicate whether a business or trade is being practised under the name a writer intends to use.

This series is based on the use of a film unit which moves very quickly across a number of locations. The nature of our film operation itself very much determines the style of our films. In general terms, we can cope with action more readily than we can with multi-handed dialogue. Unlike television, where extensive rehearsal facilities and the use of several cameras for any given scene enable fairly complicated sequences involving several actors to be staged quite easily, we have to light every shot individually for one camera. Also we cannot enjoy the luxury of extensive rehearsal. This makes complicated dialogue comparatively difficult for us.

On the other hand, the mobility of our equipment and the sophistication of our editing and dubbing techniques allow us to produce action sequences which can attain a considerable degree of pace and excitement. This is not to say that we do not need good dialogue in our scripts. Clearly an investigatory police thriller does depend, to no small extent, on good dialogue but in general terms it is better to write uncomplicated story lines which deal straightforwardly with crime and criminals where dialogue scenes are short and sharp rather than intriguing but perhaps involved plots dependent on expository dialogue.

However, when talking of action, it must be made clear that we are not in the

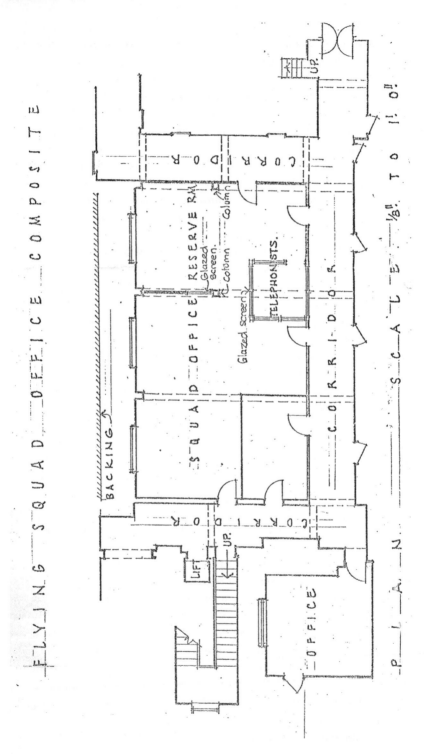

The Flying Squad set built at the Euston Films offices at Colet Court

'Bondiana' league. We can cope with a limited number of fight scenes, car chases, shoot-outs, etc. We cannot blow up 'Jablite' representations of St Paul's nor bring the whole of Oxford Street to a grinding halt in order to wreck three police cars inside Selfridges' front window!

Major crime is very often violent and one does not wish to flinch from the reality of this. Nonetheless, the series is being produced for transmission in both afternoon and evening family viewing hours. Accordingly, we must respect the rules laid down by the IBA in respect of language and the detailed description of pathological forms of behaviour. Four-letter words are not permissible, nor can we indulge in 'souped up' horror, eg. represent, in slow motion, a security guard having his head blown off by a shotgun.

Action, within our brief, does not mean continual violence. With the techniques at our disposal, it is possible to show characters in a variety of interesting real situations, where movement and action serve to underline the pace and style of cinematic story telling based on short dialogue scenes. This is the particular style we are trying to set.

The main character in *The Sweeney* is Detective Inspector Jack Regan (36), a tough, resourceful detective who is to be played by John Thaw. Regan has been a policeman since he came to London from Manchester when he was 22. He served the statutory two years as a probationary police constable then applied to join the CID. He served as a temporary detective constable and following this was made up to substantive detective constable and served within a division as a CID officer until he was promoted Sergeant and transferred to the Flying Squad. Following his promotion to Detective Inspector, he worked within a divisional unit once again before returning to Flying Squad where he has been for the past four years.

Regan is the 'total professional', a 24-hours-a-day cop. His commitment to his career led to the break-up of his marriage. He is divorced but visits his eight-year-old daughter fairly regularly. His ex-wife is now preparing to re-marry. Regan finds it difficult to develop lasting emotional relationships with people. With women he is prone to casualness, although not promiscuity. He is proud of the Flying Squad and its reputation. Like most Squad officers, he enjoys the considerable freedom the work pattern affords. This is one reason why he has not actively pursued promotion since this would probably result in his transfer. Regan is contemptuous of the formality and bureaucracy which characterises much of the police service. His casual style of dressing is one of his methods of articulating this resentment.

His basic philosophy is 'Don't bother me with forms and procedures, let me get out there and nick villains.' He fears the current developments taking place within the Metropolitan Police Criminal Investigation Department. Attempts are being made to rationalise the work of the department. A number of specialist crime fighting units have been formed at Scotland Yard in recent years – the Serious Crimes Squad and the Robbery Squad. With the freedom of action that top detective work demands, it has been difficult to prevent a measure of 'empire building' and it is often alleged that the different squads are inefficiently and ineffectively covering the same ground and wasting too much time in conflicts engendered by in-house politics.

For story purposes, we are assuming that an amalgamation of the various 'top squads' is being enacted. With some justification Regan fears his wings are about to be clipped. The new top detective is likely to be much more 'an organisation man' working through committee and much more heavily dependent on specialist forensic and other services.

Regan has been a successful detective. He has made his name by being very much 'his own man'. Intuitive, with a keen understanding of human nature, he can appear an emotive, mercurial man. He will sometimes pursue criminals with a degree of ruthlessness which can shock people used to seeing him as a cynically humorous but compassionate human being.

Regan, then, is a good detective but a man approaching middle age whose fears for his own emotional stability and long-term job security sometimes float to the surface.

It is against the background of the life and times of a particular policeman dealing day to day with major crime in a modern city that the series is to be set.

Regan works regularly with a subordinate with whom he enjoys a very good relationship. Detective Sergeant George Carter (26) is a tough, sharp cockney who hails from Notting Hill. A working-class lad on the make. Were it not for the fact that a concerned schoolteacher had instilled in him notions of public service, he might have ended up 'on the other side'. Several of his school friends have. A keen sportsman, a former amateur boxing champion, he maximised use of the extensive sporting facilities which are available to young policemen. By chance he found he had a naturalistic detective skill and was eventually offered an appointment within the Flying Squad. He admires Regan very much and enjoys working with him, although they often argue over detailed methods of approach and styles of working.

Carter is now in the Flying Squad for the second time. He returned to the more staid life of a Divisional detective after he married. His wife – a secondary school teacher with ambitions – realised that promotion and a stable marriage are unlikely to come the way of a young Flying Squad detective, particularly one who has fallen under Regan's charismatic influence. Mrs Carter believes her husband should endeavour to climb on to the promotional 'gravy train' the CID amalgamation has engendered instead of hanging round pubs and clubs with informants. She feels her husband would be better employed studying for promotion examinations and indulging in that measure of sycophantic behaviour necessary for advancement in any highly structured organisation.

Carter argues that his return to the Flying Squad will offer him the most likely chance of appointment to a higher rank. His wife remains unconvinced and Carter does run into trouble from time to time. His standing excuse is that if he comes home that particular night he might miss the big break which will lead to his promotion. The argument is wearing thin.

Detective Chief Inspector Frank Haskins (46) is Regan's immediate boss in the Squad. He is an intelligent man (Southampton Grammar School Matric.) A logical, almost academic detective, Haskins made something of a name for himself in the Fraud Squad. He was transferred into the Flying Squad to reinforce the intellectual calibre of its middle management and mitigate against the rough, tough image some senior Flying Squad officers had fostered. Haskins is an ambitious man, and the transfer was, in police terms, a prestigious promotion he could not refuse. His aim is to become Chief Superintendent in charge of one of the Crime branch's intelligence departments. To achieve this he must prove competent in his Flying Squad appointment. That is difficult for Haskins. He is a highly strung, insecure man. The secure, ordered structure of the police service has always attracted him. Yet the pressures of responsibility within an elite unit present him with difficulties. He is fast developing a duodenal ulcer. He knows he must prove he can handle the 'mavericks' like Regan but he is not sure how best to achieve mastery. He has used a number of ploys, friendship, antipathy, humour. Regan has remained impervious. Regan clearly thinks Haskins is a weak, devious man. Haskins believes Regan to be undisciplined, irresponsible and uncouth. He also suspects Regan of subverting the loyalty of junior officers like Carter. Regan is careful never to cross the boundary line which would render him liable to a formal charge of insolence or indisclipline. Carter is more sympathetic than Regan. He recognises that Haskins is a clever, often perceptive detective. He sometimes questions Regan's attitude to Haskins, believing Regan gives him a hard time unnecessarily.

Haskins is a better detective than he gives himself credit for. He has none of Regan's intuition but he has the capacity for cool logical analysis of complex situations. An insight which can elude Regan who often bogs down in emotive and peripheral matters when an investigation grinds to a halt.

Unlike Regan, Haskins welcomes the amalgamation of specialist detective functions at Scotland Yard and the increasing importance given to 'technocratic' detective methods. He sees the changes as likely to afford him greater opportunity to achieve his ambition. However in his anxiety to prove himself 'executive timber' he is prone to subservience and has a degree of 'political' awareness that suggests limited moral courage.

Haskins is married to a shrewish bank clerk, menopausal and not averse to giving her husband a hard time over it. They live in a detached house in North Harrow. They have two teenage children attending a local direct grant school.

The detectives of the Flying Squad are in the business of preventing major crime. For much of their information about developments in the underworld they depend on informants and being around locales where suitable intelligence can be culled. From time to time they are formed into larger units to deal with particular crimes but normally their brief is to be out around town finding out what is going on.

Their main concern is major crime, usually forms of robbery, including anything from hold-ups to hijacks. To an increasing extent they are becoming involved with 'organised' crime, where the proceeds of one crime are used to finance other crimes in addition to apparently legitimate enterprises.

An earlier draft of the document, dated February 1974, contained a different character as Regan's boss, Laker, the same character seen in 'Regan'. The section on the role reads as follows:

There is to be one more running character, Chief Detective Inspector Thomas Laker. Laker is Regan's immediate boss. At 32, Laker is young for the middle management of the Flying Squad. He is very much the 'bright young man' on the way up, the epitome of the new, technocratic, computerised Scotland Yard detective. A determined careerist who sees the changing situation within the CID affording an ideal opportunity for accelerated advancement.

Laker is from a lower middle-class, London suburban background. Grammar school (with two 'A' levels); he joined the Metropolitan Police after he failed to gain entry to Sandhurst. After quick transfer to CID he was selected for the 'Special' (High Flyers) Course at the National Police College. He then made a name for himself in the Serious Crimes Squad, was promoted to CID and reassigned to the Flying Squad as part of the new amalgamation. Laker is the antithesis of Regan. Cold and detached, he has none of Regan's intuitive understanding of crime and criminals. He believes in the firm application of logic and method. Given enough time to check and analyse the available data, most crimes can be solved, claims Laker. Unfortunately for Regan, Laker's method will often work. It may be more expensive and less exciting than Regan's way, but it does maximise the use of mediocre police talent and has enormous PR value for the public and, not least of all, the criminal fraternity.

Nonetheless, Laker knows that, in being placed over Regan, he is being tested for the next rung of the promotion ladder. To make Superintendent, Laker has to show he can handle the awkward but necessary mavericks of the Force. Regan knows the rules. He cannot openly defy Laker in matters of discipline, but he persistently avoids following in the detective methods Laker advocates. Regan has an almost ideological commitment to his hunchy, intuitive method of work. Win, lose or draw, Regan is not going to concede to Laker on that. Laker is determined to avoid abrasive confrontations. In consequence, the conflict is conducted on a variety of levels, often quite subtly.

Laker is tall, well-dressed, austere. Regan is short, scruffy, outspoken and extrovert. Laker is articulate with intellectual pretensions. Regan is idiomatic, at times coarse. Although Regan is a man of warmth and humanity, his private life is in ruins. Laker is cold and opportunistic but has all the appurtenances of a happy home life; a wife (he married well: the horse-faced daughter of a wealthy chartered accountant who is a Tory county councillor), two plain daughters and a modern detached house in Pinner. Laker attempts to turn Carter from Regan (yet another fighting for Carter's soul). Laker offers the carrot of easy advancement for 'safe' men and the stick of professional failure for those who aid and abet Regan. Carter is conscious of the validity of Laker's exhortations but cannot bring himself to be disloyal to Regan.

🚗 APPENDIX 2 🚗

THE SWEENEY FOR SALE

This appendix contains details of some of the merchandise related to The Sweeney. *Older items can still be found in the second hand market.*

THE NOVELS (1975-1978)

Ten *Sweeney* novels were published overall. The first three, by original series creator Ian Kennedy Martin, offer an interesting insight into the way *The Sweeney* may have gone had he retained artistic control over the programme. The characterisation of Carter, in particular, is very different to that of his television counterpart; rather than disapproving of Regan's methods, he is shown as an embryonic clone of his superior officer, bending the rules, ambitious for promotion, and looking to replace Regan as the Flying Squad's resident maverick. The pair's relationship is often fractious.

The Sweeney, Ian Kennedy Martin's opening novel, contains many of the elements from his pilot script (even down to an almost identical scene featuring a black nightclub singer). Regan is every inch the loner cop, at loggerheads with his superiors, in particular Haskins, who, just as in 'Regan', tries to have his rebellious DI thrown off the Squad. As well as trying to crack the case, Regan spends much of the story in opposition to two men, Carter and Ewing, who are respectively younger and more controlled versions of him, a point harshly reinforced when Tanya, Regan's girlfriend, sleeps with the visiting American. Personal and inter-departmental rivalries between the police play as significant a part in the narrative as catching the villains, also a hallmark of Kennedy Martin's writing.

Regan and the Manhattan File reads like the screenplay for a cinema thriller: there are shoot-outs, a *Dirty Harry*-style hunt for a bomb in a station, heavy drinking, sex, more sex and an impressive car/lorry trashing stunt. There was a good reason for this, as author Ian Kennedy Martin explains: 'Lloyd [Shirley] said, "Look, we can make a deal with CBS to shoot a two-hour episode of *The Sweeney* in New York. They just need to be convinced that there is a story there." So I wrote an American-based novel but CBS never picked it up.'

The liveliest of the three novels written by *The Sweeney*'s creator, *Regan and the Manhattan File* is almost a reverse take on his first book, as this time Regan goes to America and solves the case, outwitting the local law enforcement. The book also features another US character who could be a Stateside version of Regan, the alcoholic cop Cassidy. The only element that isn't handled maturely in *The Manhattan File* is Regan's attitude to Christa being a lesbian. Hurt male pride aside, his reaction is violently misogynistic, even for the 1970s: 'He felt humiliated and alternately dulled by the shock and wild with fury, and wanting to go back to that apartment and kick both fucking dykes around their phoney deep pile cathedral to perversion.' These days, it would probably turn him on.

There are some interesting, probably unintentional, parallels with the first *Sweeney* film, as the book involves a lone cop caught up in an international conspiracy, unsure of who the opposition is. The gang of businessmen Regan arrested at London Airport are all being systematically killed; a contemporary, paranoid edge is added with the revelation that their executioners were from the CIA.

The paranoia continues in Kennedy Martin's third book, *Regan and the Deal of the Century*, in which Regan is used as a patsy by Special Branch, framed by Maynon (whom he blackmails for information) and treated with mocking scorn by Carter (who only appears fleetingly). Like the preceding two novels, the story has some coincidental parallels, this time with the episode 'Visiting Fireman' and the first film: there are references to the oil business and Regan falls for a prostitute, later on avenging her murder.

All three of Kennedy Martin's novels are tightly plotted thrillers. The prose is tough, matter-of-fact, urgently paced and the police procedural aspects in the books, and the foreign locations, are all described with authenticity.

Sadly, the same cannot be said for the other seven books in this series, which were written by the pseudonymous Joe Balham. Written, it would seem, with tongue firmly in cheek, these later books began to exaggerate the more unpleasant characteristics of the series, such as the misogyny and violence. 'Booze brings lust for the money a man carries in his wallet, the sex a woman carries in her pants. And both are interchangeable, or so the promise goes. It's the oldest, and least fulfilled, of all the promises' (*Regan and the Bent Stripper*). In *Regan and the High Rollers,* a couple are interrupted in bed by villains. 'He felt the muzzles of the shot gun press into his anus, between his buttocks. "Stay still," the man in the centre said. "Or I'll blow off what's left of your bollocks."'

In Balham's books, Regan is totally humourless and presented as a bigoted hard man dedicated to nailing villains; he only feels at home in London. *Regan and the Bent Stripper* again: 'Soho. His patch. His territory. His kind of noise and smell. Neon lights, cooking oil stinking from Greek restaurants. Cars being illegally parked in the same street in which the Heavy Mob were lifting them away.' Unsurprisingly, the comic humour of the television series is often absent or handled clumsily.

Containing characters named 'Big Tit Lil' and 'Nige the Poof', the majority of these books feature racist/sexist stereotypes. In terms of quality and readability they come from the same stable as Richard Allen's skinhead tales, the *Nick Carter PI* books and numerous other contenders in the 1970s' 'cack airport fiction' canon. These days most of them can be found residing in charity shops.

THE SWEENEY

by Ian Kennedy Martin
aka *Regan, The Sweeny* [sic] and *The Sweeney: Regan*
h/b Arthur Barker February 1975; p/b Futura September 1975
Lieutenant John Ewing of the San Francisco PD comes to London in search of James Purcell, killer of patrolman Dennis O'Hagen. He is placed under Regan's supervision. Investigating the killing of his old informant Eddie Mavor, Regan discovers that the two cases are connected. Purcell is acting as draftsman for an IRA team that Mavor supplied false passports for and who now plan to steal from London banks owned by the New York Bank and Trust Company. Despite an antagonistic relationship, Ewing and Regan foil the robbers. Proving himself as uncompromising as his Flying Squad counterpart, Ewing beds Regan's girlfriend Tanya and kills Purcell in revenge for the murder of O'Hagen.

THE SWEENEY: REGAN AND THE MANHATTAN FILE

by Ian Kennedy Martin
aka *The Sweeney 2: Regan and the Manhattan File*
h/b Arthur Barker October 1975; p/b Futura April 1975
Regan goes to deliver documents confiscated from some 'businessmen' at London Airport to the FBI in New York; they are vital to a court case. However, he is tricked into handing the file to some fake FBI employees who work for the Mafia. Realising he's been conned, Regan stays in New York to recover the documents, teaming up with detectives Cassidy and Ciales and beginning an affair with Cassidy's friend Christa. The DI resists several attempts on his life, finally discovering that the paperwork was central to a CIA investigation of arms dealing to Libya, with the Mafia acting as middle men in laundering the money which financed the weapons shipments. Regan is furious to discover that Christa is bisexual, and despite her attempts to rescue their relationship, leaves America without a reconciliation.

THE SWEENEY 3: REGAN AND THE DEAL OF THE CENTURY

by Ian Kennedy Martin
p/b Futura November 1976; h/b Arthur Barker January 1977
Regan almost witnesses the murder of Sheik Abu Asif ben Heffasa in a massage parlour, and having caught a glimpse of the killer, is then coerced by Special Branch into taking the case. Accompanied by a 'security consultant' known as Hijaz, he follows the suspect's trail to France, uncovering similar murders. He also begins a relationship with Jo, a high-class call girl. It turns out that the dead Arabs were trying to purchase fissile material for a nuclear device from the French government, and Israeli intelligence is behind the assassinations. Working with the French police, Regan arrests the assassins, but they are then all killed in an Arab revenge attack on Nice police station; Jo dies in the crossfire. Led by Hijaz, the Arabs flee to London on a private plane and then hole up in a flat in Bayswater. By taking advantage of the

Arabs not having adjusted their watches to British time, Regan engineers a situation in which they are all shot, getting revenge for Jo. A disgusted Maynon tells him to take leave. But Regan regrets nothing. 'Sod them all, he'd live to be a hundred and not lose one hour's sleep over it.'

THE SWEENEY 4: REGAN AND THE LEBANESE SHIPMENT
by Joe Balham
p/b Futura February 1977; h/b Arthur Barker June 1977
Regan tries to prevent a huge quantity of smack being smuggled into Britain.

THE SWEENEY 5: REGAN AND THE HUMAN PIPELINE
by Joe Balham
p/b Futura April 1977; h/b Arthur Barker June 1977
In order to bust an illegal immigration racket, Regan goes undercover at the Pussy Club in Hamburg's red light district.

THE SWEENEY 6: REGAN AND THE SNOUT WHO CRIED WOLF
by Joe Balham
p/b Futura July 1977
The squad are fed false information in order to distract them from the intended robbery of an upmarket department store.

THE SWEENEY 7: REGAN AND THE BENT STRIPPER
by Joe Balham
p/b Futura October 1977; h/b Arthur Barker March 1978
Bombs explode in Soho strip clubs, which are apparently receiving threats from the League of Decency. Regan is mistaken for a flasher and beaten up by some builders.

SWEENEY 2: THE BLAG
by Joe Balham
aka *Sweeney 2: Blag*
p/b Futura March 1978)
Novelisation of the second film.
From page 101: 'Damn and sod and damn sod and bugger and blast and damnsodbuggerblast. Slowly, viciously but methodically [Regan] began to kick [his] flat to pieces.'

THE SWEENEY 8: REGAN AND THE VENETIAN VIRGIN
by Joe Balham
p/b Futura March 1978
Regan investigates the international art world, which takes him to Venice with attractive art expert Bobby Winkles.

THE SWEENEY 9: REGAN AND THE HIGH ROLLERS

by Joe Balham

p/b Futura October 1978

Shotguns are stolen in Scotland by a vicious gang who then hit the Smoke.

THE ANNUALS (1976-1978)

Three *Sweeney* annuals were produced and published by Brown Watson between 1976 and 1978. They consisted of both narrative and cartoon stories, features on John Thaw, Dennis Waterman and Garfield Morgan, as well as informative pieces on criminals and policing, guides to cockney rhyming slang, puzzles, quizzes and crosswords. The stories retained the action of the series but the language was toned down for the younger market.

THE SWEENEY ANNUAL (published 1976)

price: £1.10

Features include – the real Flying Squad; the making of the programme; John Thaw 'Thaw-ing the Regan Image', Dennis Waterman and Garfield Morgan. The quiz involves scoring enough points to become a DI. Narrative stories include 'Flyaway', 'Inside Job', 'Old Enemy', 'Knife Edge' (relocating the action from the streets to a gig by rock band 'Everest', thus catering for the youth market) and 'A Necessary Evil'; Comic strips: 'One Man's Courage' and 'Double Trouble'. Dice game – *The Sweeney.*

THE SWEENEY ANNUAL (published 1977)

price: £1.25

Three comic strip stories: 'Hyena in London', 'Boy Wonder' and 'Right Time, Right Place', in which Regan challenges the reader to solve the crime and turn to the back page for the answer! Narrative stories – 'New Firm' and 'The Banker'. Features on stunts, famous East End criminals, forensic techniques and 'Dull it isn't' – a photo-montage of scraps, cars etc. Dice game – *The Big Chase.*

THE SWEENEY ANNUAL (published 1978)

price: £1.50

Comic strips – 'Double Cross Ambush', 'Blow the Fuses'; narrative stories, 'A far too tidy corpse', 'Devil or the Deep' and 'Gold Fever'. Interviews 'interrogating' John and Dennis ('They didn't like it, not much. They wanted out…'), plus features on courageous cops, famous detectives and police training. Dice game – *Prison Breakout.*

MISCELLANEOUS

THE SWEENEY Board game (Omnia 1975)

The game consists of a two-piece game board with a number of moulded plastic figures representing the cops and robbers, 16 target cards in blue and red and a score ladder featuring a still from title sequence.

'The Sweeney is no simple game of chance. Nor is it for the faint hearted. You need cunning, craft and guts. So don't expect favours and don't give any. Get them before they get you. To win, you and your partner must work closely together. So figure out your tactics and play them close to your chest.'

'Sweeney'(blue) and 'Villains' (red) teams both build up scores by successfully raiding targets which their opponents defend and can recapture. The winner is the first team to score 14 points.

SWEENEY TARGETS: fence: 3-6; jail break: 1-5; hide out:1-3 points.

VILLAIN'S TARGETS: bank: 3-6; jewellers: 1-5; mansion: 1-3 points.

THE SWEENEY Jigsaw puzzles (1976)

Two *Sweeney* jigsaw games, 'Public Execution' and 'Masked Ball', featured a 750-piece jigsaw accompanied by a 'Sweeney File' resembling a criminal record docket, with authentic cup-ring marks on the back and a reminder for Regan to phone Kojak in New York. The blurb from Regan warned, 'Before you do the jigsaw, read the story and the dossier, try to solve the crime, then see the solution in your completed puzzle!'

THE SWEENEY T-shirts and sweat shirts (1976)

Featuring cartoon drawings of Jack and George and the Ford Granada.

THE SWEENEY: HIJACK! Super Action Heroes! (Letraset, 1976)

In a series of that also featured *Doctor Who* and *Superman*, Regan and Carter, together with the uniform branch of the Met, took on the blaggers of a meat lorry. The set came with an illustrated background for the rub-down transfers of the characters to be placed on.

THE SWEENEY FORD Granada Consul 3 litre V6 GT (Cat no R1009)
(Richmond Toys, 2002)

A scale model, complete with opening doors and bonnet.

RECORDINGS

THE SWEENEY Main theme from the Thames TV Series (EMI 2252, 1975)
The Harry South Orchestra

45rpm single of commercial version of the opening and closing title music. Sheet music was also available.

REGAN'S THEME from the EMI film Sweeney! (EMI 2578, 1977)
Denis King and his Orchestra

45rpm single of commercial version of the theme to the first feature film.

SHUT IT! THE MUSIC OF THE SWEENEY (SANCD092, 2001)
Produced by the Cinephile imprint of Sanctuary Records, this funk and wah-wah fest features 25 original music tracks from the series interspersed with soundbites from Regan and Carter, taken from stories including 'Night Out', 'Abduction', 'Regan', 'Ringer' and 'Taste of Fear'. The album includes Harry South's commercial re-recordings of *The Sweeney* theme and much background music used in the programme, as provided by libraries such as KPM, Music De Wolfe and Zomba Production Music.

The composers include Johnny Pearson (who led the BBC's *Top of the Pops* Orchestra for 16 years), Keith Mansfield (who worked with Dusty Springfield, Tom Jones and Robert Plant), Brian Bennett (the drummer with The Shadows) and Herbie Flowers (who worked with David Bowie and Marc Bolan.). The CD includes a 16-page booklet with images and text about the series, produced by the authors of this book. The album is also available as a double vinyl album, on SANDV092.

SELECTED VIDEOS (1987 to present)

1987
Regan (Thames Video Collection: TV 9909 PAL)
Jackpot (Thames Video Collection: TV 9943 PAL)

1991
Sweeney! (Warner Bros: WTB39274)
Sweeney 2 (Warner Bros: WTB39275)

1993
Ringer (Thames Video Collection: TV 8176)
Sweeney! 1 & 2 (Lumiere LUM 2096)
Released with two different covers

1994
Queen's Pawn / Night Out (Thames Video/TV Gems: VR1701)*
Initial copies were issued crediting the episodes on
the tape as 'Ringer' and 'Jackpot'
The Placer / Cover Story (Thames Video/TV Gems: VR1720)*
Golden Boy / Big Spender (Thames Video/TV Gems: VR1728)*
Contact Breaker / Abduction (Thames Video/TV Gems: VR1751)*

1995
Trap / Poppy (Thames Video/TV Gems: VR1764)*
I Want the Man / Big Brother (Thames Video/TV Gems: VR1768)*

1996
Supersnout / Hit and Run (Thames Video/TV Gems: VR1664)
The Golden Fleece / The Trojan Bus (Thames Video/TV Gems: VR1011)
Thou Shalt Not Kill / Country Boy (Thames Video/TV Gems: VR1018)

1997
Selected Target / In From the Cold (Thames Video/TV Gems: VR1025)**

1998
Tomorrow Man / Taste of Fear (Thames Video: TV8273)

2000
Sweeney! (Warner Bros: S038443)
Sweeney 2 (Warner Bros: S038444)

2001
The Sweeney Vol 3 – Diamond Geezers (Thames PTVID8077)
(Poppy/I Want the Man/One of Our Own) digitally remastered

*Repackaged by UK Gold/Thames Video
**Repackaged UK Gold/Thames Video release

DVDS

2000
The Sweeney Vol 1 – Bank Jobs (Thames PTVID8049)
(Contact Breaker/Night Out)

The Sweeney Vol 2 – Car Chases (Thames PTVID8048)
(Stoppo Driver/Faces)

Both these Special Edition DVDs have been digitally remastered from the original 16mm film negatives and are presented in Widescreen (16:9); they each include some history text, a photo gallery, biographies and car trivia.

2001
Regan (Digital Entertainment DED6042)
Stills gallery (video grabs) and normal TV format

⚘ INDEX ⚘

SELECTED RELATED FILMS

🚗 SELECT BIBLIOGRAPHY 🚗

Alvarado, Manuel & Stewart, John, *Euston Films – Made For Television*
    BFI/Thames (1985) ISBN 0423 013106

Cops on the Box, BBC documentary, (1992)

Cornell, Paul, Day, Martin, and Topping, Keith, *The Guinness Book of Classic British TV*
    Guinness Publishing Ltd (1993)
    ISBN 0-85112-543-3

Ewbank, Tim, & Hildred, Stafford, *John Thaw – The Biography*
    Andre Deutsch Ltd, (1998) ISBN 0233 99482 3

Halliwell's Film Guide 2002 edition,
(ed John Walker)
    HarperCollins (2002) ISBN 0 00 653013 3

Interviews conducted by the authors with *The Sweeney* cast and production team, and Euston Films personnel, between 1998-2002

Hunt, Albert, 'The Sweeney'. Article in *New Society* (1976)

Kennedy Martin, Troy, 'Four of a Kind' essay, *Crime Writers* (ed H R F Keating),
    BBC (1978) ISBN 0563 16263

Pixley, Andrew, 'The Sweeney – Compulsive Viewing'. Article and interview with Roger Marshall, *Primetime* No. 13.
    Wider TeleVision Access (1987)
Photoplay, (1978)

Stage and Screen, (1978)
Sweeney, The, Annuals, (1977, 1978) Brown Watson

Waterman, Dennis, (with Jill Arlon), *Reminder*
    Hutchinson/Random House, (2000)
    ISBN 0 09 1801087

Plus the following: *Daily Express, Daily Mail, Daily Mirror, The Guardian, TV Times, Radio Times*